CITIZENSHIP, MARKETS, AND THE STATE

Citizenship, Markets, and the State

Edited by

COLIN CROUCH, KLAUS EDER,
and DAMIAN TAMBINI

OXFORD
UNIVERSITY PRESS

OXFORD

UNIVERSITY PRESS

Great Clarendon Street, Oxford OX2 6DP

Oxford University Press is a department of the University of Oxford.
It furthers the University's objective of excellence in research, scholarship,
and education by publishing worldwide in

Oxford New York

Athens Auckland Bangkok Bogotá Buenos Aires Calcutta
Cape Town Chennai Dar es Salaam Delhi Florence Hong Kong Istanbul
Karachi Kuala Lumpur Madrid Melbourne Mexico City Mumbai
Nairobi Paris Sào Paulo Shanghai Singapore Taipei Tokyo Toronto Warsaw

with associated companies in Berlin Ibadan

Oxford is a registered trade mark of Oxford University Press
in the UK and in certain other countries

Published in the United States
by Oxford University Press Inc., New York

© the several contributors 2001

The moral rights of the authors have been asserted
Database right Oxford University Press (maker)

First published 2001

British Library Cataloguing in Publication Data

Data available

Library of Congress Cataloging-in-Publication Data

Citizenship, markets, and the state / edited by Colin Crouch, Klaus Eder, and Damian Tambini.
p. cm.
Includes bibliographical references and index.
1. Citizenship. I. Crouch, Colin, 1944– II. Eder, Klaus, 1946– III. Tambini, Damian.
JF801 .C5736 2000   323.6–dc21   00-060634

ISBN 0-19-924121-X

1 3 5 7 9 10 8 6 4 2

Typeset in Minion
by Best-set Typesetter Ltd., Hong Kong
Printed in Great Britain by
T. J. International Ltd.,
Padstow, Cornwall

ACKNOWLEDGEMENTS

This volume is one of the products of the European Forum: a year-long collaborative research project on citizenship held at the European University Institute in 1995/1996. We thank the Institute, especially Yves Meny, for providing the material and intellectual environment, Steven Lukes and Massimo La Torre as co-directors of the European Forum, and Kathinka España for her organizational and practical help. We also have to thank the authors for their patience. Special thanks are due to those members of the European Forum who commented on earlier versions of the chapters: Carlos Closa, Will Kymlicka, Yuri Kazepov, and Yasemin Soysal. Finally thanks go to Wenke Nitz and Katja Kerstiens for skilful editorial assistance.

CONTENTS

LIST OF FIGURES

LIST OF TABLES

LIST OF CONTRIBUTORS

VEIT MICHAEL BADER, Professor of Sociology, Department of Practical Philosophy, Free University of Amsterdam

COLIN CROUCH, Professor of Sociology, Department of Social and Political Sciences, European University Institute, Florence

KLAUS EDER, Professor of Sociology, Institute of Social Sciences, Humboldt-University Berlin

MARK FREEDLAND, Professor of Law, University of Oxford, St. John's College, Oxford

ANTON HEMERIJCK, Professor of Public Administration, University of Leiden

JANE JENSON, Professor of Political Science, University of Montreal

SUSAN D. PHILLIPS, Associate Professor, School of Public Administration, Carleton University

GIOVANNA PROCACCI, Lecturer in Sociology, Department of Sociology, University of Milano

MARGARET SOMERS, Professor of Sociology, Institute of Humanities, University of Michigan

DAMIAN TAMBINI, Research Fellow, Institute for Public Policy Research, London

1

Introduction

Colin Crouch, Klaus Eder, and Damian Tambini

The Dilemmas of Citizenship

Around a decade ago the theme of citizenship suddenly sprang to prominence in academic debate in a number of Western countries. An initial pamphlet and article literature was consolidated into books (Jordan 1989; Kolberg 1992; Oldfield 1990; Turner 1993; Janoski 1998). T. H. Marshall, whose early post-war contributions to the concept of social citizenship in the British welfare state had remained quietly in the background literature, leaped into prominence as a major figure (Bulmer and Rees 1996). Unusually for sociological and political science discourses, the theme was quickly taken up in public political debate. The British government even launched a Commission on Citizenship (UK 1990); and the European Union developed policies for a European citizenship (Commission of the European Communities 1997).

There were three main forces behind this phenomenon. First, and with particular importance, there were anxieties about the problematic citizenship status of the large numbers of immigrants and their descendants who were clearly settling permanently in the advanced industrial societies (Bauböck 1994; Brubaker 1989; Rex 1996). This raised particular difficulties for Germany, where citizenship has long been based on an ethnic concept of German-ness (Brubaker 1992; Joppke 1998); and also for the USA, where demands for the recognition of ethnic rights within a multicultural citizenship seemed to challenge earlier notions of the 'melting pot' (Kymlicka 1995). The newly emerging idea of a European citizenship also ran into immediate difficulties since, by stressing the common identity of Europeans, it almost inevitably drew attention to differences between Europeans and non-Europeans at a time when important minorities of the latter were coming to terms with permanent settlement within the territories of the European Union (Einhorn et al. 1996; Lehning and Weale 1997; Meehan 1993; Sörensen 1996).

Second, there were problems concerning the welfare state, which had in the post-war period become a major embodiment of citizenship rights. During the 1960s and 1970s public spending on education, health, welfare, and other social policies rose very considerably in virtually all countries. Shortly after this had started began the steep rise in unemployment and other forms of exit from the labour market (especially among men) which was later to become a major characteristic of societies at the end of the twentieth century. As Hemerijck discusses in Chapter 7 below, social policies that had originally seemed to have a purpose in supporting a dynamic society and active citizenship increasingly became the support of inactivity and passiveness. In the eyes of some, welfare policy actually encouraged inactivity; even for devoted supporters of the welfare state the development was a matter of disappointment.

At the same time major developments in technology and marketing were expanding the range of consumer goods available for purchase in the shops. In several countries there was evidence of resentment that taxation paid to support the welfare state was reducing individuals' private spending possibilities. By the 1980s there was added to this process the growing globalization of capital and the threat of many businesses that they might leave countries with high taxation rates. The threat was not necessarily realistic, but it combined with other discontents to raise question marks over the welfare citizenship model. Politically the main form taken by this was a growth of individualism, a rejection of the role of the state in imposing its own taxation on the expenditure decisions of individuals, and a general assertion of the superiority of unimpeded markets.

This raises a related problem of welfare citizenship. Certainly in terms of continental concepts of *Sozialpolitik*, the welfare state did not simply mean entitlements to benefits; it also incorporated the occupational citizenship rights of employees within their work organizations: rights to union representation; legal entitlements to certain standards of health, safety, and good working conditions; possibly rights to consultation and co-determination. These too might be threatened by the new mobility of capital (Streeck 1997).

Finally, there were worries about symptoms of rising criminality and marginality in contemporary societies, especially in large cities. This tendency had started in the USA but was spreading to Europe. Not only did there seem to be a growing minority of people, especially perhaps young people, who felt themselves to be outside the bonds of citizenship, but there were fears that there might be a more generalized indifference to criminal and violent behaviour. This implied that large proportions of the general public were not taking their citizenship responsibilities seriously. These anxieties, though very widely expressed, were perhaps particularly concentrated among conservative political leaders, and it was in this form that the question of citizenship often forced itself on to the political agenda.

This final issue might be seen as the other side of the coin of the crisis of the welfare state. Supporters of the welfare state argued that if welfare citizenship rights were being reduced, it must be expected that there would be a rise in the number of people who felt marginalized and alienated; welfare rights had been the most important bonds giving poor people a stake in the general society. This theme is discussed in more historical detail by Procacci in Chapter 3. Conservatives countered by arguing that it was the welfare state which, by making it possible for people to live in idleness, had broken the bonds of work that had also been an integral part of a general social ethic.

While there is room for considerable debate over this question, there was a particular problem which conservatives, locked into partnership with neo-liberals in most societies, had to recognize. Nowhere has it produced a formal break between conservative, Christian groups concerned to defend a communitarian model of citizenship and neo-liberals to whom community is anathema (Janoski 1998). Neo-liberalism deals with problems of collective life by trying to privatize as much as possible. For example, if there is a problem of pollution of some natural resource, then let private enterprise acquire that resource as private property; it will then have an incentive to prevent it from becoming polluted. However, certain essentially collective aspects of modern life cannot be so easily dispatched. Social interdependence is if anything increased rather than reduced in complex and advanced market economies. Free markets and the uneven economic developments they produce, at least in the short and medium term, encourage population movements and therefore help to produce the waves of immigration which raise worries about definitions of social membership. Growing income inequalities produced by both free markets and reduced taxation and welfare tend to increase the number of poor and socially excluded people in a society. Most important of all, by no means all natural resources currently threatened by environmental damage can be saved through privatization; no entrepreneurs can offer to buy the ozone layer. The collective, the sphere of matters of common concern, cannot be eliminated.

As a result, disillusion with welfare citizenship did not lead simply to an embrace of privatized life and free markets. Rather, citizenship became an issue of debate. Supporters of the welfare model have wanted to redefine it in the light of recent difficult experience. Advocates of free markets have wanted to find ways of reconciling these with an irreducible public sphere and democratic politics. Those concerned with both new social issues and post-state approaches to reconciling individualism with public discourse have also turned to the concept of citizenship as a useful frame within which to stake out their claims. And amid this theoretical activity, the politicians launched new policy experiments.

Evaluating the Experiments: The Theoretical Background

The result of all this has been a lively and innovative academic literature and some interesting policy initiatives. It now becomes useful to reflect on what has resulted from all this ferment. Have any master concepts or new orthodoxies of citizenship emerged? Have any of the policy experiments been of particular significance and success? In this book we shall try to answer some of these questions. First, however, it is necessary to review the intellectual debate in more detail.

Since Marshall we have been aware of the tension between citizenship as an ideal and citizenship as a set of institutions. This book examines how that tension has fared since Marshall: first the development and subsequent crisis of institutions of political and social citizenship in national states, and then a series of experiments in marketization and deliberation that have preserved and transformed the ideal of citizenship whilst re-inventing the institutions of citizenship.

Competing ideas of citizenship offer differing views of the mechanisms governing the relationship between membership of a political community, participation in the decisions governing the community, and access to public goods and resources. Neo-liberals are more likely to suggest rights as a capacity to take individual actions to protect one's personal space, while social democrats and conservatives are more likely to stress contributions to a wider community. Civic republicans emphasize the virtues of citizenship as formal and impersonal, and able to allocate rights irrespective of personal, social, or ethnic characteristics. For communitarians, in contrast, citizenship can only be fully effective where citizens are bound together by many community ties. All however are likely to agree on both the basic definition and on viewing active citizenship as somehow superior to passive. Again there will be differences here: neo-liberals are likely to complain that the welfare entitlements that socialists see as major achievements of citizenship are 'merely passive'; while the latter will similarly criticize the neo-liberal's concern for rights that protect the individual from the collectivity rather than orient her toward it.

Citizenship should therefore be understood as an ideal, in relation to which social and political institutions are created and evolve, always imperfectly institutionalizing this ideal, partly because the means used to achieve participatory citizenship themselves have unintended consequences for, and interactive effects upon, the nature of social membership and the reproduction of inequalities. The ideal of citizenship stipulates that subjects of a state should be sovereign: hence equally represented, and actively integrated in political life. In theory, social and political rights fostered that integration in national states. In ever more complex societies, however, whose membership is increasingly challenged by multiculturalism, inequality, and the break-up of welfare systems, the ideal of citizenship can no longer rely on the same apparatus. The main problems facing current institutions of citizenship are brought about by the new structural conditions of globalization, economic liberalization, and increasing institutional scale and complexity.

Within the terms of globalization, there has been the shift of power away from levels where at least elements of citizenship institutions (nation-state, local community) have been erected and the increased cross-national mobility of persons away from locations in which any citizenship rights they might possess have been embedded. Economic liberalization has meant, broadly, the withdrawal of states and other sources of regulation from economic transactions, leaving firms autonomous within markets. Whatever limitations there may have been on citizenship rights within states and other public agencies, the firm is solely a private institution. In terms of institutional scale and complexity, both technological advance and growing capacity for large-scale co-ordination—including the globalization already mentioned—produce a growing complexity both of the content of public business and issues of public importance and of the public and private organizations which manage them. This can be seen particularly clearly in the area of environmental damage, but similar arguments apply to such questions as the construction of welfare policy.

Whereas the post-war Marshallian model implied that the state should provide the social and educational resources for the making of citizens, therefore, this no longer seems feasible. The proponents of privatized citizenship have more recently tried to perfect the market as an integration mechanism, and others have tried to integrate citizens through redesigning the forum—the mechanisms of democratic representation and debate. This book investigates how these various models of social integration and democracy interpret and transform citizenship.

Marshall saw social rights as a necessary condition for the exercise of civil and political rights, and in a more controversial move implied that the progress of citizenship consisted in the successive extension of civil, political, and then culminating in universal social rights. We acknowledge that the story has moved on considerably from Marshall's time. Whereas Marshall tended to see the realization of social rights as the end point of an endogenous process of development, we acknowledge that the ideal of citizenship was neither realized nor abandoned with the construction and subsequent crisis of national welfare states. Rather, the ideal of citizenship has been invoked in a series of newer experiments, grouped in this book around the marketization of citizenship (which we argue also invokes the ideal, claiming to offer more efficient ways of realizing it); and deliberative, discursive responses (which seek to achieve the integration of citizens by improving the participative integration of citizens, independently of social rights). These experiments bear the imprint of the ideological and structural context in which they were conceived and, as each of the studies shows, are already revealing that they, like previous attempts to realize the ideal of citizenship, will succeed only partially and transform the ideal of citizenship in the process.

Since the 1980s these questions have been opened to a broad debate, leading to the policy experiments in refounding citizenship which form the focus of this book.

The Re-Emergence of T. H. Marshall

The sudden resurgence of interest in T. H. Marshall's work in the 1980s was due to the breadth, simplicity, and vagueness of the theory, together with the fact that it offered elegant and memorable means to approach a number of pressing practical problems. The 1980s citizenship debate focused on critiques of Marshall's theory of citizenship in terms of the aforementioned problems: dissatisfaction with welfare state solutions, the questioning of categories such as 'nation' that Marshall took for granted, and the increasing complexity of modern societies. Marshallian citizenship theory generally was attractive because it appeared to offer a way of conceptualizing these processes of social integration in relation to welfare, class realignment, participation, and inclusion, and to do so in an institutionalist way: one that did not reify such categories as nation or society, and had a strong notion of the role of ideas in shaping large-scale trajectories of social change.

In so far as it was related to and engendered the 'experiments in citizenship' with which this book is concerned, the 1980s debate on citizenship engaged with Marshall's account in the following respects: his account of the development of citizenship, and the functional and causal relationships between rights, participation, and (in)equality that he posed.

Marshall was criticized for neglecting the role of struggle and social movements in the development of rights (Barbalet 1988: 108; Mann 1987); for taking national belonging for granted (Turner 1986, 1990); and for neglecting gender (Fraser and Gordon 1994). He saw the development of citizenship as a result of a dynamic created by the tension between abstract granting of rights, and the institutionalization necessary for the enjoyment of those rights in practice. Hence, for example, social rights (to education or welfare) are necessary if civil and political rights (to justice or voting) are to be realized. As Somers (1996) points out, he located the engine of citizenship's development in the inherent conflict between the class inequalities resulting from capitalism and the equality of status resulting from citizenship. Marshall is vague enough about the 'carriers' or 'agents' to be read as claiming that classes (Somers 1996) or social movements (Turner 1986) were responsible for driving the process.

Is citizenship won or imposed (Turner 1990: 199)? Michael Mann's (1987) well-known critique of Marshall implied that citizenship is imposed from above, whereas others, such as Turner, have defended Marshall's position and the idea that social movements are ultimately responsible, or at least a position that allows for both (Turner 1990: 207). Critics are right to point out that Marshall is ultimately ambivalent regarding the status of his theory: whether it is an explanation or merely a description, or whether it was meant to be a theory applicable to cases other than England (Mann 1987).

The Second Wave of Citizenship Theory

For Marshall, civil, political, and social rights were interdependent: there was a natural tendency for them to be woven into a single fabric even in capitalist society. The second wave of citizenship theory in the 1980s and 1990s thus returned to the first wave of theorization on citizenship and welfare with a critical eye. Whilst the basic normative commitments to participation and status equality were retained, 1980s commentators frowned upon Marshall's focus on Anglocentric 'civilization', and further questioned the issue of membership. The abandonment of state universalist assimilation and homogenization programmes led to the presence of culturally different citizens, and a problematization of the relationships between culture, community, and citizenship. Two main discussions emerged: on one hand, older debates about political culture and civil society were reopened in terms of citizenship (Putnam *et al.* 1993; Oldfield 1990; Miller 1992) and, on the other hand, issues of self-determination and group rights for minorities were raised by communitarians (Etzioni 1996; Sandel 1992). In this way previously taboo questions about the consequences of immigration could be discussed in terms of the relationship between national membership, political culture, and civic participation.

According to Turner (1990: 193) the extension of universal citizenship to all adult subjects was followed by a new rights discourse applied to animals, children, and the environment. At the same time this was in a context where the meeting of most basic economic needs was taken for granted by the majority in the core societies. Thus social rights were downplayed, particularly in the influential new right critique, and a new discourse of obligations emerged (Kymlicka and Norman 1994).

Thus, according to Turner (1990: 195), 'the problem with Marshall's theory is that it is no longer relevant to a period of disorganized capitalism . . . Marshall's theory assumed some form of nation-state autonomy in which Governments were relatively immune from pressures within the world-system of capitalist nations'. The consensus surrounding the post-war ideal of welfare as guarantor of national citizenship was thereby challenged from both right and left. The following questions demanded answers.

If nation-states can no longer guarantee the social rights necessary to protect political and civil rights, what other mechanisms can prevent dominant and class interests distorting political processes? When the new complexity of multicultural, class-fragmented, and (majority) post-scarcity advanced societies presents such a variety of lifestyles and preferences, how can mechanisms of participation be provided that improve upon the clearly malfunctioning apparatus of mass democracy? Are the three threads of civic, political, and social rights that Marshall saw woven into national citizenship unraveling? Thus debates emerged over whether guest workers should be granted formal citizenship (and the nature of cultural differences that can be tolerated by a citizenship regime) or whether dual citizenship, or denizenship, should be instituted.

These discussions were both cause and consequence of the undermining of the previous model of welfare-based citizenship. Through them, citizenship theory and experimentation has focused on the question of the links between formal membership, rights, and participation. Various ways of conceptualizing post-national citizenship have been outlined, from Turner's (1990: 211) globalization of citizenship, to Soysal's (1994) post-national citizenship and the slowly unfolding scenario of European citizenship, which was first officially mentioned in the Maastricht Treaty of 1992 (Eder and Giesen 2000; O'Leary 1996; Wiener 1998; Martiniello 1995).

Plan of this Book

The two main parts of the book address the two types of experiments with citizenship: those concerned with the extension of the market; and those concerned with trying to transcend formal political patterns with more social and participative approaches. Part I addresses what has been called the marketization of citizenship. In identifying globalization, economic liberalization, and the rising social importance of the firm as among the problems currently being faced by the welfare-state model of citizenship, we are following in the well-established tradition of setting the forum and the market against each other. This issue is taken up by Somers in this volume. But an equally venerable tradition puts them together: in the historical rise of citizenship rights against arbitrary aristocratic authority, the freedom afforded by property and markets played a major role in the emergence of citizenship. The *Bürger* is both a citizen and a bourgeois. Not surprisingly, therefore, an important component of the current dialectic between politics and markets, citizens and customers, has been the re-expression of market freedoms as integral to, rather than in conflict with, citizenship.

However, the neo-liberal form taken by this response in many countries is strikingly aggressive in its approach to the previously dominant concept of citizenship through politics. Although the struggle between politics and markets was at the forefront of political conflict in virtually all modern societies throughout the nineteenth and twentieth centuries, for much of the past half-century it was a debate that afforded ground for compromise and even consensus. There had at least been some understanding that neither the artificial construct of the state citizen nor that of the market customer, one-sided abstractions that both are, could satisfy the full range of human needs. For example, to the extent that the market is a precise allocator and the political process a rather crude one, the best solution to a public policy problem is often recognized to be one that works through markets rather than by suppressing them. The payment to retired people of pensions rather than of baskets of goods selected for them by a welfare officer is a widely recognized example. Even though greater efficiency might be achieved if pensions were replaced by social services departments buying in bulk and allocating those goods that it would be most sensible for pensioners to have, most people would consider that such a strategy would not be worth the loss in freedom and dignity it involved. From the other side, public systems of allocation have been recognized as acceptable and even superior for certain kinds of collective goods and elements of social infrastructure (education, roads, at least basic health provision).

This is now changing. Originating with certain kinds of neo-liberal political economy theory in the USA and then in the 1980s spreading to the practical politics of the US Republican Party and the British Conservative Party, intellectual and political hegemony has been won by the view that there will be gains to utility if, far from there being some kind of compromise between these forces, the idea of achieving goals through citizenship should be completely set aside and all force given to free markets.

Nominally Christian and social-democratic groups in most advanced countries, which had in the past defined themselves in terms of a critique of markets, have also begun to adopt this reasoning. International agencies have also followed, most recently the Organization of Economic Co-operation and Development, which in its *Jobs Study* of 1994 (OECD 1994) advocated virtually the complete dismantling of labour-market regulation as the best means of securing future employability. What happens under such a regime is that employment security and decent working conditions cease to be citizenship rights and become something that employers choose to extend to different types of employee dependent on market considerations alone. Since 1994 there has been some move back from this extreme position by the OECD, with more recent policy statements accepting that complete deregulation brings various negative consequences (such as reduced incentives to employers to train and increased social inequality) (OECD 1996). In general, however, more and more policy areas are being declared off-limits to democratic influence and passed to the control of market forces and private business. The task of democracy is reduced to legislating the privatizations and deregulations which make this possible.

There are three related but ultimately distinct reasons for this major triumph of the market over citizenship: economic, cultural, and political. Full-employment strategies based on Keynesian demand management—both itself a guarantor of social citizenship rights and the safeguard of the welfare state that was their main embodiment—lost their capacity to avoid inflation during the 1970s. In democratic and pluralistic societies such policies were vulnerable to a ratchet effect: there were strong pressures to increase spending during recessions, but equally strong ones to prevent the downward adjustments necessary during high-growth periods if demand management was to be inflation-neutral. However, policy change is never a merely technical matter. The structure of political interests and the balance of power among them also changed. The decline of manufacturing employment weakened the electoral strength of social-democratic parties; international competition in global labour markets generally weakened the bargaining power of labour against capital; and liberalized financial markets freed capital from dependence on (and hence from the need to come to terms with or care about the quality and conditions of) any particular national labour force.

In these conditions there has been a major weakening of political forces pursuing labour interests, seeking redistributive taxation, or egalitarian access to identified basic needs through public provision based on citizenship rights rather than market power. Ideas for rolling back, not just Keynesian demand management, but the whole edifice of high (and more or less redistributive) taxation, public social services, and the protection of employee rights through legislation and industrial relations arrangements have met a warm welcome in the policy-making community. The climate has been very different from the decades when the employed manual labour force exercised considerable influence through its scarcity on the labour market and its preponderance in the ballot box.

A different but major initiating motive in the rise of 'exit politics' was concern over what to do about the rebelliousness of the 1960s, which threatened to undermine the essential non-market base on which conservatives know that social order ultimately rests: loyalty and obedience. This was the cultural challenge. After some panic in the 1970s, when conservative intellectuals wrote about 'ungovernability' and expressed doubts whether democracy could ever again be made adequately safe for capitalism (Brittan 1975), the neo-liberal right adopted a highly creative strategy: to encourage demands for freedom from constraints by authority, provided these took market form. Despite its concern with dialogistic participation and its association with collective causes, much of the rebelliousness of the 1960s was intensely individualistic, even narcissistic. It was a time of the liberation of the self, its demand for expression, its right to indulge appetites free from constraints of orthodoxy and rule—including those of citizenship obligations.

Finally, at the political level neo-liberals argue in effect that markets and customership are preferable alternatives to citizenship. The market does not, at least at first sight, involve the difficulties entailed for participation by collective membership and by scale and size of the forum in a modern mass society. Within most markets, at least those for consumer goods, we can participate directly and specifically in many different decisions, whereas we participate as citizens in the polity only indirectly and in formal and awkwardly aggregated ways at rare intervals in time. We confer a mandate on representatives, who continue to claim democratic legitimacy for their actions even if these run directly counter to the express preferences of large majorities of the citizenry. In the mass polity we do not really enter a dialogistic process, but are called upon to exercise trust in leaders, or loyalty in Hirschman's (1970) terms. This is likely to be a particular problem of poor people, those most remote culturally from decision-makers and decision-making processes. They are also, of course, those weakest within the market; but at least the market leaves some areas of personal action open to them.

The difficulties of managing highly complex societies and economies have led virtually all governments to lose credibility as efficient actors. Many policies turn out to be highly ineffective; politicians promise things they cannot deliver. Worse, there is widespread apprehension that politicians are corrupt and self-seeking. Meanwhile, as marketing techniques advance and most of us have more private wealth at our disposal, it becomes easier to meet various needs through shopping in the market. If the state is likely to be incompetent, it is better to keep things to oneself and spend in ways one can control. This supports the demand for low taxes and reduced public spending. The area of citizenship shrinks, that of the market grows. There is a political asymmetry here. If a government which believes in collective provision performs badly, not only does it acquire a bad reputation, but it has provided reasons for not trusting collective decisions as such. If a government hostile to collectivism performs badly, it is still blamed for error, but it gains from having further discredited the idea of collective as opposed to private action.

This new triumph of the market over citizenship has become the most important feature of social politics at the *fin de siècle*. It is therefore timely to submit it to critical attention. We do so here primarily through a series of case-studies of recent individual policy experiments. Chapter 3, by Giovanna Procacci, places the general issue in a wider theoretical and historical perspective, linking the ideas of individualization and marketization. She traces the emergence of social citizenship as a collective response to poverty, by pointing out that citizenship not only emerged as a means to guarantee that those subject to states have the ability to participate as citizens within them (Marshall) but that social rights were the result of a state strategy of governance in which poverty was no longer viewed as an individual problem but as a social (national) one. This, she argues, was a political development, and the consequences of this socialization of poverty are made most clear only now, as a new form of individualized social policy response emerges as states find they are unable to underwrite social rights.

Procacci identifies the costs of abandoning social citizenship rights: in particular, the clear differences between social policies based on social rights and social policies that construct poverty as a problem of the individual are illustrated with reference to the case of France, where new individualized social policies, as Marshall would have predicted, fail to provide the necessary conditions to exercise participatory political citizenship and, further, fail to provide an efficient way of dealing with the problem of poverty. Also, responses to social problems reflect anational responses, focusing on cities or ghettos rather than 'society' as a whole. However, she points out, such attempts to individualize poverty transform a social outlook on poverty, one which has evolved over the last 200 years. Poverty, she argues, must be seen as social.

Jane Jenson and Susan Phillips examine the consequences for the practice of public service of various experiments in marketizing and eventually privatizing many of the activities of the Canadian health service. One interesting implication of their analysis is the close relationship between neo-liberal reforms and a very traditional conservatism. This form of conservatism might be said to represent some elements of Somers's third sphere (see above). In Western European societies it has more often taken political form as Christian democracy, and as such has been more cross-pressured by social concerns than such politics in North America.

Two of the case-studies (Freedland and Crouch) concern the United Kingdom, where the Conservative governments in office between 1979 and 1997 carried out a more thoroughgoing experiment in marketization than in probably any other country. In a similar analysis to Jenson and Phillips, Freedland examines the implications for citizenship of placing the delivery of many public services in the hands of commercial firms or privatized agencies. He examines the triangular relationship that this produces between state, citizen, and privatized service provider. Perhaps surprisingly, the limb of the triangle that has the most momentous implications for citizens' relations with their political representatives is not the direct link between citizens and state, but that between the state and the privatized providers. He sees very negative implications for the concept of public service here, and makes a particularly original contribution in seeing public employee interests as allied with those of the public at large, where many other observers have seen inherent conflicts.

Like Margaret Somers, Colin Crouch makes use of the third sphere of community when considering the complex case of education policy. Dialectical processes have been particularly strongly at work here. Education is at once essentially individual and collective: individuals are clearly the immediate beneficiaries of education, often in a zero-sum sense, while nations and other collectivities share certain interests in having the generality of people achieve certain cultural and knowledge standards. The role of families in education also sustains the third sphere. There can therefore never be a decisive shift into either statist or individualist policy. As a result, the dialectic of policy conflict always produces new attempted syntheses. While Crouch is as sceptical as Freedland and Jenson of the marketization project, he does see interesting compromises emerging among citizenship, market, and community criteria.

Finally, Anton Hemerijck examines the issue of the relationship between the welfare state, inactivity, and the work ethic that has stood at the centre of much recent debate. In addition to discussing these themes at the general theoretical level, he also looks at possible ways out from the apparent impasse by considering some syntheses between citizenship and markets in recent Dutch employment policy. The Netherlands has been a country where particularly interesting syntheses have been produced between neo-liberal policies, and a revivified role for dialogistic processes and corporatist organizations. Significantly, Christian democracy has played a key role in this (Visser and Hemerijck 1997). To some extent the Dutch example, in demonstrating a continued vitality for institutions of social dialogue, also belongs among the experiments in political citizenship discussed in Part II. Marketization, then, was in part a response to generalized dissatisfaction with the workings of democratic political institutions.

Part II deals with attempts to address the problems of how to realize participative political institutions and thus political citizenship in complex societies characterized by increasing functional differentiation and communicative density. Political participation, the central normative ideal of citizenship, can be understood either as the last step in the unfolding of citizenship, or as the only procedure through which collective identity and social justice can be realized in a non-exclusive way. Independently of whether we take the teleological or the procedural stand, political citizenship is the litmus test of citizenship.

Whether we look at motives for engaging in political action (overcoming the problem of collective action) or problems of consensus formation or efficient decision-making, political citizenship has trouble meeting the expectations that it generates. We can see political citizenship as an illusion, as a euphemistic representation of real politics or as a wild struggle over symbolic capital, over defining what the real problems are. Such attacks on the idea of political citizenship have put liberal thinkers (especially neo-liberal ones) in a strange situation: given that the complete marketization of political citizenship is not a feasible project, the problem of democracy has to be addressed within a different discursive universe. Hence the new vogue for proposals of community-building, of civil society taking over state competencies, and for deliberative democracy.

The central dilemma into which political citizenship runs is the dilemma of mobilizing moral feelings, the problem of moralizing politics. Political citizenship, in contrast to markets, conceives the members of a society as political beings, as beings morally responsible for their community, for the *res publica*. Thus political citizens are carriers of moral resources for the political community. The institutionalization of political citizenship has struggled with the ambivalence of the moralization of politics. Two ideal type solutions can be identified: the Rousseauian solution where the individual moral will is subordinated to (or dissolved into) the collective will and thus civilized by the general will; and the procedural solution where regular participation in formal procedure disciplines the moral anger and moral mission of the individual and where morality is built into the logic of procedural rules which then channel moral feelings.

These solutions, however, are not immune to perverse effects. The collective moral will can result in terror: the procedural solution does not exclude amoral participation in authoritarian politics. Both critiques have historical and social-scientific empirical evidence on their side. The non-intended consequences of mobilizing the people, of doing politics for mass publics are well known, but none the less often set aside in normative debates. The participation of people in mass politics is an ambivalent process. Its pressing problem, the transformation of uncivilized moral feelings out there in society into responsible political citizenship, has to take into account the reality, historical experience as well as social-scientific evidence, of political citizenship.

How to solve this problem? The solutions of the nineteenth and twentieth century, representative political institutions, seem inadequate. The loss of trust in traditional political institutions (especially electoral procedures), and the rise of mass media politics call for other solutions. These problems with traditional political institutions increase as more complex issues such as environment and migration have to be decided by these institutions. Political citizenship dealing with complex issues such as the environment or migration immediately generates moral noise that is difficult to contain and transform into responsible political citizenship.

The contemporary political debate oscillates between (*a*) demands for market solutions (which include people as consumers, a strategy especially widespread in environmental politics), (*b*) upholding national institutions of representation (even counterfactually), (*c*) building trust in such institutions by regular ritual enactments of politics, that is, strengthening national identity and commitment to 'one's own institutions', and (*d*) experiments in a new type of political institutions characterized by deliberative procedures, in dialogistic institutions. The basic ideological orientations underlying these debates are organized along the dichotomy of liberal-individualist versus civic-republican conceptions of citizenship. Whereas a liberal-individualist conception would rather foster arguments of the type (*a*) and (*b*), a civic-republican conception is more concerned with arguments of the type (*c*) and (*d*). Communitarian and anti-communitarian conceptions of citizenship parallel this discursive universe on political citizenship. Civic-republicanism normally implies some idea of a community, whereas liberal individualism believes in some kind of implicit co-ordination (rational co-ordination) of actors.

The experimental solutions for the rational transformation of moral feelings of people into some kind of 'rational moral will' radicalize the discursive aspect of democratic participation. A first type is to involve concerned people in real deliberative procedures because participation in such procedures binds people to what these bodies recommend or decide. Once engaged in such a procedure of deliberation, one has to accept its results. This is the idea on which the debate on discursive designs for political institutions in complex societies is based. A second deliberative solution is the idea of an additional fourth branch of government, of deliberative bodies of experts (legal, financial, economic, social, religious, ecological, etc.) who represent the different interests of a society and have to decide through deliberative procedures among those best suited to find answers for complex problems while knowing the interest of (fractions of) the people. Both solutions have to pay a high cost: the inclusion of only a small number of people in such deliberative processes. Multiplying such deliberative bodies and combining both forms might involve more people, which then raises the problem of co-ordinating myriads of deliberative bodies.

The idea of this new political citizenship, then, is that mobilizing and binding the moral resources of people in complex societies will be achieved by channelling, testing, and rationalizing such resources through deliberative procedures. The new political citizenship is thus a demanding role, as we find with such procedures in the fields of the environment, of social policy, and migration/ethnic relations.

The alternative is to make people participate through mass communication. This is to maximize the number (not the discursive aspect of political citizenship) of people in political processes. This alternative way of making people political citizens is dependent on the structure and functioning of public debates and the participation this allows. Negative descriptions of such citizenship as political spectacles raise the problem of non-intended negative consequences, of perverse effects of too many people talking on complex topics. The other side is the integration of the moral resources of people in a process of public communication, tied to the hope that such public communication will civilize by its mode of functioning (argumentative constraints, limits of self-presentation in public, emotional outlet, getting tired of too much moralism in public) the moral energy of a society and will transmute it into some common good. Evidence on such processes is scant, and certainly we will need more than economic analyses of the behaviour of political citizens to understand and explain such processes.

The contributions to Part II address these questions not with the intention to find answers but to describe the ambivalence built into citizenship, identify the central questions which arise, and propose some of the analytical means that help us understand better the way in which political citizenship can be institutionalized in complex societies.

Papadopoulos develops the problem of competent citizens in a complex democratic institutional system by arguing that direct (referendum) democracy does not seem to be an appropriate means for democratizing the polity, enhancing the practice of citizenship and empowering people. The record of direct democracy is described as ambiguous. It fosters political stratification and individualistic or utilitarian behaviour, it can lead to majority tyranny, and it is prejudicial to the development of moral resources among the citizenry. The conclusion is that the need for democratic forms of politics requires even more political citizenship, which is to be found in new ideas about actors acting in increasingly plural, sectoral, and fragmented spheres of the political. The citizen needed for such a political environment will have to contribute to the promotion of moral resources in society. Thus a deliberative conception of a political citizen is postulated as an alternative to the referendum citizen who simply uses participatory claims for maximizing his individual (moral and material) interests.

Bader poses the problem of democratic institutions in an age when not only citizenries, but the political problems that institutions must confront tend to defy national boundaries, and traces the implications of the various ways that political loyalty and participation can be conceived. Eder develops these ideas further by showing that the dependence of political citizenship on staging in public spaces makes political citizenship vulnerable to the logic of public theatre. Against this, a non-idealizing notion of public spaces is developed, characterized by a triangulation of state, market, and civil society in which a public consisting of competent and self-conscious citizens can exert the control constitutive for democratic societies. Using the examples of environmental and ethnic mobilizations, he provides a framework for a form of citizenship beyond mere membership in a national community. Tambini adds a technological component to the discussion of a new type of political citizenship: the emergence of an Internet community of political citizens. Whilst this could indeed contribute to lowering the (transaction) costs of participation, it might at the same time foster what Papadopoulos already criticized: the individualist motivation characterizing this form of citizenship. Whether this ambiguity can be overcome while creating a new technologically sophisticated political citizenship is still in fact speculation.

As we discuss in the final chapter, the contributions underline the centrality of the links between states, political communities, and sovereignty. In the modern period, national states were the principal guarantors of basic freedoms and material security, and the main sites for democratic decision-making. The institutions of citizenship—of membership, rights, and participation—were the links between those states and their individual members. There is a rising awareness, however, that nation-states can no longer deliver the benefits that they once could, and that this is due not only to ideological change, but to irreversible structural changes. The search is on for other ways of organizing membership of society, and of distributing the benefits and duties that come with membership. As the organizations of national citizenship appear to get into difficulty, the values and ideals surrounding citizenship—commitments to equality, to democratic participation, and to basic freedoms—remain in place and form the framework against which alternative institutions of society—such as markets or direct democracy—are evaluated. This book examines these current experiments in citizenship, and asks to what extent they appropriate, transform, or realize the fundamental values of citizenship.

The examples in this book do not leave us with clear indications for a means of resolving ambiguities in our approach to citizenship. However, in the final chapter we try to identify the more promising potential lines which might emerge.

REFERENCES

BARBALET, J. M. (1988). *Citizenship. Rights, Struggle and Class Inequality* (Milton Keynes: Open University Press).

BAUBÖCK, R. (1994). *Transnational Citizenship: Membership and Rights in International Migration* (Cheltenham: Edward Elgar).

BRITTAN, S. (1975). 'The Economic Consequences of Democracy', *British Journal of Political Sciences*, 5/2: 129–59.

BRUBAKER, W. R. (1989). *Immigration and the Politics of Citizenship in Europe and North America* (New York: University Press of America).

——(1992). *Citizenship and Nationhood in France and Germany* (Cambridge, MA: Harvard University Press).

BULMER, M., and REES, A. M. (eds.) (1996). *Citizenship Today: The Contemporary Relevance of T. H. Marshall* (London: UCL Press).

Commission of the European Communities (1997). *Citizenship of the Union: Second*

Report from the Commission (Luxembourg: Office for Official Publications of the EC).

EDER, K., and GIESEN, B. (eds.) (2000). *European Citizenship between National Legacies and Postnational Projects* (Oxford: Oxford University Press).

EINHORN, B., KALDOR, M., and KAVAN, Z. (eds.) (1996). *Citizenship and Democratic Control in Contemporary Europe* (Cheltenham: Edward Elgar).

ETZIONI, A. (1996). *The New Golden Rule: Community and Morality in a Democratic Society* (New York: Basic Books).

FRASER, N., and GORDON, L. (1994). 'Civil Citizenship against Social Citizenship?', in B. Van Steenbergen (ed.), *The Condition of Citizenship* (London: Sage), 90–107.

HIRSCHMAN, A. O. (1970). *Exit, Voice and Loyalty: Responses to the Decline of Firms, Institutions and States* (Cambridge: Cambridge University Press).

JANOSKI, T. (1998). *Citizenship and Civil Society* (Cambridge: Cambridge University Press).

JOPPKE, C. (ed.) (1999). *Challenge to the Nation-State: Immigration in Western Europe and the United States* (Oxford: Oxford University Press).

JORDAN, B. (1989). *The Common Good: Citizenship, Morality and Self-Interest* (Oxford: Blackwell).

KOLBERG, J. E. (ed.) (1992). *Between Work and Social Citizenship* (Armonk, NY: Sharpe).

KYMLICKA, W. (1995). *Multicultural Citizenship: A Liberal Theory of Minority Rights* (Oxford: Clarendon Press).

—— and NORMAN, W. (1994). 'Return of the Citizen: A Survey of Recent Work in Citizenship Theory', *Ethics*, 104: 352–81.

LEHNING, P. B., and WEALE, A. (eds.) (1997). *Citizenship, Democracy and Justice in the New Europe* (London: Routledge).

MANN, M. (1987). 'Ruling Class Strategies and Citizenship', *Sociology*, 21: 339–54.

MARSHALL, T. H. (1950). *Citizenship and Social Class and other Essays* (Cambridge: Cambridge University Press).

MARTINIELLO, M. (ed.) (1995). Migration, Citizenship and Ethno-National Identities in the European Union (Aldershot: Avebury).

MEEHAN, E. (1993). *Citizenship and the European Community* (London: Sage).

MILLER, D. (1992). 'Community and Citizenship', in S. Avineri and A. De-Shalit (eds.), *Communitarianism and Individualism* (Oxford: Oxford University Press).

OECD (1994). *The OECD Jobs Study: Evidence and Explanations* (Paris: OECD).

—— (1996). *Employment Outlook 1996* (Paris: OECD).

O'LEARY, S. (1996). *European Union Citizenship* (London: Institute for Public Policy Research).

OLDFIELD, A. (1990). *Citizenship and Community: Civic Republicanism and the Modern World* (London: Routledge).

PUTNAM, R. D., LEONARDI, ROBERT, and NANETTI, RAFFAELLA Y. (1993). *Making Democracy Work: Civic Traditions in Modern Italy* (Princeton, NJ: Princeton University Press).

REX, J. (1996). *Ethnic Minorities in the Modern Nation State: Working Papers in the Theory of Multiculturalism and Political Integration* (Basingstoke: Macmillan).

SANDEL, M. J. (ed.) (1992). *Liberalism and its Critics* (Oxford: Blackwell).

SOMERS, M. R. (1996). 'Where is Sociology after the Historic Turn? Knowledge Cultures, Narrativity, and Historical Epistemologies', in T. J. McDonald (ed.), *The Historic Turn in the Human Sciences* (Ann Arbor: University of Michigan Press).

SÖRENSEN, J. M. (1996). *The Exclusive European Citizenship: The Case for Refugees and Immigrants in the European Union* (Aldershot: Avebury).

SOYSAL, Y. (1994). *Limits of Citizenship: Migrants and Post-National Membership in Europe* (Chicago: University of Chicago Press).

STREECK, W. (1997). 'Industrial Citizenship under Regime Competition: The Case of European Work Councils', *Journal of European Public Policy*, 4: 643–64.

TURNER, B. S. (1986). *Citizenship and Capitalism: The Debate over Reformism* (London: Allen & Unwin).

——(1990). 'Outline of a Theory of Citizenship', *Sociology*, 24/2: 189–217.

——(ed.) (1993). *Citizenship and Social Theory* (London: Sage).

United Kingdom, Commission on Citizenship (1990). *Encouraging Citizenship: Report of the Commission on Citizenship* (London: HMSO).

VISSER, J., and HEMERIJCK, A. (1997). *A Dutch Miracle* (Amsterdam: University of Amsterdam Press).

WIENER, A. (1998). *'European' Citizenship Practice Building Institutions of a Non-State* (Boulder, Colo: Westview Press).

I

The Marketization of Citizenship

2

Romancing the Market, Reviling the State: Historicizing Liberalism, Privatization, and the Competing Claims to Civil Society

Margaret Somers

In the wake of the Eastern European revolutions of the 1980s citizenship has been rediscovered even while it is being continually reinvented. Its rediscovery is a result of world events: we live in a post-1989 geopolitical world stunningly reconfigured by revolutionary transformations in Eastern Europe. Its ongoing reinvention results from the wild unpredictability of this new world set off against the limitations of those few theories we have available to make sense of it all. Central to this project has been the recuperation of the concept of civil society.[1] One of the most significant in a conceptual cluster I call the citizenship concepts,[2] the civil society concept holds immense promise. It promises a fresh political vocabulary liberated from the stifling constraints of cold war Manichean dichotomies, and it resonates to the desiderata of conceptualizing more generally the necessary conditions for democratic and participatory social organization.[3]

In proportion to its theoretical promise, however, the civil society concept also bears an enormous burden. It is being asked to carry the weight of conceptualizing a seemingly novel political and social terrain—a space of popular social movements and collective mobilization, of informal networks, civic associations, and community solidarities oriented toward sustaining a participatory public life—widely believed to have been the foundational form of

---

[1] Wolfe (1989) and Cohen and Arato (1992) document their reading of the exclusion of civil society from social science research; but see Alexander (1993), Calhoun (1993), Seligman (1992), and Taylor (1990) for an idea of the polysemic nature of the term.

[2] Elsewhere I have explored in detail the past and current uses of two others—the public sphere and political culture concepts: Somers 1995*a*, 1995*b*.

[3] e.g. the early work of Habermas (1989 [1962]) on the public sphere and the work of Almond and Verba (1963) on civic culture. On the conceptual rediscovery of civil society, see Cohen and Arato (1992) and Adam Seligman (1992).

social organization that made possible the Eastern European revolutions. The burden is made even more enormous by the *place* the concept is being asked to occupy and defend in the social and political landscape—a landscape long carved out into a binary framework with firm boundaries and epistemological closures between two mutually exclusive zones of public versus private, the state versus the market, what Bobbio has called the 'great dichotomy' of modern political thought (Bobbio 1992: 2). It was in the effort to break apart this dichotomous closure and to liberate a new conceptual space of participatory citizenship—one in between and independent of both markets and state authority, hence free of both coercion and competition—that Eastern European intellectuals and political activists alike rejuvenated the civil society concept. And it was for reasons of this 'in-betweenness' that civil society came to be seen as a 'third sphere', an intermediate and protected zone, one situated in between and not reducible to either the ruthless individualism of unregulated capitalism or the bureaucratic apparatus of the communist state (Entrikin 1991; Somers 1993).

The revival of the civil society concept, then, expresses not only the attempt to keep pace with history's exigencies. Equally important, it expresses a normative ideal: to conceptually capture and extend for future policy the processes and practices of the 1980s that successfully produced such a third realm of democratic practices and collective solidarities.

The Privatization of Citizenship

The premise of this chapter is that, a decade after 1989, it now appears that the burden has been too great. Rather than being increasingly instituted into public discourse and social policy as a third sphere independent of market and state, the conceptual space into which the civil society concept increasingly has been placed—appropriated and subsumed, more accurately—has been in that of the private, anti-political, free market. Citizenship is being privatized.

Romancing the Market, Reviling the State

As stateless cash frenetically circles the globe and foreign policy is all but dictated by central bankers, the evidence for this privatization of citizenship is everywhere. With a bullying muscularity not seen since before the American New Deal and the post-war Keynesian social contract, public policy discourse in liberal democratic societies braggardly reviles public institutions even while it seems barely able to contain its giddy romancing of global markets. In the newly emerging capitalist societies of Eastern Europe and Russia, vanishing social safety nets and burgeoning inequalities have been naturalized as inevitable to democratization.[4] In the west ('third way' governments not withstanding), there is no serious challenge to neo-liberal anti-statist explanations for collapsing welfare states and dramatically increasing degrees of social exclusion.

Anti-statist denigration of public institutions permeates even the discourse of those who promote civic culture and the value of voluntary associational life, even while it couples such normative talk with earnest messages to the poor about austerity and social discipline. Once lively ideas about the value of civic forms of social organization have disappeared into the rubric of how civic freedoms depend first on market discipline. When public debate appears fixated on speculation about whether central bankers—and not citizens—will decide to lower interest rates (a decision that will profoundly influence our collective lives), or about why privatization inevitably must replace public pension schemes, we are seeing citizenship morph from that of public participation into that of obligatory customership in the ever-expanding world of consumer and financial markets.[5]

Lost in this conflation of three spheres to two is citizenship and civil society as the domain of collective, deliberative participation, just as lost by making the 'public' a codeword for a coercive Behemoth is the common-sense notion of the public as the people in common (Wolin 1961; Taylor 1990). Also lost is therefore what T. H. Marshall (1992 [1949]) famously identified as social citizenship: the right of all to the dignity bestowed on fully participating members of a community, not merely through legal but also through social rights. Instead, the punitive language of moral degradation, dependency, and failed personal behaviour has been resurrected to explain social exclusion and poverty. This is the dark underside of romancing the market and reviling the state; here, the indignities of poverty are but collateral damage in the exigency of ministering first to the ever-expanding demands of stateless cash.

---

[4] Obscured by this reinvigorated anti-statism, Holmes (1997) suggests we take a sobering look at the tragedy of 1997 Russia to be reminded that only a muscular legal apparatus backed by a strong state has the power to stand behind a civic culture's normative principles.

[5] Recent immigration law in the USA presents one of the clearest examples of citizenship's increasing privatization. Under intense lobbying and financial incentives from Silicon Valley, Microsoft, and the high-tech industry more generally, and against active opposition from the unions and labour movement, in 1998 the Congress overturned a long-standing yearly quota on the number of Southeast Asian skilled computer technicians allowed to enter for work—and extremely low wages. In the same period of time, several hundreds of African women seeking asylum from female mutilation have been either jailed and/or eventually turned away. To be sure, private capital needs have long—informally—dictated immigration policies; the endless pull-factor from California agribusiness for illegal Mexican workers is but the most obvious example. But to formalize and legitimize practices in which immigration policy is dictated by the private needs of Microsoft, and against the will of a collective public, is to formalize and legitimize a significant increase in the privatization of citizenship.

The significance of this privatization of citizenship signals nothing less than the ominous diminishment of public life. But why? Given the extraordinary influence of the 1989 revolutions on social and political thought, this puzzle of why the civil society concept has been appropriated by the private sphere— this failure of conceptual space—calls out to be explained.

The Problem of the Third Sphere

At the simplest level the answer seems obvious. The civil society concept, after all, like all important concepts, is 'essentially contested'. Despite the recent revival of a quasi-Tocquevillian conception of civil society as a third sphere, the foundational institutions of political liberalism have for much longer claimed ownership over civil society as the anti-political sphere of free exchange, individual, civil, and political liberties, and freedom of private property from the potential tyranny of the state.[6] While essential contestation is arguably a fate to which are doomed all important concepts, civil society has a special problem; call it *the problem of the third sphere*. The problem is the difficulty—if not the impossibility—of fitting three conceptual pegs into only two available conceptual holes. On the one hand we have the only recently rejuvenated and still somewhat fragile idea of civil society as one of three spheres; and on the other hand—and here is where the problem surfaces— we have political liberalism's historically entrenched dyadic framework between market and state alone.

The problem must be framed this way because history shows clearly that the contest over the civil society concept is an unequal one. Despite challenges and varying degrees of legitimacy accorded to competing theories to that of liberalism (for example, civic republicanism, Tocquevillianism, Hegelianism), since Locke modern political theory has been fixed by the vision of only two protagonists in the forging of the modern world: the administrative state and the market economy. This reading of the past was mapped onto a conceptual landscape with firm boundaries and epistemological divides demarcating between the two mutually exclusive conceptual zones of public and private: Bobbio's (1992: 2) great dichotomy.[7] In this dichotomy the two mutually exclusive concepts of public and private, and the parallel ones of state and

---

[6] Taylor (1990) talks about a similarly competing historical notion of civil society by use of the terms 'L-stream' and 'M-stream' approaches, named, respectively, after the figures he chooses to represent them: Locke and Montesquieu. More accurately, at a minimum four rival definitions compete to control its meaning since for moral conservatism it is the anti-political private sphere of religious morality and culturally traditional civility, and I leave out entirely the added complexity offered by Hegel's triadic inclusion of the family, because it does not change the basic claim regarding the relationship of state and market.

[7] Bobbio's argument here dovetails with the work of Alexander (1992) and Alexander and Smith (1993) who have charted the 'great dichotomies' in the binary codings of 'citizen' and 'enemy' in the discourse of civil society.

market, divide the world into two zones which together are exhaustive of social and political reality. Every element of the world is thus covered between the two of them:

[they are] mutually exclusive in the sense that any element covered by the first term cannot simultaneously be covered by the second . . . from the moment that the space defined by the two terms is completely covered they arrive at the point of mutually defining themselves in the sense that the public domain extends only as far as the start of the private sphere (and the reverse is also true) . . . (Bobbio 1992: 1–2)

In a world in which all concepts must conform to one of only two binary possibilities, the conceptual space for a third terrain of participation and solidarity simply does not exist. The crucial task of theorizing civil society is thus blocked by the contradiction between a discursive claim to a zone of social organization located outside the dual arenas of public and private, and the absence of such a third space in what has been the prevailing conceptual landscape.

But this observation only reveals still deeper questions. For one, why is political liberalism so recalcitrant to challenge? The new political language of the third sphere, after all, was not merely a product of playful linguistic experimentation but of empirical forces overpowering social movements, and driving historical changes. And while it may have been just newly rejuvenated, civil society as a third sphere is hardly a weakling *ingénue* in our political vocabulary, but one with a long distinguished heritage in the Tocquevillian and civic republican tradition. So why—and how—does this dichotomy persevere so tenaciously? Moreover, even if we accept the premise of liberalism's dualistic framework, we should still go on to question and problematize the move to appropriate the civil society concept by its private sphere rather than by its public one—something, arguably, more fitting?

Fear and Loathing of the State

One answer to the second question is to be found in the nature of the 1989 revolutions—their militant anti-communist struggles were, of course, directed against tyrannical, indeed villainous, coercive states. In a conceptual landscape limited to only two choices, the 'orphan' third sphere of civil society, its recuperation wholly reinvigorated by these anti-statist, anti-communist revolutions, and motivated by dreams of individual freedom, democratization, and prosperity, would inevitably go into the only available non-state conceptual domain: the private sphere with its associated attributions of political freedom, free markets in ideas, and individual rights. But even this answer is inadequate in itself; for while we have a historically obvious explanation for the anti-statism of the East European revolutionaries, we do not yet have an explanation for the unquestioned association of freedom with private markets, and of unfreedom with a coercive and 'vampire-like' state (Block 1996).

The answer I propose here is that the great dichotomy of liberalism is embedded in and constrained by the metanarrative of Anglo-American citizenship theory (Somers 1995*a*, 1995*b*, 1999). It is this metanarrative that drives the concept of civil society to the private side of the divide; it is this metanarrative that has so firmly entrenched a foundational fear and loathing of the state; and it is the metanarrative's epistemology of social naturalism that gives it the paradigmatic capacity to triumph over the slings and arrows of time and rival theories, and potentially disconfirming counter-evidence. Attributions of such power to an enduring cognitive structure suggest a deep pessimism about the possibility of change (Stinchcombe 1982 [1978]). But there is, none the less, a research programme I believe well-suited for the challenge. A historical sociology of concept formation is designed to analyse 'how we think and why we seem obliged to think in certain ways' (Hacking 1990: 362; Foucault 1973 [1970], 1978 [1966]). The method is designed to account for how concepts do the work they do by reconstructing their construction, resonance, and contestedness over time, and thus to help us 'unthink' (Wallerstein 1991) seemingly natural assumptions. Its premise is that social-science concepts are cultural and historical artefacts embedded within and assigned meaning by their place in historically constructed cognitive and epistemological structures: whether a paradigm (Kuhn 1970), a metanarrative, or a knowledge culture (Somers 1996, 1999)—what Hacking calls 'words in their sites' (Hacking 1990: 362). A historical sociology of concept formation thus requires reconstructing the historical processes by which such cultural structures have taken shape and by which their epistemological boundaries and divides have been created and sustained. Such work of reconstruction usually reveals that concepts often taken for granted as what Durkheim called 'social facts' actually are but products of contingent histories, networks, and narratives which can be subjected to historical and empirical investigation. In what follows, I use this method to do just that: to subject the histories, networks, and narratives of the civil society concept to historical and empirical investigation by reconstructing its construction and its sedimentation over the course of the seventeenth to the twentieth centuries (Somers 1995*b*, 1999).

Reconstructing Anglo-American Citizenship Theory

Anglo-American citizenship theory is the cognitive and cultural structure in which the civil society concept is embedded. By citizenship theory, I refer not to one particular theory but to the deeper common features of liberalism shared by those who have attempted to provide accounts of the conditions

guaranteeing individual protection by the state, individual freedom from the
state, as well as the rights of civil and political citizenship (but not social,
which sits uneasily within liberalism) made famous by T. H. Marshall (1992
[1949]). First adumbrated in the seventeenth century by Locke, explicitly
articulated by the eighteenth-century Scottish moralists (such as Adam Ferguson and Adam Smith), appropriated into the foundations of nineteenth-
century modern sociological theory, and still the basic core of liberal political
thought today, this is less a theory than a story—a 'conjectural history'—of
how popular sovereignty triumphed over coercive absolutist states to ensure
individual liberties.[8] My reading of this conjectural history is that it is a narrative political fiction less about citizenship *per se*, and more about the rise of
a market and a private sphere and its heroic role in establishing the social
foundations for individual freedom and autonomy against the tyranny of the
state—what we now recognize as classical modernization theory.

Anglo-American citizenship theory explains, theorizes, and makes claims to
truth through a narrative structure. Hence it is the integrity of its temporal,
spatial, and sequential relationships that does the explanatory work, and the
success or failure of the explanation depends more on the logic and rhetorical
persuasiveness of the narrative, more on how well the elements of the story are
rationalized into a cohesive narrative logic that can convince us of the empirical world it narrates, and less on positive empirical verification.

Theorizing through Narrative and Crisis: What is to be Explained?

At the heart of every narrative is a crisis or flashpoint that cries out for a solution. So to gain access to the internal logic of a narrative requires first identifying the narrative's 'problematic': what is the crisis to which this narrative
account is being presented as a solution or explanation? The crisis driving
Anglo-American citizenship theory is an obsessional, albeit historically
driven, fear and loathing of tyranny, embodied in the institution of the state.
How to escape the state's ever-present threat to individual liberty? In this
problematic/crisis we see how the story is set to be a Manichean one: the
central antagonist and the constant threat is the public realm of the administrative state—a domain of unfreedom constituted by coercion, domination,
constraint, backed up with physical compulsion, and generative of arbitrary
personal dependencies. The job of the narrative is to solve the crisis and
remove the danger: to theorize an epic struggle led by a heroic protagonist
worthy and capable enough to meet the danger—a danger invented in the first
place by the narrative's definition of the problem as embodied by the chronic
tyranny of the public domain of the state.

[8] The concept of conjectural history I take from Dugald Stewart's characterization of Adam Smith's
historical sociology. See Collini *et al.* (1983), Meek (1976), and Winch (1978).

The unprecedented suppression of personal liberties in seventeenth-century England catalysed the first formulation of this problematic. Locke's revolutionary narration was a direct response to what he considered to be the limits to Hobbes's earlier solution to absolutist authority. Hobbes had been the first to conceptualize the 'problem of order'—so-called because it asked how and from where, in the absence of traditional monarchy, would authority and order come (Parsons 1937; Pocock 1985). Locke took as his starting-point the new problem he believed flowed from Hobbes's solution: how could personal liberty be maintained if the end of the story was again the inevitably coercive all-powerful Leviathan? How could that Leviathan be truly contained? Over the course of the seventeenth, eighteenth, and nineteenth centuries, the narrative has been driven by an amalgam of successive formulations of this same problem, each new incarnation of the problem resulting from the deficiencies of the previous narrative in accounting for new events. But it is Locke's original narration of the solution that cemented the association of the public with the coercive administrative state, and thus set the stage for the privatization of citizenship.

Narrating Place: Theorizing through Political Geography

A narrative requires a sense of space and place—a social and political geography (Entrikin 1991; Somers 1992, 1993, 1997; Somers and Gibson 1994). The prevailing one in Locke's time was represented in the famous frontispiece to Hobbes's Leviathan. In this allegorical engraving of political authority, Hobbes depicts the giant body of a wise, benevolent, and patriarchal-looking king standing God-like above a miniature landscape of everyday people's country farms and churches. What at first glance appears to be merely the king's suit of metal armour is actually hundreds of miniature people all facing reverently towards the giant head of the king and crown. What Hobbes has done here is wholly to insert into the spatial body of the king and state 'the people'—more aptly, the 'subjects'—of his kingdom. Embedded as they are within the king's one spatial corporality, there is no separate terrain available for people to inhabit other than that of the king's own body. Hobbes's narrative contained only one place of social organization—the state itself—leaving no separate place for the people. Driven by the tyrannical experience of English absolutism, Locke fiercely rejected the conflating of the people into the singular political space of the king's body/state. He had an alternative vision that would permanently relocate the place of the people and in turn reverse the direction and the source of political power—away from the state to that of the people. Even though Hobbes had imagined a one-time 'reversal' by narrating an original social contract, his theory of Leviathan revealed his reversal to be only a one-time event that settled power back with the state.

In Locke's contrary problematic of the tyrannical state, Hobbes's was a topography that called for its own negation. To endow the people with the capacity for freedom, Locke envisioned a collective terrain distinct and independent from that of the state. He envisioned, in short, a 'civil (non-state) society'.

Locke found this through a revolutionary remapping of the prevailing topography. He invented, and narrated, a new locus of social organization—a pre-political and pre-state private entity spatially separate and distinct from the state, a new place for the people alone. It was to be a permanent place of individual freedom and property that would establish the grounds for an enduring collective entity; it would also serve as a normative reference point from the state. In this permanence of a private sphere, Locke's political vision broke decisively from Hobbes's and introduced the most enduring formulation of the conditions for popular freedom. In attributing a separate and pre-political social space as the sole realm of true freedom, he forever imprinted on our political imaginations a binary spatial divide between public and private. In this revolutionary narration, he recast forever our vision of politics.

Locke thus narrated a Manichean dualism. The free-born English people are faced with an emergent crisis of evil in the vilified Goliath-like character of the state; like a *deus ex machina* a new heroic character appears in the form of the autonomous social space of a non-coercive pre-political (hence private) realm of (civil) society—only within its private boundaries are the people's liberties safe from state power. Indeed, in typical narrative form there is even an element of surprise: it is actually the people themselves who create this new realm of social organization through their own heroic act of consenting to an enduring social contract. And also consistent with most narration, the face of evil is never absolutely eliminated but remains in the shadowy background motivating a constant vigilance. Even after the sovereign people create a tamed representative government strictly under their control, the state as Leviathan hovers as a permanent potential threat always ready to rear its coercive head in popular tyranny. Fear and loathing of the state is the wellspring in the story of freedom; it is this that gives civil society its continuous *raison d'être*.

We think of the nineteenth century as the age of the discovery of modern social theory. But in this narrative it is clearly Locke who first imagined the spatial possibility of a non-political domain of life that could exist *sui generis* free from political authority and control. Civil society was the realm of popular freedom because it was a collective society with the robustness to exist independently from the state. It is this notion of an autonomous pre-political society that by the eighteenth century explicitly takes on the terminology of civil society.[9] Since Locke, the story of ever-fragile popular liberties

---

[9] Locke still used the traditional language of political theory in which the terms 'civil society' and 'political society' were used interchangeably to refer to the state-centred domain of social organization.

has been narrated as the fierce struggle of civil society to remain free from the overly regulative reaches of the public state.

Narrating Time: Establishing Causality through Sequence

Locke's invention of the new site of pre-political commercial society, as revolutionary as it was, was not in itself sufficient to ensure permanently the people's freedom from state control. After all, what would prevent the potentially Leviathan state from subordinating anew even this separate society? To solve this problem, Locke invented a new narrative sequence: rather than civil society emerging after the state, he tells a story that begins with the people and their making of the social contract, who then subsequently agree to a representative popular government. By narrating the temporal sequence of the plot in this way, Locke is able to depict a government that exists as nothing more than an outcome of the prior activities of the pre-political community: their voluntary consent to form a government. But because literally created by the temporally anterior sphere of civil society, this consent to government can be revoked at any time—sovereignty resides resolutely in the hands of the people in civil society.

Locke's imaginative use of time was political; he uses civil society's temporal anteriority to explain, thus justify, its political authority over the government it had, after all, created. The temporality of the narrative is also doing the work of establishing moral justification for the subservience of the state to the people. Thus the syntax of narrative is used to establish ideological authority. In this temporal order, a legitimate government is one morally reduced to being a contingent outcome of the people's consent endowed to them only contingently in pre-political civil society.

A clear causal plot has begun to emerge from Locke's mapping of the narrative structure of the Anglo-American citizenship story. He has taken as his point of departure in time the epic problem of free people with natural rights (the protagonists of a 'natural community') confronting the chronic tyranny of an absolute state. The danger to individual liberties and rights lies explicitly with this visible institutional and administrative state power (its personnel and bureaucracy): 'A right of making laws with penalties of death' is how Locke defines political power—a definition echoed two centuries later by Weber's characterization of the state bureaucracy as an iron cage of coercion. A resolution to the crisis can only emerge through a complete realignment of power and legitimacy, something that can only be accomplished by renarrativizing the state/society developmental story on which the original problem was based. Locke's dramatic resolution is causally plotted not only by the establishment of the domain of pre-political/society, but also by the people newly establishing a representative government that is morally and scientifically a mere 'provisional' product of the social. In this new story the rule of law, the participatory aspects of common law (such as juries), constitutions, and so on are narrated to be the outcome of the temporally and causally prior and independent (of political rule) sphere of a pre-political/society. We now have a more balanced epic struggle framed by a fiercely protected boundary between a tamed government under the control of the people and the chronic threat of the potentially tyrannical state.

Through narrative Locke has established political causality: civil society is not only separate and autonomous from the state, but existed before it and thus, quite literally, caused government's very existence by its voluntary consent. Something that comes before something else, in this schema, gives it causality.[10] This is not chronological time, but epistemological time—a narrative that endows cause and effect.

The Place of Civil Society: The People's Sociological Glue

With the invention of a private sphere of commerce, property, and exchange has come a novel sociological challenge: what would hold this society together? If 'the people' were to have any sustained power against a tyranni-cal state—and this is of course the driving aspiration of the narrative—it had to be counter-balanced not by an atomistic aggregation of individuals but by a coherent and robust body. The authority of civil society over the state could not only be based on its being separate and prior to the state; equally impor-tant, it would have to be capable of self-organized autonomy such that it did not need the state, or at least only minimally. The presumption of a society self-organized enough to be able to make and break government rule, indeed to snub all government intervention except that of security and protection of property, pushed Locke into developing a theory of social organization to account for a robust normative social cohesion beyond theology or the indi-vidualism of market exchange. Only with such cohesion could true autonomy be achieved.

Locke found this in his notion of a civil community held together through a political culture of public opinion and social trust. Added to the interde-pendencies of the market, the common moral concerns he believed charac-terized a civil community based on public opinion would ensure for order, freedom, and moral cohesion—outside the channels and institutions of the state (Dunn 1984; Taylor 1990). Unlike state authority, the authority of civil public opinion is free of 'the legislative authority of man' because vol-untary, spontaneous, and non-coercive. The idea of a civil society based on a

---

[10] In this he capitalizes on a generic quirk built into English-language narratives themselves. Linde (1993: 11) explains the 'natural logic of English is post hoc ergo propter hoc', or that which comes before causes that which comes after.

normative political culture thus provides the glue of popular sovereignty and representational consent. Locke exalted civil society's harmoniousness by virtue of the absence of public external political authority.

A sociological theorization of robust and durable societal self-activation thus emerged in necessary parallel with the normative claim that authority and right of resistance and consent must be located within the private sphere. The radical change was in rejecting the notion of ordered social relationships sustained by the power of a political centre, in favour of a conception of society as a self-activating unit capable of generating a common will—spontaneous in its workings, self-activating and functionally independent of the state. To endow 'the people' with the capacity to make and unmake political power and sovereignty, Locke had to endow the people with a collective glue independent from the political cohesion supplied by the state. For this he needed to find the social foundations to subordinate permanently the state to a cohesive popular authority. Civil society cohered in this story through what we today call 'informal social control'—not in any recognizably institutional form. Thus liberal theory's social foundations were found in a story of the private world of civil society.

An Epistemological Infrastructure of Social Naturalism

The privatization of citizenship and its concomitant fear of the public domain of the state has shown remarkable resilience over the years despite multiple challenges from both history and theory. Why has Anglo-American citizenship theory been so invincible to direct empirical criticism—even in the face of such repeated competing evidence? The answer lies in the epistemology of social naturalism.

Standard epistemology, rather than a particular theory or truth, is the theory of knowledge itself—those rules and criteria (the 'lie detectors' of intellectual claims) that are used to evaluate whether any given piece of information should count as truth, knowledge, and fact. To evaluate the truth-claims of knowledge, epistemology uses criteria that transcend the particularities of any given theory or phenomenon and relies upon what is believed to be universal and unchanging. These criteria have been called 'foundational' as the history of epistemology has been a quest for the foundations of certainty (Douglas 1982 [1970]: 52; Rorty 1979). The laws of nature—because they are universal and not subject to the vicissitudes of culture, place, and time—have always served as the foundational point of reference in the territory of epistemology. Only nature escapes the fickleness and fortuitousness of history, only nature is credited by philosophers with having absolute regularities. That which is 'natural' is thus ontologically independent of political or human

Exogenous/Natural Given in the nature of things	Endogenous/Cultural Historically constructed
Laws of nature	arbitrary
God-given	historical
universality	particularism
foundations	manifestations
rationality	irrationality
'representations which cannot be gainsaid'	artificial
certainty	fickleness and fortuitousness
universal criteria	particularities
scientific	magical
discovered	constructed
regularities	contingencies
in-the nature-of-things	externally imposed

FIGURE 2.1. The discovery of society: Anglo-American citizenship's
seventeenth-century spatial identities

intervention, be it natural law (seventeenth century), natural liberty (eighteenth and nineteenth centuries), or the natural science of political economy (nineteenth century). In contrast are those things represented as costructed-/artificial/ideological; they lack the quality of certainty because they are a product of the thinker's conceptual schemas rather than natural phenomena which exist independently of the mind.

Social naturalism extends the criteria of the laws of nature from natural to social phenomena. In social naturalism, the world of knowledge is divided into a set of binary relationships along the classic axis of nature/culture. From there it evaluates the truth of social knowledge by apportioning its conceptual arguments across this epistemological divide (see Figure 2.1)—attributing higher epistemological status to all that falls on the natural side of the bifurcation (Somers 1995*b*). In this dichotomy 'culture' and 'historically constructed' are taken to mean those non-natural, hence arbitrary, dimensions of the social universe. Social naturalism thus creates a hierarchical delineation between that which is designated as 'given' (unchanging, spontaneous, voluntary, natural, God-given, law-like) versus that designated as 'contingent' (socially or historically constructed, hence temporal, coercive, arbitrary, vulnerable to change or manipulation).

Because of philosophy's association between nature and truth, those things located on the natural, exogenous side—and so believed to be ontologically independent of political or human intervention—are deemed epistemologically more valid and foundational to knowledge and science than those located on the culturally constructed side. This method of distributing epistemological privilege makes social naturalism a grid for the all-important task of epistemological adjudication: the process by which truth is separated from dangerous fraud. According to this grid of social naturalism, social knowledge is scientific, admissible, and true to the extent that it corresponds with the foundations established by that which is natural—be it natural law (seventeenth century), natural liberty (eighteenth and nineteenth centuries), or the natural science of political economy (nineteenth century).

The Metanarrative of Anglo-American Citizenship Theory

When a narrative structure is grafted onto the binary code of social naturalism the narrative is transformed to the much more potent cultural schema of what historians and social scientists have recently come to call a metanarrative (Lyotard 1984; Skinner 1985; White 1987).[11]

A metanarrative is a narrative structure that has been epistemologically 'naturalized' by its conjoining with the binary coding of social naturalism. Thus the birth of Anglo-American citizenship theory: Locke created a metanarrative by grafting his narrative to the binary epistemological coding of social naturalism, as Figure 2.2 illustrates. Figure 2.3 shows the outcome of this process in its skeletal binary form. The temporal sequences and spatial mappings characteristic of a narrative structure have been redistributed across the binary nature/culture divide. The narrative has been transmogrified into a set of mutually exclusive abstract oppositions (public and private, state and civil society, tradition and modernity, the free/autonomous and unfree/dominated agent); to define any one category presupposes its oppositional Other. From this come Bobbio's great dichotomies of modern social and political thought, dichotomous and zero-sum concepts such that each can only be the negation of the other: 'from the moment that the space defined by the two terms is completely covered they arrive at the point of mutually defining themselves in the sense that the public domain extends only as far as the start

---

[11] Metanarratives are all around us. They are the stories in which we are embedded both as social actors as well as in our analytic role as social scientists. Our sociological theories and concepts are encoded with aspects of these metanarratives—Progress, Decadence, Industrialization, Enlightenment, etc.—even though they usually operate at a presuppositional level of social science awareness. They can be the epic dramas of our time: Capitalism vs. Communism, the Individual vs. Society, Barbarism/Nature vs. Civility. They may also take the form of macrosociologies of teleological unfolding: Marxism and the triumph of class struggle, Liberalism and the triumph of Liberty, the Rise of Nationalism, or of Islam (Somers 1992, 1995a, 1995b). The 'new institutionalists' have been especially lucid (in both their own research and building from others' work in economics, organizational psychology, and anthropology) in demonstrating that metanarratives can be found at work in everyday social life by recognizing them in the form of cultural schemas around which institutions and organizations stake their everyday routine identities—consciously or not (DiMaggio and Powell 1991; Lamont and Fournier 1992).

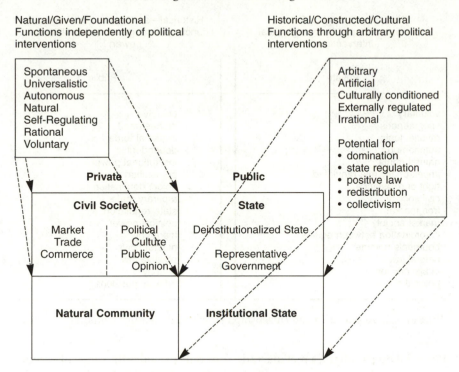

Natural/Given/Foundational
Functions independently of political
interventions

Historical/Constructed/Cultural
Functions through arbitrary political
interventions

Spontaneous
Universalistic
Autonomous
Natural
Self-Regulating
Rational
Voluntary

Arbitrary
Artificial
Culturally conditioned
Externally regulated
Irrational

Potential for
• domination
• state regulation
• positive law
• redistribution
• collectivism

Private **Public**

Civil Society **State**

Market Political Deinstitutionalized State
Trade Culture
Commerce Public Representative
Opinion Government

Natural Community **Institutional State**

Epistemological Grid of Social Naturalism Mapped Onto the Narrative
Structure of Anglo-American Citizen Theory

FIGURE 2.2. Hobbes's spatial structure

of the private sphere (and the reverse is also true)' (1992: 2). The naturalism
of the private, of modernity, civil society, and markets is fixed in opposition
to the arbitrariness of the public, of institutionalism, the state, and legal
regulation.

Social naturalism, as we know, epistemologically empowers that which it
endows, thus making metanarratives structures of supreme—thus 'meta'—
conceptual authority. They have an extraordinary power to define conceptual placement because their epistemological naturalism establishes rules
of hierarchy and inferiority, patterns of privilege and disdain, boundaries
of inclusion and exclusion, normative tropes of good and bad, rules of
rationality and evidence—all the characteristics of an epistemological
gatekeeper.

Figure 2.3's binary table shows how Anglo-American citizenship theory
exercises its adjudicative authority through inviolable epistemological divides.
These boundaries categorize evidence, argumentation, and hypothesis formation, into prestructured categories (Lamont and Fournier 1992; Zerubavel

Margaret Somers

Natural—as Original Force (functions independently of political interventions)		Historical—as Constructed Force (functions through arbitrary political power)
Private		Public
voluntary		coercive
spontaenous		orchestrated
rational logic		irrational force
autonomous		dependent
natural rights		institutional power
impersonally rule regulated		personified power
right of resistance		abject domination
civil society		arbitrary state
free market		state regulation
market society		political power
co-ordination between equals		hierarchy
bourgeois homme		master/slave
natural law		positive law
public opinion		tyranny
political culture		artificial passions

FIGURE 2.3. Anglo-American citizenship's seventeenth-century temporal structure

1991). Like a paradigm, a metanarrative not only provides the range of acceptable answers but also the terms of rational argument, the criteria for worthwhile questions, and the rules of procedure by which they can rationally be answered. Arguments that fall on the wrong sides of their usual distribution across the epistemological divides do not enjoy the privilege of being considered reasonable candidates for competing explanatory validity. Nor can a metanarrative be easily destabilized through competing evidence or routine empirical investigation. In fact when a metanarrative confronts inconvenient evidence it is able to redefine, almost domesticate it, or else to rule it inadmissible by its own standards of rationality.

Thus social naturalism—an epistemological modality which is normally intended to adjudicate the criteria by which knowledge is judged to be true or not—becomes embedded into the substantive content of the story. Locke's anti-political private sphere of civil society and the market, for example, is not only judged by its association with epistemological naturalism as more foundational and valid as the grounds for argument; it is also redefined as being natural—foundational, and hence privileged. Indeed, as I will argue, Locke's use of social naturalism to naturalize markets and the private sphere of civil society was the defining moment in modern political thought.

Figure 2.4 shows how Anglo-American citizenship theory distributes its political and sociological categories, its temporal and spatial relationships,

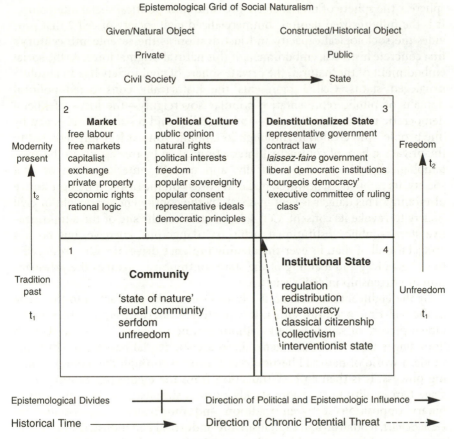

FIGURE 2.4. Place of the political culture concept in Anglo-American citizenship's narrative structure

across its epistemological divides. On the vertical axis the sequential path from unfreedom to freedom is represented; on the horizontal axis the spatial divides between the private naturalism of society and the arbitrary power of the public state. Locke's narrative begins with the 'golden age' version of the state of nature in cell 1.

Because it is natural and God-given its time is the abstract 'past' rather than the concrete past of the early 'primitive' stage of eighteenth-century social theory or the 'traditional/feudal' past of nineteenth-century theory. Its very naturalism and God-given qualities give it both narrative and epistemological primacy as the original foundational force of Locke's normative justification for popular sovereignty. But it is cell 2 that embodies the first sphere of true social naturalism: society is an autonomous self-activated natural sphere—the sphere of non-coercive pre- and non-political social intercourse. It is the fully realized natural commercialized civil society of cell 2 that provides the sociological capacity and justification as the seventeenth century's first concrete historical embodiment of this natural original force. As the social embodiment of the 'natural', the private sphere of civil society has an absolute privileged status. Cell 3 represents the historically constructed political domain of public representative popular sovereignty—the locus of liberal democratic political institutions—to be recalled and resisted, if necessary, by 'the people' who created it. Although in a public zone, it is firmly tethered to the private sphere of contractual interaction taken by free agents in the epistemologically, historically, politically, and morally anterior realm of civil society. Its publicness, however, makes it always on the brink of being a source of tyranny. This danger is kept in check by the contingency and right of civil society to revoke its consent. Cell 4, by contrast, is the site of the administrative state—public, institutional, arbitrary, dangerous, coercive, but no less crucial for all of that. Its ever-threatening presence drives the flow from cell 2 to cell 3 as fear and loathing of the state continuously justifies the privatization of citizenship in civil society.

By the eighteenth century, cell 1 bursts out of the abstract onto the scene as the real-time primitive Other. It is portrayed alternatively as either a full-blown picture of savage society without private property (as in the Scottish 'four stages theory'), or as a generalized archaic feudal past from which the modern world of natural liberties (cell 2) evolves through the natural civilizing process. It is then an easy transition from the eighteenth-century four-stage temporality to the more starkly posited simplistic nineteenth-century binary oppositions between tradition and modernity, *Gemeinschaft* and *Gesellschaft*, feudalism and capitalism, pre-industrial and industrial, status and contract, each represented by cells 1 and 2 respectively. Note that when the 'past' is specified as a traditional community organized through kinship, even though it is still clearly a locus of unfreedom, it is none the less viewed as natural, hence a necessary stage of progression to modern freedom. This contrasts with the fully aberrant non-natural arbitrary domain of public rule in the absolutist state whose presence lurks in the foreground of Anglo-American citizenship theory as the reason for the ongoing effort pre-political/society must put into maintaining cell 3—the tamed and deinstitutionalized public arena of private representation where the only rules made are those necessary to ensure the protection of cell 2's essential natural freedom (for example, contract and civil law).

The epistemological divides and the gatekeeping demarcations depicted in Figure 2.4 thus represent the three core elements originating in the seventeenth-century metanarrative of Anglo-American citizenship theory: (1) the institutionalized state of the public domain embodies external coercion, domination, constraint, backed up with physical compulsion, and generative of arbitrary personal dependencies; it is thus the domain of unfreedom; (2) private pre-political/civil society is the realm of freedom because it is autonomous from the state, impersonal, self-activating through objective interdependencies (for example, property contracts, division of labour, markets) and naturalistic; a unitary entity whose normative roots are in the idealized harmony of the market; (3) in lieu of government authority in the work of maintaining social cohesion, the norms and pressures of public opinion provide the means for both order and freedom in civil society. Combined, these comprise the essential infrastructure of Anglo-American citizenship theory, with its binary opposition between the spontaneous free forces of pre-political/civil society and the normative order of civil society on the one side, versus the tamed representative state and, in the background shadows, always the potentially coercive, dominating, and enforced dependencies of public administrative power. It is a metanarrative born out of the ongoing 'itch' (Baker 1990: 6) to find the solution to the fear and loathing of the public state, the social foundations for a spatial domain of society where liberties and rights of representation could be organizationally grounded outside the powers of the coercive state. To ensure these rights were themselves foundational and not at the behest of the crown or the positive laws of the land, Locke made them natural rights, hence God-given and part of the pre-political natural community; by this means he 'naturalized' the organizational autonomy of society.

Theoretical Implications

The Privatization of Civil Society

The privatization of civil society clearly can be traced back to its origins in the metanarrative of Anglo-American citizenship theory. Driven by a fear and loathing of the state, Locke invented a private/anti-political sphere of social organization, entirely separate from the state and strictly limited to the site of the private. His moral vision of an autonomous civil society supplied liberal theory with a mechanism of social cohesion that could not be found in a limited exchange-based notion of community. It is within this separate and pre-political site of civil society that Locke locates the origins and practices of citizenship. In this paradoxical sense, what is 'political', 'public', even 'civil' about citizenship in Anglo-American citizenship theory is that public opinion and individual rights, though firmly rooted in the private sphere of civil society, are contingently entrusted to a representative government—a government entirely accountable to the private interests from whence it came and from whom its authority derives. The invention of a civil society inhabiting a space outside of, and anterior to the public sphere of the state's political institutions, disembodied citizenship from the participatory aspect of the political, devoid of the power and practices characteristic of public decision-making activities (Taylor 1990: 109–11). The citizenship born of civil society may culminate in a government but is none the less decidedly anti-political in the sense commonly associated with citizenship as participation in a public sphere.

Constrained within this conceptual matrix, the civil society concept has been frozen in its place—firmly on the non-political, naturalistic, and anti-statist side of the epistemological divide between public and private, nature/rationality, and the arbitrary power attributed to the public sphere. The demonization, the fear and loathing of the public and the state is what made a non-political private sphere a necessity; the civil society concept is what endows this private sphere with the capacity to thrive independently of the state. The privatization of citizenship through civil society solidifies the bulwark against the constant threat of the public state.

The Metanarrative as Gatekeeper

By grafting social naturalism to his story of civil society and the state, Locke hardened his story's temporal and spatial divides into a set of durable epistemological criteria for legitimate theories of democratization and freedom. The effect was paradigmatic. The metanarrative took on the role of an epistemological gatekeeper—adjudicating over how evidence could be rationally distributed across the epistemological spectrum. If a historian's research into the 'pre-modern' world, for example, points to evidence for political rights in the wrong temporal or spatial frame—the rights of citizens in medieval cities, say—she learns very quickly that historiographical legitimacy is only accorded when these same rights have been renamed and redefined as 'traditional' 'pre-modern' rights, 'pre-political' 'paternalistic' forms of a 'moral economy' or the 'lagging' remnants of a feudal order—thus stripped of any potentially destabilizing impact on the metanarrative's story about political rights.

The hallmark of an epistemological gatekeeper, like a paradigm, is the capacity to demarcate the boundaries of what counts as rational (hence admissible) investigation into truth or falsehood; not just answers but, more importantly, the criteria for what counts as reasonable evidence to be brought to bear are delimited within the gatekeeping parameters of a metanarrative—hence Anglo-American citizenship theory's gatekeeping power over the distribution of evidence and the adjudication of what counts as knowledge and truth. Once this kind of closure has been established, evidential competition always runs the risk of being made to seem irrelevant or even irrational. No alternative empirical challenge to the privatization of citizenship or the anti-statism of Anglo-American citizenship theory can have long-term success until the gatekeeping power of the dominant metanarrative is challenged and transgressed by denaturalizing through historical reconstruction its epistemological foundations.

The Contemporary Legacy

From the metanarrative of Anglo-American citizenship theory, we have inherited the ineluctable connection established between freedom, the naturalism of market exchange, and individual rights on the one side; potential tyranny or, at a minimum, massive inefficiency, waste, and corruption in the institutional domain of the state on the other. Since the seventeenth century Anglo-American citizenship theory has proclaimed the normative guide for political organization to be the anti-institutional privatized norms of civil society. Only by mandate of the political culture of a marketized notion of civil society can true democratic rules be legitimate.

Hence from the Physiocrats' notion that public opinion reflected the *ordre naturel* emanating from civil society (Calhoun 1992) to Marx's utopian postulation of freedom, as emancipation from both the exploitation of capitalist labour as well as from the dominion of institutional politics, we can observe a continuity in the idea that it is the rationality of private exchange in civil society that gives rise to democratic beliefs, values, even practices, of public discourse. For Locke, Smith, and Marx, the freedoms of the liberal state embodied private interests alone. And although Marx, of course, saw these as bourgeois freedoms that supported the exploitation of labour, this did not in any way affect his view of the state as an expression of private interests. In perfect harmony with Anglo-American citizenship's metanarrative, Marx's source of freedom was also to be found in civil society—only for Marx it would be a more developed stage of civil society, one that followed the demise of capitalism and the bourgeois democratic state.

Indeed, as Habermas points out, for classical liberalism even the rule of law could only be made acceptable by appropriating it as the symbol not of the state but of societal norms: 'In the "law" the quintessence of general, abstract, and permanent norms, inheres a rationality in which . . . the exercise of power is to be demoted to a mere executor of such norms' (Habermas 1989 [1962]: 53). Where do ideals of liberty come from? asked Locke. From the norms of propertied society was his answer. The 'public spirited man', Adam Smith echoed a century later, was he who respected the powers and opinions that operated in the everyday life of exchange and transactions, not one who wanted to legislate and rearrange through institutional 'meddlings' (Wolin 1961: 299). It is much the same answer, driven by much the same metanarrative, that is given by decision-makers (even those of 'the third way') some 300 years later.

I cannot trace the entire historical trajectory—the institutionalized path-dependency—of Anglo-American citizenship theory and its associated arguments in liberal theory. Suffice it here to show how the earlier work set a template, and that recognizing this template gives insight into later arguments. In so doing, I demonstrate how the method of a historical sociology of concept formation differs from the usual approach to intellectual history (Somers 1995*a*, 1995*b*, 1999). Intellectual historians tend to operate on the assumption that ideas are passed along in chains from one individual thinker to another, so the key proof of continuity is to demonstrate these explicit chains of 'influence' by one thinker on another. But influence does not necessarily work in quite that way. While finding direct connections does not hurt, they would not mostly be one-to-one connections, but rather ones mediated by larger currents of thought. To demonstrate influence, a historical sociology of concept formation must find a basic continuity between the organizing assumptions and conceptual imagery of the modern approaches, and the earlier ones; it must show, for example, how the Anglo-American citizenship metanarrative's epistemological divides and narrative presuppositions remain the adjudicators of what counts as valid empirical argument in modern political social science. Recursive use of the metanarrative, from this perspective, occurs through the 'exclusion of competing aspects that might turn choice in another direction' (DiMaggio and Powell 1991: 19). Such processes of exclusion are the outcome of the naturalized boundaries, classifications, distinctions, and metanarrative assumptions we have seen at work in Anglo-American citizenship theory. Information from 'outside the boundaries' is ignored, redefined, or even 'polluted' (Douglas). For the task at hand, then, reconstructing the inner logic of the arguments and demonstrating a continuity in the underlying logic of the arguments is more important than searching for chains of direct influence.

The paradox and the puzzle I posed at the outset was that the newly rejuvenated civil society concept—recalled to theoretical service to represent a third sphere of participation, solidarities, and a robust public discourse of rights—has again been privatized in political argument, now seemingly reduced to a cluster of non-political, anti-public, and marketized attributes. Neo-liberalism has been able increasingly to hail true citizenship as a form of social activity reflecting the ethically superior private sphere of market priorities.

At the causal heart of this problem we have found the remarkably tenacious metanarrative of Anglo-American citizenship theory and its enduring, driving themes of romancing the market and reviling the state. It was not only the recent revolutions in Eastern Europe that were profoundly anti-statist; classical liberalism, the dominant paradigm of our time, was itself born of the need to theorize a modality and a sphere of life believed to be free and, above all, autonomous from what seventeenth-century thinkers saw as the chronic threat of state tyranny. For 300 years an essential element of the dichotomous conceptual mapping of political and social space has been the Manichean dimension of the great dichotomy—an overwhelming fear and loathing, an imputed sense of 'evil', tyranny, and corruption (in modern times, also inefficiencies) associated with the institutional public domain of the state. Fear and loathing of the state, its demonization and vilification, has from its inception been the dominant template of modern Western political theory, and it is this 'push factor' away from the public domain that makes the privatization of citizenship a recurrent inevitability.

The newly (seventeenth-century) invented sphere of civil society, with its foundations in a naturalized vision of market exchange, was the heroic protagonist in the metanarrative of Anglo-American citizenship theory. Civil society became the realm of popular freedom because it was declared autonomous from and prior to the state, spontaneous in its workings, self-activating and naturalistic—a unitary entity whose normative roots are in the idealized freedom of the harmonious state of nature, coupled with a romanticized vision of the market that alone could nurture the prosperity, safety, and freedom of the people's individual rights, property, and families. Hence just as there is a push factor (vilification, fear and loathing of the state) that directs the civil society concept away from the public side of a dichotomy limited to only two choices, there is also a 'pull factor' towards the private sphere that helps account for its conceptual placement. Placing civil society on the private side of the limited public/private state/market dichotomy of political thought is what allowed liberalism to be complete—to be a social as well as a political theory by adding the essential mechanism of social cohesion to the otherwise overly brittle sphere of individualized market exchange. Indeed once it was clearly accepted that such autonomy from the state was the essential precondition for human freedom, then the most urgent task at hand was to establish and fortify the private sphere as a viable counter-domain to the state, one robust enough to maintain that autonomy. The concept of civil society has long served as the social glue that gives the private market the social cohesion necessary to be able to exist autonomously from the chronic threat of the institutional state. The civil society concept has an integrative role to play in the private domain. Its theoretical job is to do what markets and individual property exchange alone could not do: solidify the social foundations of cohesion.

The resilience of the Anglo-American citizenship theory is remarkable. Its foundational elements—shifts of balance and power over the years not withstanding—have survived intact over the course of three centuries and continue to shape public discourse and social policy. One purpose of this chapter has been to demonstrate how a historical sociology of concept formation can help to destabilize the metanarrative by showing how its epistemological foundations were fixed through the convention of social naturalism, thus historicizing the seemingly primordial distinctions between nature and culture. We have seen how, for some 300 years, what is natural and what is marketized have been intimately joined as the foundational grounds for political and epistemological argument—the natural side of the divide being tethered to the morally superior and historically anterior side of the divide between private and public, society and the state. But if social naturalism's very standards of validity are historically constructed, then so too are the epistemological hierarchies between natural and constructed, private and public, market and state—and most important, so too the classical and neo-liberalism's Manichean zero-sum dichotomous choice structure. A historical sociology of concept formation challenges us to call into question that which is and is not considered natural and to destabilize the naturalizing of private over public. Perhaps, then, the greatest pay-off of exploring the privatization of citizenship and the civil society concept through historical reconstruction is the challenge it poses to the idea that epistemological boundaries and normative hierarchies are given in the nature of things; no political, social, or conceptual boundary comes without a history.

REFERENCES

ALEXANDER, J. C. (1992). 'Citizen and Enemy as Symbolic Classification: On the Polarizing Discourse of Civil Society,' in M. Lamont and M. Fournier (eds.), *Cultivating Differences: Symbolic Boundaries and the Making of Inequality* (Chicago: University of Chicago Press), 289–308.

—— (1993). 'The Return to Civil Society', *Contemporary Sociology*, 22: 797–803.

—— and SMITH, P. (1993). 'The Discourse of American Civil Society: A New Proposal for Cultural Studies', *Theory and Society*, 22: 151–207.

ALMOND, G. A. (1980). 'The Intellectual History of the Civic Culture Concept, in G. A. Almond and S. Verba (eds.), *The Civic Culture Revisited* (Boston, Mass.: Little Brown), 1–36.

—— and VERBA, S. (1963). *The Civic Culture: Political Attitudes and Democracy in Five Nations* (Princeton, NJ: Princeton University Press).

BAKER, K. M. (1990). *Inventing the French Revolution: Essays on French Political Culture in the Eighteenth Century* (Cambridge: Cambridge University Press).

BLOCK, F. L. (1996). *The Vampire State: And Other Myths and Fallacies about the U.S. Economy* (New York: New Press).

BOBBIO, N. (1992). *Democracy and Dictatorship* (Minneapolis, Minn.: University of Minnesota).

CALHOUN, C. (1992). 'Introduction', in C. Calhoun (ed.), *Habermas and the Public Sphere* (Cambridge, Mass.: MIT Press).

—— (1993). 'Civil Society and the Public Sphere', *Public Culture*, 5: 267–80.

—— (1994). 'Social Theory and the Politics of Identity', in C. Calhoun (ed.), *Social Theory and the Politics of Identity* (Oxford: Blackwell), 9–36.

COHEN, J. L., and ARATO, A. (1992). *Civil Society and Political Theory* (Cambridge, Mass.: MIT Press).

COLLINI, S., WINCH, D., and BURROW, J. (1983). *That Noble Science of Politics: A Study in Nineteenth Century Intellectual History* (Cambridge: Cambridge University Press).

DiMAGGIO, P. J., and POWELL, W. W. (1991). 'Introduction', in W. W. Powell and P. J. DiMaggio (eds.), *The New Institutionalism in Organizational Analysis* (Chicago: University of Chicago Press), 1–38.

DOUGLAS, M. (1982 [1970]). *Natural Symbols: Exploration in Cosmology* (New York: Pantheon).

DUNN, J. (1984). *Locke* (Oxford: Oxford University Press).

ENTRIKIN, J. NICHOLAS (1991). *The Betweenness of Place: Towards a Geography of Modernity* (Baltimore: John Hopkins University Press).

FERGUSON, A. (1995). *An Essay on the History of Civil Society* (Cambridge: Cambridge University Press).

FOUCAULT, M. (1973 [1970]). *The Order of Things: An Archaeology of the Human Sciences* (New York: Vintage).

—— (1978 [1966]). *Introduction to 'On the Normal and the Pathological' by Georges Canguilhem* (Dordrecht: D. Reidel Publishing).

HABERMAS, J. (1989 [1962]). *The Structural Transformation of the Public Sphere: An Inquiry into a Category of Bourgeois Society* (Cambridge, Mass.: MIT Press).

HACKING, I. (1990). 'Two Kinds of "New Historicism" for Philosophers', *New Literary History*, 21: 343–64.

HOLMES, S. (1997). 'What Russia Teaches us Now: How Weak States Threaten Freedom', *The American Prospect*, 33: 30–9.

KUHN, T. S. (1970). *The Structure of Scientific Revolutions* (Chicago: University of Chicago Press).

LAMONT, M., and FOURNIER, M. (eds.) (1992). *Cultivating Differences: Symbolic Boundaries and the Making of Inequality* (Chicago: University of Chicago Press).

LINDE, C. (1993). *Life Stories: The Creation of Coherence* (New York: Oxford University Press).

LOCKE, J. (1960). *An Essay Concerning the True Original Extend and End of Civil Government* (Chicago: Great Books Foundation).

—— (1967). *Two Treatises of Government* (Cambridge: Cambridge University Press).

—— (1975). *An Essay Concerning Human Understanding* (Oxford: Clarendon Press).

LYOTARD, J. F. (1984). *The Postmodern Condition: A Report on Knowledge* (Minneapolis, Minn.: University of Minnesota Press).

MARSHALL, T. H. (1992 [1949]). *Citizenship and Social Class* (London: Pluto Press).

MEEK, R. L. (1976). *Social Science and the Ignoble Savage* (Cambridge: Cambridge University Press).

PARSONS, T. (1937). *The Structure of Social Action* (Glencoe, Ill.: Free Press).

POCOCK, J. G. A. (ed.) (1985). *Virtue, Commerce and History* (New York: Cambridge University Press).

RORTY, R. (1979). *Philosophy and the Mirror of Nature* (Princeton, NJ: Princeton University Press).

SELIGMAN, A. (1992). *The Idea of Civil Society* (Princeton, NJ: Princeton University Press).

SKINNER, Q. (1985). *The Return of Grand Theory in the Human Sciences* (Cambridge and New York: Cambridge University Press).

SMITH, A. (1993). *An Inquiry into the Nature and Causes of the Wealth of Nations* (Oxford: Oxford University Press).

SOMERS, M. R. (1992). 'Narrativity, Narrative Identity, and Social Action: Rethinking English Working Class Formation', *Social Science History*, 16: 591–630.

——(1993). 'Citizenship and the Place of the Public Sphere: Law, Community, and Political Culture in the Transition to Democracy', *American Sociological Review*, 58: 587–620.

——(1995*a*). 'Narrating and Naturalizing Civil Society and Citizenship Theory', *Sociological Theory*, 13: 221–65.

——(1995*b*). 'What's Political or Cultural about Political Culture and the Public Sphere? Toward an Historical Sociology of Concept Formation', *Sociological Theory*, 13: 113–44.

——(1996). 'Where is Sociology after the Historic Turn? Knowledge Cultures, Narrativity, and Historical Epistemologies', in T. J. McDonald (ed.), *The Historic Turn in the Human Sciences* (Ann Arbor: University of Michigan Press), 53–90.

——(1997). 'Deconstructing and Reconstructing Class Formation Theory: Narrativity, Relational Analysis, and Social Theory', in J. R. Hall (ed.), *Reworking Class* (Ithaca, NY: Cornell University Press), 73–106.

——(1999). 'The Privatization of Citizenship: How to Unthink a Knowledge Culture', in V. Bonnell and L. Hunt (ed.), *Beyond the Cultural Turn* (Berkeley and Los Angeles, Calif.: University of California Press), 121–61.

——and GIBSON, G. D. (1994). 'Reclaiming the Epistemological 'Other': Narrative and the Social Constitution of Identity', in C. Calhoun (ed.), *Social Theory and the Politics of Identity* (Oxford: Blackwell), 37–99.

STINCHCOMBE, A. L. (1982 [1978]). 'The Deep Structure of Moral Categories: Eighteenth Century French Stratification and the Revolution', in E. Rossi (ed.), *Structural Sociology* (New York: Columbia University Press), 67–95.

TAYLOR, C. (1990). 'Modes of Civil Society', *Public Culture*, 3: 95–118.

WALLERSTEIN, I. (1991). *Unthinking Social Science: The Limits of the Nineteenth Century Paradigms* (Oxford: Polity Press).

WHITE, H. (1987). *The Content of the Form: Narrative Discourse and Historical Representation* (Baltimore: The Johns Hopkins University Press).

WINCH, D. (1978). *Adam Smith's Politics* (Cambridge: Cambridge University Press).

WOLFE, A. (1989). *Whose Keeper? Social Science and Moral Obligation* (Berkeley, Calif.: University of California Press).

WOLIN, S. (1961). *Politics and Vision* (London: Allen & Unwin).

ZERUBAVEL, E. (1991). *The Fine Line: Boundaries and Distinctions in Everyday Life* (New York: Free Press).

3

Poor Citizens: Social Citizenship versus Individualization of Welfare

Giovanna Procacci

Modern Western polities have governed individuals as citizens. Citizenship has been a strategy of governance which has developed to the extent that social rights and public services have been integrated into the social contract and an important part of our experience as citizens. Current displacements in social policies and social services risk undermining their crucial links to citizenship issues, because of a tendency to individualize social problems and their treatment.

The strength of T. H. Marshall's (1963*a*) model of the development of citizenship—the evolution of citizenship rights from civil to political and social—is that it theorizes the dynamic nature of citizenship beyond rigid legal definitions of membership. Citizenship proves to be a process based on the evolution of rights; this is why historical analyses are necessary for any theory of citizenship (Turner 1990), and Marshall's account is grounded in the British welfare experience. There are several problems, however, with his treatment. According to Marshall's scheme, social citizenship appears on a continuum with civil and political citizenship. Such a view underestimates the specificity of social rights and creates the illusion that social citizenship is a less political issue.

The sociological literature since Marshall's classic work has often reduced the dynamics of citizenship to evolutionary simplifications, making it synonymous with modernization or democratization. Legal theorists, in turn, tend to favour a rigid definition in its original meaning of membership of a political community, overlooking the fact that the modification of rights is a social, not merely a legal process (La Torre 1995; Ferrajoli 1993).

To avoid both evolutionary generalizations and disciplinary oversimplifications, I propose to consider citizenship as a strategy to govern processes of social change by creating citizens (Burchell 1995). A strategy can shift its own objectives; thus, citizenship and citizens' rights are not mere expressions of membership ties, but move with changing conditions, expectations, and citizen practices. This strategic view demands that we analyse the set of questions that citizenship is to address, and the effects it is expected to produce. I will consider the development of citizenship strategies in France in order to show how social citizenship differs deeply from civil and political citizenship, rather than developing endogenously out of them. In this chapter I thus argue that citizenship is a political issue not only at a particular stage, when political rights are at stake, nor exclusively because of its juridical codification. Social citizenship itself is political, and not simply as an endpoint of the emergence of rights (Marshall 1963*a*) but as the result of a relatively independent process with its own trajectory.

Current orthodoxy in social policy analysis often ignores the political implications of social citizenship. This leads to the assumption that social citizenship might safely be eroded, given that this erosion allegedly depends upon economic reasons linked to the financial crisis of Western states. Indeed, during the current crisis of welfare systems, social policies have become more disconnected from concerns with citizenship. On the one hand, debate over social policies is largely dominated by analyses of the American welfare model, which has always relatively neglected citizenship implications (Fraser and Gordon 1994; Abraham 1996). On the other hand, the current debate over citizenship seems more focused on cultural differences and identities than on issues of inequality: current emphasis on 'multiculturalism' tends to limit citizenship issues to civil and political rights, reviving an interpretation of citizenship as an exclusively political relation to the nation-state. In short, social citizenship—the provision of social rights to welfare that are equal for all citizens—is no longer the dominant response to social problems.

Citizenship is hence undermined in current social reforms under the dominance of orientations such as individualization, contractualization, flexibility, marketization, humanitarianism—all promoted as 'new' solutions to social problems. While marketization is mainly at work reforming social services, individualization most often inspires current displacements of social policies.

This chapter attempts to evaluate such a tendency to individualize social problems and the responses to them from the vantage point of the impact on social citizenship, particularly in policies directed against poverty. What kind of strategies do individualized social policies pursue? What are their aims? Can they, in fact, offer solutions to social problems? To answer such questions, we need better to define social citizenship, at both the theoretical (social rights) and the institutional (welfare state) levels distinguished by Marshall (1963*a*), in order to recover a sense of its specific character.

To this end, in the first part of this chapter I shall confront the Marshall model with the emergence of social rights in France. We shall see social rights taking shape out of a more general process of socialization, of poverty, of labour, of social risks—a specific strategy aimed at changing the entire relation between individual and state via the administrative apparatus, as well as the definition of a good citizen. Translated into an institutionalized field of welfare services, social citizenship has enhanced a more active meaning of citizenship.

In the second part, I discuss a twofold process of individualization of poverty policies which is nowadays reacting against socialization. Poverty is identified with individual trajectories of social exclusion and the idea of shared social risk as the basis for organizing solidarity is rejected. The desocialization of poverty reinforces the political exclusion of the poor, and risks strengthening a process of *décitoyenneté*, raising anew a question that we had thought solved once for all: when poverty is no longer treated as a social problem, are the poor still citizens? But the question can also be put the other way round: if they lose the idea of some shared social risks, are not citizens becoming poorer? The frailty of the citizenship of the poor today is symmetrical with the fragilization of social citizenship for everybody—no wonder, after all, since 'the history of citizenship entitlements is a history of freedom and not a history of compassion' (Ignatieff 1989).

Towards a Definition of Social Citizenship

Social Citizenship and Social Rights

For Marshall (1963*a*), civil rights represent the contractual bases on which a social dimension of citizenship takes shape. He intended thus to support the British social-democratic turn towards a welfare state, by attributing to social rights the same theoretical legitimacy as civil and political ones (Barbalet 1994). He also suggested, however, that the politics of social rights have some specific features. He regarded, for instance, the 1834 English Poor Laws as an alternative to a recognition of rights of citizens, because the reform renounced interference with the functioning of the free market (by means for instance of intervening in the wage system). Thus, residual relief to the poor was given only on the condition that the poor would give up their rights as citizens (internment in the workhouse). Charity and workhouses were practices opposite to citizenship. Intervention in poverty based on a principle of rights, therefore, does imply for Marshall (1963*b*) an interference with the market: social rights acknowledge that the market value of an individual is not the measure of his right to welfare. Furthermore, he characterized social rights, with respect to personal rights, as being public duties; even though an individual person eventually enjoys the right, the aim really pursued through it is an improvement of society. His classical example was compulsory education, where the public duty of education aims at the benefit, not only of the individual, but of the whole society. 'Political democracy and scientific manufactures needed an educated electorate' (Marshall 1963: 82).

The French case helps us better to understand the specific nature of social rights, originating in such a combination of public duties interfering with the market. Although the literature on citizenship characterizes France as offering a strongly egalitarian, national-republican notion of political citizenship (Brubaker 1992; Rosanvallon 1992, 1995a), I argue, following Turner (1990: 208), that France has also known a highly articulated concept of citizenship, particularly of active citizenship built on the notion of 'useful work'. This is a criterion for an ethics based on social processes, rather than on individual choices, and has played a crucial role in regulating inclusion and exclusion from the status of citizen. As a result of such tensions, a new field of policies, institutions, and sciences was promoted: the social. This offered a framework in which to treat poverty separately from its economic implications (the labour question) and from conflicts about individual rights. Its task has been to provide a rationale for governing problems of inequality in a society of equals.

If the traditional notion of citizenship takes into account that, in order to be a citizen of the *polis*, one needs some economic independence, the peculiar situation of never-ending social crises in nineteenth-century France helped to spread awareness that inequality is a dangerous source of instability, that desperate need interferes with deliberation, and that society needs some cohesive link among its members. Historically, the constitutionalization of citizenship in France was constantly challenged by the rise of a social question (Procacci 1993). While citizenship did provide the egalitarian basis for individual rights, it also pointed out the need to eliminate any restrictions on the independence indispensable to be a good citizen. Poverty was therefore no longer regarded as an individual problem, nor as a scandal, but as a social concern which required political intervention. In a liberal society, poverty was 'normal' but nevertheless raised a difficult political problem: how to govern inequality effects from within a social order based on equality.

Citizenship as a unifying concept is not only contradicted by the exclusion of non-citizens, but has never worked otherwise than through distinctions, internal borders separating different categories of citizens. As early as 1791, the French constitution, inspired by Sieyès, distinguished between active and passive citizens. The notion of useful work regulated this kind of internal barrier as a social function. However, some conditions are required: excluded people have to accept their exclusion, or be unable to influence decisions concerning it. Once the social structure of inequality is challenged, political citizenship also goes into crisis. When in 1848 Parisians claimed 'rights as citizens and rights as workers' (Sewell 1980), they revealed their conception of the political status of citizens as being different from the social status of labourers—and they claimed that both are equally essential to their membership in the Republic. Actually, this dissociation was not only in the claims of workers, but also in the political response to them: the constitution granted them rights as citizens (universal manhood suffrage) in order to deny them rights as workers—the right to vote instead of the individual right to labour or to assistance. The very extension of political rights modified the framework, and challenged the neutrality of liberal order. Some sought policies of rights that would reduce inequality.

The history of French citizenship was therefore marked by a reaction against the inefficiency of individualism—charitable, economic, and juridical—and the insufficiency of contract. Contract is characterized as an agreement between individuals rendered free and equal by their status as citizens; but civil rights regulating contracts are not only insufficient against inequality, they are affected by inequality in so far as it may create obstacles to the realization of the autonomy of the subject. Civil rights are therefore indispensable to the functioning of a market society, but unable to protect it from the dysfunctions of inequality. Civil contract provides the egalitarian foundations supporting the structure of social inequality. An equal juridical capacity is not enough to eliminate the need to act on the social structure in such a way as effectively to guarantee individual autonomy against the limits raised by its social environment. This is the specific role for social rights.

At first, the reaction was moral, interpreted by French philanthropy throughout the first half of nineteenth century (Duprat 1993). Its failure in the revolution of 1848 opened the way to a different perspective, calling for an authoritative foundation of social morality, obligatory rather than voluntaristic moral ties. From the Physiocrats' tradition of *droit social naturel*, the need was acknowledged for some synthesis between the liberal conception of individual rights and the anti-contractualistic idea that society is necessary and involuntary. Elaborating on this idea, early French social science—from Saint-Simon and Comte to Durkheim—offered strategic support to a political need to defend the state from an obligation towards the poor as much as one to defend society from the danger of disorder (Procacci 1993). In order to do so, they addressed the problem of finding a balance of rights and duties reconciling morals and politics (Donzelot 1984), while transforming charity into an obligation of pure justice. Universal individual rights interpret equality and liberty, but are unable to organize the social unit since they cannot regulate disintegrating levels of inequality. In a word, they fail to provide security. As a result, the search for security (to secure the realization of people's autonomy as well as to secure the survival of the association) has inspired a continuous attempt to re-establish a reciprocity between rights and duties, as a way of limiting the scope of rights in the interest of society.

Social rights and social policies arose from the idea that society is a subject of demands, needs, interests, and rights that are not reducible to those coming from the state or the individuals. Society was acknowledged as the space where specific, necessary, and involuntary processes take place; 'social' means that society is the legitimating reference, not social actors. A political process affecting the relation to the state is originated neither at the level of the state nor that of individuals, but at the level of society. It is what Costa (1996) calls a 'sociocentric paradigm' in his discussion of historical citizenship models. The difficulty of deducing the common good from the contractualistic premises of the liberal order led to the establishment of society as an autonomous field of knowledge and practices *vis-à-vis* economic and juridical ones. Thus it is not just the market which cannot really work without some kind of social protection, but society as a whole. The challenge of poverty *vis-à-vis* citizenship has been crucial in acknowledging society's needs.

Under the Third Republic the institutional answer to such claims took the form of a process of socialization of rights, the French way of solving the conflict that Marshall assigned to social citizenship between a democratic orientation towards equality of rights and capitalist valorization of inequality. At stake was the need to find a politically viable way towards a legitimized inequality (Bec 1994). Inequality, in this new conception, was interpreted as a problem of socialization, regulated by institutional devices that socialize risk and responsibility. When social laws establishing social rights emerged by the end of the nineteenth century, they built upon an insurance principle which had the aim of socializing risk (Ewald 1986). Individuals are entitled to social provisions only as members of a collective body, aggregated by occupation, by age, etc.; even more than gaining new rights, they gain their integration in a network of mutual obligations, as Durkheim (1895) was to theorize through his critique of contractualism. The absolute character of universal rights is here replaced by the relative character of circumstances influencing the social life of people, such as accidents, old age, and sickness (Santoro 1994).

The French social laws provided the underpinnings for an administrative state, and eventually laid the bases of the modern French welfare state. They illustrate that social rights providing their juridical foundations are not just another category of rights added to the civil and political. They reconcile rights and duties, they have not only a compensatory, but also a legitimating function. They shift the claim for distributive justice from the state towards administrative agencies. As such they therefore have a very specific logic, as Ewald has convincingly shown, and a logic that differs from that of civil and political rights. They are not judicial; rather than a judgement, they require evaluations and surveys (Ewald 1986: 275). They locate law outside responsibility and fault, and rather open a parallel law based on distribution of risk (Ewald 1986: 364). They are not comparable with subjective universal rights because they transform a claim for a negative guarantee into a claim for a positive one, for a service. They do not ask for more freedom from state power, and are compatible with state intervention in assuring services. The case of France shows that there is no simple progression from civil and political to social rights, but a genuine rupture between these forms of rights. And in fact French liberals had always firmly resisted the legal acknowledgement of duties, of positive guarantees and the like, from the Declaration of Rights during the Great Revolution (Gauchet 1989) until the parliamentary debate on social laws at the end of the nineteenth century.

Criticism of social rights usually fails to acknowledge their specificity. Legal theorists tend to criticize the very notion of social rights because of the low level of procedural definition, and therefore of uniformity, that they present, and the high level of economic expense that they usually require. Social rights appear too dependent on economic and political resources to achieve the certitude and non-contingency of genuine rights. Some critics of Marshall's approach thus claim that social rights lack the normative strength of civil and political rights, and are not in fact rights at all (Zolo 1994): they might indicate necessary social services, but they cannot transform into real rights, universal rights, giving any sort of entitlement to such services. Talking about social citizenship rights would thus be illegitimate, since this would mean they had reached the status of universal rights. Other critics tend to deny their 'social' nature and rather view them as belonging to the person. Ferrajoli (1994) defines social rights as expectation rights, and opposes them to autonomy rights, in so far they present a substantive legitimation and call for a substantive democracy. According to him, they are not attributed to the citizen, but to the person. The few exceptions we should try further to dissociate from citizenship, making all of them rights of the person. The citizen only enjoys political rights, depending upon national belonging.

In spite of all such distinctions, citizenship strategies do enter some strategic conceptions of rights. Even Ferrajoli's distinction between civil rights concerning the person and political rights concerning the citizen, according to the legal definition of citizenship, does not prevent from accounting, from a sociological point of view, for a link between the two sorts of rights. Consider how they interplay within the form of contract: not only because the practice of political rights is itself conceived as a contractual relation, but also because the political contract is based on the same principles as the civil contract, namely liberty, equality, and security. Civil and political rights might well be distinct in legal terms, but they nevertheless interact in government strategies: thus, political rights are reserved only to citizens able to fulfil the conditions for the civil contract. Instead of claiming that social rights are non-rights, a strategic approach shows, through their historical construction, that their different nature might have modified or broadened the scope of rights beyond the limits of a liberal legal conception. And today's problems of citizenship are indeed very hard to understand unless we take such a broad perspective.

Strategies of social rights have other implications for political practices: for instance, they reinforce intermediate institutions and they show that the complexity of the relation to the state cannot be expressed by the voluntaristic logic of the political contract, nor by an exclusively political notion of citizenship referred to it. We need not simply reduce the contribution of social theory to the indication of procedural ways of solving tension between contrasting principles at work in democracy, as sometimes has been the case (Habermas 1994). Such procedures only too often tend to replace substantive reasoning and historical judgement in contemporary thought about democracy.

The French case shows that social rights have been much more than a procedural solution to the political tension between individual self-realization and its social conditions; they have substantively opened a full new political space, becoming a stake for a continuous process of collective struggles. Social citizenship has therefore represented a sort of third way between pure liberalism and socialist statism. From this intermediate position, it challenged liberalism, which was thus historically forced to cope with it. To treat citizenship as a continuum with contractualistic origins, and to ignore changes which have occurred within citizenship itself, is therefore quite dangerous, since it obscures the political practices inherent to, and dependent upon, social rights.

Social Citizenship and Welfare

In this section I shall deal with the embodiment of social rights in those welfare services that Marshall indicated as an indispensable institutional component of social citizenship. Their crisis nowadays fosters attacks against social citizenship. Welfare policies are based on the idea that ensuring a minimum of well-being is not only necessary, but requires interference with the functioning of a free market, by redistributing wealth under the form of public services. Welfare services are therefore indispensable for social citizenship. Rights to education, health, and social protection are opposed to early practices and embodied in institutions based on the principle of expanded responsibility and shared risk.

Selectivity, in contrast to universal social rights, connects services to resources, inspiring means-tested access and provoking the stigmatization of recipients. By contrast, citizenship-based welfare services mean that living standards are assured to all members of the social community; they are universal, therefore avoiding stigmatization, supplication, and exposure to official discretion (Parker 1975), and build a system of expectations drawn on standards of values independent of the market. Provision to groups other than the poor has enhanced the quality of the services provided, and opened to legislation the definition of standards, thus giving to citizens the possibility of influencing choices and decisions. In this way the development of welfare systems has deeply transformed contemporary democracies, and has broken up the reliance on market criteria to regulate social solidarity. It has transformed the role of the state, its relation to the economy, and the nature of social conflict.

Thus, citizenship has expanded. It no longer consists only in national belonging and political participation; the right to welfare has become an essential part of citizenship as such, like property and voting rights, integral to our sense of belonging (King and Waldron 1988). Even more, as Freedland argues in Chapter 5 below, social citizenship is determined to a significant extent by the nature and character of public services provision.

Marshall's normative reason to associate welfare and social citizenship was less redistribution of income than equalization of status among citizens: social rights give equal access to common services, they therefore tend to reduce inequality to a legitimized level by strengthening practices where people experience equality of status. Other reasons can be invoked in order to explore how welfare enhances citizenship practices; and in France, as we have already mentioned, revolutions played a big role in spreading concerns about assuring stability, organizing solidarity, etc. All such reasons are and ought to be other than the market and charity, since welfare systems were originated to combat their insufficiency.

From this vantage point, citizenship has offered to welfare policies a more efficient framework than the market, allowing the realization of non-marketable services aimed at generalizing acceptable living standards. Citizenship restores reciprocity outside market rules, where it is regulated by an exchange between money and services, and outside family relations, where it is regulated by mutual aid. But it is of course also outside charity, where there is no reciprocity at all. This demands that society acknowledges that some standards of living are required, 'irrespective of individual bargaining power' (Parker 1975: 145). To formulate these standards in terms of rights does transform the dependencies that they try to solve into conditions for autonomy.

Nevertheless, debates about the crisis of welfare states seem nowadays dominated by the logic of economic rationality: within a resurgent market and monetarist approach, the privatization of social services and 'user pays' philosophy justify a rejection of welfare systems based on social citizenship rights. It is true, as many authors notice (Pierson 1994), that attacks on welfare have not so far had the success often loudly claimed, and this can be held to demonstrate the structural position of welfare in our political systems and citizenship regimes. However, the basic logic of these attacks is rarely challenged, and they are becoming a sort of popular truth. The political reasoning is reversed: welfare, and not poverty, is a handicap to individual independence; standards and universal rules are inefficient, since they exceed in abstraction. This leads to a focus on the elimination of welfare dependency, overlooking the more general crisis of our solidarity systems, though there is no evidence so far that non-universal services would enjoy more consent than universal ones.

Although it would be difficult to deny that welfare is in trouble everywhere, the current debate on the welfare crisis is dominated by the analysis of the American model, which in fact has never gone beyond a 'residual' conception, as Titmuss (1987) put it, of the public intervention in assistance matters, temporarily to replace such 'natural' solutions as market and family. Even when the Great Depression revealed the need for a public intervention to replace voluntary company programmes, contributory welfare programmes were reminiscent of private welfare: they explicitly refused to redistribute income (Quadagno 1984), and eventually substantiated a firm distinction between social security paid by workers and welfare given to the poor (Skocpol 1988). The 'undeserving poor', a moral category expressing the degrading nature of relief within American poverty discourse, was never eradicated by universal programmes of social security (Katz 1989). In fact American welfare has mostly dealt with social dependency rather than inequality.

The tendency nowadays to claim no contradiction between liberalism and welfare (Welch 1989), encouraged by the success of Rawls, increases the confusion even further. Welfare systems did not follow as a natural consequence of the 'utilitarian sympathy' which was the liberal key to justice; rather, they required an autonomous system of values. As Sen (1986) puts it, social welfare is not a function of individual achievement; and 'self-sufficiency welfare' just represents a misdiagnosis of the crisis of welfare (Goodin 1988). Such dominance of the unique American model becomes then quite problematic when it is a question of evaluating the crisis of European 'institutionalized' welfare systems, according to Korpi's distinction (Korpi 1983). This becomes even more problematic when the discussion focuses on social citizenship.

As Fraser and Gordon (1994) remark, social citizenship has practically no place in the contemporary debate about welfare in the USA. The reason is that social provisions there remain largely outside the aura of dignity surrounding citizenship; recipients of welfare are usually regarded with disrespect, and welfare has been generally viewed as a threat to citizenship, rather than its realization. Instead there is an overwhelming emphasis on civil citizenship, and within it, an unlimited predominance of the contractual model, increasingly assimilating all forms of reciprocity except for family ones. Such a hegemony of contract also means, Fraser and Gordon argue, that all that cannot be assimilated by it is described as its exact opposite—that is, as unreciprocated charity. The US conception of welfare rests on this binary logic opposing contract to charity, which is at work in the distinction between contributory insurance programmes and non-contributory public assistance. This masks the fact that public assistance is also based on contributions, the only difference being the way they are collected. Current trends trying to assimilate welfare to contract, under the form of agreed obligations for the recipient to perform work or training activities, are nourished, the authors claim, from a mythology of civil citizenship.

Maybe the myth also consists in taking for 'natural' the content of civil citizenship itself. As we have seen in relation to the French case, the basis for citizenship to regulate inclusion and exclusion has been, alongside the national bond, 'useful work'. This is why the poor have raised a problem, since they could not be integrated through their active contribution. Contract itself, as the central pattern for civil citizenship, refers explicitly to the restructuring of work relations under a free market model (Castel 1995*a*); it demands not only habits and virtues (Bader 1996) but above all work. If we investigate relations between citizenship and welfare, this helps us to see that social citizenship is not an undue extension of an exclusively juridical concept to socio-economic matters. Citizenship itself is a more complex concept, having a juridical definition shaped on a social form of labour relations, and therefore a socio-economic application and relevance.

Social citizenship thus expresses all that could not go under the contractual form of citizenship, all non-contractual compensation indispensable for a market-oriented citizenship to function. In this way, it means that the relation to the state in our societies is by no means merely a juridical and contractual one; the normative ideal of citizenship cannot be reduced to contract. There are people for whom this ideal might just be too difficult to match; therefore, this argument can only lead to a bipolarization of people between the ones who are able to take advantage of destructuration of our systems of social protection, and those who cannot profit from it and will only experience a more vulnerable position (Castel 1995*a*).

The conjunction of welfare with citizenship could foster further the transformation of welfare, from a traditional paternalistic paradigm where government defines welfare needs, to an improved social rights paradigm where a new consumer-based community voice may emerge to determine them (Culpitt 1992). Social citizenship enhances public action, making citizenship a way of acting, more than a way of being; it makes it possible to dissociate citizenship from nationality, for it is related to public activity rather than to a moral quality of the subject. In spite of its unpopularity today, social citizenship could inspire a better reorganization of welfare services, which they certainly often need. These services need the crucial role of citizenship at the centre of modern political debates on socio-economic arrangements that allow participation to be enhanced. This is the danger implicit in the current individualization of poverty policies.

Social Citizenship under Attack

Individualization of Poverty

The need for society to reduce poverty has long been acknowledged as an integral part of welfare systems, and of policies for employment and social security. Today, however, the crisis of the welfare state puts in question the legitimacy and efficiency of welfare as a response to the risk of poverty. A fundamental suspicion surrounds practices of social rights: rather than favouring the realization of citizenship by eliminating the burdens of poverty, social rights would contribute to keeping the individual in a condition of subordination simply by participating in a system of social protection. The dismantling of welfare provisions corresponds, then, to displacements in new policies towards the poor that reflect the main directions pursued by a more general attack against the institutional setting of social citizenship. Reviving an indistinct category such as 'poverty' and identifying all poverty problems with the extreme form of a growing marginalization are all ways of individualizing problems of poverty and denying their social nature. In this way, current analysis of poverty puts into question the basic assumptions on which welfare was grounded: namely that the poor are citizens like everyone else and have therefore the right to some standards of living considered essential in order to be a citizen.

Such analysis, influenced by the US debate, contributes in a substantial way to scepticism towards social citizenship institutions. From a cultural-biological emphasis by conservatives to an insistence on ethnically delimited innercity ghettos by progressives, current conceptual strategies have a common point: the root cause of poverty rests in individual behaviour. It is true that the present dominance of economic analysis helps dispel the idea that poverty can be referred to universal standards of economic, social, and cultural well-being to which everyone is entitled. Poverty is most often viewed as a phenomenon of a statistical nature, based on a poverty line calculated on the cost of a food basket, eventually bringing the analysis back to economic data, usually referred to income distribution. However, as Sen (1992) forcefully shows, the loss of income is not the main problem of being left without a job; poverty means not only exclusion from material welfare but also social degradation, confirming the idea of a link between poverty and delinquency.

To such economic orthodoxy, the social analysis of poverty replies by recasting the whole problem in a subjective frame: cultural features should explain poverty better than any structural hypothesis about the labour market or supply of services. However, this can lead, as in the US conservative analysis, to emphasizing moral, ethnic, or cultural 'characteristics of the poor', centring the analysis not on work, but on the work motivation of poor people. In this way, poverty is separated from labour problems, especially unemployment. It can be objected that there are no assured means to influence such characteristics; but after all, as Cruikshank (1997) notes, inculcating virtue by force is nothing but the core of conservatives' strategy to take politics out of poverty. The crucial point is rather that individual responsibility of the poor is not a wrong response: it is just a response that excludes social policy, and therefore increases the 'risk of poverty' within our affluent societies.

The progressives' reaction in the USA both to the increase in poverty and the conservative reduction of it to bio-cultural problems has led more recently to similar difficulties (Greenstone 1991). It has emphasized concepts like underclass, where the structural components of poverty due to deindustrialization are stressed. Born as a purely economic concept, indicating the persistence of poverty in spite of post-war economic growth, it has acquired new meanings. Thanks to its success with the media, the concept has taken on a behavioural and a racial dimension. It identifies blacks and to a lesser extent Hispanics in inner-city ghettos, particularly their behaviour in matters of sexuality, family, school, job, and the like. Social scientists have tried to take this perception back to the structural phenomenon of persisting poverty, focusing on the 'black male joblessness' analysis (Wilson 1987), and adding to the concept a further spatial dimension: the concentration and social isolation of the ghetto. The emphasis on such crucial spatial factors of persisting poverty has in turn contributed to orient the empirical definition of underclass towards behaviour; in the end, underclass tells us much less about being poor in an advanced society than it tells us about sexuality, family models, job, or school refusal, propensity to crime, violence, and drug abuse (Aponte 1990). Little by little, the analysis shifts from the causes of poverty to the behaviour of the poor as being the problem, finding once again the ambiguity of any cultural definition of poverty (Gans 1990).

Recently, Wilson himself has acknowledged that 'concerns about civil and political aspects of citizenship in the US have overshadowed concerns about the social aspects of citizenship . . . because of a strong belief system that denies the social origins and social significance of poverty and welfare' (Wilson 1990: 49). He further argued that Americans tend to be more concerned about the social obligations of the poor than about their social rights as American citizens. Welfare programmes in the USA have concerned mainly the working and middle classes, and had virtually no effect on poverty rates among the non-elderly. After having practically ignored it in his influential book on the underclass, Wilson seems eventually to take into account that the underdeveloped welfare state and weak institutional structure of social citizenship rights in the USA might have been a cause of economic deprivation and social isolation of the urban poor. As a consequence, he advocates a development of race-neutral programmes enhancing social rights for all groups, better able to alleviate problems of poor minorities than race-specific measures. But this seems more likely to lead towards eliminating reserved quotas than any other effect. Class confinement does not seem to be contested: welfare services reserved to the poor will be separated from services for the middle class; Medicaid will continue to pay doctors much less than other insurances; social citizenship rights will still be out of reach.

The current questioning of the European welfare systems under the political dominance of monetarist imperatives has amplified the impact of the US debate on poverty and some similar analytical strategy has taken ground on this side of the Atlantic. In spite of certain differences, the notion of social exclusion (*exclusion sociale*) which has largely dominated poverty research, particularly under the guidance of the European Community, has much in common with that of the 'underclass' (Procacci 1996). Talking about social exclusion might be a claim for re-inclusion into citizenship—and indeed many progressive analysts would pretend it is so. But at the same time, treating people as excluded takes the analysis outside the sphere of the 'city'. This means that poverty is analysed as a condition on the margins, of drop-outs, and becomes the state of living if one falls outside society, rather than a predicament which can occur within society—the condition of marginalized people, rather than a process of inequality rooted in the social structure (Castel 1995*b*).

But social exclusion is also sociologically significant. As a matter of fact, it is not as a class that the *exclus* are torn from society. They are indeed a group apart, but the notion of social exclusion is a purely negative one: they have no positivity whatsoever; they represent only a breaking down of the social fabric (*fracture sociale*); they have no common interests; they are not the *nouveaux prolétaires* (Rosanvallon 1995*b*). There is no collective identity to describe, only individual trajectories; classification becomes less important, and statistics less telling. So the debate becomes a subjective one as in the USA, centred on individual paths and, reciprocally, on personalized treatment, versus the impersonal character of general provisions. By doing so, it obscures the fact that poverty is a system of social relations (McAll 1995); it rather describes a social disintegration, but imputes it to the individual actors who suffer from it. Intervention against exclusion must foster social integration (professional, family, community) in a holistic concept of society with all problems of normative models of performing integration (Messu 1994). It consists in individual trajectories of reintegration opposed to individual trajectories of marginalization. The concept of social exclusion describes a dual society (ins–outs), and in so doing it confirms the break in social relations. It pretends to eject from society the problems which produce poverty—vulnerability, precarity of labour, reduction of resources, weakening of social protections—all processes which produce a polarization of society well before they push people into extreme poverty.

The policies that the concept of social exclusion has fostered tend to turn social problems into urban problems, where they take a specific feature of urban structure, that is replacing inequality by segregation (Touraine 1991). Therefore, the unique meaning of citizenship at work in such policies seems to be local integration. Citizenship, or the lack of it, becomes from this vantage point a question of sociability, at the most a question of animating people to do something for themselves; a culture, an identity, a set of behaviours whose frame is the urban location where the exclusion takes place (Donzelot 1991). Going back to localized treatment of social problems might be a way of reorganizing social exchange in a more individualistic way, activating reciprocity on a territorial basis, against the abstraction of universal rights (Castel 1995*a*: 470). Yet localism also implies a twofold illusion: that contract can be enough for social integration—in spite of long contrary historical evidence—and that decentralization can be a remedy against all evil. Localism does not respond to the resentment of being no longer treated as citizens; it only reinforces the sense of exclusion by pretending that problems of the poor are no longer a collective issue, a public concern.

Amartya Sen's theory of poverty (Sen 1993) centred on capabilities and functionings is often interpreted as shifting from income-based to consumption-based analyses of poverty. In fact, it does claim much more than just such a shift to a different set of data. In an analysis inevitably relative in terms of income, he introduces anew the idea that there is an absolute component of poverty, in terms of what kind of life one can achieve, that capabilities and functionings express. Poverty is absolute in so far as we have chosen a system of values which define the basis of human existence, whatever the relative conditions are. The most crucial for poverty and citizenship issues is, according to Sen (1992), to consider participation as such a value, and capability to participate an integral part of well-being impossible to renounce. He shares with Marshall the conviction that poverty, if not inequality, has to be eliminated. But participation is exactly what the association of poverty and citizenship issues had been focusing on; in a situation like nowadays, where poverty is more and more the cumulative result of several levels of mutually reinforcing marginalization, only an active defence of social citizenship can inspire policies aimed to reinforce participation.

Individualization of Risk

Social citizenship is being contested well beyond the debate on poverty. Not only is the status of the poor as citizens in question, but the erosion of social citizenship institutions affects social rights in a much more general way. In the critique of the welfare state, citizenship has been considered as expressing the normative ideal of an individual freedom, and therefore of being intolerant of social rights and social services, of their administrative organization, and of the very idea of universal standards. Indeed, the crisis involving our social institutions is not just financial, but a more general one of social regulation (Gauchet 1993). The share between universal principles and particularisms is no longer assured and needs to be reformulated. Citizenship bears the meaning of the relationship to the collective body, to a public space; it is, then, deeply involved in such a crisis—which might explain its salience in recent debates in the social sciences. The question is how we interpret such a crisis and what kind of solutions are possible.

According to Rosanvallon the failure of welfare systems comes from the search for universal, general criteria of social regulation. 'Redefinition of welfare state today demands a cognitive revolution . . . we must give up Quètelet's average man and Durkheim's sociological fact, giving back to data their individual values' (Rosanvallon 1995*b*: 210). Among the first effects of such individualization, crucial to the welfare state, is the failure of the principle of social insurance which has until now regulated health and social security. Social insurance has been a mechanism for organizing social solidarity, among people and among generations. The political process of socialization of risk and responsibility leading to it (Ewald 1986) is nowadays, according to Rosanvallon, decomposing, given the erosion of wage-labour on which it had been focused.

The result would be that social problems are today no longer conceived of as a risk. They have become constant, acyclical components of social life. This provokes a general decrease in uncertainty, which had been the condition for socializing risk. The only aspect decoded in 'social' terms is cost; we share expenses more than we look for shared services. Accordingly, the crisis of welfare systems would come from an individualization of risk, by now exploded in an unlimited number of individual trajectories. This could lead, in turn, to an *ad hoc* civic alternative to the insurance-based organization of welfare, replacing reference to universal rules of justice. There is no theoretical solution, only practical solutions; differences become legitimate, risk hits a victim only individually, and the agreement on justice rules which have become utterly conventional has to be found each time in the civic community. As a matter of fact, this exhausts also the political plane: politics consists in this constant search for instant rules to redistribute a solidarity for which there is no general principle. This is the basis that Rosanvallon proposes for an 'active welfare state'. To this new political culture, social progress does not coincide any longer with the reduction of socio-economic inequalities; rather, the development of procedures (*droit procédural*) centred on the principle of 'fairness of treatment' can only provide, through some kind of 'case-by-case' judicial agreement, individualized responses to individual trajectories.

This coincides with claims raised in the name of a 'politics of recognition' and strategies of quotas, reverse discrimination, and the like. Interestingly enough, such policies only refer to groups identified by gender, cultural, or ethnic differences with respect to mainstream dominant groups; they raise a question not in terms of exclusion-versus-inclusion, but of discrimination in the name of a non-economic, non-social element. Is there no discrimination towards the poor? It is as though discrimination could only be acknowledged when it does not question in a fundamental way the structure of inequality, but rather points at the structure of opportunities; and of course, opportunities are not the first concern in dealing with the poor.

The rationale for such policies seems to imply a fundamental distinction between inequality (as poverty) and difference (as discrimination of minority groups). It coincides with the distinction that Nancy Fraser (1995) presents between claims attacking inequality structures and claims referred to identity issues asking for group differentiation. Interestingly, she assumes that such contradiction is ineliminable, in so far as everyone in a modern society experiences several identities. No new political solution can be found by just eliminating one part of it, namely, social provisions; nor can the contradiction be exorcized in order to maximize private freedom and personal responsibility, since there is no more evidence today than ever that they can be achieved without citizenship entitlements.

Social citizenship had inspired a strategy to govern social risks, such as poverty, in a socialized way: that is, by building up a system of social regulation. Such a system has now gone into a crisis, evidenced by the recent strengthening of individualist approaches to welfare. As Rose (1996) remarks, the so-called 'death of the social' corresponds to the emergence of new rationalities, tending to govern 'without society'. Assuming it as a solution, however, means mistaking the symptom for the treatment: the difficulty to reconstruct any sense of common interest and collective fate proves that it is not just a financial crisis, but a more fundamental one of the collective subject—that is, a crisis of citizenship. Individualized social policies might respond to individual cases; they cannot reconstruct broken ties, but rather emphasize the separation. In the end, the poor, no longer citizens, will be confined in their poor sectors of the urban space; no policy will attempt to refill the gap between their poverty and the rest of society. But the incapacity to recover a system of solidarity will affect all with a diminished citizenship, less independent of the market value of each.

REFERENCES

ABRAHAM, D. (1996). 'Liberty Without Equality', *Law and Social Inquiry*, 21/1: 1–65.

APONTE, R. (1990). 'Definitions of the Underclass: A Critical Analysis', in H. J. Gans (ed.), *Sociology in America* (New York: Sage), 117–37.

BADER, V. M. (1996). 'The Institutional and Cultural Conditions of Post-National

Citizenship', paper presented to the IUE-European Forum Conference, 'Social and Political Citizenship in a World of Migration', Florence.

BARBALET, J. M. (1994). 'Citizenship, Class Inequality, and Resentment', in B. van Steenbergen (ed.), *The Condition of Citizenship* (London: Sage), 36–56.

BEC, C. (1994). *Assistance et république* (Paris: L'Atelier).

BRUBAKER, W. R. (1992). *Citizenship and Nationhood in France and Germany* (Cambridge, Mass.: Harvard University Press).

BURCHELL, D. (1995). 'The Attributes of Citizens: Virtue, Manners and the Activity of Citizenship', *Economy and Society*, 24/4: 540–58.

CASTEL, R. (1995a). *Les Métamorphoses de la question sociale* (Paris: Fayard).

——(1995b). 'Les Pièges de l'exclusion', *Lien social et politiques*, 34: 13–23.

COSTA, P. (1996). 'Models of Citizenship in the Nineteenth Century', paper presented at the IUE-European Forum Seminar, Florence.

CRUIKSHANK, B. (1997). 'Culture Wars: Personal Autonomy and Political Reproduction', paper presented at the conference on 'Displacement of Social Policies', University of Jyvaskyla, Finland.

CULPITT, I. (1992). *Welfare and Citizenship: Beyond the Crisis of the Welfare State?* (London: Sage).

DONZELOT, J. (1984). *L'Invention du social* (Paris: Fayard).

——(ed.) (1991). *Face à l'exclusion* (Paris: Seuil).

DUPRAT, C. (1993). *Le Temps des philanthropes* (Paris: Éd. du CTHS).

DURKHEIM, E. (1895). *Leçons de sociologie: Physique des mœurs et du droit* (Paris: Presses Universitaires de France).

EWALD, F. (1986). *L'État providence* (Paris: Grasset).

FERRAJOLI, L. (1993). 'Cittadinanza e diritti fondamentali', *Teoria e politica*, 9/3: 63–76.

——(1994). 'Dai diritti del cittadino ai diritti della persona', in D. Zolo (ed.), *La cittadinanza. appartenenza, identità, diritti* (Milan: Laterza), 263–92.

FRASER, N. (1995). 'From Redistribution to Recognition? Dilemmas of Justice in a Post-Socialist Age', *New Left Review*, 212: 68–93.

——and GORDON, L. (1994). 'Civil Citizenship Against Social Citizenship?', in B. Van Steenbergen (ed.), *The Condition of Citizenship* (London: Sage), 90–107.

GANS, H. J. (1990). 'Deconstructing the Underclass', *Journal of the American Planning Association*, 56: 271–7.

GAUCHET, M. (1989). *La Révolution des droits de l'homme* (Paris: Gallimard).

——(1993). 'Le Mal démocratique', *Esprit*, 195: 67–89.

GOODIN, R. E. (1988). *Reasons for Welfare: The Political Theory of the Welfare State* (Princeton: Princeton University Press).

GREENSTONE, J. D. (1991). 'Culture, Rationality, and the Underclass', in W. B. Katz (ed.), *The Urban Underclass* (Princeton: Princeton University Press), 399–408.

HABERMAS, J. (1994). 'Human Rights and Popular Sovereignty: The Liberal and Republican Versions', *Ratio Juris*, 7/1: 1–13.

IGNATIEFF, M. (1989). 'Citizenship and Moral Narcism', *Political Quarterly*, 60: 63–74.

KATZ, M. B. (1989). *The Undeserving Poor: From the War on Poverty to the War on Welfare* (New York: Pantheon).

KING, D. S., and WALDRON, J. (1988). 'Citizenship, Social Citizenship, and the Defence of Welfare Provision', *British Journal of Political Science*, 18: 415–43.

KORPI, W. (1983). *The Democratic Class Struggle* (London: Routlege & Kegan).

LA TORRE, M. (1995). 'Citizenship and Beyond: Remarks on the Political Membership and Legal Subjectivity', paper presented at the IUE-Forum Seminar, Florence.

MCALL, C. (1995). 'Les Murs de la cité: Territoires d'exclusion et espaces de citoyenneté', *Lien social et politiques*, 34: 81–92.

MARSHALL, T. H. (1963a). *Class, Citizenship, and Social Development* (Westport, Conn.: Greenwood Press).

——(1963b). 'Value Problems of Welfare-Capitalism', *Journal of Social Policy*, 1: 15–32.

MESSU, M. (1994). 'Pauvreté et exclusion en France', in F.-X. Merrien (ed.), *Face à la pauvreté* (Paris: L'Atelier), 139–69.

PARKER, J. (1975). *Social Policy and Citizenship* (London: Macmillan).

PIERSON, P. (1994). *Dismantling the Welfare State? Reagan, Thatcher, and the Politics of Retrenchment* (Cambridge: Cambridge University Press).

PROCACCI, G. (1993). *Gouverner la misère: La Question sociale en France 1848–1989* (Paris: Seuil).

——(1996). 'Exclus ou citoyens? Les Pauvres devant les sciences sociales', *Archives européennes de sociologie*, 37: 323–42.

QUADAGNO, J. (1984). 'Welfare Capitalism and the Social Security Act of 1935', *American Sociological Review*, 49: 632–47.

ROSANVALLON, P. (1992). *Le Sacré du citoyen: Histoire du suffrage universel en France* (Paris: Gallimard).

——(1995a). 'Citoyenneté politique et citoyenneté sociale au XIX ième siècle', *Le Mouvement social*, 171: 9–30.

——(1995b). *La Nouvelle Question sociale* (Paris: Seuil).

ROSE, N. (1996). 'The Death of the Social?', *Economy and Society*, 25: 327–56.

SANTORO, E. (1994). 'Le antinomie della cittadinanza: Libertà negativa, diritti sociali e autonomia individuale', in D. Zolo (ed.), *La cittadinanza* (Bari: Laterza).

SEN, A. K. (1986). *Welfare Economics and the Real World* (Memphis: F. E. Seidman Foundation).

——(1992). *Inequality Reexamined* (Oxford: Clarendon Press).

——(1993). 'Capability and Well-Being', in A. K. Sen and M. Nussbaum (eds.), *The Quality of Life* (Oxford: Clarendon Press), 30–53.

SEWELL, W. H., JR (1980). *Work and Revolution in France: The Language of Labor from the Old Regime to 1848* (Cambridge: Cambridge University Press).

SKOCPOL, T. R. (1988). 'The Limits of the New Deal System and the Roots of Contemporary Welfare Dilemmas', in M. Weir, A. S. Orloff, and T. R. Skocpol (eds.), *The Politics of Social Policy in the United States* (Princeton: Princeton University Press), 293–311.

TITMUSS, R. M. (1987). *The Philosophy of Welfare* (London: Allen & Unwin).

TOURAINE, A. (1991). 'Face à l'exclusion', *Esprit*, 169: 7–13.

TURNER, B. S. (1990). 'Outline of a Theory of Citizenship', *Sociology*, 24: 189–217.

WELCH, C. E. (1989). 'Liberalism and Social Rights', in Claude E. Welch and Murray Milgate (eds.), *Critical Issues in Social Thought* (New York: Academic Press), 163–85.

WILSON, W. J. (1987). *The Truly Disadvantaged* (Chicago: Chicago University Press).
—— (1990). 'Citizenship and the Inner-City Ghetto Poor', in B. van Steenbergen (ed.), *The Condition of Citizenship* (London: Sage), 66–75.
ZOLO, D. (1994). 'La strategia della cittadinanza', in D. Zolo (ed.), *La cittadinanza* (Bari: Laterza), 3–46.

4

Redesigning the Canadian Citizenship Regime: Remaking the Institutions of Representation

Jane Jenson and Susan D. Phillips

Canadians cannot rely on a common religion or ethnicity or centuries of myths and legends to provide an easy answer to the question of national identity. . . . Public health insurance has the . . . enormous advantage that it is a concrete, practical example of a common citizenship right.[1]

[Ontario] Health Minister Jim Wilson said at hearings in Toronto that he had no intention of greasing the squeaky wheels [of] 'special interests' affected by the health care provisions in the bill. 'This government is not going to give special treatment to people who shout the loudest' . . . Roxanne Felice does not shout but she believes the government should be listening to her anyway. She resents the notion that the non-profit social-service agency she runs in Niagara Falls is a 'special-interest' group but she fears that is how it is being perceived. 'I think groups are often labelled as special-interest groups but I believe people form groups because they have public interests'. (Campbell 1996)

Why do cutbacks and reform of the Canadian health-care system evoke threats to national identity and disputes over citizens' rights to participate? Why, in other words, are the basic dimensions of citizenship—national identity, social rights, democracy—on the table when the federal government and the provinces begin tinkering with funding formulae and closing hospitals beds? This chapter addresses these questions via an analysis of the current dismantling of the post-war citizenship regime.

These randomly selected yet typical quotations from Canada's 'national newspaper' provide a point of the departure. The public hearings described in the second quotation were organized by the Conservative government of Ontario in January 1996. It had been forced to hold them after opposition erupted to its Omnibus Bill (Bill 26), introduced in November 1995 and

---

[1] Valpy 1996: these words are those of an economist, Lars Osberg, approvingly cited by Valpy.

designed to give the government the flexibility to deal swiftly with Ontario's stubborn budget deficit. It would give Queen's Park [the provincial government] the power to tell doctors where to practice and the power to close hospitals. It would allow munici-palities the right to levy new taxes and adjust license fees. It would deregulate drug prices and tell arbitrators how to set wages for police and firefighters. (Campbell 1996)

With such 'flexibility' the government would not have to consult the legisla-ture on any of these changes. As this only partial list of powers indicates, the government intended a fundamental realignment between levels of government, state and citizens, the public and private sectors, and of democ-racy. More than 1,200 witnesses registered for the hearings; only 367 were accepted.

   This incident, albeit affecting only one of Canada's ten provinces, is emblematic of the sea-changes in the citizenship regime of the whole country that took place in the 1990s. Two decades earlier the situation was very dif-ferent. By the mid-1970s Canada's post-war citizenship regime included country-wide institutions which addressed citizens as individual 'Canadians', thereby and for a few short decades mapping the whole of Canada as a single political space with which its citizens might identify. Simultaneously, however, there was symbolic and programmatic acknowledgement of particular cate-gories of citizens, thereby granting legitimacy to the intermediary associations of civil society representing those particular interests. Initially, intermediary associations had been recognized as vital aspects of the citizenship regime because, by organizing more marginal groups, they reinforced a fledgling national identity and built loyalty to it. By the 1970s they were accepted as important in helping citizens advocate for social rights and enhance the fair-ness of the democratic process by giving a voice to disadvantaged segments of the population.

   Construction of the regime had been a long-term project, beginning in the war years and reaching its most elaborated form in the Charter of Rights and Freedoms which was embedded in the constitution during the 1982 round of reforms. The citizenship regime was institutionalized in a variety of ways. Most obvious were the constitution and attendant documents such as the Citizenship Act. But the state bureaucracy, parapublic advisory bodies, feder-alism, and other institutions of representation, especially the federal party system, all made important discursive and practical contributions to it. While institutionalized and materialized via a number of associational and state practices, the norms of the regime were never uncontested. Definitions of the nation and the pan-Canadian identity were challenged at least from the 1960s by nationalist movements of Quebecers and Aboriginal peoples. Pockets of populism objected to the active role of the state, as did traditional right-wingers.

None the less, for a period of decades there was a remarkable consensus about citizenship, that is, about the norms and practices regulating the relationship between state and society, the terms of inclusion and exclusion, and the boundaries of the national. This consensus is no more. It has been effectively exploded in the political struggles over economic restructuring in the context of globalization and government deficits, the construction of the North American Free Trade Area, and the remapping of political space associated with nationalist disputes. In all of this, a politics of neo-liberalism, firmly anchored in the state as well as civil society, is providing many of the terms in which citizenship is now being reconstituted.

This chapter presents a conceptualization of 'citizenship regime', created out of a neo-institutionalist approach to political economy, and then uses the concept to examine change over time (Jenson and Phillips 1996). The basic proposition is that if the post-war years were marked by regime-like discursive and practical coherence in a wide range of institutional connections between state and citizens, states' and citizens' responses to the economic and political conditions of the late twentieth century are dismantling and reconstituting citizenship, so that the post-war regime exists no more.

In Canada the direction of movement has been from equity towards marketization. Not only has the growing support for neo-liberalism's definition of the relations among markets, states, and citizens been central to this transformation, but the analogy of the market has been superimposed directly on the concept and practice of citizenship. Under the analogy, the representation of interests is described as a competitive market, and ideally a free market, whose appropriate players are individuals. A role for intermediary associations in narrowing the gap between formal rights of citizenship and actual access to them is assumed to be unnecessary and, indeed, undesirable. Free market competition implies minimal interference by the state in supporting equality of access to the rights of citizenship, either in ensuring that a wide range of citizens are actually being represented or in assisting disadvantaged categories of citizens develop the capacity to participate at all. Because the neo-liberal market-place of citizenship is focused on the representation of interests, rather than on the social rights of citizenship or distribution of well-being, there is little recognition of any positive spillover effects of the organization and participation of citizens in associations. This further reinforces a preference for involvement of citizens as individuals, rather than as members of collectivities.

The trajectory of this transition may very well mark a reduction of the space in which citizens can act together as social and political citizens. None the less, in this ongoing reconfiguration of the citizenship regime, positions still remain fluid, interestingly enough because the rights of democratic citizenship remain a powerful mobilizing concept within civil society.

Citizenship Regimes: Space and Time;
Stability and Change

The work of historical sociologists, from T. H. Marshall's writings in the late 1940s to the recent 'explosion of interest' described by Kymlicka and Norman (1995: 352), teaches that citizenship is a social construction. As such, it varies across both space and time. As so many authors, Marshall included, have remarked, the story of progress from civil to political to social rights which he recounted was the story of Britain.[2] Other countries were destined to live their own histories. A second legacy from Marshall is the idea of change through time. His story is one of new rights won, of new groups gaining access to citizenship, of definitions of community altering through time.

Taking these two Marshallian insights as its foundation, the concept of citizenship regime stands on two theoretical legs. The first follows from the notion that, because citizenship is an historical construction, its form will vary. Particular political struggles, particular trajectories of development, and institutional legacies underpin the forms of citizenship as well as the timing of acquisition of rights. The result is that one may speak of citizenship regimes, just as one can speak of social-welfare regimes. We can say that the concept of citizenship regime denotes the institutional arrangements, rules, and understandings that guide and shape concurrent policy decisions and expenditures of states, problem definitions by states and citizens, and claims-making by citizens.[3]

This theoretical leg generates a logic of comparison across space. Moreover, embedded in this definition is an analytic proclivity for uncovering and attributing importance to ideas as well as practices (Hall and Taylor 1996; Bradford 1998). A citizenship regime encodes within it a paradigmatic representation of identities, of the 'national' as well as the 'model citizen', the 'second-class citizen', and the non-citizen. It also encodes representations of the proper and legitimate social relations among and within these categories, as well as the borders of 'public' and 'private'. It makes, in other words, a major contribution to the definition of politics which organizes the boundaries of political debate and problem recognition in each jurisdiction.

---

[2] Marshall is quite clear about the 'reach' of his thesis about timing and ordering of rights acquisition. His references are all to British history, as are his explicit presentations of what he is trying to do. See e.g. Marshall (1965: 91). It is perhaps to his populizers that we owe the widespread notion that he meant his schema to be a general story of 'modernization': see S. M. Lipset's introduction to the Anchor collection (Marshall 1965), which locates Marshall in the modernization literature.

[3] This definition is a modified version of that of a welfare-state regime in Esping-Andersen (1990: 80). While we have adapted this definition, it is worth noting that, being a case-study, the goal of this chapter is not to follow his procedure of identifying regime types. Comparison of types rather than individual regimes was obviously at the root of his 1990 analysis. One might do the same with citizenship regimes, but this chapter elaborates no typology of regime types.

These representations of identities and social relations are the foundation for claims-making. It is only by representing their identity that groups and individuals can make sense to themselves and others of their interests. In other words, representation of self is an integral aspect of representation of interests. The state also has a role, in that it has the power to recognize citizens, both in general and as particular categories of citizens. The state uses such recognition to make sense of the claims addressed to it.

The second theoretical leg of the concept of citizenship regime is drawn from the regulation approach's notion of stability and change in the patterning of social relations. Without revisiting this approach to political economy in detail, it is sufficient to say that regulationists accept that in some historical moments there is a certain stability in basic social, economic, and political relations which allows us to say that regimes exist. Then, with the arrival of crisis—defined essentially as an intensification of contradictions always present in the regime—profound change and redirection may result. Organizing and legitimating principles can break with one model and give rise to a quite different conceptualization. Moreover, the content, direction, and long-term stability of such movement is not given in advance; it is the product of concrete struggles in particular places.

Adopting this perspective, we argue here that citizenship regimes exist as the concretization in a particular place of a more general model of citizenship corresponding to the general form of regulation. Just as one can speak of 'Fordism' only in the abstract and must qualify the form Fordism takes in each instance, one can identify a general model of post-war citizenship, which took different forms as it was concretized in each case.[4] Each regime is forged out of the political circumstances of a national state.

This theoretical leg of the argument leads to an analysis over time. Being a regime, citizenship does not alter quickly or even easily. None the less, we can expect and seek change at moments of economic and political turbulence. In such moments of fundamental restructuring of the role of the state, the division of labour between state and market, and between public and 'private', definitions of the 'national' as well as of the 'model citizen' may alter. Citizenship regimes are likely to come under pressure at such times precisely because they are a crucial component of the model of development which orders and stabilizes social relations. When the model of development enters into crisis, it is very likely that the citizenship regime embedded within it will also do so.

The theoretical stance of regulationists is that the outcome of these struggles on all dimensions of citizenship, that is over rights, identities, and access is never given in advance.[5] The uncertainty is such that, while one would

---

[4] For this argument about the variability of 'Fordisms' as well as the specific characteristics of Canada's permeable Fordism, see Jenson (1989).

[5] For a discussion of these three dimensions of citizenship, see Wiener (1998).

obviously expect historically created repertoires as well as institutionalized policy legacies to have some weight in the choices of future directions, there is no guarantee that the politics of crisis will maintain the same trajectory. Rupture and redirection are possible. Thus, only cumulation of case-study material can inform us about the solidification of likely general patterns. As a contribution to this enterprise, we present Canada's dismantling of its post-war citizenship regime, focusing particularly on new forms of political access and new forms of recognition of citizens.

Recognizing Citizens

At its most general, citizenship establishes a system of inclusion and exclusion. It defines boundaries, recognizing the citizenship status of the included and denying that status to the excluded. This notion of inside/outside leads directly to a further specification of two dimensions of the concept: citizenship as the conferring of rights and citizenship as grounding for feelings of identification with a particular community (Kymlicka and Norman 1995: 352). Some studies of citizenship have made inclusion and exclusion correspond to the political border of nationality (the citizen of a country).[6] But boundaries have never been confined to national frontiers; internal borders have always separated the full citizen—the person entitled to full rights—from the national with limited rights—a sort of 'second-class citizen'.[7] Attention to internal distinctions makes it evident that schemes of recognition of citizens' access are important.

Much analysis of the identity dimension of citizenship proceeds from the relatively unproblematic assumption that citizenship practice generates a sense of community loyalty among those grateful to be included. Indeed, since the nineteenth century many have assumed that extension of the political rights—and even more so the social rights—of citizenship would calm the revolutionary fervour of the working class. In this formulation we see that the arrow of causality is from rights to identity: having access to rights will create a feeling of belonging.

---

[6] This is the element of citizenship which Brubaker (1992) addresses, essentially eliding the two concepts of citizenship and nationality. Soysal (1994) also focuses on nationality, but in order to demonstrate the permeability to non-citizens of citizenship regimes in countries with guestworkers.

[7] As a result, studies have further specified the rights dimension of citizenship so as to assess the extent to which there is an inequality or hierarchy of rights within the same citizenship regime. The basic question is: which citizens have access to which rights? Analysis also measures the reality of access against the constitutionally defined ideal of 'universal rights'. For example, studies of citizenship and gender have focused on the ways in which the social rights of citizenship were often unequally distributed by social-welfare regimes which took the male breadwinner as the model citizen. They have also documented the ways in which some social programmes may be defined as citizenship rights while others on a secondary track continue to be viewed as no more than assistance or charity, with all the consequences in terms of the disempowerment of citizens which follow.

Such a formulation fails to address the content of citizens' identity. How does one recognize a citizen? What does a model citizen look like in each citizenship regime? What is the model relationship between citizens and the state? The silence around such questions arose, no doubt, because of three tendencies: to see citizenship as part of nation-building, and therefore to assume that a 'national' identity results from the extension of rights; to take the 'universalist' claims of citizenship discourse for reality, without realizing that 'second-class' citizens may exist; and to have a 'society-centric' theory of the state, which does not attribute an 'interest of state' to particular representations of citizens' identities.[8] Once we realize that citizenship involves a lot more than the boundary between nationals and non-nationals, that distinctions among citizens may exist, and that state institutions engage in the politics of recognition, then we must begin to ask when the state will alter its representation of its citizens and when citizens' claims-making will change.

This chapter proceeds from this perspective, seeking the ways state institutions consciously as well as inadvertently engage in a politics of recognition. In effect, state definition of rights and grants of access engage the state in representing citizens to themselves. State institutions never have the power to establish these identities, however. Claims for recognition arise within civil society, often in the form of demands for altering power relations. The state may choose to recognize some claims, and thereby to shore up some identities, but the identity remains the property of the claimant, a creation of collective action.

In Canada, and many other countries, the citizenship regime is in crisis, being restructured under pressure as state and non-state actors seek to make sense of the conditions of the world which they now face, one quite different from Marshall's world, which completed the famous triptych of rights, or even from the world of social movement politics seeking differentiated citizenship. More than a decade of politics driven by a neo-liberal agenda has resulted in offers of a new definition of marketized and individualized citizenship.

Equitable Citizenship: Recognizing Categories, Opening Access

The Canadian post-war citizenship regime was an integral part of the post-war model of development. As were those of many other industrialized

---

[8] Social democrats of various stripes have been the most likely to see citizenship politics as a 'politics of struggle', usually led by the organized working class. But classical Marxists, who demonstrated little interest in 'citizenship' and saw the state as (some version of) the 'best political shell for capitalism', also saw rights following from the needs of bourgeois society. Various correctives to these views have been offered, but there is relatively little yet available which addresses the question of why the state might begin to alter its recognition of certain identities.

countries, Canada's model was Fordist, albeit one that was unusually permeable and open to the effects of the international economy, as well as less social-democratic than many European citizenship regimes (Jenson 1989). It owed its form to a shift in power relations between the federal and provincial governments. As a result of the fiscal crises which struck the provinces in the 1930s, as well as the needs of wartime mobilization, the federal level had been able to accumulate much more authority to direct the Canadian economy and society than it had enjoyed previously. It shaped Canada's welfare state, which extended the citizenship regime, incorporating new social rights in two waves, one at its beginnings in the 1940s and the other in the 1960s.[9]

The establishment of the legal concept of Canadian citizenship in the 1946 Citizenship Act coincided with the first years of the Fordist model of development. The turbulence of wartime political and economic conditions gave impetus to the creation of a citizenship discourse which would inform the citizenship regime for the next four decades. Wartime fears about the loyalty of immigrants from combatant countries, as well as the need to mobilize support for the war effort by those not in the armed forces, laid the groundwork for the state institution, housed in various departments, which came eventually to reside in the Secretary of State. In 1944 this new citizenship branch was given a grab-bag of responsibilities, including promoting women's participation in the war effort and 'fitness programs, incorporating folk dancing'. The keystone, however, was a citizenship training programme (Pal 1993: 75–6).

In the post-war years, concerns about identity replaced those about loyalty. In introducing the Bill which became the Citizenship Act, the Secretary of State said that it would 'provide an underlying community of status for all our people in this country that will bind them together as Canadians' (Pal 1993: 79). But the state did not have exclusive responsibility for fostering this identity or even organizing training for citizenship. It was to be shared, indeed 'contracted out'. As early as 1951 the branch was providing funds to voluntary organizations for programmes in the area of citizenship (Pal 1993: 85).

Thus, the principles underpinning the post-war citizenship regime were not simply liberal; collective responsibility existed and the state had its place as the expression and guarantor of this collectivity.[10] The citizen identity being nurtured was also clearly a national one, and as such it matched that fostered by other institutions regulating Fordism. Indeed, the societal vision of the citizenship branch informed many more state institutions than simply one

---

[9] None the less, federalism remained the central political institution of Canada. As a result, the national institutions created in the era of Canada's permeable Fordism were somewhat particular. They did provide Canadians with the same social and economic rights and benefits no matter where they lived, despite the fact that the provinces had constitutional authority over many social and labour realms, as well as education and health. The mechanism was a system of intergovernmental financing and transfers. Federal–provincial negotiations and agreements became the heart of the model.

[10] This notion of state responsibility for assuring collective goals, as well as the notion that such goals exist, is a legacy of the Canadian Tory and social-democratic traditions. See Horowitz (1966) for the original expression of this idea.

branch. A pan-Canadian party system was being created for the first time (Smith 1996). The notion of a 'national' culture, distinguished from that of the imperial centre(s), and whose own integrity was defensible, was identified in the Massey Commission on the Arts in the early 1950s, as well as in the emerging self-consciously Canadian literature of the time. Economic institutions were creating a country-wide labour market and consumer society. Also, the state was extending pan-Canadian social and economic rights of citizenship, several of which established a direct link between individuals and the federal government.

That government entered into a direct relationship with each Canadian via several important new social programmes. Cheques came from the federal government for family allowances and pensions, and Unemployment Insurance became a country-wide programme. Thus, for the first time, the vision of individual Canadians, linked by a set of national institutions, made everyday sense. An additional central aspect of these programmes was the creation of an Equalization Programme in the late 1950s that used federal-provincial fiscal transfers to offset regional and provincial differences in tax base and resource endowments.[11] The notion was that all Canadians should have more or less the same life chances, whether they lived in wealthy Toronto or poverty-stricken Newfoundland.

These first three decades of the post-war years were all of a piece. The extension of social and economic rights continued through the 1960s, which were the zenith of Canada's Fordism. There was no radical break with the post-war regime. A discourse of equity and social development supplemented the liberal grounding of social rights in previous decades. The 1960s brought a second wave of expansion of Fordist institutions, bringing concerns about equity and social change again to the fore, so that, for example, in these years social rights of Canadian citizens became even more distinct from those available in the USA.

The discourse of equity and social justice was pervasive, shaping proposals for everything from reforming party financing to health care. A wide variety of institutions also shared a conceptualization of how citizens should gain access to the state. Individuals were not the primary actors in this vision; organizations were. In the 1940s and again in the 1960s, trade unions increased in size and gained collective bargaining rights to represent their members to employers and to the state. Parties changed shape, developing more elaborate internal machinery for selection of leaders and policy discussion. Indeed, the New Democratic Party organized itself finally to provide representation to workers' organizations as well as to individuals. The Quebec nationalist movement spawned parties and associations from the early 1960s and was soon joined by organizations of the English-Canadian nationalist movement and

---

[11] The federal Equalization programme which transfers money to the 'have not' provinces to bring their per capita incomes up to a national average began in the late 1950s, just before the second wave of social programme expansion.

then the Aboriginal nationalist movement, all designed to represent a political position to the state.

Concerns about 'Canadian' identity flowered. In part, but only in part, this was because nationalists in Quebec challenged the rest of Canada to decide what difference the presence of two language groups made to the country's definition of self. Two effects of this challenge were the Official Languages Act (1969) and the multiculturalism policy (1971), as well as new life in the citizenship branch of the Secretary of State, which gained responsibility for multicultural programmes and for Official Language Minority Associations.

The challenge was not simply about language, however. The strategy of nationalists in Quebec was to use the state to realize their development project, in particular to build a sophisticated, secular, and above all activist state with the capacity to catapult Quebec society into modernity. A central element of this construction was the elimination of the responsibility of religious institutions for health and education and the development of an array of social programmes in which French-speaking Quebecers would recognize themselves. Thus, the completion of the Canadian welfare state became both a response to the initiatives coming from Quebec and a consequence of the reinforced discourse of social justice overlaid with nation-building motives. Matters of equity were now also matters of national identity.

A similar blending of themes of fairness and national identity was provided by the English-Canadian nationalist movement which arose in the 1960s. Warnings came from both left and right that Canada risked losing its sovereignty and its identity because of the growing influence of the USA in the economy and cultural affairs. Only a state actively pursuing an economic strategy to promote Canadian culture and investment and to sustain Canadian distinctiveness could fend off the threat to its cultural, economic, and political autonomy.

The discourse of social justice was accompanied by a boom in state support for intermediary organizations to assure representation of citizens to and in the state. Reform of the electoral system and party financing was prompted by the goals of assuring equitable treatment of parties by the media and by the recognition that resources were not evenly distributed among social groups. Therefore, the electoral regime established in 1974 recognized political parties for the first time and then proceeded to regulate their access to the media, limiting their campaign expenditures, so that the richest parties and candidates would not overwhelm the less well-endowed; and provided public funding for their campaigns (Seidle 1996). The logic of these actions was that equitable access and fair competition were integral to the well-being of democracy. Realization of the political rights of citizenship required both regulation and state support for these basic institutions which guaranteed access to citizens.

But the discourse of equitable access encompassed more than political parties, elections, and lobbyists. The state also increased its support for other intermediary organizations of representation. The activities of the citizenship branch of the Secretary of State provide one example here. That agency amplified its identity-building activities in the first years of the 1970s. It extended its funding of those associations which organized citizens whose identity state policy sought to affirm, in particular multicultural groups, official language minorities, and Aboriginal political organizations. In 1974, a separate Women's Program was created to foster collective activities by providing both core and project funding to women's groups. As Bernard Ostry, a former Assistant Under Secretary in charge of citizenship said, the goal of the branch was to 'develop and strengthen a sense of Canadian citizenship, chiefly through programs that would aid participation and assuage feelings of social injustice' (quoted in Pal 1993: 109). In addition to the provision of funding, several quasi-independent advisory bodies, notably those responsible for women, social welfare, and the elderly, were established with the intent of conducting research and providing advice to government on matters pertaining to these particular constituencies. Particularly in the case of the Canadian Advisory Council on the Status of Women, the goal was to connect the state more directly with the women's movement (Jenson and Phillips 1996).

We might summarize the citizenship regime of the golden age of Canadian Fordism in the following way. Goals of social justice and equity were central to the citizenship regime. Citizens gained new social and economic rights, with equity and justice being distributed in a pan-Canadian system. Efforts were made to smooth out distinctions across social groups and across space so as to minimize differences in access to social citizenship rights. Efforts were made to foster equitable access to political power and the state via public funding for electoral and lobbying activity. Limits on the political power of those with resources were part of this regime, as was support for citizen advocacy groups.

The regime's discourse linked the solidification of Canadian identity to the realization of equitable treatment of the disadvantaged. As a result, it gave advocacy to groups whose goal was the achievement of social justice for women, the disabled, Aboriginal peoples, and discursive space to minorities of all sorts to make their claims for 'categorical equity' (Jenson 1991). Moreover, a citizenship regime which recognized the particular needs of disadvantaged groups for access to the state provided protection and institutional space for claims-making. The culmination of this regime was the Charter of Rights and Freedoms. On the one hand, the Charter endows individual citizens with pan-Canadian rights, thereby affirming that differences across provincial jurisdictions must be minimized and equal treatment guaranteed. At the same time, the Charter entrenched collective rights and their protection, recognizing both the multinational composition of Canada and the responsibility of the state for overcoming past economic and gender inequities. In all this, the Charter gave constitutional recognition to many of the same groups that had already been recognized via government funding in previous decades.

It is important to understand that the Charter was simultaneously the culmination of the post-war citizenship regime and the beginning of its destabilization. The constitutionalization of the regime was occurring just as the policy-makers were coming to realize that the Fordist model of development had reached its limits. Slowly but surely, a neo-liberal agenda began to emerge in the federal government, within the business community, in the party system, and among interest groups. Opposition to 'special interests' as well as to state spending and economic equity began to emerge. Because the post-war citizenship regime had come to involve public funding for advocacy groups making claims for more state support, a potential contradiction was obvious. As the state lost its enthusiasm for intervening to foster social and economic equity, it would find itself funding its opponents. A mismatch in the citizenship regime occurred.

As the crisis of Fordism intensified, and as the neo-conservative agenda took form, such contradictions became blatant. The Canadian state started to cut back social programmes. Each time it did so, it encountered government-funded groups critical of its intentions to cut pensions, to renege on promised childcare programmes, to reduce funding to women's centres. When it moved from cutbacks to redefining the basic principles of social and economic citizenship, via social policy reform, it also encountered opposition from advocacy groups of all sorts.

By the 1990s the state had begun to reconsider the wisdom of funding its critics. None the less, the cutbacks in support for intermediary institutions cannot be explained only as a consequence of the state 'coming to its senses', or as an effort to rid itself of irritating criticisms. A much larger change was going on. The citizenship regime was being reconstructed. The recognition of citizens would no longer pass through intermediary institutions. Individualization of responsibility for life's hardships, from which Canadians had previously been protected by the economic and social rights of citizenship, was the new model. The discourse on access changed in a similar way, emphasizing competition over fairness and bringing the marketization of representation.

Shifting the Relationship between State and Society

The crisis of the post-war Fordist model of development which struck all advanced industrial countries in the mid-1970s took form and generated specific responses in Canada. The country's position as both a highly industrialized economy and resource producer meant that the economic effects of the oil shock and shifts in patterns of trade affected it differently than they did countries whose economies were more exclusively shaped by industrial production. In particular, recognition of the seriousness of crisis and the mobilizaton of a political strategy to respond was delayed until well into the 1980s. Moreover, because the political regulation of the post-war model had implicated the institutions of federalism more than partisan politics, the crisis was manifested politically as a constitutional crisis (Jenson 1989). Constitutional politics was the terrain on which much actual debate about economic restructuring occurred. These two aspects meant that implementing change was often difficult. Constitutional reform is a cumbersome way to make changes in economic and social policy. It involves moving eleven governments simultaneously. Not surprisingly, to the extent that changes were made, those affecting individuals were often done 'by stealth' involving arcane and poorly understood technical changes to programmes, such as de-indexing and clawbacks in the tax system. Those affecting federalism often involved changes imposed on the provinces by the federal government. Thus, concerns about the restructured economic future were expressed not only in economic terms; demands for democracy and openness also began to resonate.[12]

The reconfiguration of the relationship between state and society had several implications for the representation of citizens. First, many institutions have been reorganized to give less visibility to categories of citizens and to remove their means of advocacy from within the state. Second, the credibility of advocacy groups is under attack, and their capacity to represent citizens to the state is being diminished. In the process, the nature of public consultation is being reoriented. Third, modes of service delivery are being recast under a rubric of partnerships. Finally, economic restraint and the politics of federalism have forced social programmes to abandon the principles of social justice and the pan-Canadianism that underpinned the former regime. There has been a marked move to a much more decentralized system of social programme delivery which is likely to produce wide variations in access and levels of service and to refocus identities from the national to the provincial or local level. Therefore, as the quotations at the head of this chapter indicate, cutbacks to health care call into question everything from the definition of the nation, national and other identities, the role of the state, and the right to be heard as change is being made and programme delivery is being designed.

Weakening the Advocates for 'Categorial' Citizens

Institutional change within the federal government has reduced recognition of many group interests and shed centres promoting potentially critical policy

---

[12] For example, the debate about free trade involved not only issues of winners and losers, but also disputes about how the decision could legitimately be made and who should participate.

perspectives. One step was simply to dismantle the government department which had been most visibly involved in promoting citizenship via social development. In a major reorganization under the Conservatives in 1993, the Secretary of State was closed down and its programmes either cancelled or placed in a variety of other departments. Such reassignments and breakup of bureaucratic linkages obviously had effects on civil servants' capacity to continue to deliver programmes according to the long-standing philosophical principles. In addition, political representation of many societal interests at the cabinet table was eliminated. Using the rhetoric of 'reducing waste' in government, the number of cabinet seats was cut to twenty-five by the Conservatives and to twenty-three under the post-1993 Liberal government. The peak had been forty in the 1980s and had at various times had included representatives for youth, seniors, and small business, among other interests (Swimmer 1994: 192–3). Moreover, under the Liberals the portfolios of multiculturalism and status of women were combined and then demoted from having a full-fledged cabinet minister to a new designation of 'secretary of state', a second-tier minister with limited resources.[13]

Restructuring also eliminated the parapublic bodies which had stood at the interface of civil society and the state, providing access for ideas via policy research as well as for individuals. In 1992 the government eliminated both the Economic Council of Canada and the Science Council, bodies that had been created to advise the government by bringing the expertise of non-governmental sources 'into the loop'. It argued that private-sector research institutes were more appropriate sources of advice and recipients of public monies for specific programmes.[14]

A good example of targeting within-state advocates for categories of citizens was the swift dismantling of the 'Women's State' in 1995 (Jenson and Phillips 1996). The Canadian Advisory Council on the Status of Women (CACSW) was dissolved and the Women's Program in the Department of Labour that funded advocacy organizations was absorbed into the Status of Women, a small transversal department with no line policy responsibilities. The justification that such moves would save money and increase service efficiency, with a resulting improvement in service to the public, is less than convincing. In the case of the Women's State there was very little duplication of functions across the three agencies, other than the fact that all had 'women' in their title. Not much money was saved by this reorganization, nor in the larger scheme of things did they spend much to begin with. For officials in

[13] This minor ministerial appointment should not be confused with the department of Secretary of State, whose important role we have described above.

[14] For example, the federal government 'contracted out' to private research institutes the organization of public consultations about constitutional reform in 1992 and about the Budget in 1994. It also contracts out research which previously would have been done by the Economic Council or the Science Council. The Minister Responsible for the Status of Women will also contract out research which CACSW would have done in-house.

the central agencies preoccupied with deficit reduction and shrinking the role and size of the state, however, the women's movement and its advocates within the state seemed out of touch with the current political environment. Therefore, these institutions were entirely expendable.

Another interpretation is that the government wished to bring the extensive network of regional offices of the Women's Program and the research budget of the CACSW under the control of the Minister Responsible for the Status of Women. These regional offices had been used by the Women's Program as an 'ear to the ground', moving information upward as well as providing support and funds directly in communities. Since reorganizing, it appears that Status of Women has used the regional offices primarily as a way of 'informing' citizens about the activities of the department and its minister. In addition, Status of Women was interested in absorbing the research budget of CACSW but it had little intention of supporting independent research as CACSW did. Thus the surviving institution of the former Women's State has taken a form that can be easily controlled by its 'political masters' and is less able to act less as an advocate for women within the state bureaucracy. The political message was clear. Groups should be self-supporting and voluntary. The experiment in the state facilitating and even promoting the collective voice of women outside and within the state ended.

Reducing Interest Group Capacity and Credibility

A related manifestation of the shift in the citizenship regime has been a direct attack on the credibility and organizational base of groups and their role in policy consultation. A first step involved reducing direct funding to public interest groups. The Tory government began to cut grants and contributions to groups selectively in 1986–7. Often there was a 'testing of the waters' to assess reactions. For example, the funding practices of the Women's Program were a target.[15] The 1990 budget made cuts to three women's magazines, a 20 per cent reduction to five feminist groups, and eighty women's centres. The country's largest women's group, the National Action Committee on the Status of Women (NAC) was spared at first, however, because the government feared an uproar if it were touched and widespread demonstrations did succeed in having some funding to the women's shelters restored. None the less the pressure for reductions was relentless. Each year further cuts were announced and a change in government did not alter the situation. The Liberals did abandon the across-the-board cuts popular with the Tories, preferring selective ones specifically targeting advocacy groups.

[15] One type of group was not cut, however. The Tories continued to fund associations representing official language minorities and multicultural groups (Phillips 1991).

In addition, under the Liberals the purpose of interest-group funding has changed. A new funding strategy identified a number of criteria that were clearly intended to stress the role of groups as service providers. Groups that spend more effort on service delivery and less on advocacy are much preferred. One criterion is to test funding against the organization's benefit to the public. Another is its ability to get access to other funds. Finally, the 'fit' between the groups' activities and government priorities is important. Overall, these criteria constitute a test of the importance of particular programmes, not just groups, to departments. Those departments that use groups to deliver their programmes and support their policies could fund them. The result of using these criteria, rather than ones of justice or equity in access, means that the state has reduced its role in service provision. But in others it has taken a strong hand in setting direction and policy, using groups as its clients and occasional allies.

Further rethinking of the role of interest groups and the institutions of representation has come from within Parliament and the political parties. Over the last decades there has been a decline in the legitimacy of political parties. Public opinion's distrust of politicians is one manifestation. A second is the rise of right-wing populism. Indeed, the right-wing Reform Party has reaped the greatest benefits of this disgruntlement and renewed emphasis on the role of parliamentarians. The language of 'special interests' has resonated far beyond right-wing politicians, however. The conflict between groups and Members of Parliament often comes down to an 'us or them' mentality, with many stressing that parties and Parliament must monopolize representation, sharing legitimacy only with individual voters. For example, the 1992 Report of the Royal Commission on Electoral Reform and Party Financing insisted on maintaining a distinction between the 'good' representation provided by strong parties, and the representation of 'special interests' by advocacy groups.

This backlash against citizen groups has also been reflected in subtle changes to the format of public consultations organized by federal departments, parliamentary committees, and independent commissions. The shift began in 1990 with the Citizens' Forum on Canada's Future which used the opportunity of a national consultation exercise to hear individuals as individuals, not as members of interest groups, and which judged its success by the number of participants involved, no matter how minimally these individuals participated: a phone call to a 1-800 number was sufficient to be counted. This approach has become the norm of national consultations. For example, in 1992 the Canadian Panel on Violence against Women used a substantial part of its $10 million budget to travel to 139 communities across the country. It heard from 4,000 individuals who were encouraged to recall their personal experiences with violence. At the same time it severely limited opportunities for representatives of groups from the shelter and women's movements to engage in discussions of policy alternatives. Similarly, the Liberal government's major consultation on the social security review in 1994 included not only a parliamentary standing committee that led the consultation hearing from a variety of interest groups, but also a variety of supplementary exercises, including focus groups, 1-800 phone lines, public-opinion surveys, and policy 'workbooks' that were designed to provide input from individual citizens.

Redefining Government through Partnerships

The language of 'partnership' became the buzzword for a new form of governance in the 1990s under both Conservative and Liberal governments. Indeed, one of the six tests used under a major review of all federal government programmes in 1994 was the scope for public–private partnership as an alternative for provision of programmes or services.[16] The intent is to encourage a wide array of partnering arrangements with both the private and third sectors. While reducing costs is an important goal of public–private partnerships in an environment of economic restraint, it is not the only one. The claim is also made that partnerships have the potential to improve the quality of service delivery and programme design because the partnering organizations are often more aware of the needs of the clients with whom they have frequent contact and can be more flexible in responding to these needs (Seidle 1995). In addition, partnerships permit variations in services and facilitate local control, thus being compatible with the retreat from national standards.

In spite of the potential of partnerships, the current approach being pursued in Canada is detracting from, rather than enhancing, the maintenance of a vibrant third sector. First, true partnerships involve power-sharing. Initial indications of the experimentation with partnerships by Canadian governments, however, suggest that they have not invested wholeheartedly in such relationships and have been unwilling to share power with the partners, preferring instead to maintain a traditional top–down approach. Many of the so-called partnerships are, in fact, merely contracts in which the state, as the contracting party, sets all the rules. In spite of the constraints of these contracts, many third-sector organizations are drawn into them, either because they need the project money as a substitute for the loss of core funding or because the state has withdrawn direct provision of services and their constituencies will only be served in this way.

Second, partnerships may alter the nature of third-sector partners, especially social movements. The originality of the new social movements that

---

[16] The other tests are serving the public interest, the need for government involvement at all, the appropriate federal role, scope for increased efficiency, and affordability.

arose beginning in the late 1960s was that they were not tied to specific places, but represented broader, often quite diverse, social communities and were dynamic, fluid networks, rather than conventional, institutionalized organizations. The sometimes elaborate rules of contract partnerships, however, may force them to become more place-bound (by delivering services to specific geographic communities), and may transform the informality of movements into formalized, professionalized organizations.

Third, the current approach is creating a hierarchy of groups, with those focused exclusively on service delivery placed at the top and those focused on advocacy deemed irrelevant. For the partnering organization, opportunities for action may be diminished because it is difficult to act as an advocate for policy changes from within a partnership arrangement, especially if the state has held on to the cords of power. From the outside, it is more difficult to lobby multiple partnerships rather than a single government body.

In the face of economic restraint, an even more difficult problem arises. Frequently, once a partnership arrangement has been established and a clientele has become dependent upon it, the state's contribution to the contract is cut significantly. Contrary to the popular myth that such cuts enliven a sense of voluntarism to fill the gap left by state funding, experience indicates that the common response by third-sector partners is not a growth in voluntary activity, but a rise in commercialism. Voluntary organizations turn to user fees and other sources of market income, thereby becoming more business-like and more integrated into the private market economy. In addition, for-profit firms begin to seek out this niche, often gradually crowding out the voluntary organizations (Picard 1998).

Restructuring Federalism

Finally, the model of federalism based on activist intervention by the federal government in social policy is being fundamentally redesigned. The capacity of the federal government to use its spending power, especially through intergovernmental transfers and programme cost-sharing in areas of provincial jurisdiction, has been voluntarily constrained. In 1995, the federal government created a new block-funded transfer to the provinces, called the Canada Health and Social Transfer (CHST), which replaced existing cost-sharing for welfare and transfers supporting health care and post-secondary education. The concomitant withdrawal of $6 billion in cash over two years—a cut of 37 per cent—marked a significant retraction of the federal spending power that had been actively used in the post-war years to ensure equity among individuals, as well as across regions, by providing redistribution from richer to poorer citizens. In 1996, the federal government made the commitment that it would refrain from undertaking any new cost-shared programmes in areas of provincial responsibility. The rationale for these moves was threefold: to stabilize and reduce federal spending; to offer greater flexibility to the provinces to design their own route through post-Fordism; and to demonstrate to Quebec that its demands for constitutional reform were being partially satisfied by federal respect for provincial jurisdiction (Boismenu and Jenson 1996).

At the same time as it cut the transfers nominally covering social programmes, the federal government increased allocations for unconditional equalization payments. The clear symbolic message, suggests Banting (1995: 5), is that 'equalization is our most important social programme' and that '[w]e are a people who reject greater inter-regional inequality but accept inter-personal inequality' (Banting 1995: 8). Debates over the distribution of income and the well-being of individuals may be destined to become matters of significance only at the provincial and local level. Finally, many programmes once provided directly by the federal government, notably labour market training, have been devolved to the provinces. As the responsibility for designing and supporting social programmes is downloaded, identities and communities are also being refocused. Increasingly, it may be difficult to support the notion that 'Canadians share experiences'.

Concluding Remarks

Citizenship regimes define who 'we' are, both to ourselves and to others, thereby establishing the boundaries of solidarity and difference. In the last decades the citizenship regimes constructed in the post-1945 years have come under strain in many countries, under the pressure of economic restructuring, restraint on state expenditures, and new nationalisms. If the pressures are similar in many cases, the results may widely vary. In Canada the debate over state–citizen relations has to a large extent occurred as part of societal discussions about the economic role of the state and about Canada's very existence, in the face of demands from Quebec for independence and the NAFTA. Therefore, exclusion of representatives of certain categories of citizens from state and parastate bureaucracies, as well as dismantling of meaningful consultative mechanisms, have been portrayed by actors in both the state and civil society as a requisite of fiscal restraint rather than as a matter of representative democracy. Devolution of responsibilities from the federal government to the provinces and a lack of interest in maintaining country-wide standards of social protection is rationalized as a step towards national unity. Both types of changes have major implications for the future of the citizenship regime. Citizenship has become more individualized: activities of interest groups and social movement organizations have been delegitimated. It is as if only individuals may address the state. Citizenship has also become marketized: the relationship between the citizen and the state is defined as one of client to provider. Any disputes about service must be settled in the 'market-place of ideas', and any interest which cannot demonstrate its capacity to accumulate resources in that 'market' is not worth recognizing.

With this latter change, a potential contradiction and space for mobilization of an alternative opens up, however. The state has become increasingly reliant on groups to deliver its services. If such 'partnerships' have been thus far unidirectional and if supposedly apolitical and non-advocacy groups have been privileged, such service-providers are likely to come into contact with the social costs of decentralized, underfunded non-uniform programmes. Indeed, they already are beginning to demand attention to the needs of their constituencies, and new forms of collective action may result.

REFERENCES

BANTING, K. (1995). 'The Social Policy Review: Policy-Making in a Semi-Sovereign Society', *Canadian Public Administration*, 38/2: 283–90.

BOISMENU, G., and JENSON, J. (1996). 'La Réforme de la sécurité du revenu pour les sans-emplois et le dislocation du régime de citoyenneté canadien', *Politique et société*, 30: 27–45.

BRADFORD, N. (1998). *Commissioning Ideas: Canadian Policy Innovation in a Comparative Perspective* (Toronto: Oxford University Press).

BRUBAKER, W. R. (1992). *Citizenship and Nationhood in France and Germany* (Cambridge, Mass.: Harvard University Press).

CAMPBELL, MURRAY (1996). '1,289 Squeaky Wheels', *Globe and Mail* (20 Jan.), D1.

ESPING-ANDERSEN, G. (1990). *The Three Worlds of Welfare Capitalism* (Princeton: Princeton University Press).

HALL, P. A., and TAYLOR, R. C. R. (1996). 'Political Science and the Three New Institutionalisms', *Political Studies*, 44: 936–57.

HOROWITZ, G. (1966). 'Conservatism, Liberalism and Socialism in Canada', *Canadian Journal of Economics and Political Science*, 32: 143–71.

JENSON, J. (1989). '"Different" but not "Exceptional": Canada's Permeable Fordism', *Canadian Review of Sociology and Anthropology*, 26/1: 69–94.

——(1991). 'Citizenship and Equity: Variations across Time and in Space', in J. Hiebert (ed.), *Political Ethics: A Canadian Perspective* (Toronto: Durndurn Press), 195–228.

——and PHILLIPS, S. D. (1996). 'Regime Shift: New Citizenship Practices in Canada', *International Journal of Canadian Studies*, 14: 111–36.

KYMLICKA, W., and NORMAN, W. (1995). 'Return of Citizen: A Survey of Recent Work on Citizenship Theory', in R. Beiner (ed.), *Theorizing Citizenship* (Albany, NY: State University of New York Press), 283–322.

MARSHALL, T. H. (1965). *Class, Citizenship, and Social Development* (Garden City, NY: Doubleday).

PAL, L. (1993). *Interests of State* (Montreal: McGill-Queens University Press).

PHILLIPS, S. (1991). 'How Ottawa Blends: Shifting Government Relations with Interest Groups', in F. Abele (ed.), *How Ottawa Spends 1991–1992: The Politics of Fragmentation* (Ottawa: Carleton University Press), 183–228.

PICARD, A. (1998). *A Call to Alms: The New Face of Charities in Canada* (Toronto: The Atkinson Foundation).

SEIDLE, F. L. (1995). *Rethinking the Delivery of Public Services to Citizens* (Montreal: IRPP).

——(1996). 'The Canadian Electoral System and Proposals for Reform', in A. B. Tanguay and A. G. Gagnon (eds.), *Canadian Parties in Transition* (Toronto: Nelson), 282–306.

SMITH, D. E. (1996). 'Canadian Political Parties and National Integration', in A. B. Tanguay and A. G. Gagnon (eds.), *Canadian Parties in Transition* (Toronto: Nelson), 32–51.

SOYSAL, Y. N. (1994). *Limits of Citizenship: Migrants and Postnational Membership in Europe* (Chicago: University of Chicago Press).

SWIMMER, G. (1994). 'Public Service 2000: Dead or Alive', in S. D. Phillips (ed.), *Maling Change: How Ottawa Spends 1994–1995* (Ottawa: Carleton University Press), 165–204.

VALPY, MICHAEL (1996). 'Health Care under the Knife', *Globe and Mail* (7 Feb.).

WIENER, A. (1998). *'European' Citizenship Practice: Building Institutions of a Non-State* (Boulder, Colo.: Westview Press).

5

The Marketization of Public Services

Mark Freedland

When they were developing the project from which the present volume results, the editors proposed, as one of the starting-points, a framework of analysis which argued for *different locations* of citizenship as a way of recognizing the separation of market citizenship from state or community citizenship.[1] In this chapter it will be argued that one can go further and identify these not just as different locations but to a certain extent as *rival conceptions* of citizenship. We can contrast private, economic, individualistic conceptions with public, social, communitarian ones. In political practice, these conceptions place each other under tension; each can operate so as to subvert the other. The marketization of public services has been a very important way of promoting the former conception of citizenship and subverting the latter.

In order to develop this argument, I shall first set up a structural paradigm to explain how I understand the marketization of public services. In this paradigm, marketization consists in ensuring that public services are provided on the basis of a certain particular type of triangular relationship. That is to say, an intermediate public-service provider (IPSP) is placed between the state or the government and the citizen—which is not novel in itself—and, which is much more novel, the relationships between the state and the IPSP, between the IPSP and the citizen, and between the citizen and the state, are designed or conducted according to marketized conceptions of those relationships. In the first part of this chapter, those structures and conceptions are described and explained.

Exercises in imposing these paradigms are often only partially successful in creating meaningful markets, and may be counter-productive in terms of the

---

[1] Thus Klaus Eder, in a communication to the proposed authors on 26 Mar. 1996: 'Citizenship has three social locations: in the state (as membership in a state), in the market (as social citizen, tied to his role as producer and consumer), and in the community (as political citizen, identifying with the other by marking the boundaries of the community. . . . A central assumption is that these three locations are increasingly decoupled.'

economy and efficiency in the name of which they are conducted. Those engaged in such exercises often do not regard this as invalidating their efforts. That may be because their underlying aims are still achieved even if the marketization is only partially realized and at high transactional costs. We can understand this by interpreting the underlying aims in terms of the promotion of market citizenship and the subversion of public or social citizenship. The remainder of this chapter is concerned with those aims, or those effects, of marketization of public services.

This marketization effects the subversion of public or social citizenship in a number of different ways, some of them relatively obvious and some of them much less so. These can be identified by concentrating in turn on the different relationships in the triangular structure of state, citizen, and IPSP. That inquiry is undertaken in successive sections of the chapter. The development is from the more obvious impacts on citizenship to the less obvious ones. Thus we begin with the relationship between the citizen and the IPSP. By identifying this relationship in commercial terms (with the citizen as the customer), marketization places the citizen in a conflictual, individualistic relationship with the public institutions with which he or she immediately deals. It will be argued that, on any view, we radically amend our conception of citizenship when we identify the citizen as a shopper in the market-place.

We then turn to the, somewhat less obvious, effects on citizenship of the remodelling of the relationship between the citizen and the state in a marketized triangular public-service structure. By rendering the relationship between the citizen (as customer of the IPSP) and the government (which operates through the IPSP) an indirect and incidental one, these remodelling exercises downgrade the citizen's voice in government, both by denying the directness of that voice and by commercializing the subject-matter of the discussion between citizen and government.

Finally, we consider the much less obvious implications for citizenship of the marketization of the relationship between the state and the IPSP. This might, on the face of it, seem to be important purely as a relationship between institutions and therefore as not important to citizenship. It will be argued, to the contrary, that it is the construction of marketized rationales and marketized patterns of operation for this set of relationships which is the under-recognized and perhaps crucial way in which citizenship is transformed by the marketization of public services.

The chapter will conclude by recognizing and considering the complexities and ambivalence of this set of arguments. Thus, views differ as to the positive and negative values of the reducing of individual deference on the part of citizens and the humbling of public-service professionalism, as deployed in relation to citizens, which are involved in the marketization of public services. The conclusion will consider how far there are alternative conceptualizations of public-service relationships which capture these effects as virtues and avoid them as vices.

Paradigms of Triangular Public-Service Relationships

It will be argued in this section that the phenomenon which is central to, indeed almost definitive of, the marketization of public services is the imposition of certain paradigms of triangular public-service relationships. I will seek to demonstrate that this argument does not extend to all forms of triangular public-service relationships, and to identify what is singular about those paradigms which can be thought of as marketization. I will also attempt to show in what sense the marketization paradigm itself takes more than one form, and what is the nature of the differences between those forms.

Triangular public-service relationships are those which arise when a separation is made within the institutions of executive government and public-service provision so that they are split into two distinct levels or capacities, and significant relationships arise between the two levels or capacities, and between the citizen and each of the two levels or capacities. A central example, though not one which should be thought of as the central paradigm, for there is no one such central paradigm, is that of the Next Steps programme in the United Kingdom, by which executive agencies have been separated off from very many government departments.[2] These executive agencies have thus been established as intermediate public-service providers.

It is important to emphasize that the executive agency does not constitute the universal paradigm of triangular public-service relationships because the diversity between different patterns of such relationships is highly significant. It is not even the case that the intermediate institution will necessarily be a 'public-service provider' in any meaningful sense. Thus, I am far from convinced that it is satisfactory, for instance, to regard a social security contributions collecting agency as a 'public-service provider', though, for reasons which we shall discuss later, the rhetoric of the Next Steps programme insists on regarding it as such. It may simply be that a triangular public-service relationship arises because the central state or central government has seen fit to entrust to an intermediate institution one of its tasks or functions which impacts upon the citizens. Although that formulation could apply to triangles arising between central government, local government, and the citizen, it is not intended to include those relationships in this analysis; they present a further set of issues which are tangential to the concerns of this chapter.

---

[2] For my analysis and evaluation of the Next Steps programme in the context of constitutional law, see Freedland (forthcoming).

In order to understand this diversity between different kinds of triangular public-service relationships, and to relate that diversity to the marketization of public services, it may perhaps be useful to try to establish a typology of these relationships. We can best do that by considering the different purposes for which, or different rationales with which, intermediate public-service institutions are separated off from the central state or central government and entrusted with public-service functions. I suggest that there is in fact a broad spectrum of these. At one end of that spectrum lie wholly public-sphere and administrative purposes or rationales. At the other end of this spectrum we find wholly private-sphere and economic or commercial ones. Most actual intermediate public-service institutions find their rationale and purpose somewhere away from the extreme ends of the spectrum, but their point of location on it is still very significant. This typology obviously needs elaboration and illustration, which I seek to provide in the following paragraphs.

Let us begin that exercise at the public and administrative end of the spectrum. Probably the clearest illustration of this kind of purpose or rationale for separating off intermediate institutions is the doctrine of separation between policy and administration which is specially associated with Woodrow Wilson in his pre-presidential capacity as a professor of political science (Foster and Plowden 1996). Wilson argued that the checks and balances needed to secure constitutional democracy were inadequately provided by the doctrine of separation of powers unless this further separation was included, that is to say, the separation of administration from policy within the executive arm of government. It is an argument for separating off and insulating a civil service bureaucracy from the political and policy-making level of executive government, so that the execution, implementation, or administration of policies determined at the political level can take place in a way which is not arbitrary, over-discretionary, or over-exposed to political influence.

The argument for separation between policy and administration has not in and of itself been a general rationale for creating separate intermediate institutions in the twentieth-century history of British government and the British state. The doctrine in a sense has its counterpart in the (now sadly diminished) notion of the independence of the British civil service from the government of the day.[3] It has even served on particular occasions as a reason for formal separation of intermediate institutions where a particular importance has been attached to manifesting the political neutrality with which the administrative task in hand is carried out, as with the separation off in 1975

---

[3] This conception is integral to the design of the British civil service as it resulted from the implementation of the Northcote–Trevelyan Report of 1853 (Hennessy 1989: 31–51). The assertion that this independence is now sadly diminished is my own, and refers principally to the so-called Armstrong doctrine, a restatement of the duties of senior civil servants in terms which prioritized their obligations to pursue the policies of the government of the day (Hennessy 1989: 344–6).

of the mediatory functions of the Department of Employment into a distinct Advisory Conciliation and Arbitration Service (Freedland 1992). But generally in British public administrative history, civil service independence has been asserted or expressed as an intellectual detachment rather than an institutional one.[4]

That being so, the main influence of the doctrine of separation between policy and administration on current practice in the UK is, as we shall see, in the shape of a belief that the distinction between policy decision-making and *operational* decision-making is unquestionably valid and legitimated in terms of the theory of public administration. That belief has been harnessed, as we shall see, to the cause of institutional separation with rationales very different from those which animated Woodrow Wilson and the other proponents of policy/administration separation. This is disturbing, since the inherent unsatisfactoriness of the policy/operational distinction as applied to actual administrative processes makes it a dangerous weapon in the hands of managerial ideologues.[5] This takes us to the other end of our spectrum of rationales, which I now address.

Here lies a set of purely economic rationales for entrusting public-service tasks to intermediate institutions, ideally in the form of private commercial corporations.[6] Since the early 1980s, these rationales have been pursued, and the structures which they suggest have been created, very extensively in many countries. The leadership, both by rhetoric and by example, has come from Britain, the USA, and, quite surprisingly, New Zealand. This is at once acknowledged and at the same time very powerfully related to Australian experience by Michael Pusey (1991). The impetus for creating structures of this kind is that of a perceived need on the part of governments to limit public expenditure (Foster and Plowden 1996: chs. 1 and 2), and to do so by transferring the burden of providing and paying for risk or investment capital, and of conducting the

---

[4] Thus Foster and Plowden (1996) identify the British doctrine as the 'Haldane model', from the Haldane Report (HM Government 1918), and argue that this, by envisaging civil servants as the (ultimately independent) *advisers* of the ministers, provided an *alternative* to institutional separation between ministers and civil servants. 'As advisers they can advise a minister on anything, and there is no need to separate their powers. . . . Since the Northcote–Trevelyan reforms, this has been the cornerstone of the British administrative tradition, and *it could not be more different from the Wilsonian tradition*' (1996: 77; emphasis added).

[5] A point very well taken by Foster and Plowden (1996: 77) in relation to the development of the doctrine in the USA: 'the distinction between policy and administration cannot be sustained practically or logically. The danger, already recognised by some critics of the Clinton–Gore reforms . . . is that it is being transformed into a different doctrine by which politicians become not only the legislators, the policy-makers and the rule-makers, but also the entrepreneurs, leaving implementation, in a much restricted sense, to the civil servants.'

[6] Though also, often equally satisfactorily from this perspective, in the form of a non-profit-making body from the third or voluntary sector—a point which has been well understood in the USA, and is attracting increasing interest in the UK. 'Third-sector bodies' defining characteristic would seem to be that they have some motive other than profit, and are thus more likely to help government achieve its mission with altruism and sympathy, while at the same time being flexible enough to be efficient' (Foster and Plowden 1996: 46).

operation for which the capital is raised, from the state to the private sector of the economy. When structures of this kind are created, for example by privatization or contractorization of public services or by private finance initiatives in relation to public services, the government or state assumes the role of entrepreneur or franchiser, and the intermediate institution has the role of commercial undertaking or franchisee (Veljanowski 1987). In essence, this is the model of the completely marketized public service.

It has gradually become evident, both to the proponents and to the critics of this model of public-service relationships, just how fundamental a transformation it effects in conceptions of the role and nature of government and of the state. This is recognized in the very title of one of the best-known tracts of this ideological movement, Osborne and Gaebler's *Reinventing Government* (1992). The bible of the movement is probably Hayek (1960). In a somewhat more critical, though by no means wholly hostile, vein, Foster and Plowden (1996: preface and ch. 12) identify the extent to which these developments indicate that traditional conceptions of the British state are under stress. They develop a metaphor that the creating of this kind of structure represents a hollowing out of the traditional state, and it is this metaphor which explains the question which forms the subtitle to the work in which they propound this argument: can the hollow state be good government (Foster and Plowden 1996)?[7] Whatever may be the right answer to that question, it is certainly clear that the hollow state is very different government from that of the decades which preceded it.

This discussion has been located towards the economic end of the spectrum of rationales for entrusting public-service functions to intermediate, and in this case private-sector, institutions. We have to be bold, and to enter a world which verges on being abhorrent to many people, to reach the extreme end-point of that spectrum. That is the point at which governments come to identify their own nature and role, and their conception of what constitute public functions, as the creation of opportunities for revenue or profit, and the enfranchisement of those opportunities to the private sector. This is the world of the eighteenth-century tax-farm. Some may detect resemblances to it in the British National Lottery, the enfranchisement of which to the private sector was an inherent and central feature of its design and creation. Governments begin to inhabit that world when they come to rely on private-sector prison services, especially if their own policies and the commercial interests of private-sector companies combine to increase the demand for prison accommodation.[8]

However, and from my own perspective thankfully, much of the phenomenon which I wish to describe in a broad sense as marketization of public

---

[7] For the notion of 'hollowing out', see especially Foster and Plowden (1996: ch. 9).
[8] Compare, for evaluation of current developments in the USA and the UK, Stern (1997).

services is not located quite so far at that end. In British experience at least, and I suspect more generally, much of the development of marketization took place somewhere in the middle of the spectrum between purely public administrative rationales and purely economic ones. In between those two extremes lies a group of 'managerial' rationales for restructuring public-service relationships. I shall argue that, from the 1980s onwards, these were subjected to a political and ideological dynamic which moved them more and more decisively towards the economic end of the spectrum, although it was not necessarily there that they had found their origin. A short narrative account will be necessary to explain this argument.

In the relatively recent history of British government, we can observe strong impulses to reform and improve the management of the civil service from the mid-1960s onwards (Hennessy 1989: 169 ff.). Very broadly speaking, we can say that the concern was to ensure that the civil service was managed in such a way as to achieve the goals of the welfare state effectively, while doing so by processes which were fair, rational, and responsive to the needs and aspirations of citizens. This was widely seen as requiring reform of the machinery of government, and in particular as pointing towards the creation of very large, overarching, government departments but within which managerial units were separated out and entrusted with particular tasks and functions. Such ideas were prominent in the Fulton Report (HM Government 1968), and informed Edward Heath's so-called 'Quiet Revolution', that is, the programme of civil service reorganization carried out during his government of 1970–4 (Hennessy 1989: 235–6).[9] This meant that the reformist zeal of post-1979 governments towards the civil service could be portrayed, both by politicians and writers, as lying within or building upon recent discourse and practice (Hennessy 1989: 589 ff.).[10]

This was only superficially true, for the underlying reality was that from the beginning of the 1980s, administrative reform was far more single-mindedly directed towards cost-cutting and financial 'efficiency'. That is what is really distinctive about 'new public management', as this 1980s genre of public administration came to be known (Foster and Plowden 1996: ch. 4). It is essentially a project of subjecting public administration to the managerial methods and disciplines of the private sector, because those are perceived by the proponents of 'new public management' to be more financially rigorous or efficient, more keenly attuned to the relationship between inputs and outputs, investment and outcomes, than the management styles of existing, unreconstructed, public administrators.

This involves a subtle set of transformations. In the earlier stages of these reforms the emphasis was most prominently on 'getting results', in terms of

---

[9] Hennessy (1989) is intensely critical of the civil-service response to this programme of reform.

[10] Hennessy, however, contrasts post-1979 radicalism with pre-1979 obstructionism towards the pursuit of managerial efficiency in the civil service.

better health, less crime, and so forth. The shift to the aim of getting the same results at a lower cost, and ultimately to formulating a more limited and economical definition of what services it is appropriate to provide, is a gradual one, and indeed not necessarily a complete one. The aspiration to retain or arrive at a high level of resource allocation, and to achieve more with it, remains a real and influential one, which has been realized in some areas. That said, the institutional framework of new public management does subject that aspiration to increasing pressure, and may make it appear as an internal survival from an earlier public-service culture, rather than an integral element in the current culture.

This analysis enables us to understand why the proponents of 'new public management' have been every bit as much concerned as their 1960s and 1970s predecessors with the creation of distinct intermediate units of management and triangular public-service relationships. That same analysis, on the other hand, also shows why the modes, purposes, and effects of their pursuit of that concern have differed from those of their predecessors. It is in that set of differences that the dynamic towards marketization is to be found; from apparently slight initial shifts of emphasis, perspective, and terminology, consequences of great practical and ideological significance have followed. Again, some expansion will be necessary to explain this argument.

Perhaps the clearest point on which to focus in the rather complex landscape of new public management is the way in which the separation of intermediate units is effected and conceptualised. Foster and Plowden identify ten principles of new public management, of which their first (and in my view identifying) one is: 'separating purchasing public services from production' (Foster and Plowden 1996: 45).

They portray this mode of separation as synonymous or closely congruent with other distinctions which are part, as we have seen, of a long-standing discourse of public administration: 'Recommending the separation of purchasing public services or, as it is often called, their provision from production, "steering from rowing", is already a well-established tradition. . . . it echoes a much older distinction between policy and administration' (Foster and Plowden 1996: 46).

In fact, the recent discourse of new public management seems more and more to prefer to express Foster and Plowden's dichotomy in terms of separating the purchaser from the 'provider', rather than the 'producer' of public services, so that the intermediate unit of management is the immediate provider, and the state or an appropriate surrogate for the state is the purchaser. That last modification should not distract us from the importance of the point made by Foster and Plowden; they correctly show how the purchaser/producer, or purchaser/provider split is at the heart of new public management thinking. It is born of the discourse of private-sector management. The transition from 'producer' to 'provider' marks the shift from a primarily manufacturing to a primarily service economy; this does not matter to the argument; the paradigm in which either the 'producer' or the 'provider' is separated from the 'purchaser' is one which is commercial in its conception. The 'producer' or 'provider' is essentially a unit of management in the business sense, as a self-contained productive or service enterprise, having a business relationship with the 'purchaser' of what it produces or provides.

It is in that discourse, in the rhetoric of financially and commercially oriented new public management, that a dynamic is created towards complete marketization. That is to say, the logic by which intermediate units of public-service administration are identified and separated off in the form of business or business-like enterprises is seen to demand that those units function in a market or market-like environment, where there will be actual competition for business or at least an equivalent commercial discipline. Hence we have, for example, the so-called 'internal market' within the British National Health Service (Harden 1992), and (at the level of local government) the system whereby the carrying out of local authority services is compulsorily put out to tender (Walsh 1991). That this is often a dynamic or incremental development is well illustrated by the way in which, in the UK, the Next Steps programme of separation of executive agencies from government departments (referred to earlier) was developed so as to place the executive agencies in competition with the private sector by means of the so-called 'market-testing programme', whereby it is periodically assessed whether to put the function of each agency out to contract in the private sector.[11]

We have thus established our paradigms for marketized public-service relationships, so far as those between the state or government and the intermediate public-service institutions are concerned. However, it remains to show in what sense these are triangular paradigms involving the citizens. The relationships are in fact to be seen as triangular in two senses or at two levels. At one level, we can say that the separation out of intermediate public-service providers necessarily and automatically creates a triangular relationship with the citizen, in the sense that if the citizen would have had a single linear public-service relationship with the state, or government, as regards the public service in question, then that relationship is rendered triangular by the very act of creating the intermediate institution. This assumes, of course, that the state, or government, remains in a direct relationship with the citizen despite the introduction of the intermediate institution, and that the citizen acquires a direct relationship with the intermediate institution; but it seems appropriate to insist that this is the case, however much the state might wish to minimize the significance of those relationships.

At another level, the triangular relationships which might arise as an automatic consequence of separating out an intermediate public-service provider

---

[11] The market-testing programme resulted from the White Paper, *Competing for Quality* (HM Government 1991c).

are in any case deliberately constituted in a certain way as part of the deliberate design of new public management. That is to say, new public management casts the citizens in the role of the customers or consumers of the intermediate public-service providers, and gives them rights of choice or reparation against the IPSPs, so that those rights may constitute part of the apparatus of economic discipline which controls the management of the IPSP. The sedulously created notion of parental choice in the British state school education system is a good example.[12]

As was indicated in a preliminary way, these paradigms of marketization may not be fully realized; the rights they appear to confer on citizens may not be effective, and the controls they offer to place on the financial efficiency of public administration may be in part illusory. The proponents of these marketized paradigms may nevertheless not be wholly or even partly discouraged by that; because they may feel, often with good reason, that they are nevertheless in the course of effecting a fundamental ideological and political reordering and reconstituting of the public-service relationships in question. We can usefully investigate that set of phenomena or possibilities under the heading of a question: does the marketization of public services affect and redefine our notions of citizenship? I shall attempt this in the next section.

Triangular Public-Service Relationships and the Marketization of Citizenship

In this section we consider how marketization of public-service relationships leads on to marketization of citizenship itself, at least in some of the important aspects of the concept of citizenship. This can best be analysed by attempting to look more deeply at the effects of marketization upon or implications of marketization for each of the three relationships in the triangle. Those effects or implications can be very broadly identified as:

(i)   the consumerization of the citizen/IPSP relationship;
(ii) the marginalization of the citizen/state relationship;
(iii) the economization of the IPSP/state relationship.

This section will be devoted to explaining and elaborating that analytical framework.

Note that these three kinds of development are cited in ascending order of importance. This might appear odd, since one might expect the marketization of citizenship to be chiefly expressed in the relationships involving

---

[12] See Ch. 6 by Crouch and, for a general discussion of the system introduced by the Education Reform Act 1988, Pierson (1993: 247–9).

citizens. One might further expect the consumerization of the citizen/IPSP relationship to imply marketization most strongly. But I shall suggest that, important though it is, that consumerization is in a certain sense incidental to the more central development which is the marginalization of the direct relationship between citizen and state so far as public services are concerned. Paradoxically, however, it is in the third relationship, that between the IPSP and the state, where the citizens seem least directly involved, that the profoundest effects upon citizenship are to be found. It is the economization of that relationship, and its effect upon citizenship, which forms the most ambitious part of the present argument and which requires the most careful justification.

We begin, then, by looking at the consumerization of the relationship between the citizen and the intermediate public-service institution, that being, of the three relationships in the triangle, the one whose transformation by new public management seems most obviously to result in the marketization of citizenship. It has already been suggested that, ironically, this may not in fact be the most significant location of the marketization of citizenship. There is a further such irony when one comes to analyse what is meant by the consumerization of this relationship. For it turns out to be useful to distinguish between consumerization as it impacts on the citizen and as it impacts on the service provider. Whereas one might expect the impact on the citizen to tell us more about the marketization of citizenship than the impact on the institution could tell us, it is in fact the other way about. This may become apparent as we go through those two stages of analysis.

In order to carry out this analysis, we can do no better than use a British government policy document which in my suggestion is the classic and quintessential expression of the marketization of public service and of citizenship, namely the *Citizen's Charter* (HM Government 1991*a*). That document was presented by the Prime Minister, John Major, himself and formed, to an unusual extent, a statement of his personal political credo and particular policy preoccupations (Drewry 1993). The extent of that personal commitment is made very evident by the message from him which accompanied that document, and which began: 'The Citizen's Charter is about giving more power to the citizen. It is a testament to our belief in people's right to be informed and to choose for themselves. I want the Citizen's Charter to be one of the central themes of public life in the 1990s' (HM Government 1991*b*). Even if we find that rhetoric slightly grandiose, we should not underestimate the significance of the policy and programme which it introduced.

At the heart of that policy and programme is the consumerization of the relationship between the public and the state and its emanations as public-service providers. Essentially, the public is atomized or disaggregated into a large number of individual citizens who are seen as consuming public services, and also purchasing those services either directly from the service-providing institutions, or indirectly by paying taxes to the state, which therefore acts as the purchasing agent on their behalf. Thus the *Citizen's Charter* is introduced with the words: 'All public services are paid for by *individual* citizens, either directly or through their taxes. They are entitled to expect high-quality services, responsive to their needs, provided efficiently at a reasonable cost' (HM Government 1991*a*: 4; emphasis added).[13] We need to identify the not inconsiderable implications of identifying relationships between citizens, the state, and providers of public services in that way.

The fundamental implication of this way of conceptualizing and presenting those relationships seems to be that they are bilateral ones between the public-service providers and each individual citizen. Each citizen has his or her own set of dealings with a set of providers, and it is the right and duty—in short, the role—of each citizen to deal on the terms most favourable to himself or herself. In other words, it is for him or her to consult his or own individual interests, thereby identifying the preferences by which alone the economically efficient functioning of the system of public-service provision can be measured and tested. Thus the *Citizen's Charter* declared the 'Principles of Public Service' to be that:

Every citizen is entitled to expect . . . explicit standards published and prominently displayed at the point of delivery . . . openness . . . about how public services are run, how much they cost, who is in charge, and whether or not they are meeting their standards . . . full accurate information in plain language about what services are being provided . . . choice wherever practicable . . . non-discrimination . . . accessibility . . . and if things go wrong . . . at the very least . . . a good explanation or an apology. (HM Government 1991*b*: 5)

The whole frame of reference for these supposedly universal rights is that of the citizen dealing as a self-regarding individual in a strictly bilateral relationship with the public-service provider in question. It is to be noted how powerfully that discourse transforms the expectations which it identifies into individualistic and self-regarding ones. The conception of wrongs ('if things go wrong') and of remedies ('at least a good explanation or an apology') are entirely localized to each individual. *I* am entitled to an apology, perhaps even compensation, because *I* was kept waiting. If I concern myself with failures in relation to other people or to in relation to the public at large, I am exceeding my expectations, and I am even interfering with the proper functioning of the market in public services.

It is debatable how far the citizens are themselves transformed by these conceptions of their role, and how far such transformations are desirable. We may see them as rendered more self-reliant and confident, as being sustained in

---

[13] The individualistic emphasis is even more strongly and succinctly evident in the Prime Minister's accompanying circular letter of 19 July 1991 to civil servants: 'The individual users and the taxpayers who pay for them deserve high quality services. *And I know you want to supply them.*'

the shedding of inappropriate deference to bureaucracy. We may on the other hand see them as encouraged towards aggressiveness, calculation, and selfishness. Or we may think that they will in general prove resistant to the blandishments of institutionalized courtesies and ubiquitous personalization, and that they will not be lured into a space of self-help and *se sauve qui peut*. That is a difficult assessment. What seems to me far clearer is that the institutions of public service, which are equally forced into these bilateralities, are thereby greatly transformed. It may or may not change the citizen to reconstruct her or him as a customer or user rather than as a passenger, a patient, or simply *un homme de bon volonté*; but it seems to me much clearer that such reconstructions are transformative of the public-service providers, and of the state which appoints them as its intermediaries. This takes us on to an analysis of the other relationships in the triangle.

The marketization of public services not only consumerizes relationships between citizens and public-service providers, it also makes those consumerized relationships more prominent than the relationship between the citizen and the government or central state. The relationship between the citizen and the public-service provider becomes the baseline of the triangle of relationships, while that between the citizen and the government is weakened and marginalized. This is a logic in which the relationship between the citizen and the provider is envisaged as the primary relationship because it is, supposedly at least, constructed as a market relationship, while the government stands outside the market, deliberately distanced from the citizen.

The application of that logic typically gives rise to a demand that the government should re-enter the marketized arena (which it has sought to create, and from which it has sought to exclude itself) in order to regulate the conduct of the public-service providers within the market.[14] It is typical of governments wishing to preserve their relative isolation from the marketized sphere that they will insist that the regulatory function is itself one which should be conducted at arm's length from them. Hence we find that governments engaged in the marketization of public services will create separate regulatory agencies (often, it must be said, in their own image) and will positively assert and lay claim to the independence of the regulators from the government or central state itself. This is especially the case when the regulator has to control the terms of 'trade' between the citizen and the public-service provider, as is to a significant extent the case in relation to public utilities in a fully or nearly monopolistic situation. It is a way in which marketizing governments marginalize their direct relations with their citizens with regard to public-service provision.

To identify the regulator in this way reminds us that the casting of public-service provision into a triangular structure is itself engaged upon by marke-

---

[14] For an admirable general account of the theory and practice of such regulation, see Ogus (1994).

tizing governments with the aim and effect of placing an intermediate institution between themselves and the public. It is a strategy of marginalizing the direct relationship with the citizen, and deflecting its dynamics into the indirect relationship which is mediated via the provider. The citizen, instead of being able to use the straight path to the government or central state, is rerouted round two sides of the institutional triangle. This triangularity is perfectly expressed when the government, or one of its departments, insists that it is not *directly responsible* for a particular kind of public service but only *indirectly accountable* for its due provision by the intermediate institution (Freedland forthcoming). This directs our attention to the third side of the triangle, the relationship of accountability between the government and the public-service provider, the economization of which is at the heart of the whole argument of this chapter and which we shall now consider.

The relationships between governments and public-service providers are seen as relationships of accountability, and they are economized relationships. These are essentially interlinked notions; they connect in the following way. Governments, which have constituted themselves as indirectly accountable for public-service provision by intermediaries, typically discharge that accountability by treating the public-service providers as directly accountable in part, as we have seen, to citizens as consumers, but in part also to themselves as purchasers on behalf of citizens. The proponents of new public management, as we have seen earlier, insist that this accountability must be first and foremost a financial one, directed at securing 'efficiency' and 'value for money'. Therein consists the economization of the relationships between governments and intermediate public-service institutions. Some theorizing will be offered in order to show how this results in a kind of transformation of the content of citizenship itself.

The central point of this argument is that the subjection of the relationship between governments and intermediate service-providing institutions to the discourse of financial accountability tends to result in the construction of descriptive and prescriptive models of public-service provision which are remote from a whole range of public and social concerns. For example, financial models of public-service provision are often delocalized, in the sense that they make little or no concession to the social importance, both at a collective and at an individual level, of providing public services to people in the communities and in the places in which they live and work. This has been a potent source of mutual incomprehension and hostility between hospital administrators, to whom it is obvious that more financially efficient provision can be made in a smaller number of specialized centres, and patients to whom it is important to have general hospitals near at hand.

This kind of phenomenon has been observed and placed in an explanatory framework by a group of scholars engaged in the critical analysis of accounting. In a recent symposium work, they show in various ways how accounting has to be understood not simply as a set of book-keeping techniques but as a much more centrally significant body of social and institutional practice (Hopwood and Miller 1994). To quote from Peter Miller's introductory chapter:

[A]ccounting techniques . . . invent a particular way of understanding and acting upon events and processes. There are complex linkages between the calculative practices of accounting and other managerial practices. These calculative practices are more than imperfect mirrors of economic reality. They do more than distort or modify results after the event. *Accounting practices create the costs and the returns whose reality actors and agents are asked to acknowledge and respond to.* . . . [They] make up the realm of financial flows to which certain Western societies have come to accord such vital significance. (Hopwood and Miller 1994: 1–2; emphasis added)

Vivid illustrations of this can be found in the various ways in which the benefits of education, at many levels, are increasingly being reconceptualized in terms of 'value added', that is to say, in terms of the value which is deemed to have been added to the attributes or qualifications of those being educated.

The final sentence of that quotation refers to the growing predominance of accounting as the discourse of management. This seems to me to be quite central to the ideas and ideology of new public management, and captures what I mean by the economization of public-service relationships. The way in which accounting has thus become a technique of public *government* as well as of private management is very well identified in a further chapter in the same work. Brendan McSweeney shows how 'management by accounting' has been asserted to be the 'one best way' of governing public-sector activity in the UK since 1979 (Hopwood and Miller 1994: ch. 10).

In a further chapter, Michael Power (Hopwood and Miller 1994: ch. 12) takes the argument even a stage further, writing about the 'audit society' and arguing that audit is tending to become a constitutive principle of social organization. In a passage which is crucial to the argument being advanced here, he says, under the heading of 'auditing and the construction of the auditable object', that:

Audit is to a large extent a question of 'making organizations auditable', a process which requires the active construction of forms of receptivity to audit. Far from being exogenous or environmental features of audit practice, modes of accountability and standards of performance are emergent features of audit arrangements. While audit may initially be mobilized by programmatic claims for 'improved' accountability, *it reconstructs these claims in specific ways, effectively creating specific patterns of visibility and performativity.* (Hopwood and Miller 1994: 308)

The emphasized passage in particular makes the point about the transformative effects of audit practice, which has been marked in relation to public-service provision. A good illustration is to be found in the way that auditing of the efficiency of the police service tends to exact a shift of resources and effort towards the formal 'clearing up' of offences which have been committed and away from crime prevention and general amelioration of behaviour in the community.

This set of arguments is pursued at what I think is a still deeper level in a recent text which examines the impact of this new ideology of economic rationalism upon the senior civil and public service of the Australian federal state in the period between the mid-1970s and the early 1990s (Pusey 1991). The author seeks to show how the new economic rationalism transformed not only the discourse, but also ultimately the actual outlook or mindset of the senior bureaucracy in Canberra. At the level of changes in discourse, he asks what has happened to the deliberative capacities of the state, and answers by contrasting the discourse of civil society and the 'public sphere' of the early 1970s with the discourse of economic rationalism of the late 1980s. He depicts that contrast as a shift from a discourse of communicatively co-ordinated action in a socio-cultural order to a discourse of systematically co-ordinated behaviour in an economic order (Pusey 1991: 169–70).

The full extent and relevance to our present argument of Pusey's concern become clear when he explores the way in which this change of discourse not only restricts deliberativeness but actually transforms the perceptions of reality held by those who engage in it, and the ways in which they understand and judge the ideas of other people. Thus he says, in a passage which I find exceptionally powerful:

It is a discourse that, ironically, draws its energy and conviction not from anything that is socially given in the human condition, but rather from its method—that is from a systems logic that turns everything into sets of equations. As with any and every form of positivism, reality is stood on its head as the method determines what can count as substance. . . . The criteria that these exceptionally intelligent people [i.e. the senior civil servants whom he surveys] use to judge the intellectual abilities of their peers is the agility and speed with which they can conjure up abstract models of a very particular kind. *What counts is a kind of 'dephenomenalising' abstraction that neutralises the social contexts of program goals in any area whatsoever, from trade promotion to industry assistance to social welfare or community support.* (Pusey 1991: 176)

The emphasized passage identifies precisely what is meant by the economization of relationships between governments and public-service institutions, and articulates the concerns one may feel about that. A good illustration is to be found in the way that provision of primary and secondary education comes to be evaluated as if it were independent of its local and demographic context. Hence poor results, in terms of attendance and achievement, come to be axiomatically blamed on bad teaching and bad management, interpreted as economically inefficient performance with little or no reference to the social situation of the pupils or students. Moreover, that kind of assessment is often associated with an insistence on the non-specific, deprofessionalized nature of good and bad performance, as in the sort of rhetoric in which it is said that 'you wouldn't put up with a bad surgeon, so why should you have to put up with a bad teacher?'

We may indeed express those concerns as worries about the marketization of citizenship itself. One of the worries about economic rationalism which Pusey hints at in the above passage is that its reasoning is not merely desocialized but actually tends towards the self-referential or circular in character—as where, in his terms, 'the method determines what can count as substance'. This may occur where a set of performance indicators has been so firmly imposed as the basis of assessment of the adequacy of a public service that it excludes all direct reference to the experience and reactions of those using or affected by the service in question. Examples of this occur when reduction of hospital waiting times is sought according to crude targets, such as 'nobody will wait for more than three months'.

As a body of reasoning verges upon the self-referential, so it becomes more and more impoverished. Ultimately, this is what one means by the marketization of citizenship; I suggest that, ironically, economization in the public sphere moves more towards that impoverishment than towards the enrichment which its advocates always claim for it. Polemic, however, becomes all too easy; I turn from it to the endeavour of positive construction with which I undertook to conclude.

Conclusion: A Reconstruction in Terms of Constitutionalism?

I shall engage in that endeavour only very briefly and tentatively. There has been much writing from those who have fully recognized the dangers of the economization of public services and the public sphere, and have explored alternatives and antidotes much more effectively than I could hope to do (Selznick 1992). Perhaps the most useful thing I can hope to do is to address the problem from a lawyer's perspective. From that particular standpoint, I see an emerging trend of reconstructing notions of civic and public virtue in the realm of constitutionalism and public law. The aim of this concluding section is to draw attention to the positive possibilities of such an approach, but also to point out the pitfalls. Although those will be shown to be considerable, it will nevertheless finally be suggested that this a path well worth pursuing.

There seem to be two main lines of thought along which constitutional lawyers are trying to come to grips with the problems and shortcomings of economic rationalism. One, which is obviously in alignment with the project of this book, consists in the assertion of a renewed need for the articulation of the rights of citizenship in constitutional law and doctrine, in a way which transcends the economic sphere. This stream of thought is very well represented, for example, by the recent writings of Dawn Oliver (1994; Oliver and Heater 1994), who summarizes the legal dimension of our present concerns in the following terms:

The legal relationship between the individual and the State has evolved over the years. The individual enjoys civil, political, and social rights which may be regarded as amounting to a citizenship of entitlement.

The revolution in public administration which has been taking place since the 1980s focuses on the importance of individuals as economic actors and consumers of public services, adding a further dimension to the relationship, though undermining social rights in some respects. . . . These developments leave open the question whether the relationships of individuals to their State . . . and the communities in which they live can accurately be described as one of citizenship. (Oliver 1994: 441)

In Britain, thinking of this kind contributes materially to the growing demand for an enacted Bill of Rights, and also to a questioning whether the needs which are thus identified are better met by development of national citizenship on the one hand or European Community citizenship on the other.

Another stream of thought among public lawyers, not at variance with the foregoing one but pursuing a rather different direction, concerns itself not so much with the theory of citizenship in relation to constitutional law, but rather with the political theory of democracy which underlies any supposedly democratic system of constitutional law. Paul Craig, as a principal exponent of this line of inquiry, has sought to explore the competing conceptions of democracy which have informed present and recent ways of thinking about constitutional law in Britain and the USA (1990). His main point of departure consists in identifying the generally accepted inadequacies of the Diceyan construction of constitutional law as resulting from Dicey's unduly *unitary* conception of constitutional democracy (focused, as it was, almost exclusively upon the sovereignty of Parliament) (Craig 1990: ch. 2).

This leads on to an exploration of alternative theories of pluralist democracy. Especially relevant to our present discussion is the distinction he draws[15] in the British context between, on the one hand, versions of pluralism which concentrate on *political* liberty and autonomy (both for individuals and groups) in civil society, and, on the other hand, versions of pluralism which concentrate on *economic* liberty or individual market freedom. Of these two, the political version opposes itself to state authoritarianism more reliably than the economic version. Indeed, Craig shows (1990: 153–7), picking up on a line of argument advanced in the 1980s by Andrew Gamble (1988) in

---

[15] Or, perhaps more precisely, which I read from what he writes; I hope the text to which this note relates correctly captures the argument of Craig (1990: ch. 5).

relation to the style of government espoused by Margaret Thatcher, how the economic version may be positively conducive to certain kinds of state authoritarianism.

Craig carries his discussion beyond that analysis of different species of pluralism to a description and evaluation of the different political theories which in his view underlie the different conceptions of democracy competing with each other in the practical and doctrinal experience of constitutionalism in the USA. In particular, he explores theories of liberalism and republicanism, and radical developments of participatory democracy (Craig 1990: chs. 8–11). Two very important points emerge from that treatise which have a crucial bearing upon our present discussion. The first is that there is a very significant interrelationship between different versions or models of democracy and different versions or models of public or constitutional law, even within a broadly common legal tradition or legal discourse such as that of Anglo-American common law.

The second, and equally important, point is that these different approaches to public law, reflecting different conceptions of democracy, tend to be more sharply identified and focused where there is the formal articulation of constitutional norms in a written constitution. This is one of Craig's bases of comparison between public law in the UK on the one hand and the USA on the other. In his own words:

Lawyers in the United Kingdom have much to gain by reflecting upon the experience in the United States. At the most fundamental level this serves to remind us that the existence of a written Constitution is not the end of constitutional controversy, but rather a watershed and the beginning of contestable interpretations concerning the 'proper' direction for public law. (Craig 1990: 10)

My suggestion is that this line of thought, coupled with the thinking about citizenship and public referred to earlier, may be helpful in devising positive responses to concerns about the marketization of public services.

In advancing the suggestion that heightened articulation of constitutional legal principles may be of value in combating the impoverishment of public service which marketization brings, I am nevertheless aware of great dangers. It is essentially a perilous voyage between Scylla and Charybdis. On one side lies the risk that one is laying claim to a discourse of legal constitutionalism but actually simply replacing the *false objectivity* of economic rationalism with an equally false objectivity of cultural or political morality.[16] On the other side lies the risk that, having steered a course as far as possible from shoals of value-loaded constitutional law, one founders on the opposite rocks by articulating legal principles which are *self-referential* or self-justifying in just the same way

---

[16] This is a set of hazards very powerfully explored by Greenawalt (1995: 165–82).

as we found economic rationalism to be.[17] It is, for example, hard to speak about 'the rule of law' without being aware of that set of risks.

Nevertheless, the legal theorists who point out these hazards still leave one with a sense that there is some room for manœuvre, a navigable though narrow channel for legal exposition of ideas of constitutionalism which oppose themselves to the cruder extremes of marketization. It seems to me just possible, for example, that efforts towards this kind of articulation and application of legal constitutionalism may help to elaborate and reinforce the idea of 'politics as mutual education' which David Marquand (1988: ch. 8) put forward by way of positive prescription at the conclusion of his overwhelmingly powerful critique of the path of political discourse being followed in Britain in the 1980s.

REFERENCES

CRAIG, P. P. (1990). *Public Law and Democracy in the United Kingdom and the United States of America* (Oxford: Clarendon Press).

DREWRY, G. (1993). 'Mr. Major's Charter: Empowering the Consumer', *Public Law*, 27: 248.

FOSTER, C. D., and PLOWDEN, F. J. (1996). *The State under Stress* (Buckingham: Open University Press).

FREEDLAND, M. R. (1992). 'The Role of the Department of Employment: Twenty Years of Institutional Change', in W. McCarthy (ed.), *Legal Intervention in Industrial Relations* (Oxford: Blackwell), 274–95.

—— (forthcoming). 'The Changing Crown', in M. Sunkin and S. Payne (eds.), *The Nature of the Crown* (New York: Clarendon Press).

GAMBLE, A. (1988). *The Free Economy and the Strong State: The Politics of Thatcherism* (London: Macmillan).

GREENAWALT, K. (1995). *Law and Objectivity* (New York: Oxford University Press).

HARDEN, I. (1992). *The Contracting State* (Buckingham: Open University Press).

HAYEK, F. (1960). *The Constitution of Liberty* (Chicago: University of Chicago Press).

HENNESSY, P. (1989). *Whitehall* (London: Secker & Warburg).

HM GOVERNMENT (1918). *Report of the Machinery of Government Committee* (London: HMSO).

—— (1968). *Report of the Royal Commission on the Civil Service* (London: HMSO).

—— (1991a). *The Citizen's Charter: Raising the Standard* (London: HMSO).

—— (1991b). *The Citizen's Charter: A Guide* (London: HMSO).

—— (1991c). *Competing for Quality* (London: HMSO).

HOPWOOD, A. G., and MILLER, P. (eds.) (1994). *Accounting as Social and Institutional Practice* (Cambridge: Cambridge University Press).

---

[17] This is the problem which has been identified and extensively explored, especially by Gunther Teubner (1988, 1993).

MARQUAND, D. (1988). *The Unprincipled Society: New Demands and Old Society* (London: Jonathan Cape).

OGUS, A. I. (1994). *Regulation: Legal Form and Economic Theory* (Oxford: Clarendon Press).

OLIVER, D. (1994). 'What is Happening to Relationships between the Individual and the State?', in J. Jowell and D. Oliver (eds.), *The Changing Constitution* (Oxford: Clarendon Press), 441–62.

——and HEATER, D. (1994). *The Foundations of Citizenship* (New York and London: Harvester Wheatsheaf).

OSBORNE, D., and GAEBLER, T. (1992). *Reinventing Government* (Reading, Mass.: Addison-Wesley).

PIERSON, C. (1993). 'Social Policy', in P. Dunleavy, A. Gamble, and G. Peele (eds.), *Developments in British Politics* (London: Macmillan), 100–20.

PUSEY, M. (1991). *Economic Rationalism in Canberra: A Nation-Building State Changes its Mind* (Cambridge: Cambridge University Press).

SELZNICK, P. (1992). *The Moral Commonwealth: Social Theory and the Promise of Community* (Berkeley, Calif.: University of California Press).

STERN, V. (1997). 'Crime Pays Big Dividends', *Guardian*, Society Supplement (15 Jan.), 3–5.

TEUBNER, G. (ed.) (1988). *Autopoietic Law: A New Approach to Law and Society* (Berlin: de Gruyter).

——(1993). *Law as an Autopoietic System* (Oxford: Blackwell).

VELJANOWSKI, C. (1987). *Selling the State* (London: Weidenfeld & Nicolson).

WALSH, K. (1991). *Competitive Tendering for Local Authority Services: Initial Experiences* (London: HMSO).

6

Citizenship and Markets in Recent British Education Policy

Colin Crouch

Although we are concerned here mainly with the contrast between citizenship and customership as differing forms of social participation, we must also see both in the context of a third: community. Under customership goods and services are acquired through purchase within a free market. In citizenship they are allocated as of right, and financing their cost is separate from the act of acquisition. Within community goods and services are allocated according to criteria of affect and custom, again with payment separated from acquisition.

Customership requires a basic collectively imposed framework of rules within which market transactions may be conducted, but beyond that it does not make use of a sense of the collective or the public. Participation and entitlements are acquired through private capacity to act in the market by selling and purchasing. Customers play an active role in the sense that their aggregated choices give signals to producers and suppliers, indicating the goods and services that are wanted. Passive customership involves choosing from among the goods and services provided and paying for them.

Citizenship, in contrast, assumes a core of collective business, an arena of public space in which decisions are made by a recognizable public authority and then imposed by that authority on pain of sanction. Citizens in the active sense are those persons within the community who have a right to join in deliberations over how such business is dispatched. Passive citizenship takes the form of receiving certain goods and services by virtue of membership of the collectivity. Citizenship in both active and passive meanings is therefore defined in terms of orientation to a public space, that is a space not claimed by private ownership. It is quite possible, and in pre-modern times was

I am grateful to Anton Hemerijck for his comments on an earlier version of this chapter, and to various local government officers and teachers in the UK who provided me with information on the operation of recent education policies.

normal, for possession of citizenship rights to be closely associated with property rights, but the processes remain distinct.

Communities are collectivities, but they are not formally defined as are citizenries and they do not normally claim to embody universal values.[1] The major examples are families, households, and informal groups. Both active and passive participation in community are defined by a complex web of rules, but there are no formal processes of appeal to claim one's rights as exist for both citizens and customers.

In conflicts over the relative advantages of citizenship and customership advocates of both are likely to try to co-opt aspects of community to their side.[2] For example, socialist defences of citizenship will often claim the attributes of community or altruistic moral commitment in their critique of the market;[3] but the formal, professional, and bureaucratic institutions of citizenship and the welfare state differ in crucial respects from this third sphere and have often been its enemy, the arbitrariness and lack of universality of community often being seen as a major impediment to egalitarian goals. Advocates of the market will use the family and religion as part of their attack on the state, claiming that while the welfare state undermines their role, the market, by virtue of being non-dirigiste and decentralized, is friendly to them. But this is also untrue. Extensions of the market commodify these areas, drawing them into its grasp and away from the community sphere. The extension of commercial activity on sacred days (such as Sunday trading) and the spread of concepts of individual maximization and use of exit options to the institution of marriage are examples. As Somers reminds us in Chapter 2 above, Polanyi's (1957 [1943]) great work on the growth of capitalism demonstrated how much of the history of the rise of markets was the story of a struggle against traditions of this kind.

The contrast between citizenship and the market is often depicted as one between the collective and the individual, but this is a distortion. Citizenship rights are exercised by individual persons in relation to the collectivities of which they are members; they can use freedom of choice in their active roles as citizens, and can enforce individual claims to the passive rights to which membership entitles them. If individuals within citizenship differ from individuals in the market it is because of the highly specific meaning given to that term in economic theory. The individuals of economic theory are not human persons, in at least two respects. First, firms are often treated as individuals;

---

[1] Citizenship is never in practice universal but stops at the borders of nation-states, which institutions are themselves defined in arbitrary, affective terms similar to those of community. This central inconsistency of citizenship concepts is passed over in virtually all political discussion by a kind of convention that the nation-state enjoys some kind of universalist validation.

[2] For good discussions of the problematic relationship of community and citizenship see Oldfield (1990) and, for a study which adds markets to the equation, Miller (1989).

[3] For example, see Richard Titmuss's (1970) analysis of the UK's voluntary blood transfusion service as the embodiment of the principles of the welfare state; in practice the model of a voluntary service based on altruism is not paradigmatic for British or any other welfare state service delivery.

and second, economic individuals are entities with very limited characteristics. They are completely dominated by profit maximization and unaffected in their decision-making by human loyalties and passions; they act solely by sending and receiving signals through the price mechanism.

The citizen, the customer, and the community member are all artificial constructs. The citizen is oriented to a public collectivity, within which it[4] uses the Hirschmanian concept of voice (Hirschman 1970), or Habermasian idea of dialogistic processes and speech communities (Habermas 1976), to indicate its desires. It also claims membership rights in order to receive certain outcomes. The customer indicates its desires through market signals, corresponding to Hirschman's 'exit' in the sense that, if one does not like a particular item on offer, one does not try to change it but simply goes elsewhere. Neither of these constitutes a whole person; not only does each lack the other, but both omit the domestic or community aspect of the person, rooted in face-to-face small-group and intimate contexts and motivated by emotional and traditional bonds and diffuse exchanges rather than precise calculation. However, this too is partial since it fails to note the extent to which such persons are also embedded in the more formal worlds of citizenship and markets.

One could say that community embodies something of Hirschman's idea of loyalty, in that an affective bond overcomes rational calculation. Hirschman saw loyalty as acting as an adjunct to both voice and market, providing stability and a gentling of the criticism and constant re-evaluation of commitments that take place under fully rigorous application of the others. Similarly, Hirschman (1993) has also argued (in a discussion of the collapse of the East German state) that a minimal capacity for exit is probably necessary for voice to be exercised, even if the two principles are in general alternatives. The differences between citizens, customers, and community members, and the limitations and artificiality of each, being understood, we should have no difficulty in recognizing mixed forms. For example, such cash transfers as state retirement pension payments constitute a citizenship right that permits one to participate in the market. A scheme for improving a state hospital service through partnership with charitable associations is a mix of citizenship and community. Local shops are often mixes of market and community.

Distortion, Degradation, and Residualization

As suggested in the Introduction, there has in recent years been a new ascendancy of the customer principle over that of the citizen. In this chapter I shall

---

[4] In keeping with this artificiality I shall use the impersonal pronoun for both citizens and customers, thereby also evading the usual problems of gender.

draw attention to some of the problems caused by this, making use of an extended empirical example drawn from the introduction of market criteria into education policy in the United Kingdom during the period of the neo-liberal Conservative governments of 1979–97. The place of community in the conflicts between citizenship and customership that this involved will also be considered.

A critique of the effect of marketization on citizenship turns on three principal problems: distortion, degradation, and residualization. Neo-liberalism limits its concept of relevant human wants to those things for which demand is expressed in the market. If people do not signal a willingness to purchase, they do not want the good or service in question. Provided the distribution of income has itself been produced by competitive labour markets, there is no need to consider the implications of relative wealth for expressed demand. From the point of view of citizenship this can be problematic. A citizen can voice many kinds of wants. Whether the polity can satisfy them depends partly on pure feasibility, partly on the power of the citizen making the demand, and partly on the economic criterion of the public authority being able to fund the provision in a non-inflationary way. From this point of view, the market *distorts* the voiced demand by redefining it.

Distortion caused by markets often results ironically from the fact that markets are highly sophisticated mechanisms. For goods or services to be provided through markets involves an elaborate procedure of creating barriers of access so that we cannot get them without using market means (that is, payment). Sometimes the character of a good itself has to be changed to do this. We accept these distortions or most goods and services would not be provided at all; most obviously, traders would not be willing to set up shops if we did not accept cash desks and the whole procedure of money exchange. There are instances, however, where the extent of distortion required so damages the quality of the good in question or erects barriers so artificial that one may reasonably doubt whether the gains from any efficiency improvement are worth the losses incurred: for example, when entrepreneurs are allowed to buy pieces of coastline and charge for access to beaches or cliff walks. Another example is the interruption of television programmes by the advertisements which are needed to fund their production.

A more specific example was provided by the record of the Child Support Agency, set up by the UK government of the 1980s to increase contributions to children's maintenance from parents (usually fathers) who were no longer supporting their former partner in the children's upbringing. As a product of a neo-liberal approach to government, the agency was not concerned with pursuing justice and even-handedness as in an elementary citizenship model of legal rights. Its task was to operate like a private debt-collection firm, and its staff had financial incentives to maximize the returns to government revenue that they could achieve. The agency found it easier to demand more money from fathers already making some payment and therefore easy to trace, rather than to track down those making no contribution at all, finding whom would take resources. Seen in terms of the ideals of justice and even-handedness among citizens embedded in the rule of law, this was experienced as a distortion of purpose and the agency was widely unpopular and regarded with lack of trust.

Distortion may mean simply changing the shape of a form of provision, but it may also mean changing it in ways which make it clearly inferior, a process of *degradation*. An important element of neo-liberal arguments for marketization is that, under state-funded or citizenship-driven schemes, there is often 'over-provision' of such resources as health, education, and social welfare, in the sense that they give many people more than they would choose to buy, as customers, if they had to secure these things in the open market. People in the lower levels of the income distribution almost certainly receive more health and education than they would be able to buy. This occurs because a publicly funded service, especially one driven by professionals (as in these cases) seeks to give the best available service to all comers. Those involved in it are reluctant to believe that its services are unimportant and need not be provided to a high standard; and they have no reason to distinguish among its clients other than on grounds of need for the service. From the point of view of citizenship, the reduction of quality or quantity of provision to some people which would follow from the full introduction of market principles constitutes a degradation of a citizenship right.

In market terms to provide more than would be produced in the free market is to provide too much, and therefore to waste. While this thought is rarely voiced openly in public debate, it is frequently expressed in terms of a criticism of 'paternalism', defined as deciding on people's behalf what is good for them and requiring them to provide it through taxes, thereby preventing them from choosing how to spend their money in the shops. From the point of view of economic theory, money spent through a mass of individual choices is always more efficient than money spent in large lumps by the state.

In practical politics it is often very difficult to secure public acceptance of the degradation of a public service that would follow from placing it under market rules. In these cases there can sometimes be a creative and interesting compromise: the erection of inspectorial and regulatory offices designed at least in principle to guarantee standards of service. There are several examples of this from the British privatization process. The British nationalized sector was almost solely limited to 'basic' goods and services which are likely to be monopolistic under any form of ownership (telecommunications, public utilities, energy, transport). Privatization and marketization have been accompanied by the establishment of regulatory agencies with a mandate to ensure certain levels of service and also limitation of the extent to which the privatized firm can use its monopoly position. The adequacy of any particular set of arrangements and strength of any particular set of rules can always be criticized, but debate over that is a proper part of what is meant by the active citizenship process.

Another device of this kind has been the innovation of 'charters' whereby providers of public services have to offer certain commitments to recipients; included among these are a *Parent's Charter* and a *Student's Charter*. The basic document by which they are all governed was in fact called the *Citizen's Charter*. They are however more analogous to the guarantees of quality and service that many commercial firms issue and therefore to a customership rather than a citizenship model (Lewis 1993; Tritter 1994). The rights conferred are limited to monitoring the performance of lower level service providers and do not permit policy to be discussed. Indeed, discussion is not envisaged at all; the charters give individual customers the right to complain. It is in this context interesting to note that the use of the genitive singular in the charter titles was a deliberate affirmation of individualism over collectivism.

Most models of even neo-liberal utopias concede the residual existence of certain public spaces: literally, in the sense of streets, or of territories that are simply unwanted by market forces; metaphorically, in the sense of marginalized parts of the population, or such issues as fresh air that defiantly remain public goods. Both theory and considerable experience tell us that such common areas will degenerate: streets that are not cared for by public authorities or police become both dirty and criminalized; uncleared derelict land becomes dangerous and toxic; people who fail in labour-market competition and lack the community resource of family also become derelict and intoxicated.

The response to this of neo-liberal theory is to marketize as much public space as possible. If, instead of public streets, there are privately owned shopping malls, the owners of these will have them policed by private security guards or video cameras since they have an incentive to encourage customers to come to the space. If the uses of land are freed from regulations and planning controls, someone will find some use for it and there will be few derelict sites. If wages and working conditions are permitted to fall, they will reach a point that even very inadequate, low-productivity people will be able to find some form of paid work. Some of these solutions raise problems in themselves, but they are not our current concern. A further issue is raised: what happens to those streets, sites, people whose problems are too severe for the market to solve? The market depends on choice, and it is this which gives private provision many of its efficiency gains over public: entrepreneurs must be able to choose *not* to provide a service. For example, if a private bus or postal service can be provided profitably to a particular area only at prices that very few people will pay, then that area will not receive such services; there is no effective demand, so such a service can be defined in market terms as unnecessary. Equivalent public services, working to citizenship concepts of demand, have to provide the service and are therefore unprofitable and inefficient.

It is at these really difficult points that at least some neo-liberals accept a role for public provision. However, such provision is under the strong constraint that it must not rival the market. If public streets are cleaner and more orderly than the shopping mall, customers might not bother to go the mall and its shops might close. If the unemployable are given more than the barest minimum, people working for very low wages in bad conditions might prefer to be unemployed. The space left to public provision within the neo-liberal framework is residual, and the process of *residualization* has important implications of level and type of provision.

Residual services are *required* to have low status and poor quality, and they are excluded from the realms of both markets and citizenship. Public services of this kind cannot be described as 'citizenship': access to them is more a penalty than a right; and the essential citizenship mechanism of voice must not be made available to residual recipients or they might seek improvements that would break the rule of no competition with market provision.

An important example may be taken from the world of employment placement and unemployment assistance. The logic of a neo-liberal market regime is to privatize as much employment placement as possible, leaving a public service to deal with the hard-to-place, the unemployable. The administration of unemployment benefit must therefore be joined to sanctions on them concerning the kinds of jobs they must take. They lose both market choice—for which they do not have the requirements for market entry—and citizenship, as they are now in a world where benefit withdrawal may be threatened, not a world of the right to security. During the 1960s and 1970s it was generally considered in advanced countries that state employment services should provide as extensive a service as possible, and that the administration of public assistance should be separated from a placement service, as the aim of placement was seen—in both efficiency and citizenship terms—as being to maximize individuals' opportunities for suitable and fulfilling work. The current orthodoxy is exactly the opposite: privatization is required under the Treaty of Maastricht and encouraged by OECD, as is amalgamation of placement and assistance services and a shift from provision of a right for citizens in difficulties to cajoling the unemployed into finding some kind of work by making unemployed life very unattractive. King (1995) has shown the negative implications that this can have for quality of service for the poor unemployed in an analysis of how these changes have affected the operation of the British and US employment services.

One problem of residualization of public provision is that pointed out long ago by Richard Titmuss (1970): if the users of a service are able to transfer to alternative, private sources of supply if they can afford it, they have no incentives to seek improvement in the initial service, which becomes left to the uncomplaining poor. The point was an early formulation of Hirschman's distinction between exit and voice; it was in fact observation of cases of the Titmuss kind that led Hirschman to formulate his thesis.[5] It follows that some goods have to be public *if* a high standard is to be achieved.

The Case of Education

We can now apply these concepts to British education during the period of Conservative government 1979–97. Under the influence of neo-liberal thinking, these governments tried to insert elements of marketization in order to address certain perceived defects of the state sector. To what extent can these policies be seen as trying to engineer a shift from citizenship entitlements to markets, involving the three problematic processes considered above? As we shall see, the case is not straightforward and leads to some surprising conclusions. Education presents particularly difficult problems for a full application of market logic without distortion and degradation. Introduction of a full market in education would mean treating it like any other good. Schools and colleges would be like shops offering items for sale according to supply and demand. This model is virtually never pursued. A purely voluntary education market would almost certainly mean that a large minority of parents would fail to have their children educated or would buy very cheap and inadequate schooling. This would create problems of social order and would also weaken considerably the capacity of these children eventually to make a contribution to the national economy. Most versions of neo-liberal theory assume the continued existence of governments concerned with the basic collectivist tasks of maintaining public order and sustaining economic stability, a national education system with compulsory components, and a general stance of encouraging the pursuit of educational opportunities. Therefore measures to ensure higher standards than would be provided for many people under a pure market model are almost universally maintained. In other words, the concept of citizenship entitlements is very important in this sector. The results in the British experiment were some interesting compromises between neo-liberal and citizenship strategies.

---

[5] Specifically, he observed that, while the carriage of freight by Nigerian railways was appallingly poor, no one ever complained. The reason was that all firms of any substance used road transport; the railways had become a residual service for very poor businesses. Not wanting to receive complaints and be under pressure to improve their service, the Nigerian railways were not interested in winning lucrative trade back from the roads.

Distortion

For example, one way in which policy tried to use market analogues to improve educational quality was through the extension of choice. There has long been an element of choice in British schools through the existence of a private fee-paying sector. The fees enable many of these schools to provide an exceptionally good, well-resourced education,[6] but it is extremely expensive and therefore involves only a small (around 10 per cent) proportion of the relevant age group. Government policy sought to increase this by subsidizing the fees of some children, whose parents would not themselves have paid fees, through the Assisted Places Scheme. This extension of the market therefore involved various forms of distortion: subsidization (which is itself a breach of market principles of allocation); and exceptional discriminatory expenditure targeted on an arbitrarily selected group.

More extensive in their distorting implications were policies towards the mainstream public sector. Public-sector schools in the UK are normally under the control of local government (local education authorities (LEAs)), which means that within a geographical area there is a monopoly supplier of public education.[7] Increased choice was therefore also attempted by a number of devices, which will be discussed in turn: (1) encouraging the formation of a different group of public-sector schools, under central rather than local government control (grant-maintained schools (GMS)); (2) giving the remaining schools more autonomy from local authorities (local management of schools (LMS)); (3) giving parents increased rights to choose individual schools within their local authority, rather than children being allocated to their neighbouring school; (4) improving information flows about schools to potential parents by carrying out standard tests on pupils and publishing the results; and (5) the maintenance of certain selective schools alongside a majority comprehensive system.

(1) Grant-maintained schools

It was provided under the Education Reform Act 1988 (ERA) that existing parents of children at an LEA school could vote in a ballot to have the school become a GMS. In order to encourage them to do so the government introduced certain inducements, which were gradually made more powerful as initial years demonstrated little enthusiasm for the idea. Schools were offered financial incentives in the form of generous capital grants (not available to

---

[6] Since there is little inspection of the private sector there is, however, a lengthy 'tail' of poor private schools, where for relatively low fees parents perhaps buy social segregation for their children at the expense of educational quality. Particularly in the case of daughters, some parents may prefer control over their children's associates to high educational achievement.

[7] Some schools have been controlled jointly by the churches (usually either the Church of England or the Catholic Church) and the LEA.

LEA schools and financed out of a total educational budget that would otherwise have been spent on schools in general) if they voted for GMS status.[8] A later Act required governors of LEA schools to discuss balloting parents on the issue every year, though once a school has become a GMS it is prohibited from discussing reversion to LEA status for a number of years.

The implications of this for markets and citizenship are complex: the introduction of a chance for parents to vote to change a school's status constituted an extension of citizenship; but the inducements to encourage them to vote a particular way were corruptions of a citizenship right; further, the use of capital grants among these inducements was a case of subsidization, a market distortion. Meanwhile, removal of GMS from the range of schools available within the provision of a particular local authority could result in a *de facto* reduction in the choice of school available to many parents. This would occur in the following manner. LEAs are required to permit parents freedom of choice among their schools, using proximity of the home from the school as the rationing criterion if a school would become heavily overcrowded as a result of the expression of parental choice. GMS were permitted to select up to 15 per cent of their pupils, this criterion trumping the geographical proximity rule. It was therefore possible for parents living sufficiently close to a school to have had their child accepted at it (if the school were an LEA school) to be denied that choice if the school was a GMS which has selected up to 15 per cent of its intake from other areas. In practice the implications of this have been rather limited: not many GMS were introduced; their distribution through the country was very uneven. Their contribution to increased choice and therefore to a market in schools was limited, arbitrary, and sometime negative, as was their contribution to citizenship entitlements to education.

(2) Local management of schools

Of more general importance has been the LMS system and new rights of parental choice. In several respects LMS marks a rare simultaneous expansion of active citizenship, community, and customership. In addition to granting increased decision-making powers to schools, the Education Act 1986 (No. 2) provided for a number of elected parent representatives on school governing bodies: a clear extension of citizenship. It was also an extension which took the form of drawing on the resources of local neighbourhoods: opportunities for a community role. The schools were then given incentives to market themselves by being rewarded financially if they could compete successfully with other local schools to recruit additional numbers of students: a market

---

[8] This was itself an example of the marketization of a citizenship concept. To offer financial inducements to vote in a certain way when establishing a voting regime is normally seen as offensive to citizenship models of choice. It is, however, common practice in the market-oriented voting of the business world. When rival groups of directors are seeking the support of shareholders for a corporate takeover it is normal for them to offer financial rewards for a favourable vote.

analogue. LEAs lost their position of tutelary authority over schools and instead became providers of services to them on a purchaser/provider basis, a pure market form that will be discussed below. In some cases these services have been completely privatized, the firms providing them no longer having any connection at all with a local government policy-making role.

The model does, however, have certain deficiencies. First, it reproduces with no attempt at resolution a classic conflict between citizenship and community. The capacity of different local communities to provide relevant expertise for governing bodies, and to be able to raise additional school funds from community resources, varies very widely. In general, the advance of citizenship and community rights in schools for people in wealthy areas accompanies an impoverishment of citizenship for those in poor areas.

Further, the increase in school autonomy was ambivalent. Schools received more financial and managerial autonomy from LEAs, but lost their previous autonomy over the content of teaching through the simultaneous introduction of a National Curriculum. Clear overall net losers in the power struggle were the LEAs; clear gainers were national government; the schools' position was ambiguous. The ambiguity demonstrates the point made above: even a neo-liberal government is unlikely to entrust the content and quality of education to the market. It was, however, happy to entrust financial and managerial responsibility to market analogues.

Further to control the ostensibly newly autonomous schools, the government effected changes in the inspection of school standards. Before the 1988 Act school standards had been supervised by two institutions: Her Majesty's Inspectors of Schools, a nineteenth-century institution established as completely autonomous of both central and local government, and the inspectorate services of LEAs. The former was replaced by the Office for Standards in Education (OFSTED), a body responsible to the Secretary of State for Education, while the role of LEA inspectors was weakened, following the change in the LEA's role away from one of authority to that of a supplier of business services on a more or less commercial basis. There was therefore an overall decline in the availability of non-partisan inspection of school quality.

(3) Parental choice

Increased rights of choice for parents accompanied these changes. This worked out in a perverse manner that both gave less choice to parents and removed from some of them the strength of their citizenship right. This results from a fundamental problem with the market analogy in education. The 'customers' are parents; the 'products' are their children at the end of the educational process. However, as the sociology of education has repeatedly shown us, parents themselves play a major part in the educational achievements of their children. This is an example of community, here in the form of the family, creating problems for both citizenship and market. It is a problem for the former in that goals of providing some kind of equal opportunities for children are constantly frustrated by parents of very different capacities trying to help their own children. It is a problem for the market in that the customers contribute their own services to the product. The nearest the true market comes to this is in repair services; customers frequently take for repair goods that they have tried to mend themselves, with varying degrees of success. If bungled attempts at repair by customers simply increase what the repair firm can charge, this is not a problem. However, if being brought damaged items to repair will hurt repair firms in some way, they are likely to take such measures as refusing to accept goods that customers have tried to mend themselves. For example, it is a frequent requirement of product guarantees that customers have not tried themselves to fix items which they then submit for repair under guarantee.

Schools cannot prevent parents from attempting to educate their own children. They can, however, do other things which involve distortions of provision. Schools know that parents vary considerably in their educational competence, and know that if they wish to improve their own performance they should admit children of parents likely to be competent educators and reject those without this advantage. If expanded parental choice leads to some schools facing excess demand, they will therefore at least in the short term respond by exercising various kinds of selection. In the long term popular schools might be expected to expand to meet rising demand, and the ERA gives them some incentives to do this—though they might prefer not to do so, to remain small, to continue selection, and thereby achieve better results. This will have been achieved by restricting parental choice.

A policy of expansion by a popular school creates different problems. The attraction of resources away from less popular schools will threaten the latter with deteriorating buildings and a vicious spiral of decline. The appropriate market response to this would be closure of the unpopular school and in some cases this happens. This might lead to inconvenient journeys for children and in the short and medium term create overcrowding problems for the surviving schools. As a result many parents would be unable to have the school of their choice for their children. It is therefore not surprising that the Audit Commission (1996) discovered the paradoxical consequence that, since the introduction of parental right to choice, fewer parents had been able to secure their first choice of school than before the reform.

It might be argued that school selection of pupils from 'suitable' families is more consistent with the market model than this discussion makes out. In a true market, if demand for the education provided by a particular school rises more rapidly than supply can increase to meet it, equilibrium will be restored by the school raising the price of its education. In the absence of fees its price takes the form of a demand for higher quality children; educating them will lead to higher academic results which will in various ways increase the 'prof-itability' of the school. However, this case is not publicly made as a defence of the process, since it constitutes an open breach with the concept of equal opportunities and free schooling that is an established and officially unchal-lenged part of the citizenship concept of British education.

(4) Improved information flows through tests

Parental choice is also aided by another innovation of the 1988 Act and its successors: the use of scores to measure schools' achievements and the colla-tion of these in published league tables to enable schools to be ranked. These derive from analogies with balance sheet and stock-exchange models of decision-making whereby performance can be summarized in a small number of quantified indicators, aiding maximizing choices by purchasers. In the case of schools, pupils' performances in national examinations and in official tests administered at various ages are published and ranked in national league tables.[9]

Such tests present problems of the selection of indicators and unfairness, but that is endemic to market indicators. Stock-exchange evaluations of com-panies often present biased and distorted estimates of a firm's long-term worth; the exchange rates of currencies often bear only a poor relationship to their respective purchasing power; relative incomes are not the only legitimate means of comparing the value of two occupations. But provided those involved wish to make use of the data provided by the indicators they become self-validating. School league tables based on examination success are a case in point. In particular, and this is a major problem where shadow analogues rather than real exchange-value prices are concerned, partial indicators encourage competitors to maximize their performance by concentrating all their efforts on those items reflected in the indicators, neglecting everything else. If success in certain examinations is measured and published, the ratio-nal school will concentrate on those examinations at the expense of other activities.

Abuses of this kind can be checked by adjusting the indicators used so that they cover all relevant areas, but there are two limitations to this strategy. First, if indicators multiply, they become too complex, and potential customers find them difficult to appraise. Second, and more important, many aspects of edu-cation are not measurable in genuinely quantitative terms, and these will con-tinue to be neglected. The use of indicators usually involves measuring that which can be measured, rather than that which is important. Behaviour then becomes determined by the artefact of measurability. A similar point has been made by British police forces in their criticism of the imposition on them of

---

[9] Something similar is done for universities, which are marked and ranked on the basis of research achievement and teaching performance.

performance indicators that would necessarily emphasize easily measured and publicly prominent data like numbers of arrests and would neglect such things as advice given to citizens. One of the reasons why advanced firms in the real market sector moved beyond the Fordist model of production is that they realized the costs that came from seeking efficiency through control in this narrow way; but adoption of business analogies to public services by British government has meant the introduction of such 'outmoded' Fordist concepts to areas formally free of them in order to increase the scope for central control.

Markets can also be 'unfair' in that they seem not to follow moral criteria of deserts. Why do hospital nurses earn so much less than advertising copy writers? Why can fortunes be made by accidents of share ownership at the time of a takeover bid, while others spend years building up an innovative company for little return? The answer from economic theory is that markets have nothing to do with fairness, but with the laws of supply and demand. (This would be all very well if wealth was not taken to denote moral worth and poverty evidence of moral blame, but they almost routinely and universally are.) Something similar happens in the application of market measures to education. Teachers complain that it is not fair that a school which recruits children from deprived educational backgrounds should be judged by the same standards as one recruiting among the privileged. Proposals have therefore been made to improve the indicators through 'base-line testing', that is, testing children at the point of entry to a school and publishing subsequent results and league tables in terms of relative improvement achieved rather than absolute performance. However, it is likely that many of the parents who are eager to use indicators have not the slightest interest in what gives a 'fair' reflection of a school's performance, but want to know something both about the school's capabilities and about the social background of the other children with whom their sons and daughters would be mixing if they attended it. Absolute measures of achievement may well serve their purpose better, even if the consequence is a distortion of schools' activities and of the means by which they are presented.

(5) The maintenance of selection

From the point of view of the individual school the logical end point of the desire to have the best pupils is to be able explicitly to select them; by definition, however, this cannot be achieved by all or even a majority of schools. From the point of view of the individual parent the logical end point of the desire to send one's child to the best school is to have some schools clearly designated both as having the highest standards and recruiting the most promising fellow pupils from the most competent families; by definition this cannot be achieved by all or even a majority of parents. There will therefore be strong demands for selective schools. Their provision within an overall system of free education can be justified in market terms through the argument already used above: the offer to a school of 'better quality' pupils by some parents can be seen as a kind of higher price paid by them, justifying their access to the better quality product of the selective school.

It was therefore Conservative government policy to to make such schools available, partly by protecting those selective schools not abolished when comprehensive education was introduced during the 1960s and 1970s, partly by permitting GMS to become selective, and partly by proposals to open new selective schools. The case for doing this was made in terms of increased freedom of choice—a market justification—leading in particular to the proposal that every LEA area in the country should have at least one such school which parents could choose.

For the majority of parents the change of a school's status from comprehensive to selective actually involves a reduction rather than an increase in choice. If before they could choose among four schools, after the policy change they would be able to choose only among three, with their child being eligible for consideration for selection by the fourth, which is not choice. This is a further distortion produced by the inappropriate use of market analogies in a field where expectations are rooted in citizenship assumptions.

In a true market this would not be a problem. Take for example a country in which there are four car manufacturers producing general family saloons. One of them decides to become a luxury car manufacturer, and its products are now removed from the reach of many potential purchasers. In market terms the inaccessibility of this firm's products is not a problem for freedom of choice, since demand is measured only in terms of effective demand; by definition, in economic theory one cannot demand something one cannot afford. If the loss of one family saloon manufacturer leaves a gap in the market that cannot be filled simply by expanded production by the three remaining firms, either a new firm will sooner or later be established or people will buy imported cars.

None of these market points apply to the schools case. Most elementarily, the import model is inapplicable except for people living on the borders of LEA areas, since parents usually want to limit the amount of travel to school their children undertake. Because of the importance of critical mass for school size, it is also extremely unlikely that a new comprehensive school would be built to replace loss of generally available provision resulting from the establishment of the selective one, unless major population expansion were taking place. But the core problem with the model is that, where publicly provided education is concerned, most people are not prepared to accept choice defined in market terms—that is as something to which one is entitled only if one can afford it. They have instead a citizenship concept of choice: if one is part of the universe defined by a certain citizenship, then one is entitled to participate in any choices which it makes available.

A thoroughgoing market model of educational provision would try to persuade people to drop this view, and in some aspects of the British neo-liberal
reforms of the 1980s and 1990s this was done. In education, however, no challenge was mounted on the fundamental citizenship model; instead therefore
one encounters partial market analogues, frequently embodying distortions.

Degradation

Some aspects of the changes in British education had a spiralling effect which
turned a distortion of provision into its degradation. According to market
logic, if schools which attracted large numbers of pupils received extra
funding, and if good examination results attracted pupils, then the funding
would give schools an incentive to improve their teaching in order to improve
their results. However, schools can more easily improve results by attracting
the most promising pupils; this enables a school to improve measured
performance without contributing any value added. Not only is this pointless
from the point of view of the system as a whole, but, since resources of
both finance and the supply of promising pupils are finite, other schools are
necessarily set on a downward spiral by the same process. The closure of a
school which has declined beyond the point of rescue is a slow and disrup-
tive process, and its replacement by a new one will take even more time. Meanwhile many children will have to spend their school careers in deteriorating
institutions.

As noted above in the brief theoretical discussion, it is politically difficult
to secure acceptance of degraded provision in some areas of policy, and therefore the longer term consequence of some attempts at marketization has been
the introduction of new citizenship devices to offset the logic of a market
reform. This is especially true of education. All governments have strong
motives for requiring that a certain amount of education be received by all
persons settled in their national territory, this kind of national-interest
requirement (be it paternalistic, authoritarian, or far-sighted) usually being
the other side of the coin of most citizenship rights. It is therefore interesting
to note how, as market analogues were extended in British schools, so new
elements of central quality control were erected to protect the system from
degradation: the National Curriculum, which removed educational autonomy
from schools at the same time that they were being given financial autonomy
and encouraged to operate in a market; a more tightly controlled inspectorate
to check on the quality of their activities.

New citizenship concepts have therefore been used to compensate for possible deteriorations consequent on marketization. Yet they are not necessarily
adequate to offset the logic of degradation embodied in marketization. Some
examples can be found within recent educational developments.

Nursery vouchers

In order to encourage the provision of pre-school education, a system of so-called 'nursery vouchers' was introduced in April 1997 following experiments in a small number of LEA areas. The scheme was abolished by the Labour government elected the following May, so there was in the event little track record to assess. However, the experiment and the period of preparation for the scheme enables us to make some judgements about how such an approach works out in practice. Funds were removed from LEA budgets and transferred to parents of pre-school children in the form of vouchers which they could use to acquire various forms of daytime supervision of their children. The value of the vouchers was not set high enough to make a contribution to the capital cost of providing new nursery accommodation, unless there were to be drastic reductions in the pay of staff or the quality of equipment and furniture. Meanwhile, the scheme sometimes led to increases in the cost of nursery provision; by encouraging new private providers it reduced the average size of nurseries and nursery classes and thereby increased unit costs. Parents could supplement the voucher with their own funds or they could limit the provision they acquired to whatever forms of childcare the voucher would purchase.

This is about as pure a form of marketization as one can envisage within a framework of public provision. Funds were to be transferred from authorities and given to individuals in a market form—the voucher—that made the parents customers. They could choose from among whatever providers appeared in the market, public or private. They could supplement the voucher with their own money, so there was no requirement of equality of provision. Since there was only a small increase in funds and mainly a redistribution from LEAs to parents, any increase in provision would result from market competition rather than from increased public spending.

The following were set to be the consequences. First, the objective of pre-school education was transformed into day-care provision, some of which might have an educational content but this was not required. Second, LEAs often responded to their loss of funds by trying to ensure that the bulk of vouchers would be spent with them rather than with private providers—an ironic consequence of a marketization reform. They did this by offering to take children of immediate pre-school age into the reception classes of existing schools. This could be done quite cheaply, partly because there were often economies of scale to be had by enlarging class sizes, but more important because regulations defining levels of staffing and facilities for normal schools are lighter than those for nurseries catering for pre-school children. Making normal school places available to younger children would also have produced a decline in the number of playgroups provided specifically for them.

Vouchers were therefore producing a degradation of educational provision in two respects. First, non-educational care was to be provided instead of education. Second, small children were being added to school classes rather than being treated in a manner designed specifically for their needs.

Training vouchers

Something very similar has been happening at the post-school end of education. Young people who do not proceed to full-time post-school education are equipped with training vouchers which they can 'spend' with an employer. This is designed partly to encourage young people to act like customers in a training market, choosing options best suited to them, and partly to give employers an incentive to train, since they exchange the vouchers for cash with a government department.

This is a pure market analogue, and it suffers from one of the central failures as an allocation device to which the market is vulnerable: poorly informed customers. School leavers of moderate or lower educational level are not well equipped to make choices of the training schemes likely to equip them for future employment. At the same time, in order to encourage provision by employers, government introduced a new range of vocational qualifications called NVQs, the initial grades of which indicate very elementary levels of skill that could be provided very cheaply. Evidence so far suggests that most NVQ provision is at the lowest levels, providing skills considerably below those that would in the past have been seen as equipping people with a serious vocational skill (Robinson and Steedman 1996). Educational quality has been degraded by the market analogue, partly because the young people are ill equipped to choose and partly because (as with the nursery case) the voucher provides only low levels of provision.

Residualization

Residualization has not happened to the core British education system, but a potentiality for it is embodied in several exit options: encouragement of the expansion of the private sector, grant-maintained schools, the retention and possible extension of selection, the differential capacity of families to take advantage of school rankings. These potentialities have been seen in the experience of at least one school. The Ridings School in northern England is located in an area with several GMS and some selective schools. As a result the pupils it takes tend to be a residuum of those who have neither chosen nor been chosen by schools with good reputations. During the course of the academic year 1996–7 its disciplinary problems reached the level of a national issue, leading to newspaper headlines, television attention, special inspectorial visits, and the installation of crisis package of reform. Ministers of the Conservative government took a keen interest in maintaining the crisis, since they saw it as vindicating their view that local authorities governed by the opposition Labour Party were not fit to administer schools. However, the fact that the school was embedded in an area in which several other schools had been removed from the reach of a residuum of parents and children as a direct result of government policy was probably a more relevant cause of the difficulties.

Re-Enter Community

These problems of markets must not obscure the fact that the citizenship model of participation also has great difficulties. While it is usually seen as an embodiment of shared moral value, its administration is often delegated to bureaucracies that can become rule-bound and anything but full of moral concern. The active, participative side of citizenship, the exercise of voice, is particularly difficult to achieve in the modern mass polity. To find answers to these problems citizenship advocates usually turn to ideas of direct participation and involvement, of delegation to very local levels. What is being attempted here is a partnership between citizenship and community. As noted at the start of the chapter, neo-liberal reformers also try to co-opt community as an element of markets.

These exercises are fruitful but problematic. Given that several deficiencies of both citizenship and markets as systems of participation relate to the distortions embedded in formalisms and abstractions that remove them from 'real, human' control, community mechanisms are an obvious recourse for both. This, at least in part, explains the current popularity of proposals for inserting a communitarian element into political strategies (Etzioni 1996; Gray 1993). However, it is these very real and human qualities that give communitarian mechanisms their potentiality for arbitrariness, partiality, and unfairness. These ambiguities can again be exemplified in recent British education policy. There are three particularly relevant community institutions in education: the professional community of education, the family, and the neighbourhood. We shall examine these in turn.

There is now a considerable literature, based on studies of normal firms producing goods and services for the market, suggesting that there can often be a general welfare gain from co-operation rather than competition among producers, which will be lost if market rules insist on competition. For example, a group of firms in the same product markets and located in the same district may find advantages in pooling their marketing activity, or in gaining economies of scale through sharing training facilities. Networks of trust developing out of a shared local and occupational community are often needed to make such sharing among competitors possible. Similar arguments apply to co-operation among local schools. There are resources that can be used more efficiently if shared, but monopoly over which a school may wish to claim if it is engaged in a dog-eats-dog contest for pupils with a neighbouring school. Similarly, all schools need to be expected to take their share of difficult or handicapped children, but schools engaged in competition will seek to dump these on each other through their use of exclusions and pressure on parents.

To make relationships take a market form includes translating all those between providers and recipients of services into suppliers and customers who make precise calculations of costs and benefits. This brings certain efficiency gains, but these come at certain costs. A proper appraisal of the marketization of relationships should therefore include a cost/benefit analysis of the process itself.

For example, relations between LEAs and schools, and between different departments of local authorities, now have to take the form of purchaser/provider, in the sense that all exchanges between these units have to be calculated, costed, and charged through some system of actual or shadow pricing. Thus the Audit Commission (1992) insisted that local education authorities in 'purchaser/provider' relations with schools must ensure very clear distinctions between themselves and the schools in question, even though in the past they saw themselves as colleagues working for the same organization. This virtually rules out acts of goodwill, attempts at establishing trust, co-operative acts by people perceiving a shared task. As such it flies in the face of much thinking within private business management itself, which encourages purchasers and providers to become permeable organizations, treating each other as colleagues to maximize the efficiency gains that come from co-operation.

This occurs partly because neo-liberalism is committed to that particular form of modern capitalism that maximizes short-term competitive gain at the expense of long-term co-operation, and partly, again, because it is in its political interests to undermine networks of co-operative behaviour within the public service. At collegiate levels, barriers have been introduced. In large schools headteachers become managers and are separated from teaching staff. More relevant has been intrusion of purchaser/provider model in relations between LEAs and schools. This reduces scope for real co-operation, and also reduces scope for LEAs to act as watchdogs for citizenship. Response to this has been centralization of that function, which sits paradoxically with markets as we shall see below.

To argue this should not lead us to adopt an unreservedly communitarian position. Acts of trust and goodwill might simply be a cover for unreflecting sloppiness. What are needed are subtle approaches which seek to sustain an equilibrium between the two. Unfortunately this cannot be achieved through an automatic pilot of the market kind, but requires constant professional input—a concept with which both community and market have difficulty.

Although, as noted, market forces have had their problems with the family during the history of modernization, they are more or less at peace with it today. Not surprisingly, in practice neo-liberal arguments are advanced by political interests representing those who have done well out of the operation of the capitalist economy. These are in turn the groups who find it easiest to help their children educationally through deployment of their material and cultural capital. They are therefore happy to see the marriage of market choice and family advantage embodied in such mechanisms as fee-paying education and selective schools. While the combination of economic and family advantage might be offensive to citizenship concepts of equality of opportunity, advocates of markets and communities can be very content with such arrangements.

A similar argument might be deployed in relation to the growth of parental and other local community involvement in school governance extended by the British reforms; it is the better educated who are best equipped to take advantage of these possibilities, and schools in the neighbourhoods where they are concentrated which will thrive. However, this is not a combination of community and market but community and citizenship. This should not be concealed by the fact that it was introduced in a general context of marketization. It was also a real response to the problem of providing accessible public spaces for contemporary citizenship. As such it presents two challenges to advocates of citizenship: how far they are prepared to exchange the universalism of citizenship for the arbitrariness and unevenness that community offers in its achievement improved participation? And can universalist social policy develop strategies for improving the participative skills of the disadvantaged, rather than use them as an excuse for retreating behind inaccessible bureaucracy?

Conclusion: Towards New Syntheses

Recent British experience presents a number of examples of the damage done by marketization to citizenship processes, but rather than conclude by summarizing them it will be more useful to draw attention to points of potential synthesis that have emerged. It was stated earlier that a significant feature of contemporary neo-liberalism is its break from the positions of the post-war consensus that compromises had to be reached between markets and moderations of them, in exchange for the view that the purer that markets the better the outcomes. While many of the British social policy experiments have been launched from that perspective, what they may have achieved is to indicate scope for new compromises.

The extension of parent and other local participation in school governance has not led to the antagonism between parents and teachers that was widely anticipated. Instead, knowledge and understanding of schools' problems have probably spread through the population. Paradoxically, an ostensibly market-oriented reform has in fact produced a synthesis of citizenship and community. The fact that this raises the anticipated problems of the inequalities of community leads to a further useful paradox. The gap between citizenship and community might be bridged by the provision of advice and support for parents and neighbourhoods who do not possess the skills for effective participation. This is a task for the professional staff of the public services. Contrary to neo-liberal beliefs that the role of public service can be reduced by co-opting the voluntary activities of community, there is in fact a new role for such services in binding together the resources of citizenship and of community.

Devolution to schools of various powers and their own local democratization has also led to useful combinations of citizenship and community, but methods need to be found to prevent beggar-my-neighbour competition among schools which prevent them drawing on the co-operation possibilities of the community network of neighbouring schools. This is a matter of institutional design and the provision of incentives for co-operation.

Because marketization of education has had to take place within a citizenship context, there have been some (though not enough) interesting new initiatives in safeguards against poor quality. Such safeguards are also essential to a proper citizenship model. The concept of users' 'charters' could be developed very creatively here. At present the charters are distorted because their role is to make lower level service deliverers the scapegoats for inadequate levels of provision and unpopular policy decisions. But the basic idea could be extended to embody entitlements to level of provision, not just the manner of delivery. This would truly make them citizens' as opposed to customers' charters. Charters for various services would lay down the level of service that could be expected without market charging. As such they would be subject to real public voice: debate, change, and scrutiny. They would create expectations and assert citizens' rights to a service. For example, a proper Parents' Charter would include commitments to class sizes and levels of facilities for particular subjects. If government was seeking to reduce public provision in a way that would break the guarantees, this would need to be openly declared and debated.

The extension of inspection and regulation that has accompanied the partial marketization of schools and the full privatization of many other former public services is similarly relevant here. Private and public providers alike must be subject to high levels of inspection to ensure that guaranteed standards are maintained. Particularly notable has been the way in which the regulatory institutions created in recent years have had a more populist, accessible role and style than the rather stuffy bodies created by earlier generations. Tough, publicity-conscious inspectorates, reflecting a wide range of interests and appraising service delivery in the light of more ambitious charters embodying standards of excellence, would be major radical tools for guaranteeing the quality of citizenship services.

REFERENCES

AUDIT COMMISSION (1992). *Getting in on the Act* (London: The Commission).

—— (1996). *Trading Places: The Supply and Allocation of School Places* (London: The Commission).

ETZIONI, A. (1996). *The New Golden Rule: Community and Morality in a Democratic Society* (New York: Basic Books).

GRAY, J. (1993). *Beyond the New Right: Markets, Government and the Common Environment* (London: Routledge).

HABERMAS, J. (1976). 'Was heißt Universalpragmatik?', in K. O. Apel (ed.), *Sprachpragmatik und Philosophie* (Frankfurt: Suhrkamp), 174–272.

HIRSCHMAN, A. O. (1970). *Exit, Voice and Loyalty: Responses to the Decline of Firms, Institutions and States* (Cambridge, Mass.: Havard University Press).

—— (1993). '*Il crollo della Repubblica Democratica Tedesca*', paper (mimeo).

KING, D. S. (1995). *Actively Seeking Work? The Politics of Unemployment and Welfare Policy in the United States and Great Britain* (Chicago: University of Chicago Press).

LEWIS, N. (1993). 'The Citizen's Charter and Next Steps: A New Way of Governing?', *The Political Quarterly*, 64: 316–26.

MILLER, D. (1989). *Market, State and Community* (Oxford: Oxford University Press).

OLDFIELD, A. (1990). *Citizenship and Community: Civic Republicanism and the Modern World* (London: Routledge).

POLANYI, K. (1957 [1943]). *The Great Transformation: The Political and Economic Origins of our Time* (Boston, Mass.: Beacon Press).

ROBINSON, P., and STEEDMAN, H. (1996). *Rhetoric and Reality: Britain's New Vocational Qualifications* (London: mimeo).

TITMUSS, R. M. (1970). *The Gift Relationship: From Human Blood to Social Policy* (London: Allen & Unwin).

TRITTER, J. (1994). 'The Citizen's Charter: Opportunities for User's Perspectives?', *The Political Quarterly*, 65: 397–414.

7

Prospects for Effective Social Citizenship in an Age of Structural Inactivity

Anton Hemerijck

The Predicament of Structural Inactivity

One of the paradoxes of the contemporary European welfare state is that, while today practically every adult male and female seeks gainful employment, jobs are hard to come by. There is a growing number of (economically) inactive citizens, people of working age who are structurally dependent on social policy for their livelihood. The predicament of inactivity is concentrated among the low-skilled, ethnic minorities, and the long-term unemployed. A comparison of six European countries, considering unemployment, sickness, occupational disability, maternity, general need, and early retirement, reveals that levels of inactivity have dramatically increased over the past decade (see Table 7.1). Moreover, in five of the six countries (not Denmark), the rise in the volume of inactivity in the 1980s went together with a decline in labour-market participation of the population aged between 14 and retirement age. In short, inactivity—paid non-work—seems to have become a mainstay of the advanced European welfare state. The peculiar combination of the growing number of inactive citizens receiving welfare benefits and the decline in active (working) citizens, threatens the financial, social, cultural, and political foundation of the welfare state. The post-war welfare state was not only geared towards the achievement of full employment, but also very much dependent on the attainment of substantial levels of (male) labour-force participation.

Financially, national economies faced with rising inactivity and declining activity, seem no longer able to preserve generous welfare standards. Especially where social security is financed through payroll contributions, growth in the number of welfare recipients pushes up the tax burden and social wage costs. Under conditions of intense international competition, high social wage costs

TABLE 7.1. *Distribution of the population (from age 14 until retirement age)*

Country	1980		1992	
	Active (%)	Inactive (%)	Active (%)	Inactive (%)
Netherlands	50	16	47	20
Belgium	54	20	52	27
Germany*	54	23	51	23
France	59	13	56	18
Denmark	56	19	59	25
UK	60	12	56	19

Source: Rourda and Uogels 1997: 245–8.
* Calculations based only on West Germany.

result in a per saldo loss of activity and, most likely, a further increase in level of inactivity, as a consequence of bankruptcies and the relocation of production to low-wage areas.

In terms of societal cohesion, structural inactivity threatens to undermine the form of organized solidarity upon which the post-war welfare state was founded. Through their social-security contributions skilled and productive paid workers are currently subsidizing the growing population of less skilled and less productive welfare recipients. This condition could in due course deteriorate into a distributive conflict between the productive 'insiders' of the formal labour market and the welfare-dependent, inactive, 'outsiders'. Ongoing polarization will provoke the insiders to withdraw their support from the inactive. Even worse, insiders could be tempted to exploit their privileged positions in the formal labour market by effectively preventing entry of inactive outsiders.

Culturally, structural inactivity generates a crisis of societal cohesion and moral aspiration, as more and more people with 'a right to work' seek gainful employment, while there are few jobs available. It has been argued that long-term inactivity invites the development of a 'culture of dependency' among welfare recipients. Not poverty *per se* but a sense of being socially redundant and economically irrelevant will provoke an emergent underclass of inactives to turn their back on the values and institutions of mainstream society.

Finally, politically, in the face of a crisis of cultural aspiration and societal cohesion, intensifying problems of organized solidarity under conditions of intense international competition, the political centre finds it difficult to muster nation-wide support for welfare state programmes, which, in the eyes of many, actually contribute to the predicament of inactivity.

How do we explain the rise of structural inactivity in conjunction with declining labour-market participation in contemporary European welfare states? Do the citizens of the welfare state no longer wish to work? Do they, pampered by generous standards of social protection, prefer leisure? Or are they sick or otherwise unable to work, as the statistics of broad unemployment would have us believe? In this chapter, I wish to explore the intimate correlation between declining activity and rising inactivity from two contrasting sets of arguments, both revolving around the 'unintended' or 'perverse' effects of post-war social policy.

The first argument, rooted in cultural sociology, centres around the alleged decline of the traditional work ethic in the welfare state. By dissolving the 'sacred' link between work and income, the welfare state has come to undermine the motivation to seek gainful employment. The lack of immediate feedback between work and income, conservative critics of social policy contend, weakens the moral fibre of welfare recipients. The resultant rise in inactivity contributes to the emergence of a 'dependency culture' of benefit claimants.

While the causal chain of the decline-of-the-work-ethic argument runs from the behaviour of citizens to the rise of inactivity, the second argument, rooted in comparative political economy, suggests that the institutional characteristics of national labour market and systems of social security structure the level of inactivity. The crisis of inactivity, following this line of reasoning, is not the result of crippling norms and values, but rather the consequence of accumulated institutional rigidities and historically perverse policy choices.

For the purpose of this volume, I will approach the arguments of the decline-of-the-work-ethic argument and the proposition of deficient welfare state institutions from the perspective of the renewed interest in citizenship in political and social science discourse. By so doing, I wish to relate T. H. Marshall's classic portrayal of the extension of citizenship and the struggle for 'equal social worth' to contemporary conceptions of citizenship (Marshall 1963). I will especially focus on issues of work and welfare in the recent literature. Next, I will empirically scrutinize the predicament of inactivity on the basis of evidence from the Netherlands. I wish to concentrate on the Dutch experience for three reasons. First, the Dutch welfare state is one of the most advanced welfare states in Europe. Second, the Netherlands did experience a severe crisis of inactivity in the 1980s. Notwithstanding, third and most important, the recent Dutch experience presents a case history of a social policy regime that has adapted relatively successfully to processes of demographic change, economic restructuring, international competition, labour-market flexibilization, and individualization, by way of social policy reform bent on reversing the cycle of declining activity and rising inactivity.

After having empirically examined the arguments of the decline of the work ethic and faltering institutions for the Netherlands, the final normative section considers policy. What are the prospects for effective social policy in an age of structural inactivity, as it were adapting T. H. Marshall's principle of 'equal social worth' to the new realities of diversified labour-market conditions and heterogeneous household patterns? I will explore two broadly debated policy alternatives which are intimately linked to particular diagnoses of the crisis of the welfare state. These are, first, 'workfare' policies, designed to repair the direct link between the obligation to work and right to welfare, which has become uncoupled in the welfare state. Alternatively, there is the idea of the introduction of a universal 'citizen's income', which, by contrast, is directed towards a radical decoupling of the conditional connection between work and income in social policy.

Relating T. H. Marshall to Novel Conceptions of Citizenship

The resurgence of the concept of citizenship in contemporary political and social science discourse has invited a critical rereading of T. H. Marshall's famous 1949 lectures, published together in 1963 under the title of *Citizenship and Social Class* (Culpitt 1992; Meehan 1993; Twine 1994; Bulmer and Rees 1996). In these lectures, Marshall portrayed the extension of citizenship rights in terms of a progressive tale of democratization and class-abatement. Based on the British experience, Marshall locates the origins of the struggle for citizenship in the affirmation of civil rights in the eighteenth century. After the establishment of liberal protection of equality before the law, liberty of the person, freedom of speech, thought, and faith, the right to own property and conclude contracts, the nineteenth century gave rise to the inauguration of political rights: the right to take part in elections and to serve in bodies invested with political authority. The struggle for citizenship reached its completion in the second half of the twentieth century with the attribution of the social rights, which Marshall defined as: 'the whole range from the right to a modicum of economic welfare and security to share to the full in the social heritage and to live the life of a civilized being according to the standard prevailing in the society' (1963: 74).

Notwithstanding the intimate historical links between the three types of citizenship rights, Marshall emphasized that social rights can never be theoretically derived from the democratic principle of majority rule. Social rights stress the right to receive (Marshall 1981). Protecting the vulnerable and preventing the disadvantaged from becoming vulnerable lies at the heart of Marshall's social ethic of 'equal social worth'. The very purpose of the welfare state is to help the disadvantaged to enter mainstream society by countering processes of societal marginalization. As such, the welfare state held out a promise of the enlargement, enrichment, and equalization of people's 'life chances': 'an equalization between the more and less fortunate at all levels—between the healthy and the sick, the employed and the unemployed, the old and the active, the bachelor and the father of a large family' (1963: 107). The introduction of a universal right to real income, 'not proportionate to the market value of the claimant' (p. 100), for Marshall, was the key institutional innovation of the post-war welfare state, representing the 'invasion of contract by status', the 'subordination of market to social justice' (p. 115).

Marshall's conception of citizenship revolves around two constitutive elements; on the one hand, the legal status of the bundle of rights, and, on the other, the particular collective identity of a political community, within which citizenship rights can be exercised. As a bundle of rights, citizenship is inspired by and in turn can surely strengthen: 'a . . . direct sense of community membership based on loyalty to a civilization which is a common possession. It is a loyalty of free men endowed with right and protected by a common law. Its growth is stimulated both by the struggle to win those right and by their enjoyment when won' (1963: 96). For Marshall, social rights not only provide citizens with a sense of material security against the adverse effects of poverty, illness, disability, unemployment, and old age, which encourage citizens to enter socially useful but individually risky wealth-creating occupations. In turn, social security encourages a sense of belonging and commitment to the kind of society, the welfare state, within which citizens live.

Contemporary students of social policy have criticized Marshall's rather 'whiggish' portrayal of the progressive extension of citizenship. While perhaps aptly capturing the British experience, Marshall's logic of social progress has been found wanting when applied to other national experiences. In Germany, for instance, social policy innovation came first, in order to compensate for deficient political rights (Bendix 1964; Esping-Andersen 1990). In defence of Marshall, I would like to emphasize that today there is much cross-national congruity in terms of citizenship rights. All the advanced democracies of the European Union are fully committed to the rule of law, parliamentary democracy, and the welfare state. An altogether different point of criticism that carries more weight is that Marshall, writing at the apex of the 'golden age' of post-war prosperity, falsely took for granted full (male-breadwinner) employment, Keynesian economics, social-democratic politics, bureaucratic social policy administration, together with a solidly entrenched class compromise between organized capital and labour. More important, Marshall did not fully appreciate the immanent tension between 'negatively' defined civil rights and 'positively' defined social rights (Offe 1993). Civil rights, by virtue of being defined in negative terms of government non-interference, are operationally precise and can be easily enforced. By contrast, social rights, defined in substantive terms of need, imply affirmative state action of meeting the different needs of the vulnerable. By their very nature, social needs can never be precisely demarcated. Moreover, welfare provisions must ultimately be provided by the free market economy. Designed to substantiate an equalization of 'life chances', social rights oblige the political community to interfere in and modify the distributive consequences of market processes. Offe rightly states that any standard of social right is inherently subject to potential upward as well as downward adjustment, depending not only on changes in political commitment towards redistribution and state capacities to administer and implement social policy legislation, but also on aggregate economic performance. Consequently, the question of 'how much' is good enough, and 'what kind' of social services are required and 'which organizational form is effective', on behalf of 'what categories of people', and at 'whose expense' can never be unambiguously settled.

The recent rediscovery of the concept of citizenship has brought together two different intellectual perspectives which are worth relating to Marshall's classic contribution to the debate. These are civic republicanism and communitarianism (Beiner 1995; Kymlicka and Norman 1995). While sharing in a critique of liberal political theory, civic republican and communitarian authors adhere to distinctly different normative foundations of their respective conceptions of citizenship. Civic republicans endorse a more restricted political understanding of citizenship, in terms of the practice of political participation in public decision-making by free, equal, autonomous, and competent citizens (Barber 1984). Communitarians, on the other hand, adhere to a more general—sociologically informed—notion of citizenship, founded on shared values and put into practice in various, not merely political, 'spheres of justice' (Walzer 1983). To employ Albert Hirschmann's vocabulary: the civic republican tradition defines citizenship in terms of a 'thick' political practice of exercising 'voice' in the political forum, whereas for communitarians the moral primacy lies with a 'broader' sociologically informed sense of 'loyalty', on the basis on shared values, as the normative foundation of citizenship.

In Habermas's civic republican ideal of 'constitutional patriotism', citizens do not derive their identity from cultural properties, but rather from the praxis of citizens actively exercising their civil rights (Habermas 1992). The quality of citizenship critically depends on the willingness of citizens to engage in public debate and collective self-rule. For the civic republican conception of citizenship to be effective, individual citizens have to be endowed with a number of inalienable civil rights, so as to protect their autonomy *vis-à-vis* the state and guarantee equality before the law, together with granting them political rights to be able to participate in public debate and collective decision-making. Following Aristotle, a civic republican citizen actively exercises his rights in the 'forum' of public deliberation and collective self-rule.

By stressing the primacy of politics, civic republican authors seem to have tacitly removed social rights from the debate, resulting in a lack of understanding of the social preconditions of citizenship, which facilitate or constrain citizens actively to engage in political deliberation (Gunsteren 1992). Civic engagement as a political practice crucially depends on sufficient material security, leisure, and adequate levels of education. In comparison to civic republicans, communitarians are far more sociologically informed in their premises, insights, judgements, and lessons. The communitarian tradition defines citizenship far more in terms of prepolitical belonging, based on shared values, not *per se* in terms of membership in the political community, but rather in the everyday spheres of the family, child-rearing, friendship, the neighbourhood, leisure, learning, and religion. Following Durkheim, communitarians argue that society precedes and constitutes the individual. Like Marshall, communitarian authors are particularly sensitive to processes of effectively enfranchising or disenfranchising different categories from the 'cultural heritage' of civil society. To be sure, social inclusion involves designing appropriate political rights, but it also bears on generating the non-political prerequisites for gaining social respect and personal dignity in the many other 'spheres of justice'.

Both communitarian and civic republican authors have articulated pointed critiques of contemporary social policy. Civic republicans fear that the welfare state, organized around a multitude of substantive categories of need, contributes to the decline of civic engagement and a widening gap between public administration and the citizenry. Social policy, it is argued, encourages a privatized retreat from the ideal of citizenship as a practice of political participation, by encouraging a consumerist clientelization of citizenship. Communitarians, in keeping with their broader understanding of society, lament the decline of the family, the waning of associational life, and (civil) religion (Lasch 1979; Bellah *et al.* 1985; Etzioni 1993; MacIntyre 1988; Sandel 1982, 1984; Selznick 1992). However much the ideology of the welfare state may underscore the affirmation of community, its operative ethos, many communitarians maintain, is decidedly anti-communitarian. Social policies, implemented through affirmative state intervention, display little concern for the integrity of the institutions of civil society.

At a time of resurgence in mass unemployment and important changes in the world of work, it is rather surprising that issues of work and the experience of unemployment do not feature prominently in civic republican and communitarian writings. Communitarians prefer to focus on other spheres of social life, like neighbourhoods and schools. In the civic republican tradition there is only one notable counter-example. Judith Shklar, inspired more by De Tocqueville's version of civic republican than Aristotle's, takes issue with Hannah Arendt's élitist disdain for the mundane world of work (Shklar 1991). In *The Human Condition* (1958), Arendt argued that industrial workers, whom she called the 'animal laborans', were effectively unfit to make informed judgements about political questions. Shklar, by contrast, maintains that self-directed economic independence through productive work took the place of honour as the object of social aspiration in nineteenth-century America: 'It is in the marketplace, in production and commerce, in the world of work in all its forms . . . that the American citizen finds his social place, his standing, the approbation of his fellows, and possibly some of his self-respect' (1991: 63).

After the abolition of slavery, Shklar argues that the values of economic independence through the 'earning of a living' took the place of the outmoded notion of civic republican virtues as the ethical basis of modern democracy. Gainful employment has become the social basis of democratic citizenship, social status, and power. Critically aware of the novel intimate link between work and citizenship, Shklar highlights how the feminist movement's quest for inclusion, after the establishment of universal suffrage, has been geared towards gaining access to and equal treatment in the labour market. For Shklar modern citizens have become members of two interlocking 'public orders'. To be a recognized as a fully fledged citizen he or she must be an equal member of the polity, as a voter, but should also be independent, which under contemporary social and economic condition means that he or she must be an 'earner', a 'free remunerated worker', finding a source of pride in being 'self-made' (Shklar 1991: 64). It is, in short, the contemporary interplay of productive work and public concern that constitutes modern citizenship. The intimate connection between work and citizenship in Shklar's understanding of citizenship, however, remains problematic. Is gainful employment, executed in hierarchically organized firms, really able to nourish the necessary competencies of independent judgement and individual autonomy necessary for active civic engagement in politics? And what are the political implications for emancipating the sphere of gainful employment to the status of a 'public order' in a free market economy?

Rereading Marshall in the context of the debate between civic republicans and communitarians, I am tempted to reclassify his lectures for contemporary use as institutional communitarianism. In line with the communtarian tradition, Marshall's lectures were empirically oriented, sociologically informed, adhered to a rather expansive conception of society, and particularly concerned with the societal processes of inclusion. Unlike contemporary communitarians, however, Marshall cannot be accused of ethnic nationalism. His understanding of social rights, although territorially bound, is guided by the universalist recognition of 'equal worth for all'. Marshall's universalist rights-based justification of the welfare state captures an empowerment strategy to enable citizens to exercise their basic civil and political rights, underscored in the civic republican tradition, so as to let them share 'to the full' in the 'social heritage' of the nation in accordance with the 'standard prevailing in society'. Marshall benignly believed that the institutions of the welfare state, based on this inclusive conception of social citizenship, were to become key sources of political and societal integration after 1945. Although he realized that full employment for those able to work and an adequate system of benefits for those who were not were crucial to the creation of post-war political identities, under conditions of post-war full employment, he conceded that it was 'no easy matter' to revive a sense of personal obligation to 'put one's heart into one's job and work hard' (Marshall 1963: 123–4).

From Calvinism to Consumerism?

After 1945, the political community took on a qualified commitment of sustaining minimum standards of income, nutrition, health, work, education, and housing, as distinct social rights of citizenship. For most of the golden age of post-war prosperity, the welfare state was supported by a positive definition of the common good, a strong consensus over a considerable degree of income redistribution, while relying on a solid and efficient private economy, guaranteeing full (male-breadwinner) employment. Male job security, with dedicated housewives, in fact allowed welfare state intervention to be kept at bay. Social policy came into play merely at the beginning (education) and near the end (old-age pensions) of relatively homogeneous biographies, with only rare and brief intermittent periods of dependence on the social-security system. The benign economic environment of the post-war era, inspired many national policy-makers to increase the levels of benefits and progressively expand the coverage of social rights (Flora 1987).

The breakdown of the Bretton Woods monetary system in 1973 and the steep rise in oil prices between 1973 and 1979 brought an end to the golden age of post-war prosperity, and stalled the progressive expansion of social rights. While the advanced industrial societies employed remarkably divergent national strategies of crisis management during the late 1970s, cutbacks in social security were introduced practically everywhere during the 1980s. Access to welfare state programmes was made more selective, levels of benefits were reduced, and periods of coverage curtailed. Many conservative governments that came to power in the early 1980s were elected on their promise to scale back the welfare state.

The rhetoric of neo-liberalism, proclaiming the superiority of 'negative' economic over 'positive' social rights appeared very convincing against the background of the rise of mass unemployment, failing Keynesian macroeconomics, and accumulated failures in social policy implementation. Social policy, following the prevalent sociological critique, did not live up to its promise of the fulfilment of citizenship because it perversely weakened the moral fibre of the citizens of the welfare state. This critique is echoed in the thought-provoking argument about the decline of the work ethic in the welfare state advanced by Daniel Bell in the late 1970s. In *The Cultural*

Contradictions of Capitalism (1976) Bell argues that welfare capitalism has—unintentionally—fallen victim to its own success, because 'the principles of the economic realm and those of the cultural domain now lead people in contrary directions'. The spectre of individualism, released by the Reformation and the Enlightenment, activated the values of industriousness, hard work, thrift, entrepreneurship, and 'deferred gratification' in early modern capitalism. Under the welfare state, ironically, individualism encouraged the development of an alternative 'hedonist' ethos, which is fundamentally at odds with the original sober mentality of early modern capitalism. Pampered by a generous system of social security, the welfare state, by virtue of having dissolved the 'sacred' link between work and income, contributed to erosion of the traditional work ethic as a central point of moral reference. This constitutes, according to Bell, the cultural contradiction of capitalism:

Capitalism has lost its traditional legitimacy, which was based on a moral system of reward rooted in the Protestant sanctification of work. It has substituted a hedonism which promises material ease and luxury, yet shies away from all the historic implications of a 'voluptuary system', with all its social permissiveness and libertinism. Hedonism as a way of life promoted by the marketing system of business, constitutes the cultural contradiction of capitalism. (1978: 84)

Bell's cultural critique of the welfare state is based upon the presupposition that, at an earlier stage, bourgeois capitalism was supported by a strongly entrenched work ethic that made work a moral obligation, like the one portrayed by Max Weber in his classical study *The Protestant Ethic and the Spirit of Capitalism* (Weber 1958). In his essays, Weber suggests that the core values of Protestantism provided the moral seed-bed for the long-term development of capitalism and industrialism. Especially Calvinism supplied an important normative source of legitimation for work, money-making, and capital accumulation. The Reformation promoted work as a purposive activity to the status of an obligation, a promise in a calling (*Beruf*): 'in the sweat of thy brow' (Gen. 3: 19). The Calvinist work ethic not only encouraged industriousness in the honour of God, but also sanctioned individual responsibility: 'Who does not work, shall not eat' (2 Thess. 3: 10). In his explanation of the development of modern capitalism, Weber placed great emphasis on the Calvinist doctrine of predestination. Because God's blessing was only given to those who worked hard in a calling, Puritans, as God's stewards, were tempted to interpret success in the sphere of productive work as a sign, but not a proof, of grace. Puritans indirectly and unintentionally helped to transpose the idea of a calling from the traditional—Catholic—religious sphere to the modern secular realm of bourgeois capitalism (Marshall 1982; Poggi 1983).

The welfare state, following Bell, fosters an illusion of security, supplying its citizens with more psychological comfort than is good for them, the economy, and society. There is a paradoxical elective affinity operative between the institutions of the welfare state and its ethos of hedonism, which runs counter to the *Wahlverwandtschaft* Weber found between Calvinist doctrines and the spirit of early modern capitalism. To paraphrase Weber: it seems that the consumerist *Gesinnungsethik* of the welfare state has driven out the original *Verantwortungsethik* of early modern bourgeois capitalism.

It should be emphasized that the thesis of the decline of the work ethic was not only popular among conservative sociologists like Bell. In progressive academic circles there was and still is much agreement that the welfare state is no longer able to reproduce the cultural resources and economic sanctions that are necessary to stabilize the moral obligation to seek gainful employment. This is, however, for altogether different reasons than the ones suggested by Bell. Claus Offe, for one, maintains that the work ethic fails as an important function of social integration, because gainful employment is being 'rationalized away' by economic restructuring. Industrialism and international competition increasingly put a premium on capital-intensive production, resulting in the structural elimination of work. Moreover, the time which people spend in gainful employment throughout their lives has drastically decreased over the past fifty years. And as levels of unemployment continue to rise, Offe believes that the moral stigmatization of living off welfare will wear off. Beyond a certain threshold, paid non-work or inactivity can no longer be plausibly accounted for in terms of moral default (Offe 1985, 1996).

Is the work ethic dead or alive, or has it changed its nature? To what extent have social policy and industrial restructuring contributed to a weakening of the work ethic? Or are we to observe, contrary to the imaginative sociological reasoning of Bell and Offe, a strengthening of the work ethic over the past decade? On the basis of three empirical research efforts I will now chart changing values orientations with respect to work and unemployment in Dutch society.

In quantitative sociological inquiry, the work ethic is commonly understood in terms of two related dimensions of the societal appreciation of gainful employment. On the one hand, the work ethic is intimately related to the conviction that people have a 'moral obligation' actively to seek employment. On the other hand, the work ethic is associated with the relative weight of gainful employment in relation to activities beyond the sphere of paid work in the lives of individuals, and by extension, society at large. The second understanding of the work ethic delineates the extent to which work is valued as a 'central life interest'. In this respect, a strong sense of the centrality of work in one's life does not *per se* have to correspond to an equally strong morally obliging conviction to work. The classic essays of Max Weber could be said to depict the historical development of the work ethic, from the Calvinist obligation of God's stewards to work hard in a calling to the institutionalization of a more generalized habitual rule of having a job in the formal economy in the wake of the industrial revolution.

On the basis of survey and panel research on value change in Dutch society, we are able to assess and interpret changes with respect to the appreciation of work as a moral obligation, on the one hand, and the norm of the work experience as central life interest, on the other. The conviction of work as a moral obligation is operationalized on the basis of survey statements like: 'If someone wishes to enjoy life, he or she has to be prepared to work hard for it' or 'Everybody who is able to work, should do so'. Survey findings from the period from 1977 to 1985 display a relative decline in the appreciation of work as a moral obligation (Ester and Halman 1994). Interestingly, the more drastic decline in the work ethic of the late 1970s and early 1980s has practically come to a halt. The negative trend of 2.25 per cent per year until 1985, is followed by a marked slowdown, stabilizing at a mere 0.8 per cent from 1985 to 1990. Additional panel research reveals intertemporal changes in the work ethic as a moral obligation, which are far from consistent with the hypotheses of its unilinear decline. Almost 40 per cent of the respondents have come to modify and adjust their work ethic in the course of their lifetime. Furthermore, the direction of change is differentiated: 15 per cent of respondents have adjusted their work ethic in an upward, affirmative direction, while 24 per cent have reassessed the appreciation of the moral obligation to work in negative terms (Ester and Halman 1994: 128). In large part, the variation can be explained in terms of personal and group characteristics. Elderly respondents endorse a stronger work ethic than younger people, and more educated respondents embrace a weaker, less obliging work ethic than low-skilled workers, while on the whole male breadwinners endorse a stronger work ethic than housewives and mothers.

The dimension of work as a central life interest is captured by the answers to survey questions like: 'How important is work for you personally and in your life at large in comparison to other interests?' Findings for the period of 1977 to 1990 reveal that paid work remains a highly valued activity in people's lives. Over two-thirds of all respondents, 68 per cent in 1985 and 69 per cent in 1990, value paid employment as a key central life interest. Behind the stable picture of the highly respected status of having a job in people's lives, there is again a hidden dynamic of contrary movements. More than a quarter of all respondents have corrected the relative value of gainful employment in their lives over time. The direction of change is differentiated: for 10 per cent of the respondent the relative value of work in their lives has increased, while for 15 per cent there have been a downward adjustments (Ester and Halman 1994: 112–15).

The strong endorsement of paid work as a central life interest in survey research concurs with the findings of numerous opinion studies of the Dutch Social and Cultural Planning Bureau (SCP 1986, 1992, 1994, 1996). The SCP found that, were they to win the lottery, an overwhelming majority of 83 per cent said they would probably continue working (Allaart *et al.* 1993).

According to SCP research, the desire to take part in the world of gainful employment may, if anything, actually be growing rather than weakening. The growing appreciation of gainful employment as a central life interest in Dutch society is, in part, the result of the increased orientation of women towards labour-market participation. This in turn reflects higher levels of education, values of economic independence, and the conviction that labour-market participation demonstrates gender equality. Today, 50 per cent of non-working women and mothers with small children aspire to a job in the future. By contrast, for a majority of elderly men (that is, above the age of 55), while they endorse a strong, morally obliging, work ethic, the appreciation of work as a central life interest seems to be receding. This does not constitute a contradiction. Older men, apparently, judge that they have worked hard for long enough (SCP 1994: 166–7). The resilience of the appreciation of work as a central life interest does not imply that work-related values and aspirations have not changed. The SCP identifies an ever greater variety in work-related values beneath the general opinion that participation in the labour market is of central importance. There is much diversity with respect to the type of jobs and particular work experiences that people seek, as a significant drop in the number of people who aspire to a traditional, regular, full-time nine-to-five job, five days a week, forty-eight weeks per year, for forty years, reveals. An ever growing part of the population are looking for 'large' part-time jobs, ranging from 20 to 30 hours a week. On average, more that one-third of the women currently holding full-time jobs, would prefer to work part-time. Of the number of women who are in 'small' part-time jobs, less than twenty hours a week, over a quarter aspire to a 'larger' part-time job. Among men too, there is a growing interest in part-time work. Next to the popular preference for part-time work, there is a growing interest in different forms of leave, allowing adult citizens temporarily to work shorter hours or interrupt the job completely for a short break to care for children or parents or take up a course of study.

Finally, there is research on the experience of long-term unemployment and welfare dependency, on the basis of which the relative strength and weakness of the work ethic can be assessed *ex negativo*. How important is having a job for people who are structurally dependent on welfare and have little prospect of returning to a regular work? Is the experience of structural inactivity particularly painful for these jobless who endorse a strong, morally obliging, work ethic? What is the effect of long-term welfare dependency on the work-related values of the long-term unemployed? Do they adjust their values to the condition of inactivity over time, following Offe's logic of the evaporation of moral stigmatization of living off welfare in the face of industrial restructuring? These questions are answered in the study *Een Tijd zonder Werk* (A Time without Work) by a research team of Dutch sociologists on the effects of long unemployment in three depressed neighbourhoods in Amsterdam,

Rotterdam, and Enschede (Kroft *et al.* 1989; Engbersen 1990). The study is modelled on the famous study of the experience of unemployment in the early 1930s in the small Austrian industrial town of Marienthal, just outside Vienna, by Jahoda, Lazarsfeld, and Zeisl, *Die Arbeitslosen von Marienthal* (Jahoda *et al.* 1972 [1933]). The unambiguous findings of the Marienthal study provide a good starting-point for comparing the experiences of unemployment of the 1930s and the 1980s. From such a comparison valuable insights can be obtained into the effects of social policy in a fully fledged welfare state. In the 1930s, the experience of unemployment inescapably created immediate financial hardship as the unemployed were entitled to benefits averaging a mere quarter of last earned wages. A downward spiral of multiple and absolute deprivation, Jahoda *et al.* found, hit over two-thirds of the community. When the research group left Marienthal in 1933, they characterized the unemployed community as *die müde Gemeinschaft* (the weary community). Five years later, tragically, a majority of unemployed of Marienthal, welcomed the *Anschluss*, though not for ideological reasons: Hitler promised jobs!

For the Dutch unemployed in the 1980s, the level of unemployment insurance and social-security benefits stood at 70 to 80 per cent of last earned wages and the level of public assistance was set at the level of the legal minimum wage. These income guarantees, to be sure, mitigated immediate financial distress. However, more than one-third of the long-term unemployed, especially those with dependent children, did experience the kind of social-psychological strain that Jahoda *et al.* found in Marienthal. An important finding of the Dutch study is that today there is much more diversity in the style of coping with long-term unemployment than there was sixty years ago. Kroft *et al.* distinguish two groups of 'cultures of unemployment'. A large majority (70 per cent) belongs to a so-called 'traditional' culture of unemployment. Like the unemployed of Marienthal, the trauma of unemployment reveals itself in the experiences of a loss of time structure, purposelessness, self-blame, strain on mental and physical health, a decline of interest in hobbies and in regular social contacts, loss of identity, a gradual loss of employability, and a distinct decline in involvement in political affairs and civic activities. Conventional role patterns of the traditional unemployed stand in the way of creative solutions. For the traditional unemployed, gainful employment continues to be the most important source of income, security, status, and prestige. Social-security benefits are perceived of as a form of charity, rather than as entitlements.

A substantive minority (30 per cent) displays novel ways of coping with unemployment. This group, adhering to a modern—individualistic and utilitarian—culture of unemployment, is far more active, able to continue their hobbies, participate in the community, and work in the informal economy. Whereas the traditional unemployed are ready to make serious sacrifices in terms of pay and working condition, the modern unemployed hold on to relatively high 'reservation wages'. Job offers have to be in line with their education, skills, and experience. Hereby, the modern unemployed live by a far more instrumental work ethic than the traditional unemployed. Gainful employment is certainly not an end in itself: it is a means, a gateway to a certain standard of consumption, the realization of a particular lifestyle, on the basis of adequate levels of income.

The overall conclusion that emerges from the above research effort confirms that paid work continues to occupy a prominent place in the lives of most adult citizens. The dynamic of contrary value reorientations over time cannot be considered as evidence for an overall cross-the-board decline of the work ethic. If anything, it could be argued that the paid job is the only 'sacred cow' that has outlived the cultural revolution of the 1960s. To say that the work ethic is alive and kicking is not the same as saying that work-related values and behaviour have not changed. Increasingly, more expressive values of self-realization, and hedonist elements of labour time reduction and a company car, are sought after in the work experience. The younger generation of the unemployed maintains a more relaxed, instrumental, work ethic. It should be emphasized that the experience of unemployment speaks about the absence of work, not of the quality of employment. The non-material—latent—meanings of work are not so much contingent on a good or a bad employer, or friendly or unfriendly organization. Looking back on her research in Marienthal, Jahoda acknowledges that other human activities may be able to enforce one or more of these categories, but none of them combines them all with as compelling a reason as earning a living (Jahoda 1982).

Reversing the Cycle of Welfare without Work

If high levels of structural inactivity cannot be explained by a decline of the work ethic, under conditions of welfare state generosity and industrial restructuring, it is germane to concentrate on the interactive effect of the operation of institutions of labour markets and the system of social security. Prima facie, persistent divergences in national experiences of reducing labour supply and facilitating labour-market exit since the late 1970s indeed suggest that structural inactivity may be highly contingent on national patterns of interaction between the institutions of labour-market regulation and different systems of social security.

The structure of the link between labour markets and the welfare state is central to the path-breaking work on national welfare states of Gøsta Esping-Andersen (1990). Following a structural reading of T. H. Marshall, Esping-Andersen highlights how social rights serve to protect the non-working population—the aged, sick, and the unemployed—by providing them with sources of income—social security and public assistance—so as to enable citizens to make ends meet without necessarily relying on their labour-market value. Esping-Andersen has called this measure of protection from the market 'decommodification' (1990: 37). The degree and scope of decommodification mitigates the immediate feedback between work and income. In the language of neo-classical economics, decommodification translates into structural disincentives actively to seek employment, undermining the proper functioning of the labour market. Esping-Andersen's comparative study, however, reveals that any exhaustive decoupling of work and income in various welfare state regimes is the exception rather than the rule in post-war social policy. The majority of national systems of social security are conditional, organized around the status of gainful employment. While recognizing that unemployment, sickness, and disability are social risks, not caused by personal default, national systems of social security clearly put a premium on a person having had a job, preferably for a long time. Levels of social-security benefits are largely tied to previous work experience and generally are set below the level of last earned wages. In addition, welfare recipients are generally obliged by law to look for work. Sanctions, in terms of benefit cuts, can be forced upon claimants who reject job offers or refuse to take part in job-training programmes. The only welfare state regime that comes close to a fully decommodifying system, enabling citizens to make ends meet independent of labour-market participation for lengthy periods of time, is the 'social-democratic' welfare state regime exemplified by the Swedish model. The social-democratic regime type executes a universal system of highly generous and universal redistributive benefits, financed out of general taxes, which are not dependent on individual contributions.

Esping-Andersen's research reveals that the Scandinavian welfare states are not fraught with excessive levels of inactivity and suboptimal levels of labour-market participation. Ironically, it is the continental welfare state, where the conditional ties between work and income have remained far more intimate, that is confronted with a crisis of spiralling inactivity, falling levels of labour-force participation, and jobless economic growth. The 'compensatory', transfer-based, welfare states of France, Germany, Belgium, Italy, Spain, and the Netherlands are, following Esping-Andersen, trapped in a pathological vicious cycle of 'welfare without work' (Esping-Andersen 1996).

The continental welfare states seem to suffer from a negative spiral, a devastating interactive logic between the labour market and the system of social security, leading to increased inactivity and suboptimal levels of participation. During the 1980s, most continental welfare states embarked on strategies of large-scale labour-shedding in response to industrial restructuring. While the social-democratic cases remained committed to high levels of participation of men and women by way of encouraging entry and preventing exit, the continental model, by contrast, decided to subsidize exit particularly of elderly male workers, extend periods of vocational education and training for the young, discourage entry of others, especially women, while sending so-called 'guest-workers' home. In Germany and the Netherlands, the initial policy response to the emergent crisis of inactivity was founded on the idea that the continental model of high wages and generous and lenient social-security provisions could be saved. In order to maintain decent standards of social protection, the German economy has redirected its strategy of indus-trial adjustment towards international markets for high value-added prod-ucts, where competition is not based on price competition and the economies of scale of standardized mass production, but on advanced manufacturing technologies and organization structures with strong innovative capacities, stable industrial relations, good training, and education provisions. This supply-side offensive, however, did not help to overcome stagnant labour-force participation and the rise of inactivity, especially in the 1990s, after German unification (Streeck 1995). The productivity gains made possible by supply-side 'diversified quality production' strategies of upgrading the work-force did not suffice to regain full employment. In fact, novel 'supply-side' corporatist policies speeded up the contraction of industrial employment, especially, through policies of early retirement, popular in Germany, and sickness and disability pensions in the Netherlands.

A complicated pattern of mutual interaction between investments, pro-ductivity, labour participation, wage costs, and social-security arrangements is operative under the Bismarckian design of the continental welfare state. Companies in high-wage economies can really only survive if they are able to increase productivity. This is most commonly achieved through labour-saving investment strategies and/or by laying off less productive, mostly elderly, workers. At the macro-level, pressures to increase productivity set in motion a negative cycle of declining labour-force participation. In order to remain competitive in world markets, manufacturers exposed to international com-petition raise productivity through labour-saving investments. However rational such a response might be from the micro-economic point of view of individual firms, the macro-social and economic consequences certainly are not. Increased inactivity drives up taxes and social-security contributions, which in turn puts more upward pressure on wage costs, providing new grounds for reassessing the remaining workforce in terms of their produc-tivity, leading to a subsequent round of dismissals. Employment disappears, especially in sectors where productivity increases stagnate and the prices of goods and services cannot be raised significantly. Consequently, inactivity generates a further rise in inactivity. Moreover, this logic makes job growth in domestic services at the lower end of the labour market extremely expensive, as sector wages and social-security contributions are closely linked to exposed sector wage developments (Paridon 1994).

The Bismarckian principle of industrial insurance for occupational risk, the central role of the breadwinner, the quasi-private administration of social security, and the focus on income compensation rather than active labour policy, have together intensified the continental crisis of inactivity and created a new class of excluded citizens of non-employed, mostly low-skilled, permanently welfare-dependent citizens. In short, if there is a crisis of the welfare state, it is a crisis of deficient (or no longer effective) institutional design. Esping-Andersen believes that the continental model is particularly ill-equipped to respond to post-industrial structural change caused by increased international competition, transformation of the world of work, ageing, and family change. Moreover, the continental model is confronted with important obstacles to reform of its own making. There is a widening gap between a diminishing group of 'insiders', who are active and highly productive workers with high wages and expansive social rights, and a growing population of inactive 'outsiders' (elderly workers, women, and youngsters), who remain financially dependent upon either the welfare state or traditional breadwinners. The emergent 'insider–outsider' cleavage effectively blocks labour-market flexibility and undermines the expansion of the service sector, thus forestalling any possibility of increased labour-force participation in domestic services. The insiders, organized in strong, sectorally organized trade unions, will most likely oppose social policy reform initiatives which are geared towards disengaging family dependency on the earnings and social entitlements of the traditional male breadwinner. The likely result is that the existing privileges of the insiders will be safeguarded at the expense of the outsiders and a tremendous waste of human capital.

To what extent has the proverbial continental welfare state regime of the Netherlands followed Esping-Andersen's scenario of 'welfare without work'? Or does Dutch labour-market performance contradict the continental pathology of declining activity and rising inactivity?

In terms of job creation, the Netherlands today is Europe's undisputed champion. At a rate of 1.8 per cent per year on average since 1983, Dutch job growth is four times the average for the European Union (see Table 7.2). Unemployment has come down from an all-time record in 1984 to less than 6 per cent in 1997, while the EU average remained at over 11 per cent (see Table 7.3). In contrast to the American 'jobs machine', Dutch job growth is less associated with a sharp increase in earnings inequality. Inequality has increased but the Netherlands has been able to maintain a middle rank between Germany and Scandinavian countries, on the one hand, and Britain and the USA on the other (see Figure 7.1). The Dutch response to the continental crisis of inactivity is best described in terms of a process of policy-learning (Visser and Hemerijck 1997). A number of interrelated developments stand out in the Dutch experience of policy-learning. These are: (1) protracted wage moderation; (2) labour-time reduction; (3) social-security reform;

TABLE 7.2. *Employment growth in the Netherlands, the EU, and selected OECD countries*

	1983–93	1994	1995	1996	1997*
Netherlands	1.8	0.8	2.4	1.9	2.0
EU	0.4	−0.7	0.5	0.1	0.4
Belgium	0.5	−0.7	0.3	0.1	0.5
Germany**	0.7	−1.8	−0.3	−1.2	−0.9
France	0.1	−0.4	0.9	−0.2	0.2
Denmark	0.2	1.2	1.6	1.0	1.3
Sweden	−0.6	−0.7	1.6	−0.6	−0.4
UK	0.6	1.2	0.8	0.5	1.3
USA	1.8	3.2	1.5	1.4	2.3

Source: OECD, *Employment Outlook*, issues of July 1994 and July 1997 (Paris: Organization of Economic Co-operation and Development).
* Projection.
** Until 1993 West Germany only.

TABLE 7.3. *Unemployment in the Netherlands, the EU, and selected OECD countries*

	1983	1990	1993	1994	1995	1996
Netherlands	9.7	6.2	6.6	7.1	6.9	6.3
EU**	9.2	8.5	10.6	11.4	11.1	11.5
Belgium	11.1	6.7	8.9	10.1	9.9	9.8
Germany*	7.7	4.8	7.9	8.4	8.2	9.0
France	8.1	9.0	11.7	12.3	11.7	12.4
Denmark	—	7.7	10.1	8.2	7.1	6.0
Sweden	3.9	1.8	9.5	9.8	9.2	10.0
UK	11.1	7.1	10.5	9.6	8.8	8.2
USA	9.6	5.6	6.9	6.1	5.6	5.4

Source: OECD, *Employment Outlook*, issues of July 1996 and July 1997 (Paris: Organization of Economic Co-operation and Development), table A.
* Until 1993 West Germany only.
** Not standardized (commonly used definition, see *Employment Outlook* (1997), table B).

(4) the growth of part-time jobs; (5) the popularity of temporary jobs; and (6) a record increase in female labour-market participation.

Real wage moderation, agreed in collective bargaining at the sectoral level by trade-union and employers' representatives, has contributed to curbing wage costs over the past fifteen years. Inaugurated by a major Social Accord, concluded between central union and employers federations in 1982, the sustained policy of wage moderation has helped to preserve and create jobs. Wage

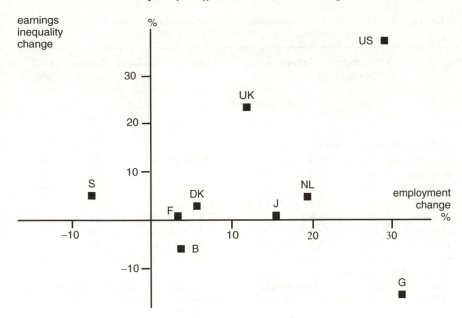

FIGURE 7.1. Employment growth and changes in earnings inequality in the
Netherlands and selected OECD countries, 1982–1995

Source: Roorda and Vogels 1997

moderation has had an especially favourable impact on employment in sectors
that produce mainly for the domestic market, making low-wage, labour-
intensive production again profitable. Wage moderation has also helped to
improve the price competitiveness of Dutch industry (see Table 7.4). Because
of continued appreciations of the guilder, the level of inflation has been sup-
pressed, which, in turn, had a favourable effect on domestic wage trends.
Dutch exporters have therefore been able to preserve their shares in world
markets, contributing to employment and output growth. The concerted
strategy of wage moderation entailed two political exchanges which followed
each other in time and importance: one between workers and employers, the
other with the government. In the first exchange wage moderation was traded
against a modest reduction in annual and weekly working hours. Dutch trade
unions have been able to shorten the average working week for full-time
workers from forty hours in the first half of the 1980s to thirty-eight hours in
1987. Although the trade unions have been aiming at a thirty-two-hour
working week, progress in labour-time reduction stalled in many sectors after
a 5 per cent reduction in working time. Labour-time reduction has positively
affected job growth, especially in small and medium-size firms.

   In the second exchange, between the social partners and the government,

TABLE 7.4. *Labour costs in manufacturing in the Netherlands and in selected OECD countries, changes 1980–1994, and 1994 levels*

	% change in labour costs per hour (DM)			Level	Indirect costs as % of direct labour costs	Labour costs*	Unit labour costs**
	1980–9	1989–94	1980–94	1994			
Netherlands	31.3	19.8	57.5	DM 34.87	80	79	89
Belgium	24.3	28.1	59.2	DM 37.35	94	85	90
Germany	54.9	30.6	102.4	DM 43.97	82	100	100
Denmark	40.9	19.5	68.4	DM 34.41	22	78	93
Sweden	43.9	−6.8	34.1	DM 31.00	70	71	94
UK	61.4	13.4	63.1	DM 22.06	40	50	106
USA	59.1	5.8	68.3	DM 27.97	43	64	99

Source: SZW 1996a: tables 2.1–2.3.
* Index total labour costs per hour worked in manufacturing (see column 4), Germany = 100.
** Index of total labour costs per unit produced in manufacturing, Germany = 100.

which gained more prominence in the late 1980s, wage restraint was compensated by lower taxes and social charges, made possible not only by improved public finances and a broader tax base as a result of record job growth but also by hard-won social-security reform. The sharp increase in unemployment in the early 1980s had saddled the Dutch welfare state with a serious fiscal imbalance. The public deficit increased from 5.2 per cent in 1975 to 10.7 per cent in 1988. The initial measures, including a freeze of benefits, tightening of eligibility to programmes, a reduction of the duration of benefits and lowering of maximum entitlements of earnings-related benefits from 80 to 70 per cent, did bring about initial cost-savings but were partly undone through collective bargaining and could not stop the rise of inactivity throughout the 1980s. In 1989 the centre-left Lubbers–Kok government announced a policy package of financial incentives aimed to discourage the use of the sick leave and disability schemes. Beneficiaries already enrolled in the disability scheme were to be re-examined on the basis of these more stringent rules. In early 1993 parliament agreed to a reduction in the level of benefits and a shortening of the duration of coverage of new claimants. These harsh measures provoked widespread protests and nearly wiped out the two political parties—Christian Democrats and Labour—who took responsibility for them in the 1994 general elections. Both coalition parties lost about a third of their electoral support in the elections. Ironically, because the Labour Party, overtaking the hegemony held by Christian Democracy in Dutch politics since 1918, became the largest party, Labour leader Mr Wim Kok was able to forge

TABLE 7.5. *Incidence of part-time employment in selected OECD countries, by sex, 1973–1996*

	Men			Women		
	1983	1990	1996	1983	1990	1996
Netherlands	6.8	14.8	16.1	22.0	36.4	38.0
Belgium	2.0	2.0	3.0	19.7	25.9	30.5
West Germany	1.7	2.6	3.6*	30.0	33.8	33.8*
France	2.5	3.3	5.3	20.1	23.6	29.5
Denmark	6.5	10.4	10.8	43.7	38.4	34.5
Sweden	6.2	7.4	9.3	45.9	40.0	39.0
UK	3.3	5.2	5.6	41.3	44.3	42.7
USA	10.8	10.1	10.9	28.1	25.2	26.9

Source: OECD, *Emplyment Outlook 1997* (Paris: Organization of Economic Co-operation and Development), July 1997, Table E.
* Figures for 1995.

a new coalition government with the Liberals of the right and the centre. The Kok administration, despite popular discontent, stepped up social-security reform. In 1996 the sickness scheme was transferred to the private sector, on the basis of very stringent public rules with respect to levels and duration of benefits. The possibility of opting out of the public disability system is foreseen in the future.

The extraordinary growth in part-time jobs has contributed to the massive entry of women in the labour force, and the replacement of older workers by younger, cheaper, and possibly more flexible and skilled workers. With some delay, the Dutch trade unions have come around in support of these changes and taken a positive attitude towards part-time employment and flexibility. The share of part-time work has surged from less than 15 per cent in 1975 to 35 per cent in 1994, a share well above that of any other OECD country. Of all part-time employment, 75 per cent of jobs are held by women: 63 per cent of all female workers are employed part-time. The incidence of part-time work among men is at 16 per cent the highest among OECD countries (see Table 7.5). The EU 15 average of male part-time employment is only 5 per cent. The Netherlands has the highest rate of part-timers among young people in Europe (25 per cent). This suggests that entry into the labour market is commonly channelled through part-time work.

Next, the use of temporary work agencies in the Netherlands is the most extensive in the OECD area. The numbers of hours supplied through these offices has more than tripled over the past decade, with over 10 per cent of all workers currently employed holding temporary jobs (see Table 7.6).

TABLE 7.6. *Incidence of temporary jobs in the Netherlands and major OECD countries, 1983–1994 (% of all employees in paid jobs)*

	1983	1990	1994
Netherlands	5.8	7.6	10.9
Belgium	5.4	5.3	5.1
West Germany	—	10.5	10.3
France	3.3	10.5	21.0
Denmark	—	10.8	12.0
Sweden	—	9.7	13.5
UK	5.5	5.2	6.5

Source: OECD, *Empolyment Outlook 1996*. (Paris: Organization of Economic Co-operation and Development) July 1996.

TABLE 7.7. *Employment/population ratios by sex in the Netherlands, the EU, and selected OECD countries*

	Men			Women		
	1983	1990	1996	1983	1990	1996
Netherlands	69.1	76.2	76.6	34.7	47.0	55.0
EU*	75.8	74.2	69.8	42.9	46.7	48.4
Belgium	70.4	67.3	67.3	36.6	41.0	45.8
Germany**	76.6	76.4	73.4	47.8	52.8	54.3
France	74.4	70.4	67.2	49.7	50.6	52.1
Denmark	78.4	82.5	81.4	65.2	71.5	67.8
Sweden	84.7	86.9	74.7	75.5	81.8	70.6
UK	78.7	83.7	77.7	55.3	63.7	64.1
USA	78.9	83.1	82.3	57.7	65.8	68.1

Source: OECD, *Employment Outlook*, issues of July 1996 and July 1997, (Paris: Organization of Economic Co-operation and Development), tables B and C.
* Not standardized (commonly used definition), see *Employment Outlook* (1997), table B.
** West Germany until 1993.

The growth of female participation is perhaps the most dramatic development in the Dutch labour market's dramatic improvement. Female labour-force participation was extremely low in the Netherlands in comparison to most OECD countries. Participation of women in the labour market increased from under 35 per cent in 1983 to 55 per cent in 1996 (see Table 7.7). The growth in labour-force participation is concentrated among women who are either married or cohabiting: they now represent a quarter of the active labour

TABLE 7.8. *Average annual working hours per employee in the Netherlands and selected OECD countries*

	1973	1979	1983	1990	1996*
Netherlands	1,724	1,591	1,530	1,433	1,372
West Germany	1,804	1,699	1,686	1,562	1,508
France	1,771	1,667	1,558	1,539	1,529
Sweden*	1,557	1,451	1,453	1,480	1,554
UK*	1,929	1,821	1,719	1,773	1,732
USA	1,896	1,884	1,866	1,936	1,951

Source: OECD, *Employment Outlook*, 1997 (Paris: Organization of Economic Co-operation and Development), July 1997, Table G.
* Total employment.

force. The majority of working women find employment in the commercial and non-commercial service sectors. The demand for a flexible workforce in the service sector agrees with general preference of women for part-time work. As a consequence of the increase in labour-market participation of women, there is also a growing interest in part-time work on the part of men, so as to combine gainful employment work with unpaid family care.

Following protracted wage moderation, labour-time reduction, increase in part-time, and temporary work, and the surge in female market participation, average annual working hours per worker have come down significantly since 1973 (see Table 7.8). However, net labour-market participation has increased from 52 per cent to 64 per cent from 1983 to 1994. To be sure, it should be emphasized that, in terms of participation in full-time equivalents, the rate in the Netherlands, at 50 per cent, is still lower than in neighbouring countries (Table 7.9).

Hard-won social security reform, initially opposed by the unions, and the revived confidence in negotiated adjustment, endorsed by unions and employers, gradually concurred with a general shift in the definition of the alleged crisis of the Dutch welfare state. Policy-makers came to realize that the low level of labour-market participation was the Achilles' heel of the continental system of social protection. Gradually, the central policy objective of fighting unemployment by subsidizing easy exit and reducing entry was replaced by maximizing the rate of labour participation and is now embraced by the government and the social partners alike. In addition, the Minister of Social Affairs and Employment, Mr Ad Melkert, has introduced a series of special programmes geared towards the reintegration of unskilled and low-paid workers. This late inauguration of an active labour-market policy stance appears to have had modest success in bringing down youth and long-term unemployment.

Anton Hemerijck

TABLE 7.9. *Net labour participation (employment as % of population between 15 and 64)*

Country	Persons		Standardized labour years of 1,800 hours	
	1983	1994*	1983	1994*
Netherlands	52	64	44	50
Belgium	55	56	—	—
Germany	62	63	60	55
Denmark	72	74	—	—
Sweden	79	70	63	60
UK	64	67	—	63
USA	66	73	66	72
Japan	71	74	83	79

Source: OECD, 1995*b*: 204, table A. Labour years based on SZW calculations based on this source: employment in labour years is calculated by multiplying the ratio of the average number of hours worked per person by a standard labour year of 1,800 hours (SZW, 1996*a*).
* 1993 for United Kingdom.

In terms of performance, the Dutch experience, currently praised by many observers, flies in the face of Esping-Andersen's scenario of the continental pathology of 'welfare without work'. However, all that glistens is not gold. The present state of nearly full part-time employment may be judged a second-best solution only. The current low unemployment rate of under 6 per cent does not reflect the true state of slack in the Dutch labour market. The level of structural inactivity, although declining in absolute and relative terms, including all unemployed and inactive persons of working age receiving a social-security benefit and persons enrolled in special job-creation programmes, remains high at 20 per cent of the current labour force. New jobs have gone predominantly to younger and better skilled recruits to the labour market and many are part-time, sometimes for a limited number of hours only. Inactivity is concentrated among the low skilled, older workers, immigrants, and women. The participation rate of older males, between the age of 55 and 64, before legal retirement, has dropped to one of the lowest in Europe. The rate long-term unemployment has started to decrease but is still, at about 50 per cent, extremely high by international standards (see Table 7.10).

Considering Policy Alternatives

Towards the end of the twentieth century there is much anxiety over the future of the advanced welfare state based a universalist rights-based conception of

TABLE 7.10. *Long-term unemployment in the Netherlands and selected OECD countries (% unemployed longer than 12 months)*

	1983	1990	1996
Netherlands	48.8	49.3	49.0
Belgium	64.8	68.7	61.3
West Germany	41.6	46.8	48.3*
France	42.2	38.0	39.5
Denmark	44.3	30.0	26.5
Sweden	10.3	4.7	17.1
UK	45.6	34.2	39.8
USA	13.3	5.5	9.5

Source: OECD, *Employment Outlook 1996* (Paris: Organization of Economic Co-operation and Development, 1996).
* Figure for 1995.

social citizenship, formulated by T. H. Marshall fifty years ago. Critics point out that post-war social policy has accumulated a vast array of rigidities which impede flexible adjustment, block technological innovation, and hamper necessary economic and employment growth. From this kind of diagnosis, the obvious recipe is to scale down the ambitions of social policy by way of curtailing the level, content, and scope of social rights. Encouraged by the American job-machine miracle, the OECD recommended European policy-makers to deregulate their labour markets, abolish or lower minimum wages, scale back social security, and give up progressive taxation (OECD 1994). European policy-makers, however, are reluctant to follow the American example of recommodifying labour, as the unparalleled expansion of jobs in the US economy has been accompanied by the emergence of an underclass of 'working poor' who are unable to acquire a decent standard of living through regular earnings. But is there really any choice? Are there alternative policies, conceivable, functional, feasible, fair, and sustainable, through which the inactive of continental Europe would not have to bear the brunt in terms of increased poverty or inequality? The persistently high level of unemployment in the European Union, affecting more than eighteen million citizens, and the concurrent steep rise in the volume of inactivity, provides ample evidence that the days of the comprehensive welfare state are numbered.

The challenge of social policy lies in the need to find novel ways of linking Marshall's normative aim of 'equal social worth' to programmes and institutions which are able to respond to the new rules of global competition, deal with the new shape of working life, and answer for the new realities of family life and the predicament of demographic ageing. For universalist social rights to be effective, we have to consider policy, to strike the right balance of policy instruments, institutions, and idea(l)s, in relation to a number of structural changes which have fundamentally recast the social and economic environment of welfare states over the past twenty years. It should be emphasized that for our purposes policy options have to be considered from two angles. From a citizenship perspective, policy alternatives should not merely be adequate to the problem at hand: they have to be rated in terms of their citizenship content. Social policy is only citizenship-related when it is based on rights and universalism. From this perspective, one constraint remains highly relevant: the 'right to work' as a right of social citizenship cannot be effectively guaranteed in a market economy (Elster 1988). The right to work may be anchored in a qualified public commitment to help provide the opportunities to earn a living wage for citizens who need and demand it, which can be underpinned by an 'active labour-market policy' but in a capitalist economy the right to work is overwhelmingly dependent for its implementation upon the voluntary co-operation of autonomously employing firms.

In the academic debate over the prospects for effective social citizenship, two diametrically opposed policy proposals are often advocated. These are the policy of 'workfare' policies and the proposal for a 'citizen's income'. Workfare policies are designed to strengthen and repair the conditional links between work and income, which have been lost with expansion of the welfare state. As such, workfare involves a form of forced labour or community care in exchange for public assistance and welfare services. For Lawrence Mead, an ardent defender of workfare, it serves the purpose of 'remoralising' the welfare state (Mead 1986). He here largely follows Bell's diagnosis of the demise of the work ethic in the welfare state. Welfare recipients must be obliged to accept 'employment as a duty' in order to receive benefits. Mead's normative claim is that (undeserving) recipients, who do not actively seek work and refuse to partake in job-training programmes, should have their social benefits taken away from them. In mere practical terms, workfare programmes, as they mostly involve additional public-sector employment initiatives, are rather expensive. They require intensive efforts of supervision and implementation. Most successful are policies of vocational training and education that focus on marketable skills, along the lines of Swedish active labour-market policies. However, many additional public-sector job programmes, based on a workfare philosophy, have not been all that successful in achieving lasting integration of disadvantaged groups into the regular labour market. Not only is it particularly difficult actually to reach disadvantaged groups, but turnover from workfare programmes to regular employment proves to be problematic. Many initiatives appear to result in 'dead-end' solutions, which is demoralizing for participants and policy-makers alike. Far more important from a citizenship perspective is that Mead's policy option of workfare fails to meet the citizenship criteria of rights and universalism. In fact, the citizenship content is completely lost in Mead's proposal selectively to put the deserving poor to work for the sake of remoralizing mainstream society.

The foremost advocate of an unconditional citizen's income, in line with the principles of individual liberty and equal treatment, is Philippe Van Parijs (Parijs 1991, 1992, 1995). A basic income, a right to real income, due to material standards prevailing in society, is granted as a universal right to all citizens as a component of their citizenship. This is clearly perfectly compatible with citizenship. In fact, it represents an extreme form of citizenship in terms of rights and universalism. A basic income fundamentally recasts the role of the welfare state. Central to a citizen's income policy is the fundamental disengagement of real income entitlements from employment status, wage-earning conditions, and the readiness actively to seek employment. Instead of providing income support for inactive workers and their families, social protection would take place outside the labour market.

By endowing every person with wealth, basic-income protagonists argue that government could quit the business of providing social welfare, since individual citizens would be able to take care of themselves (Veen and Pels 1995). To be sure, a basic income helps to reduce the costs of social policy administration and implementation, and is likely to curtail fraud. But despite these cost reductions, an unconditional basic income, given to all adult citizens, at the level of the present standards of a social minimum, would be extremely expensive. A large number of citizens who are at present neither engaged in gainful employment nor receiving conditional social-security benefits—think for example of housewives—would be entitled to a basic income. A less expansive alternative would be a 'negative income tax', which is more narrowly targeted on the needy. But both the unconditional basic income and the negative income tax require far-reaching restructuring of present system of taxation, social assistance, social insurance, pensions, and wage setting, incurring massive transformation costs of regime change.

While the advocates of workfare policies believe in the prospect of the return of full employment as we know it, protagonists of a basic income policy, by contrast, argue that a return to full employment is wholly unrealistic. Claus Offe strongly defends a basic-income strategy on the presupposition that the restoration of traditional full employment, as a consequence of 'jobless growth' is illusory, economically undesirable, ecologically indefensible, and socially unacceptable (Offe 1996, 1997; Dore 1994). Under conditions of jobless growth, a basic income makes it possible for people to participate more in voluntary activities beyond the sphere of gainful employment, such as community care and learning.

For radical policy alternatives, like the introduction of an unconditional basic income, to be adopted, they not only have to be 'adequate to the problem' at hand, they also have to be normatively 'acceptable' to the citenzenry at large. It remains difficult to translate Parijs's 'right to surf' in a normatively convincing way to a world in which people's real-life understanding of social justice and reciprocity is rooted in conditional social policy (Jordan 1989). Large majorities in advanced welfare states of the European Union repudiate the 'something for nothing' philosophy that a basic-income policy seems to endorse.

Given the financial constraints faced by present systems of social security and the lack of normative support for a basic-income alternative, in face of massive administrative and institutional uncertainty, it is rather unlikely that the introduction of an unconditional citizen's income will be implemented in the near future. On the whole, policy-makers and mainstream political parties in the European Union favour workfare strategies (Weir 1992; King 1995).

Rather than proposing a fundamental overhaul of the contemporary welfare state, many of the financial constraints and moral scepticism with respect to a basic-income policy can be avoided, however, by a modest, less costly, and more feasible policy option. For the continental welfare state of Germany, Fritz Scharpf has, in a number of recent publications, suggested employing the logic of a negative income tax, in the form of regressive wage subsidies, to create a low-wage job-intensive sector in the fight against inactivity (Scharpf 1995, 1997a, 1997b, 1997c). Wage subsidies for low-earning workers, Scharpf believes, are likely to encourage the expansion of the low-wage labour market through a reduction of gross wage costs for employers and an increase in take-home pay of low skilled workers. Scharpf's scheme is fully compatible with citizenship, since it is made available as a matter of right, and it does not threaten to undermine social services provision. However, as the proposal is geared towards job creation, it should be emphasized that it hinges on the assumption that jobs are available, a presupposition challenged by most basic-income protagonists. Scharpf maintains that in Germany and other continental welfare states there is a considerable potential for an expansion of low-skilled jobs in services like wholesale and retail trade, personal services, tourism, and recreation. In the USA, where wages are comparatively flexible, there was a considerable increase in low-skilled jobs in the 1980s. In North America the problem is the rising class of 'working poor', who work below the subsistence level. The European dilemma is welfare-dependent inactivity; jobs rather than income. Banking on the large reservoir of social and political support for a comprehensive welfare state in Europe, Scharpf maintains that targeted wage subsidies, following a negative income tax logic, could permit a scenario of 'labour-cheapening' and job growth, without an American style surge in poverty and inequality. As wage subsidies are likely to increase labour demand at the bottom end of the labour market, Scharpf believes that, when successful, subsidies could pay for themselves in terms of reduced outlays for full-time unemployment. Moreover, normatively, Scharpf's proposal of targeted wage subsidies is consistent with the prevailing work ethic. In reply to the kinds of objections raised by Offe, it should be highlighted that the new jobs to be created in personal services are neither confronted with the kind of productivity pressure prevalent in manufacturing in the exposed sector nor do they create environmental problems.

By its very logic, a negative income tax solution contains important advantages for the working of the labour market. Unlike workfare policies, which always revolve around additional public-sector employment programmes, a negative income tax has the advantage of mobilizing private resources. Many job creation and hiring decisions remain in the hands of private firms. In theory, a negative income tax logic provides a comprehensive solution to the poverty trap and the predicament of inactivity, which by analogy with the poverty trap can be called the 'inactivity trap'. The poverty and inactivity traps are perhaps the two most perverse, wholly unintended, effects of post-war social policy, producing a cleavage between full-time employment and full-time inactivity. The poverty trap relates to the condition whereby benefits are cut when people make an effort to increase their disposable income. High marginal tax rates clearly undermine the incentive to work extra hours. The poverty trap is particularly problematic for people who are considering moving from full-time welfare dependency to part-time or temporary employment. The inactivity trap relates to generous and long-term social-security benefits, guaranteed minimum-wage requirements, tied to productivity levels, and an adequate level of social assistance. The inactivity trap can be understood as a productivity trap: the minimum level of productivity of a potential job seeker in Germany and the Netherlands is, due to the structure of the welfare state, considerably higher than that in the USA. The inactivity trap engenders important disincentives for employers considering the hiring of less productive, low-skilled workers. Both the poverty and the inactivity traps produce 'lock-in' effects, cutting a substantial number of people off from labour-market opportunities.

Targeted wage subsidies can help overcome the perverse effects of being trapped in poverty and inactivity. It could encourage the utilization of low-skilled workers, while countering the emergence of a large population of 'working poor' who are compelled to work overtime to achieve incomes that remain below the poverty level. There are essentially two policy options for targeted wage subsidies. Permanent income subsidies can be provided to workers or employers. One could give a tax credit to individual workers or, alternatively, one could reduce social security charges for employers. For the Anglo-American welfare states, where unemployment benefits are low and of short duration, individual tax credits and social services to support workers and their families who work for wages below the poverty line would be most appropriate. Earnings-related subsidies to working families, the so-called 'Earned Income Tax Credit', is currently the largest assistance programme for low-income American citizens (Haveman 1995). Similar programmes have been introduced in Canada, the United Kingdom, Ireland, and Australia (Atkinson 1995). For the advanced welfare states of continental Europe, which guarantee levels of minimum-income protection above the subsistence level though social security and social asssistance, it is more appropriate to subsidize the employers who are willing to hire low-skilled workers. Here the solution to the predicament of structural inactivity should be accompanied with a reduction of non-wage labour costs, that is, the social-security contributions, of employers hiring low-skilled workers.

Notwithstanding the favourable verdict of wage subsidies following a negative income tax logic, it is important to mention a few practical difficulties. As long as policies of this kind are part of a special scheme, they are likely to be limited in their impact and will evidently require constant policy initiatives. When they become general, on the other hand, they are liable to massive abuse by employers, who can simply lower their wage rate without necessarily creating new jobs. Furthermore, a policy alternative of lowering social-security contributions for employers hiring low-skilled workers could have a considerable unintended disincentive effect on the educational ambitions of young people, who might think that they stood a better chance of getting a job if they had low skills. A more serious objection is how public finances lost by cutting employers' social-security contributions would be compensated for. For reasons of globalization there has in recent years been a shift in the burden of taxation away from capital on to labour. This tendency to increase the tax burden on workers could lead to tax resistance, which in turn would incite mainstream political parties to compete on the basis of their ambitions to cut taxes, with the result of reducing public spending at the expense of the quality of welfare citizenship. It is possible that consideration will have to be given to taxing firms, not on the basis of the employees they hire, but in terms of the capital, equipment, and energy they use and the kinds of environmental damage they engender.[1]

Conclusion

The post-war welfare state is founded on the normative principle of protecting vulnerable citizens—the aged, the sick, the unemployed—from poverty and from social and political marginalization. While Marshall could assume stable families and properly functioning male labour markets, today's social policy-makers have to answer for demographic ageing, less stable families, the new shape of working life and the new realities of double-income households, and the new rules of global competition. The Dutch experience, highlighted above, gives reason for moderate optimism. It reveals that, despite constraints,

[1] I am grateful to Colin Crouch for these observations.

there is still considerable scope for maintaining a comprehensive welfare state. While the modernization of the Dutch welfare state is still incomplete, there are some useful lessons that can be drawn.

First of all, the Dutch success of sustained economic growth, low inflation, responsible wage moderation, extraordinary full-time, part-time, and tempo-rary, job-creation, together with a revolutionary increase in female labour-force participation, accompanied by important social policy reform, represents a significant departure from the scenario of 'welfare without work' so typical of the continental welfare state, given its particular mode of financ-ing social security. The Dutch experience reveals that wage moderation, after a first phase of boosting competitiveness in the exposed sector, can help to create more jobs in personal services, reduce the number of people depend-ing on social benefits and hence reduce the social wage component, allowing the government to use the improved public finances to lower the tax and con-tribution wedge at or near the minimum and get more unskilled workers back into jobs.

Second, the Dutch job miracle largely contradicts the spectre of jobless growth, on the basis of which many observers advocate a basic income. The Dutch policy priority of maximizing employment opportunities for everyone appears realistic. To be sure, this implies what might be judged to be a second-best solution: a shift away from the traditional expectation of full employment on the basis of full-time working hours and lifetime, open-ended employment contracts for men, towards more varied ways of combining paid employment, family responsibilities, education, and leisure for both men and women at dif-ferent stages of their lives. The growth of double-earner families is a positive trend as it reduces the households' narrow dependency on one 'family wage' and breadwinner's job security, and also because two-income families are the best defence against child poverty.

Third, evidence from the Netherlands challenges the intuitively appealing cultural thesis of the erosion of the work ethic as a consequence of the decou-pling of work and income by way of social policy. Gainful employment remains an important source of social integration and economic indepen-dence for both men and women. People seek gainful employment, not merely to earn a living, but also for reasons of security, social status, prestige, com-panionship, and engagement in collective purposes. Studies of the experience of unemployment essentially confirm this state of affairs, which, however, does not imply that the work ethic has remained unchanged. Overall, work-related values have undergone a transition from the biblical (Calvinist) obligation in a calling to the more broadly endorsed norm of social participation through paid work. To be sure, consumerist elements have also entered the work ex-perience. For these reasons, a majority (65 per cent) of the Dutch population reject an unconditional basic-income scheme (SCP 1994: 230).

On the whole, over the past twenty years, the Dutch welfare state has adapted to the new realities of post-industrial working life and family relations with a surge of voluntary part-time work, including larger numbers of men working in part-time jobs, the revolutionary increase in female participation, and the rapid expansion of the service sector. This is significant, because the Dutch welfare state, as a specimen of continental social security, is generally believed to be hardest type to change!

In order to maintain the universal and rights-based conception of social citizenship, changes are necessary in the design of social security. In particular, the paradigmatic shift in the world of work and the world at home in a globalizing economy implies a refocusing on achieving a new balance between flexibility and security. On both sides of the Atlantic Ocean, social policy has to respond to the universal downward shift in the demand for low-skilled work, especially in internationally exposed sectors, as a consequence of globalization and technological change (Ehrenberg 1994; SZW 1996*b*; Snower and Dehesa 1997). Two policy avenues which may help to increase employment opportunities for the low-skilled are relevant. First, policies geared towards raising the quality of the workforce, through vocational education and training, are likely to reduce the number of less skilled workers. However, increasing the employability of disadvantaged groups through training and education is not a recipe for everyone. A truly positive-sum solution, however, requires, as well as a social investment strategy, a concerted policy effort to increase the chances of low-skilled workers in the regular labour market by making less productive work economically viable. A further crystallization of wage subsidy arrangements, along the rights-based proposal suggested by Fritz Scharpf, ranging from family credits to reduce the poverty of workers accepting low-wage jobs to employer-based reductions of social-security contributions, could stimulate the demand for low-productivity work, and thus help to curtail the poverty and inactivity traps inherent in traditional social policy regulation. This could open up a wide range of additional, economically viable employment opportunities at the lower end of the labour market, which would allow the less skilled, less productive workers to be absorbed in a labour market of easy-entry jobs, which are currently unavailable in most European welfare states. So far continental welfare states have been slow to expand in this direction. However, in the Netherlands we can observe a gradual policy shift away from workfare experiments (labour pools, youth work guarantee plans) towards fiscal measures to subsidize low-paid employment at the bottom end of the labour market. Minister Melkert has significantly reduced employers' wage costs, through reductions in taxes and social-security contributions, instigating a decline in the tax wedge for employers who hire the long-term unemployed. These reductions can add up to as much as 25 per cent of the annual wage. An employer hiring someone who has been out of work for a year or more, who will earn less than 130 per cent of the minimum wage, does not have to pay social-security contributions for a four-year period (Visser and Hemerijck 1997: 173–6).

Additional policy measures should make it easier for people to move in and out of employment, maximizing opportunities for labour flexibility and job mobility. This can be achieved through the introduction of a legal right to work part-time, also for elderly workers, and the right to take sabbaticals and other more differentiated forms of leave, such as educational leave, parental leave, and care leave, whereby temporary vacancies are filled by unemployed persons hired on a fixed-term contract. Policies of voluntary inactivity, in turn, are likely further to increase the demand for part-time and temporary jobs. Also workfare policies of public employment, following the Swedish example—not the Anglo-American version which fails to meet the basic citizenship criteria of rights and universalism—remain relevant as a bridge to regular employment, especially for the young.

The current predicament of structural inactivity not only adds to the fiscal crisis of the welfare state, it reinforces labour-market segmentation. By contrast, activating welfare policies that put men and women into work, help households to harmonize work and family obligations and train the population in the kinds of skills that the modern economy demands, strengthens, in words of Marshall, the 'loyalty to a civilization which is a common possession' (Marshall 1963: 101). If the underlying normative criterion is to counter involuntary inactivity and poverty, there is all the more reason to support rights-based policies which are likely to result in an increase in labour-force participation and a decrease in hours worked, which in due course could foster a more nuanced and relaxed work ethic.

REFERENCES

ALLAART, P. C., KUNNEN, R., PRAAT, W. C. M., VOOGD-HAMELINK, A. M., and VOSSE, J.-P. M. (1993). *Trendrapport aanbod van arbeid* (The Hague: OSA-rapport 12).

ARENDT, H. (1958). *The Human Condition* (Chicago: University of Chicago Press).

ATKINSON, A. B. (1995). 'On Targeting and Family Benefits', in A. B. Atkinson (ed.), *Incomes and the Welfare State: Essays on Britain and Europe* (Cambridge: Cambridge University Press), 223–61.

BARBER, B. R. (1984). *Strong Democracy: Participatory Politics for a New Age* (Berkeley, Calif.: University of California Press).

BEINER, R. (1995). 'Why Citizenship Constitutes a Theoretical Problem in the Last Decade of the Twentieth Century', in R. Beiner (ed.), *Theorizing Citizenship* (Albany, NY: State University of New York Press), 1–28.

BELL, D. (1976). *The Cultural Contradictions of Capitalism* (London: Heinemann).

BELLAH, R. N., MADSEN, R., SULLIVAN, W. M., SWIDLER, A., and TIPTON, S. M. (1985). *Habits of the Heart: Individualism and Commitment in American Life* (New York: Harper & Row).

BENDIX, R. (1964). *Nation-Building and Citizenship: Studies of our Changing Social Order* (Berkeley, Calif.: University of California Press).

BULMER, M., and REES, A. M. (eds.) (1996). *Citizenship Today: The Contemporary Relevance of T. H. Marshall* (London: UCL Press).

CULPITT, I. (1992). *Welfare and Citizenship: Beyond the Crisis of the Welfare State* (London: Sage).

DORE, R. (1994). 'Incurable Unemployment: A Progressive Disease of Modern Society?', *The Political Quarterly*, 65: 285–302.

EHRENBERG, R. G. (1994). *Labor Market and Integrating National Economies* (Washington, DC: Brookings Institution).

ELSTER, J. (1988). 'Is there (or should there be) a Right to Work', in A. Gutmann (ed.), *Democracy and the Welfare State* (Princeton: Princeton University Press), 53–78.

ENGBERSEN, G. (1990). *Publieke Bijstandsgeheimen: Het ontstaan van een onderklassein Nederland* (Leiden and Antwerp: Stenfert Kroese).

ESPING-ANDERSEN, G. (1990). *The Three Worlds of Welfare Capitalism* (Princeton: Princeton University Press).

—— (1996). 'Welfare States Without Work: The Impasse of Labour Shedding and Familianism in Continental European Welfare States', in G. Esping-Andersen (ed.), *Welfare States in Transition* (London: Sage), 66–87.

ESTER, P., and HALMAN, L. (eds.) (1994). *De cultuur van de verzorgingsstaat: Een sociologisch onderzoek naar waardenorintaties in Nederland* (Tilburg: Tilburg University Press).

ETZIONI, A. (1993). *The Spirit of Community: Rights, Responsibilities and the Communitarian Agenda* (New York: Crown Publications).

FLORA, P. (ed.) (1987). *Growth to Limits: The Western European Welfare State since World War II* (Berlin and New York: de Gruyter).

GUNSTEREN, H. (1992). *Eigentijds burgerschap* (The Hague: WRR).

HABERMAS, J. (1992). 'Citizenship and National Identity: Some Reflections on the Future of Europe', *Praxis International*, 12/1: 1–19.

HAVEMAN, R. (1995). *Reducing Poverty While Increasing Employment* (Paris: OECD).

JAHODA, M. (1982). *Employment and Unemployment: A Socio-Psychological Analysis* (Cambridge: Cambridge University Press).

—— LAZARSFELD, P., and ZEISL, H. (1972 [1933]). *Marienthal: The Sociography of an Unemployed Community* (London: Tavistock).

JORDAN, B. (1989). *The Common Good: Citizenship, Morality, and Self-Interest* (Oxford: Basil Blackwell).

KING, D. S. (1995). *Actively Seeking Work? The Politics of Unemployment and Welfare Policy in the United States and Great Britain* (Chicago: University of Chicago Press).

KROFT, H., ENGBERSEN, G., SCHUYT, K., and WAARDEN, F. (1989). *Een tijd zonder werk: een onderzoek naar de levenswereld van langdurig werklozen* (Leiden and Antwerp: Steufert Kroese).

KYMLICKA, W., and NORMAN, W. (1995). 'Return of Citizen: A Survey of Recent Work on Citizenship Theory', in R. Beiner (ed.), *Theorizing Citizenship* (Albany, NY: State University of New York Press), 283–322.

LASCH, C. (1979). *The Culture of Narcissim* (London: Abacus).

MACINTYRE, A. (1988). *Whose Justice? Which Rationality?* (London: Duckworth).

MARSHALL, G. (1982). *In Search of the Spirit of Capitalism: An Essay on Max Weber's Protestant Ethic Thesis* (London: Hutchinson).

MARSHALL, T. H. (1963). *Sociology at the Crossroads, and Other Essays* (London: Heinemann).

——(1981). *The Right to Welfare and Other Essays* (London: Heinemann).

MEAD, L. M. (1986). *Beyond Entitlement: The Social Obligations of Citizenship* (New York: Free Press).

MEEHAN, E. (1993). *Citizenship and the European Community* (London: Sage).

OECD (1994). *The OECD Job Study, Evidence and Explanations: Part 1 and 2* (Paris: OECD).

OFFE, C. (1985). 'Work: The Key Sociological Category?', in C. Offe (ed.), *Disorganized Capitalism* (Cambridge: Polity Press), 129–50.

——(1993). 'A Non-Productivist Design for Social Policies', in H. Coenen and P. Leisink (eds.), *Work and Citizenship in the New Europe* (Cheltenham: Edward Elgar), 215–32.

——(1996). 'A Basic Income Guaranteed by the State: A Need of the Moment in Social Policy', in C. Offe (ed.), *Modernity and the State: East, West* (Cambridge: Polity Press), 201–21.

——(1997). 'Towards a New Equilibrium of Citizens' Rights and Economic Resources', in OECD, *Societal Cohesion and the Globalizing Economy: What Does the Future Hold?* (Paris: OECD), 81–106.

PARIDON, C. W. A. M. (1994). 'Verzorgingsstaten en arbeidsmarktregimes: Een verkenning van de samenhang tussen inactiviteit en arbeidsparticipatie', in G. Engbersen, A. C. Hemerijck, and W. E. Bakker (eds.), *Zorgen in het Europese Huis: Verkenningen over de grenzen van nationale verzorgingsstaten* (Amsterdam: Boom), 89–112.

PARIJS, P. (1991). 'Why Surfers should be Fed: The Liberal Case for an Unconditional Basic Income', *Philosophy and Public Affairs*, 2: 101–31.

——(ed.) (1992). *Arguing for Basic Income: Ethical Foundations for Radical Reform* (London: Verso).

——(1995). *Real Freedom for All: What (if Anything) can Justify Capitalism?* (Oxford: Clarendon Press).

POGGI, G. (1983). *Calvinism and the Spirit of Capitalism* (Amherst, Mass.: University of Massachusetts Press).

ROORDA, W. B., and VOGELS, E. H. W. M. (1997). 'Arbeidsmarkt bescherming en prestaties', *Economisch Statistische Berichten*: 245–8.

SANDEL, M. J. (1982). *Liberalism and the Limits of Justice* (Cambridge: Cambridge University Press).

——(ed.) (1984). *Liberalism and its Critics* (Oxford: Blackwell).

SCHARPF, F. W. (1995). 'Subventionierte Niedriglohn-Beschäftigung statt bezahlter Arbeitslosigkeit', *Zeitschrift für Sozialreform*, 41: 65–82.

——(1997a). 'Economic Integration, Democracy and the Welfare State', *Journal of European Public Policy*, 4: 18–36.

——(1997b). *Employment and the Welfare State: A Continental Dilemma* (MPIfP Working Paper 97/7; Cologne: Max-Planck-Institute for the Study of Societies).

SCHARPF, F. W. (1997c). 'Wege zu mehr Beschäftigung', *Gewerkschaftliche Monatshefte*, 48: 203–16.

SCP (1986). *Sociaal en Cultureel Rapport* (The Hague: Sociaal-Cultureel Planbureau).

——(1992). *Sociaal en Cultureel Rapport* (The Hague: Sociaal-Cultureel Planbureau).

——(1994). *Sociaal en Cultureel Rapport* (The Hague: Sociaal-Cultureel Planbureau).

——(1996). *Sociaal en Cultureel Rapport* (The Hague: Sociaal-Cultureel Planbureau).

SELZNICK, P. (1992). *The Moral Commonwealth: Social Theory and the Promise of Community* (Berkeley, Calif.: University of California Press).

SHKLAR, J. N. (1991). *American Citizenship: The Quest for Inclusion* (Cambridge, Mass.: Harvard University Press).

SNOWER, D. J., and DEHESA, G. (eds.) (1997). *Unemployment Policy: Government Options for the Labour Market* (Cambridge: Cambridge University Press).

STREECK, W. (1995). *German Capitalism: Does it Exist? Can it Survive?* (WZB Papier 95/5; Cologue: Max-Planck-Institut für Gesellschaftsforschung).

SZW (1996a). *De Nederlandse Verzorgingsstaat in Internationaal en Economische Perspectief* (The Hague: Ministerie van Sociale Zaken en Werkgelegenhied).

——(1996b). *Employment and Social Policies under International Constraints* (The Hague: Ministerie van Sociale Zaken en Werkgelegenhied).

TWINE, F. (1994). *Citizenship and Social Rights: The Interdependence of Self and Society* (London: Sage).

VEEN, R.-J., and PELS, D. (eds.) (1995). *Het basisinkomen: Sluitstuk van de verzorgingsstaat* (Amsterdam: Van Gennep).

VISSER, J., and HEMERIJCK, A. (1997). *A Dutch Miracle: Job Growth, Welfare Reform and Corporatism in the Netherlands* (Amsterdam: Amsterdam University Press).

WALZER, M. (1983). *Spheres of Justice: A Defense of Pluralism and Equality* (Oxford: Martin Robertson).

WEBER, M. (1958). *The Protestant Ethic and the Spirit of Capitalism* (New York: Charles Scribner).

WEIR, M. (1992). *Politics and Jobs: The Boundaries of Employment Policy in the United States* (Princeton: Princeton University Press).

II

The Limits of Political Citizenship

8

Citizenship through Direct Democracy? The 'Broken Promises' of Empowerment

Yannis Papadopoulos

Direct Democracy: The Panacea?

It is a well-established tradition in political thought to consider that civic life hardly makes any sense if it does not have a pronounced participatory character. This goes back to Pericles' discourses in the Athenian democracy (or at least as they were reported by Thucydides in *The Peloponnesian Wars*), and later in European history to people like Jean-Jacques Rousseau, Thomas Jefferson, or Victor Considérant. Recent epigones are the members of the participatory school, among whom one can count prominent political thinkers, like Carole Pateman, Crawford Macpherson, Benjamin Barber, Nicos Poulantzas from the French Marxist school, or even Robert Dahl in his later works.

However, it often remains unclear how participatory theorists conceive of the concrete ways to achieve a more sustained involvement of the citizenry in civic affairs. To be sure, a number of them advocate various forms of economic democracy, such as the democratization of decision-making and profit-sharing within the firm. Nevertheless, corporations cannot be assimilated to the public sphere as a whole, and participation in political decisions is not touched, at least directly, by such provisions. Offe and Preuss (1991: 170) argue, in an essay which is of central interest to the questions raised here, that: 'The potential contribution to the formation of "good citizens" of "good schools" or egalitarian industrial relations within an arrangement of "economic democracy" seems limited unless it is complemented by new constitutional procedures which will help to improve the quality of citizens' involvement in the democratic process.'

Thus, I would like to turn to direct democracy as a way to empower people. Although I am aware that not all participatory thinkers would agree with this

option, direct democracy is commonly viewed, if not as an alternative, at least
as a complement to the imperfections of representative democracy. Furthermore, a participatory 'strong' democracy is deemed favourable to the arrival
of 'a spirit of reasonableness' (Barber 1984: 160), and of a 'sense of community' (Graham 1986: 152). In fact, for some theorists, representative democracy hardly approximates the democratic ideal, particularly as in its modern
forms it excludes the binding mandate to elected deputies: 'democracy is too
important to be left to the elite of politicians' (Berry 1989: 58), and 'representation is incompatible with freedom because it delegates and thus
alienates political will at the cost of genuine self-government and autonomy'
(Barber 1984: 145).

I must clarify now that by direct democracy (or direct legislation as it is
phrased in the American literature) I do not have in mind town meetings or
'Landgemeinden' at the local level. I am rather interested in contemporary
forms of non-delegated decision-making which cope with the problem of size,
and which may also exist at a wider level, such as the national or even the
supranational one. For example, frequent referenda at the European level are
considered by Schmitter (1996), one of the most prominent specialists of the
question, as a possible antidote to the present democratic deficit in the 'Euro-
polity'. These procedures are often called semi-direct democracy, indicating
thereby their compromise character with the constraints of large and densely
populated communities. Although this concept covers a wide range of provisions for referenda throughout the world, I select here only the referendary
mechanisms that can be considered at first glance as the most democratic
ones. As I would like to discuss to what degree direct democracy seems compatible with the goal of citizens' empowerment, I think it is useful to focus
strictly on those provisions that cannot be criticized for their élitist or
personalistic orientation. In other words, I concentrate on referenda whose
impulse comes 'from below' and thus cannot be controlled by people in power.
This is the opportunity given to a group of citizens to put on the ballot for
popular ratification decisions that were previously made by governments and
parliaments (popular veto right), or the initiative right that enables a number
of individuals to put proposals on the agenda and have the voters decide
upon them. In the first case we have a vote of control over decisions, in the
second a vote of promotion of new decisions (Uleri 1996: 10–11). In practice,
however, legal provisions sometimes combine both mechanisms.

There are mainly three political systems where one regularly encounters
referendum mechanisms designed as a source of pressure from below, and not
as plebiscitary instruments controlled by the top: in Switzerland, Italy, and the
USA (not in the national level in the latter case). Quite interestingly, citizens
in those countries seem to share with a growing intensity the negative judgement of participatory theorists about the responsive character of representative institutions.

In Switzerland, which has experience of direct democratic mechanisms at all decisional levels for several decades, we note (although this is not a Swiss specificity) growing cynicism about established politics, disenchantment with the performance of politicians, an increasing lack of identification with traditional parties, and mass support for populist leaders. This is also indicated by the steady decline of voters' turnout in federal elections, while direct democracy is highly praised, something which is reflected by a growing participation in referendum votes. These correlations seem quite logical after all: the distrust in parliamentarians, parties, government, and representative democracy as a whole is paralleled by a positive evaluation of direct democracy, as a counterweight to the power of self-interested politicians. Fishkin (1991: 58) detects similar tendencies in the USA: 'in 1990, there were at least sixty seven proposals on state-wide ballots, the largest number since 1932'. In California, which is very familiar with direct democracy, only nine initiatives were put on the ballot during the 1960s, twenty-two in the 1970s, and forty-eight in the 1980s. Also in that state they were increasingly successful: 28 per cent won majorities between 1912 and 1976, 43 per cent between 1976 and 1992 (Kobach 1993: 238). In Italy, thirty-eight votes have taken place since the introduction of the 'referendum abrogativo' at the beginning of the 1970s, but twenty-nine of them since only 1987, and twenty more propositions are pending. This accelerating movement is confirmed by the increasing popular echo of the proposals put on the ballot: although none of them won a majority before 1987, things drastically changed since then. Some findings by Putnam *et al.* (1993: 95–6) can also be interpreted in a similar way, albeit in a synchronic rather than a diachronic perspective. Thus, areas where the turnout in referendum votes is higher than the average in Italy are those where clientelistic identification with politicians (measured by the frequency of the preference vote) is the weakest.

Now, do even these mechanisms of pressure from below really contribute to the democratization of the public sphere and to the empowerment of the citizenry? I would like to introduce a number of qualifications here to that mainstream view, and to show that direct democracy also has its 'broken promises', as Bobbio (1987) said about the overall performance of liberal democracy. Stated differently, I will not here share the dominant criticism about the role of direct democracy, which is rather élitist, as it mainly highlights the turbulence and dysfunctions direct democracy may cause to the steering activities of political élites.[1] By contrast, the main thrust of my argument will be that direct democracy is not necessarily equivalent either to a larger pluralism or to a stronger and more effective peoples' participation where it is practised. Let us now review some of the disillusionment caused by the actual exercise of direct democracy.

---

[1] Although I do not consider that a concern about steering and governance is illegitimate or irrelevant. See Papadopoulos (1995*a*) and particularly concerning direct democracy Papadopoulos (1995*b*).

The Irrelevance of Direct Democracy to Deliberation

A decision by popular vote, even though it involves larger sections of the population than pure parliamentary decision-making and is thus more inclusive than the latter, hardly fulfils the conditions necessary to an ideal deliberative process. This remains the case even if the vote is preceded by a referendum campaign to help people improve their knowledge of the issues, become aware of conflicts between objectives they would like to achieve, and thus clarify the reasons for their choice, all these features being components of deliberative processes (Manin 1985: 82–4). Particularly as long as equality of resources between participants is lacking and as long as there are no institutional mechanisms that transform confrontational games into co-operative ones, blackmail[2] is always likely to be preferred as a strategy for gaining support, in the place of rational arguments that aim to persuade about their truth value. This might require some further elaboration, to demonstrate how difficult it is to achieve deliberation and to approximate a Habermasian ideal speech situation.

In fact, it is not because a great number people interact in a decision-making process that the latter becomes *ipso facto* a genuine deliberative one. The contrary has even be argued: Fishkin (1991: 101) emphasizes 'the hard choice between the nondeliberative (formal) political equality of the masses and the deliberative political *in*equality of the elites'. This antinomy is however not so clear. If the trade-off was perfect, then logically the most inegalitarian and exclusive situation ought to be simultaneously the most deliberative. Yet autocracies are not really deliberative and transaction costs in these regimes are very low (Buchanan and Tullock 1962). Experience with *small groups* where face-to-face relations are possible nevertheless shows that they do seem more propitious to deliberation, thanks to their dialogical component. One can think for instance of consociational agreements, parliamentary and expert committees, or neo-corporatist arrangements. But their compatibility with democracy is often disputed by outsiders who feel excluded from them. Moreover, although the small-group dimension is probably necessary to deliberation because it may be at the origin of richer communicational exchanges, this is by no means a sufficient condition. Vertical and authoritarian relations, where not much room is left for argumentative practices, are commonplace in small groups such as patriarchal families or sects. Deliberation is not an

---

[2] I am referring here to Crozier and Friedberg's (1981) 'blackmailing power', which results from the control of sources of uncertainty (e.g. information). To put it in a simple way: if the non-cooperative behaviour of an individual or a group is likely to cause prejudice to other participants in a decisional process, the latter will be 'blackmailed' (constrained), so that they will have to take into account the point of view of the former. Persuasion in this case plays no role, as the blackmailer only has to threaten and not to prove the legitimate character of her claims. See also the definitional distinction between 'power' and 'persuasion' by Mansbridge (1992).

inherent property of the small group. In fact, the latter has to be *egalitarian* itself to make deliberation possible.

Even egalitarian social interactions may be nothing but the actualization of power relationships: a play with mutual threats. Although this certainly sounds trivial, it should perhaps be recalled that social life is marked by both co-operation and conflict. And when actors whose mutual relations are not uneven choose to co-operate, this is not always the outcome of their deliberations. Dryzek (1993: 227) correctly holds that 'consensus can be reached under all kinds of conditions, through reference to many kinds of standards, and on the part of all kinds of groups, not all of which are equally defensible'. Agreement may well result from the need to avoid a deadlock, thus from an awareness of the power balance between these actors. Compromises result more often than not from interdependence, which makes people more sensitive to the claims of their partners.[3] This does not occur because people become more empathetic, but rather because they expect to be paid for their willingness to co-operate, or simply to be left in peace: promises and threats about our future fate are what matter to us. Exchange relationships are not necessarily deliberative ones, and the compromises resulting from bargaining are not tantamount to a rational consensus built upon the common conviction that some arguments have proved more resilient to criticism and to falsification than others. Thus, the following quotation from Ernest Barker (1942: 67) is misleading:

Discussion is not only like a war; it is also like love. It is not only a battle of ideas; it is also a marriage of minds. If a majority engages in discussion with a minority, and if that discussion is conducted in a spirit of giving and taking, the result will be that the ideas of the majority are widened to include some of the ideas of the minority which have established their truth in the give and take of debate . . . Some fusions will have taken place; some accommodation will have been attained.

Even though a multitude of durable 'mariages de raison' have no doubt originated from what the author calls a 'spirit of giving and taking', no one could bet on their 'love' component. Collective 'accommodation' may well occur for good and perhaps also legitimate reasons quite alien to the mutual acknowledgement of 'truth': 'The pluralist conception of democratic politics as a system of bargaining with fair representation for all groups seems an equally good mirror of the ideal of fairness' (Cohen 1989: 29). Interactive processes of all sorts should therefore be submitted to closer scrutiny to identify their nature and the behavioural patterns of their protagonists. Hence, it is not easy to share the optimism of a number of critical analysts who underscore the existence of a discursive component in policy processes, thus frequently

---

[3] See in that respect the distinction drawn by Cohen and Rogers (1992) between 'civic republicanism' and 'egalitarian pluralism'. Although in the first case deliberative institutions foster social justice and consensus, in the second one it is rather an even representation of interests.

overestimating their deliberative aspects and eschewing the exchange dimension inherent in them (not to speak about the frequent oblivion of power issues in their accounts!). Although empirical evidence remains to my knowledge rather scant as a whole (Forester 1989), in-depth research on deliberative institutions of environmental policy in Germany shows for example that their contribution to 'Konsensbildung' is higher when concrete decisions are not at stake, or when polarization is not so high (Eder *et al.* 1997). A good deal of Habermasian conviction is required to remain optimistic in view of such conclusions! Deliberative arenas are unfortunately not *only* 'schools of overlapping consensus', contrary to what Cohen and Rogers (1995: 256) maintain, and it can even be argued that a certain amount of consensus is a *prerequisite* for their construction. The most propitious situation for reaching an agreement to deliberate is probably that of a consensus on the nature of problems to solve and goals to achieve, in combination with a high degree of uncertainty (but not profound disagreement) as to the means available.[4] Finally, social theory should probably rely more heavily on the findings of research on micro-level interactions: the latter can indifferently generate complementary/consensual or symmetric/confrontational dynamics (Watzlawick *et al.* 1972). Consequently, an 'argumentative' turn in policy analysis is likely to help us better grasp the changing dynamics of the discursive practices—'storytelling'—that are inherent in any controversies about political issues (Rein and Schön 1993).

Direct Democracy as an Obstacle to Co-operation

Hence, direct democracy will fit the deliberative model very partially, although there are not many reasons to blame it for its failure to cope with such a difficult task. Yet it is also debatable whether direct democracy even fits the exchange model that, on strategic or even on cynical grounds, can also be conducive to mutual co-operation and compromise. Settling complex and controversial issues requires a co-ordinated action by a multitude of groups and societal segments. Direct democracy is not very relevant to that purpose, mainly because ordinary citizens have the final say, instead of members of specialized legislative bodies. This is not to say that the difference in behavioural patterns should be attributed to the idiosyncratic properties of social agents, as élitist theory would put it, drawing thus a distinction between the specialized skills of professional politicians and the incompetence of the profane. It is simply that professional and lay legislators act in very different contexts, as usually do, for example, those who elaborate agreements and

---

[4] Discussion with Joshua Cohen; I wish to thank him here for these remarks.

those who are affected by them (Scharpf 1993: 41). In the case of direct democracy, the difference of settings remains, although the previous boundary is blurred.

Especially in multiparty systems where there is no alternative to coalition-building, parliamentarians have no other choice than bargaining and log-rolling. The same applies to neo-corporatist negotiations between social partners, where each side is willing to make compromises in exchange for differed gratifications (for example, social peace for business interests, full employment for labour unions). As we mainly know from game theory, the perpetuation and the routinization of social interactions, in combination with the acquisition by social agents of a 'time capacity' (Offe 1995: 119), are helpful to mutual co-operation. This is the case simply because a long-run perspective introduces the possibility of future rewards for co-operative behaviour and of sanctions in return if people are reluctant to make sacrifices. Even in the absence of explicit positive and negative sanctions, Offe (1992: 9–10) is right in pointing out that 'das Gesetz des Wiedersehens' acts in a 'disziplin-ierend' way for the participants. Similarly, log-rolling is also possible even without any mechanisms ensuring reciprocity. It presupposes in that case mutual trust, so that free-riders will undergo symbolic sanctions: discredit by the community. Explicitly or not, people taking part in these interactions are aware of their interdependence and, as we noticed before, a feeling of common fate can bring about mutual adjustment even if partners do not share much else in common. In a nutshell, this is the way Katzenstein (1985) explains the emergence of domestic co-operative arrangements in small countries, whose economy is widely open and thus highly vulnerable to the movements of the international context. Similar phenomena of 'diffuse reciprocity' between representatives of the nation-states are discernible within the European Union policy process (Héritier 1996).

Things differ considerably in direct democracy. Social pressure in favour of log-rolling for fear of discredit is considerably higher in small groups (Miller 1983: 152), where exit, if only through deviant behaviour, becomes a very costly option. Furthermore, unlike parliamentarians or union leaders, when voters come to cast their ballot they do not have in mind forthcoming issues about which they will have to decide subsequently. Referendary decisions are made on a discrete and not on a continuous base (Sartori 1987: 224). Voters do expect their decisions to be followed by some positive or negative consequences and referendum campaigns strongly focus on these prognostic aspects. Yet voters will not make compromises because they expect to be paid in return, for the simple reason that a genuine communicative process in which future rewards and sanctions could be mentioned by each side is missing here. Future collective benefits and disagreements here are less visible than personally addressed promises and threats, and are therefore much less likely to achieve the goal of co-operative behaviour.

It could probably be objected that, if voters refuse to be 'co-operative' and thus to ratify legislative proposals or to turn down propositions rejected by the establishment, this can be regarded as a very positive sign of their empowerment. It is correct that the top–down view that stigmatizes non-cooperative attitudes on behalf of the citizenry is very partial and one with a strong élitist bias. Yet, being co-operative is a matter not of agreeing with the rulers, but of being willing to reach compromises. For the latter are badly needed in complex societies that undergo numerous centrifugal tendencies, be it under the pressure of the trans- and supranational level, of the subnational one (territorial identities), of sectoral subsystems, or of cultural minorities. 'Kompromissbereitschaft' is crucial for the preservation of social cohesion, and it can be jeopardized by the binary procedures of direct democracy where no space is left for amendments, but only for *en bloc* acceptance or rejection of policy packages.

The Marketization of Direct Democracy

Even the model of egalitarian interdependence, not to speak about genuine deliberation, remains an optimistic ideal compared to the actual allocation of resources in our societies. With the marketization of the public space in contemporary democracies, possession or control[5] of monetary resources can make the difference in access to decision-making. Stein Rokkan's formula, 'votes count, but resources decide' (Rokkan 1966: 105), was initially supposed to apply to electoral processes. It would be an error, however, to overlook its relevance to the direct legislation process as well, especially if free and equal access to the media is not guaranteed. In that case, Cronin (1989: 215) compares direct democracy to a town meeting where one side has many more opportunities to speak than the other. As Eder (*et al.* 1997: 332) notes: 'Das Problem ist, dass Öffentlichkeit nicht per se demokratisch ist, sondern ihrerseits demokratisch geregelt werden muss.' This actually implies a need to devise institutions that would have to be commonly accepted as being of a higher and more democratic order than direct democracy, institutions endowed with enough legitimacy to regulate the latter. When we know that plebiscites are often viewed both by politicians, experts, and the citizenry as a supreme source of immediate popular sovereignty, we come to realize how difficult this task may be.

---

[5] We can interpret in such a way the thesis of the structural dependence of capitalist societies (Offe 1984): private business interests have a blackmailing power for they control the lever of investment, and can thereby affect the global welfare (levels of employment, wages, consumption, etc.). The relevance of this theory was questioned by Przeworski and Wallerstein (1988).

In view of the cost of referendum campaigns, and for lack of any limiting provisions concerning fund raising, some have gone so far as to argue that vote outcomes can be 'purchased'. Were that the case, direct legislation would not only be of very little utility for the advent of more egalitarian and more pluralist regimes, it would quite to the contrary replicate the existing inequalities with respect to political influence and thus increase their impact. There is indeed some empirical evidence from Swiss referenda that sustains these gloomy thoughts: it has been said that 'options which are most in evidence on press advertising during campaign tend to win most support and the high-spending side frequently wins the vote' (Papadopoulos 1995*b*: 440). Fortunately, these conclusions are not entirely convincing because the indicators selected were rather crude or fairly partial, and we do not know whether other factors also played a role: simple binary covariations are seldom indicative of causal mechanisms.[6] Moreover, when there is a fertile ideological soil, outsiders do have a chance: for example, in the case of the optional referendum in Switzerland, almost half the bills that were opposed only by fringe groups were rejected by the people.

As for research results on this problem in the USA, Cronin (1989: 215) mentions a study of seventy-two campaigns according to which the high-spending side won in 78 per cent of the cases. On the other hand, the tobacco industry in California in 1988 spent 21 million dollars fighting a tax increase on cigarettes, and lost the vote. Here again, empirical results are rather inconclusive. Yet the monetarization of referendum campaigns goes beyond the mere influence on the vote, as it also affects in a preliminary phase the collection of the required signatures to put an issue on the ballot. This is far from easy and frequently demands a certain amount of professionalism and of specialization. Only wealthy political entrepreneurs and organizations can afford to hire PR firms who can do the job well, or make use of costly direct mail techniques. It even seems that, relying on their experience, firms are now able to produce lists where people are classified according to the particular type of issue they are likely to support, or even lists of those who are willing to sign any proposal (Cronin 1989: 65)! We are here miles away from the ideal of voluntary militancy. One of the American direct democracy entrepreneurs described his activities in the following manner: 'I have a general supervisor who gets about 2,000 dollars, and then it is about 30 cents a signature' (quoted by Cronin 1989: 62). And as another leader was putting it: 'Why try to educate the world when you're trying to get signatures?' (Cronin 1989: 63).[7] Monetarization of campaigns is not just a typically North American phenomenon; it recently spread to Switzerland as well, as is shown

---

[6] For more details about Switzerland, see Papadopoulos (1994: 148–9).
[7] Fishkin (1991: 52) confirms that the educative function of American direct democracy is rather weak.

by the case of Denner, an important supermarket firm who paid people for the collection of signatures against measures profitable to the agricultural sector and thus prejudicial to a lowering of farm products prices.

Other Resources Count as Well

Monetary resources are not the only ones of some relevance in referendum campaigns. At least two other kinds should be added to the list: organizational and rhetorical resources. In a sense, this could be an equalizing element, as financially poor organizations can compensate for their weakness by a strong mobilization potential through a powerful structure and an appropriate discourse. To be sure, the capacity to maintain a strong 'machine' may itself be contingent on financial resources. Yet ideological commitment and cohesiveness are also important cements of an organization. So is ideology the key to the problem of unequal resources, if, as I have noted, the richest is not automatically the winner? As any expert on propaganda could certainly confirm, ideological persuasiveness is far from equal to empowerment, however, and citizens are seen as easily manipulable subjects, in a long intellectual tradition since Michels, Weber, or Schumpeter.

Now, although some data can be provided to support this view,[8] this is in all likelihood a rather bold generalization, as many factors are likely to strengthen or to inhibit manipulation. Empirical studies have shown that people are more likely to understand correctly the issue at stake when this is not too technical or complex. Moreover, a high educational level and the possession of a substantial amount of cultural capital will enhance an individual's ability to make decisions. Education can thus be a remedy to manipulation; albeit only a very long-term one. Furthermore, even education and civilization (in the sense of Norbert Elias) are no guarantee that, in societies

---

[8] According to survey results in four North American states dating from 1976 a majority of voters would acknowledge themselves that issues on the ballot were too complicated and not easily understandable (Cronin 1989: 74). This is illustrated by votes on nuclear plants in the USA and in Switzerland, where a significant minority voted contrary to their intentions because they did not understand the formulation of the question. Kriesi's team, however, concludes that the average decisional competence of Swiss citizens is fairly satisfactory (Kriesi 1993). Nevertheless, this is a methodological artefact generated by the very low threshold of competence: being able to motivate one's vote, even if it is merely based on elementary slogans and simplistic stereotypes. In those cases where people only repeat what they hear in campaigns, their alleged competence is probably nothing more than a sign of their inclination to be manipulated! Besides, Graham (1986: 131) refers to a number of studies in the USA and the UK, according to which only a minority of people are sufficiently informed to be able to provide reasons for their attitudes. Although voters in California all receive a handbook with information about ballot issues, only a minority varying between 13 and 35% according to the proposition at stake make use of it (Magleby 1984: 36). In Switzerland the proportion of handbook users varied between 35 and 51% for seven votes at the national level in 1991–2. Voters however refer more frequently to the mass media (Kriesi 1994: 52).

that continue to be inegalitarian, vested interests will cease externalizing the costs of their advantages to weakly organized sectors.

One thing is sure: it cannot be asserted conclusively that the deprofessionalization of political choices leads to irresponsible collective choices. Manipulation of citizens is probably a function of the time they are able and willing to devote to issues at stake, a function of their decisional competence, both resources which are socially unevenly distributed, and a function of their subjective 'Betroffenheit': how far they feel that a decision is likely to affect them. Moreover, if citizens could be influenced in all their choices, their attitudes would be more strongly shaped by organizations to which they feel an affinity. In Switzerland, however, citizens only partially follow the recommendations of the major political parties: often they ignore them or do not consider them important (Kriesi 1994: 67)! In California too, 'even on propositions where elites representing a wide spectrum of interests can agree, a majority of voters choose to vote the other way 25 per cent of the time . . . even with a broad base of support or opposition, propositions are often decided contrary to that consensus' (Magleby 1984: 152–3). It is, however, indisputable that direct democracy procedures themselves tend to underrate the complexity of problems, for they reduce political choices to a binary yes or no alternative. Besides, they are probably more propitious than parliamentary debates to the propagation of demagoguery. In Cronin (1989: 208) we find a nice selection of slogans that could be used in the USA, all of them blatantly deceitful: 'Do you want to make politicians honest?' or 'Sign here to stop big business pollution!' The risk of manipulation does exist, and the development of modern marketing techniques is likely to aggravate it: access to them ordinarily requires a combination of monetary, organizational, and rhetorical resources. This suffices to undermine the argument of citizens' empowerment through direct democracy.

When Social Inequalities Produce Political Stratification

One should add to the previous factor the consequences of voters' self-interested behaviour. I do not maintain here either that ordinary people are more egoistic than any enlightened political élites, or that voting takes place in an ideological vacuum and that it should only be dictated by explicit strategic calculations. Contextual differences do matter, as individual action is constrained to a varying degree by pressures and incentives. Deputies who hold mandates cannot allow themselves to behave in a purely individualistic way. They may favour the local interests of their constituencies, or even the particularistic interests of some pressure groups, contrary to the modern doctrine of representation. Yet this is not the same as individualism, especially as deputies must take care to be re-elected, and must often take into account alternative points of view as well, if they want to achieve majoritarian support for a bill.

It can of course be argued that, in direct democracy too, voters do not make their choices in a privatized way, because they are exposed to referendum campaigns that can make them other-regarding. Nevertheless, one should again emphasize the critical point that makes the difference: there is no way to constrain referendum voters to behave with solidarity and to act for the 'common good' if they do not want to. In sum, there is no institutional restraint to citizens' individualism or sectoral short-sightedness in direct democracy, as there is no provision for sanctions in case of a self-interested behaviour. In a previous text I argued that: 'No question for example of functioning according to a principle of reciprocal concessions and differed gratifications as in the neo-corporatist arrangements between trade unions and business interests leaderships. . . . Governance requires empathy and self-limitation, whilst strong democracy in fragmented societies is propitious to sectoral rent-seeking with suboptimal collective effects' (Papadopoulos 1995*b*: 432–3).

Now, nothing prevents us in principle from conceiving of a society where the aggregation of individual preferences would produce collective welfare, in a Mandevillian vein. Voters' self-interest is a serious impediment, however, when we come to consider that voting turnout is highly selective. Max Weber in his *Economy and Society* underscored the risk of democratic administration causing the rise of concentrated and notabilistic power (*honoratiores*), because only wealthy people have the opportunity to devote their time to political activities (Weber 1968: 950). More recently, and following the seminal work by V. O. Key (1961) on political stratification, empirical research in several countries regularly shows that economically and culturally disadvantaged groups frequently exclude themselves and abstain from voting. People belonging to these groups have a very low expectation of the efficiency of politics, and they tend to believe that they lack the necessary competences to cope with decision-making on collective issues. Even in 'direct' democracy, voter turnout is higher among middle and upper class people, to whom other social strata thus come, although not purposively, to delegate their voice. Direct legislation does not solve all representation problems, and the distance between citizenship as a formal status and citizenship as a practice can be considerable. In the USA, 'less educated, poorer, and nonwhite citizens are organizationally and financially excluded from setting the direct legislation agenda . . . These same people are less likely to vote on ballot propositions because they cannot comprehend the wording of the proposition' (Magleby 1984: 183–4). Various studies demonstrate that income level is an important discriminating factor, and people who constantly feel excluded from benefits allocated by political or economic institutions will find it difficult to accept that voting can be of much use to them (Cronin 1989: 76–7). Particularly for the lower social strata, voting is a costly activity as it requires information, time, and skills (Graham 1986: 134): the 'ticket' for access to this form of political participation is an expensive one!

Furthermore, the same applies to more radical and unconventional forms of mobilization, in which we note similar discriminations (Memmi 1985), or to mass primaries in the USA that equally seem to have failed in their role of democratizing the presidential election. According to Fishkin (1991: 60), this 'brings into question the extent to which the interests of all strata of society are getting an effective hearing in the process'. Paradoxically, forms of participation that are usually viewed as particularly appropriate for the expression of an outsider's viewpoint replicate social and political inequalities! Immigrants' deprivation of the right to vote when they often form an important part of the total population only aggravates the absence of *isegoria*, particularly when these people become the scapegoats for all sorts of inconveniences (ranging from unemployment of the natives to environmental pollution). To be sure, political stratification affects the election of parliaments too. Nevertheless, deputies cannot act as if they were only elected by a narrow 'chasse gardée' of upper class people. In fact, they face a 'veil of ignorance' as to who is likely to participate in the forthcoming election, and are thus more eager to be other-regarding.

Utilitarian Behaviour: Why and How

Self-interest should not only be postulated, but ought to be explained too. What happens is that people are willing to turn down any policies that entail concentrated costs that are likely to affect their pocket directly, when their collective benefits are less visible: either because they are diffuse or, even worse for the achievement of support, because they mainly profit selected narrow groups, as is the case in a great deal of redistributive policies.[9] Although reactions of this kind are perfectly rational, they do not facilitate the task of governments which requires, among others, a capacity to reconstitute social cohesion. Thus, direct democracy can be a serious obstacle when it comes to developing social policies by means of taxation, and it can feed the 'nimby' (not in my backyard) syndrome against the local implementation of collective infrastructures.[10]

This perhaps needs some clarification: originally the literature on 'nimby'-type oppositions was about the difficulties of implementing 'dirty public things' (Allison 1986) which entailed high risks or caused environmental

---

[9] Schumpeter (1969: 354–5) noted with much insight in his classical work that individuals were more sensitive to concentrated and short-term advantages and costs. This has become since then a core belief of policy implementation analysts.

[10] For evidence on the Swiss case, see Kübler (1995).

pollution, such as nuclear plants, highways, hazardous waste disposal, and the like. Yet 'nimby' reactions can be found about any project whose consequences, whatever they are, are viewed as general nuisances that some will have to undergo. In a similar vein Offe (1987), in an article on the devastating effects of the neo-conservative offensive, attributes the decline of support for welfare policies to the erosion of collective identification feelings and to the diffusion of utilitarian cost–benefit cognitive patterns among the individuals. Ironically, the *homo economicus* that most social scientists considered at best as an abstract and oversimplified ideal type, at worst as a misleading notion deprived of any empirical content, seems about to become the prevailing type of individual in our societies! On the other hand, it is surprising to read that utilitarian behaviour is equally presented as a result of the atrophy of civil societies in post-communist, consequently weakly differentiated, and pre-modern East European societies, where experts note a lack in mutual trust and 'civilizational competence' (Sztompka 1992),[11] which as we all know are central determinants of social co-operation, of democratic consolidation, and of any other facet of progress.

'Mann ohne Eigenschaften' (the man without qualities): pre- or post-modern? Difficult to say, and it would probably be too bold to generalize. Here the 'institutionalist' explanatory key may be of some help to us: as mentioned before, politicians will definitely find it very difficult to justify their behaviour on purely individualistic, or even narrowly corporatist grounds. They will have to produce rhetorics of public interest (*intérêt général*), and these discourses, although they should not be all taken at face value, are never *only* mystifying, simply because they constrain the room for manœuvre by those people who use them to legitimize their choices and their actions. Nothing similar applies to ordinary citizens who have no obligations of correctness to comply with. The argument is simple: take a self-interested individual, she will not have identical opportunities to express her inclinations according to the institutional setting in which she is embedded. The problem with more direct forms of participation is that they totally lack any mechanisms of accountability for participants: unlike parliaments, accountability is not to an electoral clientele, but simply to others. Voters are not obliged to give any reasons for their choices, and they are only accountable to their own conscience. Hence, it is not really paradoxical to note that the more participation is encouraged in an inegalitarian society, the higher the risk is that some people will be excluded from those benefits (allowances, equipment, and the like) whose costs must be paid by the community as a whole.

---

[11] Anthropological studies of poor and rural South European communities reached the same conclusions about mutual distrust and lack of collective identification several years ago: communism does not seem to be the sole cause of weak civil societies. See e.g. Banfield's (1958) 'amoral familism'. On the role of trust as a cement of social relations and on its functional equivalents, see Luhmann (1979).

The Risks of Individualism in Direct Democracy

Thus, as long as 'egalitarian pluralism' (Cohen and Rogers 1992) is not achieved, 'strong' democracy is likely to be counter-productive concerning an aim of empowerment. Numerous examples can be mentioned which support this argument: and even though the outcomes of referendary votes are contrasting,[12] the *risk* remains that some measures may be taken which cause prejudice to the weakest.

Hence, anti-fiscal measures, often profitable to the wealthiest, constitute the largest category of initiatives in the USA (Cronin 1989: 205). The case of 'proposition 13' voted in 1978 is notorious: sponsored by an impressive mass of 1.5 million citizens, it was approved by 65 per cent and led to a drastic decrease in the number of state employees. Instead of jubilating in its anti-bureaucratic virtues, one can meditate on its disastrous consequences on state policies. Moreover, the anti-fiscal contagion rapidly affected a great number of other American states (Möckli 1994: 26). Votes favourable to the death penalty took place in some states in the 1970s and in the 1980s. In Colorado a small majority passed anti-abortion provisions, although 10 per cent believed that a 'yes' vote to the initiative would mean a pro-choice vote (Cronin 1989: 213): this raises again the problem of information and of decisional competence, even if in some other states the pro-life side failed in their task. To be sure, women's suffrage was adopted by way of such initiatives, but this did not prevent male voters of South Dakota from denying twice this right in 1890 and 1898 (Auer 1989: 77). Segregationist initiatives about school bussing were voted in Colorado in 1974, and in California in 1979. More recently, Californians used their initiative right in 1994 (proposition 187) to restrict access of some categories of immigrants to educational services. Minority rights can thus be damaged, or at least seriously threatened. In Switzerland, although no xenophobic initiative against immigrant workers won a majority, they had an impact on official policies that became increasingly restrictive. Is that really what should be meant by responsiveness? In California in 1978 an initiative advocated the firing of homosexual teachers from schools; fortunately it was rejected. In Switzerland the existence of cultural centres of the 'alternative' milieu at the local level was seriously undermined in Zürich, where traditionalist forces could make use of the referendum, whereas public authorities

---

[12] In the case of American initiatives, which can either introduce new proposals or simply abrogate statutory and legislative provisions (veto right), it seems that the share of liberal and conservative propositions that win majorities is approximately equal. Liberal projects are about reduction of the working hours, environmental provisions, control of toxic products. According to Cronin (1989: 85), citizens dislike extremism. Sometimes, referendum outcomes are quite surprising, as was the case in Utah, a state where approximately three-quarters of the population are Mormons with a very strict morality, and where an initiative to rule out pornography from cable TV was turned down by 61%. Cronin (1989: 212–13) concludes that this measure was viewed as an excessive governmental impediment on the exercise of individual rights.

could adopt a much more liberal policy in Geneva, simply because direct democracy provisions were not available there.[13]

In sum, giving a voice to the plausibly tyrannical aspirations of customarily silent majorities does not seem very wise when no checks and balances are provided. Highly risky issues are those which are of direct interest to individuals, such as taxation. Direct democracy is also problematic about very emotive issues, such as crime punishment, where popular reactions can suddenly dramatically change under the influence of media sensationalism (Offe 1992: 20). Besides, majority tyranny is particularly dangerous when one faces the 'intense minority' problem (Miller 1983: 151–2). Decisions that increase only marginally the satisfaction of each component of the majority are likely to harm considerably and simultaneously the satisfaction of affected minorities in uses such as the death penalty, restriction of abortion, etc. It goes without saying that this problem is acute in fragmented societies. We thus need institutional devices that limit, bind, and constrain decision-makers, especially as 'in all questions concerning human and citizen rights [the issue is] not to "win majorities" but to protect rights from being overruled by even the strongest majorities' (Offe and Preuss 1991: 166). If majority rule is nothing but a compromise with the need to limit transaction costs, while the sole base of legitimacy remains unanimous consent, then '(l)es contrepouvoirs, les freins et les contrepoids sont nécessaires parce que la volonté majoritaire n'est pas la volonté de tous' (Manin 1985: 91).

A system of checks and balances obliges majorities to find advocates that are willing and capable to elaborate their viewpoint, to argue on its base, to subject it to criticism, and to deliberate about it. Hence, the existence of some form of judicial review over decisions made by way of direct legislation is probably welcome. Here are just a few examples of votes in the USA that were invalidated by the Supreme Court because of their lack of conformity with the Constitution: the obligation to send children to state-owned schools, the legalization of segregation in educational institutions, racial discriminations concerning housing (Auer 1989: 142 n. 803). In California seven initiatives out of the eleven accepted by the citizens were subsequently declared totally or partially anti-constitutional (Magleby 1984: 53, 203). In Italy, the Constitutional Court pre-emptively rejected between 1972 and 1995 twenty-nine out of seventy-five demands for abrogative referenda. Yet judicial interference is also controversial: thus, decisions of Italian magistrates would often be disputed on the grounds of the politicization ('partitocrazia') and of the pro-establishment bias of the judiciary system. This is a typical dilemma about the role of non-majoritarian institutions: their existence is necessary in a Madisonian perspective, but it is not without raising in its turn serious accountability problems (Majone 1996: 125–34).

---

[13] I refer here to information given by Kriesi and Wisler (1996); the authors would however probably not agree with the conclusions I draw on the impact of direct democracy.

As a rule, measures initiated by way of direct legislation find it difficult to win majorities: according to Cronin's (1989: 197) calculations, only 35–40 per cent of the approximately 1,500 initiatives in the USA since 1904 have been accepted. In Switzerland, the rate is even considerably lower at the federal level; but ratification of laws is more frequently rejected. What is more important, the veto right is a threat that acts preventively and indirectly, as it is a Damoclean sword hanging over the decisional process, intimidating administrators, expert committees, and legislative bodies as a whole. This introduces a populist pressure whose majoritarian dimension is neither relevant for the 'intellectual cogitation' (Wildavsky 1979) that is required for the handling of complex problems, nor favourable to the empowerment of the weakest.

Democracy and Governance: Legitimacy Conflicts

Significantly, state bureaucracies are occasionally obliged to bypass democratic channels to achieve some of their empowering objectives. This can be the case when administrators advocate policies that are profitable to stigmatized social groups. Swiss AIDS policy is a good case in point (Bütschi and Cattacin 1994): considered to be a model in Europe, it has to rely on institutional and legislative 'bricolages', short-circuiting wherever possible the traditional legal and budgetary framework. The same applies to recent decisions to experiment with innovations in drugs policy, that could definitely not have been implemented had they stood under the constant threat of a popular vote, something that is quite customary in Swiss decision-making. In such strongly value-loaded issues, votes take place in a climate of extreme polarization that may be prejudicial to competent choices. Administrators in charge of AIDS or drugs policy significantly acknowledge that governmental initiatives became much less innovative once the debates started being vehemently politicized in the media and in the public sphere. It seems here that competent decision-making can only be confined to narrow technocratic circles, as the learning capacity on behalf of the citizenry is weak. One should of course treat this argument cautiously when one knows that it emanates from people who have an interest in preserving their predominant role in policy-making. Yet one cannot simply sweep it away, regarding it only as an illegitimate one. In the aforementioned policy sectors it would be a disastrous error to overlook the avant-gardist role played by state administrators. They do it in close co-operation with doctors and social workers with whom they build 'advocacy coalitions' (Sabatier and Jenkins-Smith 1993) and, when they can find credible counterparts in a difficult milieu, with representatives of target groups (policy-takers) too.

This is not to say that no legitimacy problems are discernible here. Policy-makers are probably aware of them themselves, as the measures taken are put under constant evaluation by experts. In addition, consensus within the policy network can also be presented as a proof of wisdom of the innovations decided on. Yet this combination of an expert legitimacy based on efficiency and of a local-sectoral one based on acceptance remains fragmentary, and can thus quite well be challenged as insufficient. Using the parliamentary circuit or, even better, the referendary one would undoubtedly confer a portion of legitimacy that would be more compatible with the traditional standards of a democratic polity. It would, however, in all likelihood dramatically affect the co-operative and trust relationships presently existing between the various policy partners, for it would introduce an external perturbation to a climate of mutual understanding that is really necessary to policy success in this par-ticular case. We are in presence of a trade-off and consequently of a serious dilemma: it seems that expert/local and democratic/global forms of legitimacy are incompatible and cannot be cumulated. This is not the same as to the tra-ditional dilemma between effectiveness and legitimacy, as we are rather con-fronted here with a strain between competing sources of the latter. The improvement of living conditions and the empowerment of the weakest seem to be achievable only if they are promoted by a cohesive coalition of tech-nocrats and professionals: democracy loses then. When these issues escape the monopolistic control of experts' coalitions thanks to the pressures of social movements and of political entrepreneurs, majoritarian democracy will win but the weakest will probably lose, as many people who thus obtain a say will not accept to 'pay'.[14] Good ideas can yield unexpected and unintended conse-quences, and hell is paved with good intentions.

To be more accurate, all this raises the central problem of *who* ought to be entitled to make decisions or, stated differently, it raises the issue of the rele-vant decision-making level, space, or sphere. Offe and Preuss (1991: 166) give the following eloquent example: 'Take the case of an airport construction project: is the universe of those affected by the decision, and for that reason the universe of those entitled to participation in making it, "all" inhabitants of the nearly villages, or is it "all" airlines and their clients who qualify as potential users of the new facility?' It would be misleading to believe that such a question is only a theoretical one. A few years ago, the citizens of the Geneva canton approved by referendum a project aiming to extend the facilities of the local airport. Needless to say, not a single citizen of the neighbouring cantons (not to mention neighbouring French departments) had a say, although these people are inevitably users of the Geneva airport and at the same time endure its nuisances. Simply broadening participation would probably not have

---

[14] We are talking about costs at large: monetary of course, by the way of taxation, but also any other sort of perceived nuisances and disagreements (safety problems, image degradation of a neighbour-hood, etc.).

solved the question of the appropriate decisional universe that would remain as an object of controversy. Keeping in mind this kind of problem, participatory theory seems poorly equipped to come to grips with the complexities of contemporary decision-making, a problem that is no doubt also aggravated by globalization.[15]

Which Alternatives to Direct Democracy as Means of Democratization?

In sum, it would be too optimistic to assert that direct democracy's record with respect to democratization is unambiguous. This is not to say that its overall performance is absolutely negative. Yet even a differentiated view ought to pay some attention to a number of risks inherent in direct democracy and one should not be fascinated by 'direct-majoritarianism' (Fishkin 1991: 24). Its deliberative and even its exchange components are rather weak and do not seem to provide sufficient incentives for co-operative behaviour. These problems are aggravated by the marketization of the referendary scene, by its selective mechanisms, and by the *de facto* delegation of decisional competences to people with much to lose from redistributive policies favourable to social justice at large. In addition, no provisions exist to discourage narrowly utilitarian attitudes or the externalization of costs to the weakly organized and those who do not have a say. The overall contribution of direct democracy to governance is therefore ambiguous, and this also applies to a view of the latter departing from the narrowly managerial one, a view that would in particular include as a major requirement the reconstruction of social cohesion in centrifugal societies (Papadopoulos 1995*a*).

There is however, perhaps even to an increasing degree, a major concern about the need to improve the opportunities for democratic feedback on political decisions and to enhance the sensitivity of political systems to the demands of their social environments. It is besides noticeable that several contemporary attempts at deepening democracy are not motivated by the ethical reasons advocated by the participatory school. They are rather imposed for the sake of governability,[16] as policy implementation research has shown: administrations need more participation to make more effective and

[15] In his essay on globalization, Held (1991: 202) gives a long and very convincing list of similar dilemmas. Cook and Morgan (1971), although by no means opposed to further democratization, were as early as a few decades ago fully aware of the problems of co-ordination, externalities, relevance of decisional levels, related to the complexity of participatory decisional styles.

[16] See e.g. Offe's (1995: 119) distinction between normative perspectives centred on citizen participation and functional ones centred on steering and guidance requirements. In a sense both perspectives are equally normative (the latter adhering to a managerial viewpoint), albeit on different grounds.

simultaneously more legitimate decisions.[17] Governments alone often do not have the huge amount of information, organization, authority, and financial resources that public policies require. The question now is whether direct democracy provisions, say the veto or the initiative right, can be considered as relevant in this respect. On the series of arguments listed so far, one would be inclined to be rather sceptical. For example, direct democracy does force legislative bodies to be more responsive and it enhances their accountability too. When responsiveness leads to irresponsible populism this becomes highly problematic however,[18] and the same applies to accountability when it awards supplementary 'voice' resources to the strongest.

What are we facing in the actual world now, apart from the particular case of the few countries with an experience in referenda? There is a revival of interest in forms of direct democracy, which is curiously mostly discernible either at the level of local communities or in the European unification process. A number of people, of parties, and of social movements are eager to see direct democracy as one of the remedies to the increased distance between élites and the citizenry. Nevertheless, direct democracy is also presently challenged by a variety of other forms of people's participation in civic affairs: negotiated arrangements in specific cases of policy implementation, delegation of welfare competences to groups and a correlative rise of the third sector, of 'associative democracy', frequent use of pluralistic methods for the conduct of responsive and inclusive policy evaluations, etc. To be sure, these procedures are still weakly consolidated and institutionalized.[19] Moreover, they have their own legitimacy deficits: a critical problem is, for example, that 'citizenship' does not seem to be a very relevant category any more, for people's participation is justified on the grounds of more fragmentary and particularistic roles and identities, such as those of consumers of private goods, users of public services, taxpayers, policy-takers, and the like. Public spaces and arenas are nowadays increasingly plural, sectoral, and fragmented and this is not without consequences. Habermas (1992: 389) stresses the decoupling of political government from parliamentary institutions and the disappearance of political issues from the public arena which put the 'democratic question' again onto the public agenda.

Yet these forms of participation might represent interesting complements and alternatives to direct democracy and its shortcomings. Offe and Preuss

---

[17] This is an important qualification to the alleged trade-off between 'system effectiveness' and 'citizen participation' (Dahl 1994).

[18] Sartori (1994: 73) correctly argues that governments need to be simultaneously responsive and responsible. This double requirement suffices to rehabilitate research on the relevance of political institutions, norms, and procedures for the achievement of governability. Nevertheless, there may well be trade-offs between responsiveness and responsibility, which are not always compatible or combinable.

[19] Jenson (1996: 22–3) points to some crucial problems of 'partnerships': insufficient power-sharing, alteration of the nature of third-sector organizations, creation of hierarchies between groups, withdrawal of the state and commercialism.

(1991: 166) give some reasons for that: to give but one example, considering the limits of regulation by legal means, 'the rule of law must be complemented at the micro-level of the principled action of conscientious citizens'. The role of every participatory mechanism should be evaluated with a particular concern about its contribution to the promotion of 'moral resources' (Offe and Preuss 1991), a task in which the performance of direct democracy is rather poor:[20] self-restraint, other-regardingness, and empathy instead of short-sightedness, trust, willingness to co-operate, openness to learning from experience, a reflexive second look on one's arguments. In a (neo)-institutionalist vein that embeds considerations of applied ethics as well, procedures and rules of the game can make the difference for the achievement of these properties that are consubstantial to a high level of democratic deliberation.[21] And to conclude with Offe's and Preuss's (1991: 168) seminal essay: 'There is a shift from quantity to quality in the sense that in order to produce more reasonable outcomes it often no longer makes sense to ask for broader participation, but instead to look for a more refined, more deliberative, and more reflective formation of the motives and demands that enter the process of mass participation already in place.'

REFERENCES

ALLISON, L. (1986). 'On Dirty Public Things', *Political Geography Quarterly*, 5/3: 241–51.

AUER, A. (1989). *Le Référendum et l'initiative populaire aux États-Unis* (Basel and Paris: Helbing & Lichtenhahn and Economica).

BANFIELD, E. (1958). *The Moral Basis of a Backward Society* (Glencoe: The Free Press).

BARBER, B. R. (1984). *Strong Democracy: Participatory Politics for a New Age* (Berkeley, Calif.: University of California Press).

BARKER, E. (1942). *Reflections on Government* (London: Oxford University Press).

BERRY, C. J. (1989). *The Idea of a Democratic Society* (New York: St Martin's Press).

BOBBIO, N. (1987). *The Future of Democracy: A Defense of the Rules of the Game* (Cambridge: Polity Press).

BUCHANAN, J. M., and TULLOCK, G. (1962). *The Calculus of Consent: Logical Foundations of Constitutional Democracy* (Ann Arbor: University of Michigan Press).

BÜTSCHI, D., and CATTACIN, S. (1994). *Le Modèle suisse du bien-être* (Lausanne: Réalités Sociales).

---

[20] More generally, Hermet (1989) provides an impressive catalogue of fictions about the popular virtues.

[21] '(R)eflection is also required with regard to the arenas of the communicative effort itself' (Healey 1993: 247). It does indeed make little sense to advocate the advent of interdiscursive practices without conceiving of the appropriate procedures to achieve them: 'different rules may lead to different results even when the participants have the same degree of consensus on substantive values' (MacRae 1993: 298).

COHEN, J. (1989). 'Deliberation and Democratic Legitimacy', in A. Hamlin and B. Pettit (eds.), *The Good Polity* (Oxford: Oxford University Press), 17–34.

——and ROGERS, J. (1992). 'Secondary Associations and Democrartic Governance', *Politics and Society*, 20/4: 393–472.

——and——(1995). 'Solidarity, Democracy, Association', in Erik Olin Wright (ed.), *Associations and Democracy* (London and New York: Verso), 236–67.

COOK, T., and MORGAN, P. M. (eds.) (1971). *Participatory Democracy* (San Francisco: Canfield Press).

CRONIN, T. E. (1989). *Direct Democracy: The Politics of Initiative, Referendum, and Recall* (Cambridge, Mass: Harvard University Press).

CROZIER, M., and FRIEDBERG, E. (1981). *L'Acteur et le système: Les Constraintes de l'action collective* (Paris: Seuil).

DAHL, R. A. (1994). 'A Democratic Dilemma: System Effectiveness versus Citizen Participation', *Political Science Quarterly*, 109: 23–34.

DRYZEK, J. S. (1993). 'Policy Analysis and Planning: From Science to Argument', in F. Fischer and J. Forester (eds.), *The Argumentative Turn in Policy Analysis and Planning* (London: ULC Press), 213–32.

EDER, K. (1995). 'Die Dynamik demokratischer Institutionenbildung: Strukturelle Voraussetzungen deliberativer Demokratie in fortgeschrittenen Industriegesellschaften', in B. Nedelmann (ed.), *Politische Institutionen im Wandel* (Kölner Zeitschrift für Soziologie und Sozialpsychologie, Sonderheft 35; Opladen: Westdeutscher Verlag), 327–45.

——BRAND, K.-W., BARTHE, S., and DREYER, M. (1997). *Reflexive Institutionen? Eine Untersuchung zur Herausbildung eines neuen Typus institutioneller Regelungen im Umweltbereich* (Abschlußbericht on die Deutsche Forschungsgemeinschaft, DFG Projektnummer ed 25/7-1; Munich: Municher Projektgruppe für Sozialforschung).

FISHKIN, J. S. (1991). *Democracy and Deliberation: New Directions for Democratic Reform* (New Haven, Conn.: Yale University Press).

FORESTER, J. (1989). *Planning in the Face of Power* (Berkeley, Calif.: University of California Press).

GRAHAM, K. (1986). *The Battle of Democracy: Conflict, Consensus, and the Individual* (Brighton: Harvester Wheatsheaf).

HABERMAS, J. (1992). *Faktizität und Geltung: Beiträge zur Diskurstheorie des Rechts und des demokratischen Rechtsstaats* (Frankfurt: Suhrkamp).

HEALEY, P. (1993). 'Planning through Debate: The Communicative Turn in Planning Theory', in F. Fischer and J. Forester (eds.), *The Argumentative Turn in Policy Analysis and Planning* (London: ULC Press), 233–53.

HELD, D. (1991). 'Democracy, the Nation-State and the Global System', in D. Held (ed.), *Political Theory Today* (Cambridge: Polity Press), 197–235.

HERITIER, A. (1996). 'The Accommodation of Diversity in European Policy-Making and its Outcomes: Regulatory Policy as a Patchwork', *Journal of European Policy*, 3: 149–67.

HERMET, G. (1989). *Le Peuple contre la démocratie* (Paris: Fayard).

JENSON, J. (1996). *Citizenship Regimes: From Equity to Marketisation* (European Forum 'Citizenship'; Florence: European University Institute).

KATZENSTEIN, P. J. (1985). *Small States in World Markets* (Ithaca, NY: Cornell University Press).

KEY, V. O. (1961). *Public Opinion and American Democracy* (New York: Knopf).

KOBACH, K. W. (1993). *The Referendum: Direct Democracy in Switzerland* (Aldershot: Dartmouth).

KRIESI, H. (ed.) (1993). *Citoyenneté et démocratie directe: Compétence, participation et décision des citoyens et citoyennes suisses* (Zürich: Seismo).

——(1994). 'Le Défi à la démocratie directe posé par les transformations de l'espace public', in Y. Papadopoulos (ed.), *Présent et avenir de la démocratie directe* (Geneva: Georg), 31–72.

——and WISLER, D. (1996). 'Social Movements and Direct Democracy in Switzerland', *European Journal of Political Research*, 30: 19–40.

KÜBLER, D. (1995). 'Problèmes de mise en œuvre de la politique sociale en milieu urbain: L'Exemple des services médico-sociaux pour consommateurs de drogues', *Revue suisse de science politique*, 1/4: 99–120.

LUHMANN, N. (1979). *Trust and Power: Two Works* (London: John Wiley).

MacRAE, D., Jr (1993). 'Guidelines for Policy Discourse: Consensual versus Adversarial', in F. Fischer and J. Forester (eds.), *The Argumentative Turn in Policy Analysis and Planning* (London: UCL Press), 291–318.

MAGLEBY, D. B. (1984). *Direct Legislation: Voting on Ballot Propositions in the United States* (Baltimore: The Johns Hopkins University Press).

MAJONE, G. (1996). *La Communauté européenne: Un état régulateur* (Paris: Montchrestien).

MANIN, B. (1985). 'Volonté générale ou délibération? Esquisse d'une théorie de la délibération politique', *Le Débat*, 33: 72–93.

MANSBRIDGE, J. (1992). 'A Deliberative Perspective on Neocorporatism', *Politics and Society*, 20/4: 493–505.

MEMMI, D. (1985). 'L'Engagement politique', in M. Grawitz and J. Leca (eds.), *Traité de science politique* (Paris: Presses Universitaires de France), 310–66.

MILLER, D. (1983). 'The Competitive Model of Democracy', in G. Duncan (ed.), *Democratic Theory and Practice* (Cambridge: Cambridge University Press), 133–55.

MÖCKLI, S. (1994). *Direkte Demokratie: Ein Vergleich der Einrichtungen und Verfahren in der Schweiz und Kalifornien unter Berücksichtigung von Frankreich, Italien, Dänemark, Irland, Österreich, Lichtenstein und Australien* (Berne, Stuttgart, and Vienna: Haupt).

OFFE, C. (1984). *Contradictions of the Welfare State* (London: Hutchinson).

——(1987). 'Democracy against the Welfare State? Structural Foundations of Neoconservative Political Opportunities', *Political Theory*, 15/4: 501–37.

——(1992). *Thesenpapier zur öffentlichen Anhörung der gemeinsamen Verfassungskommission zum Thema Bürgerbeteiligung/Plebiszite* (mimeo).

——(1995). 'Some Sceptical Considerations on the Malleability of Representative Institutions) in E. O. Wright (ed.), *Associations and Democracy* (London and New York: Verso), 114–32.

——and PREUSS, U. K. (1991). 'Democratic institutions and Moral Resources', in D. Held (ed.), *Political Theory Today* (Oxford: Polity Press), 143–71.

Papadopoulos, Y. (ed.) (1994). *Élites politiques et peuple en Suisse: Analyse des votations fédérales 1970–1987* (Lausanne: Réalités Sociales).

—— (1995a). *Complexité sociale et politiques publiques* (Paris: Montchrestien).

—— (1995b). 'A Framework for Analysis of Functions and Dysfunctions of Direct Democracy: Top–Down and Bottom–Up Perspectives', *Politics and Society*, 23: 421–48.

Przeworski, A., and Wallerstein, M. (1988). 'Structural Dependence of the State on Capital', *American Political Science Review*, 82: 11–29.

Putnam, R. D., with Leonardi, Robert, and Nanetti, Raffaella Y. (1993). *Making Democracy Work: Civic Traditions in Modern Italy* (Princeton: Princeton University Press).

Rein, M., and Schön, D. (1993). 'Reframing Policy Discourse', in F. Fischer and J. Forester (eds.), *The Argumentative Turn in Policy Analysis and Planning* (London: UCL Press), 145–66.

Rokkan, S. (1966). 'Norway: Numerical Democracy and Corporate Pluralism', in R. A. Dahl (ed.), *Political Oppositions in Western Democracies* (New Haven, Conn.: Yale University Press), 70–115.

Sabatier, P. A., and Jenkins-Smith, H. C. (eds.) (1993). *Policy Change and Learning: An Advocacy Coalition Approach* (Boulder Colo.: Westview Press).

Sartori, G. (1987). *The Theory of Democracy Revisited* (Chatham, NY: Chatham House).

—— (1994). *Comparative Constitutional Engineering* (London: Macmillan).

Scharpf, F. W. (1993). 'Versuch über die Demokratie im verhandelnden Staat', in R. Czada and M. G. Schmidt (eds.), *Verhandlungsdemokratie, Interessenvermittlung, Regierbarkeit* (Opladen: Westdeutscher Verlag), 25–50.

Schmitter, P. C. (1996). *Is it Really Possible to Democratize the Euro-Polity? And if so, What Role Euro-Citizens Play in it?* (Florence: European University Institute).

Schumpeter, J. A. (1969). *Capitalisme, socialisme et démocratie* (Paris: Payot).

Sztompka, P. (1992). *Civilizational Competence: A Pre-requisite of Post-Communist Transition* (Krakow: mimeo).

Uleri, P. V. (1996). 'Introduction', in M. Gallagher and P. V. Uleri (eds.), *The Referendum Experience in Europe* (London: Macmillan), 1–19.

Watzlawick, P., Beavin, J. H., and Jackson, D. D. (1972). *Une logique de la communication* (Paris: Seuil).

Weber, M. (1968). *Economy and Society* (New York: Bedminster Press).

Wildavsky, A. B. (1979). *Speaking Truth to Power: The Art and Craft of Policy Analysis* (Boston, Mass.: Little Brown).

9

Institutions, Culture, and Identity of Transnational Citizenship: How Much Integration and 'Communal Spirit' is Needed?

Veit Bader

Introduction

Institutions, cultures, and political identities of democratic (nation-) states are increasingly under pressure in our epoch of rapid globalization and huge migration. The theory and politics of radical democracy have to imagine answers to many new problems.

1. Global ecological problems, global insecurity (wars, civil wars, ethnic cleansings), and poverty require co-ordinated international efforts at a time when the misfit of existing inter-governmental and international institutions, worsened by neo-liberal globalization strategies (Hirst and Thompson 1996), is increasingly felt (Held 1995; Falk 1995). How to counter neo-liberal strategies in favour of the 'rich and powerful'—inside states and internationally—given the fact that movements and social movement organizations (SMOs) of negatively privileged classes and groups are particularly weak at supra- and interstate levels (Streeck 1996; Schmitter 1996)? What would be an appropriate design for international institutions to tackle the root causes of forced migration?

2. How to combine politics of 'fairly open borders', needed in order to prevent citizenship in rich northern states from increasingly becoming a morally indefensible privilege, with just and feasible politics of democratic incorporation of migrants and asylum seekers (Bader 1997b)?

3. In our age of increasing ethnic diversity and 'strange multiplicity' inside states, all state institutions, concepts of citizenship, and of political culture

have to be disentangled from ethnicity and nationhood at least to a certain degree.

I have criticized all versions of stronger communitarian particularism for not going far enough in this decoupling (Bader 1995*a*, 1995*c*) and unrooted cosmopolitanism for going too far (Bader 1997*e*). More specifically, I have tried to answer two questions. First, how far has such a disentanglement of democratic citizenship and culture from 'ethnos' gone historically in those models promising it as part of their constitutions and their official political myths: the French republican model and the pluralist models in immigration societies (the US melting pot and the Canadian mosaic)? My overly short answer has been: by far not far enough (Bader 1997*e*). Second, how far should it go? Here I criticized positions claiming that a complete and neat separation of ethnicity and citizenship would be the only legitimate moral option and upholding the unachievable ideal of a complete 'benign' ethnic neutrality of state institutions. Instead of unachievable full cultural equality in all regards which would overrule legitimate moral claims of majorities, I opted for rough complex equality and cultural fairness (Bader 1997*e*). I did not, however, address a third, empirical and explanatory question: how far can such a disentanglement go, given our—contested—sociological and social-psychological knowledge? In this chapter, I focus on this question, trying to debunk deeply rooted sociological prejudices about 'social integration', psychological prejudices about 'identity', and political philosophical prejudices about the impact of normative consensus regarding shared principles (section 2). Societies do not fall apart as easy as most sociologists assume. People can live with multilayered, shifting, and context-dependent political identities. Democratic political communities can do with much less consent and shared principles. However, projects of democratic experimentalism in general, and in particular those of democratic politics addressing urgent global ecological problems and problems of global insecurity, poverty, and structured inequalities, require more commitment than is generated by the 'live and let live' resulting from institutionalized conflicts (Bader 1995*a*: n. 60, 1995*b*: 167 n. 53). In section 3, I analyse whether the hope of all participatory democrats that a productive dialectics of institutions—cultures—habits/virtues—practices can generate, in time, enough democratic commitment, is fostered by the design of domestic and trans-domestic associative democratic institutions.

How Much Integration and Communal Spirit is Needed?

The newly developing transatlantic citizenship and political culture frame (Kymlicka and Norman 1994; Favell 1996) commonly assumes that a fairly high degree of social cohesion or societal integration is needed for well-functioning societies, and that this can be achieved only by a high degree of common political solidarity and identity. In answering the question how far can the disentanglement of demos from ethnos go, given the 'nature' of human society and human beings, I take a critical stance towards these two basic assumptions shared by most recent political philosophers—not just communitarians[1]—and also by the sociology of political culture.

Too much social-coherence-, cohesion-, and integration-talk is prevalent in the conservative diagnosis of fragmentation, dissolution of (nation-)state societies and the deplored 'decline' or 'loss' of (political) morality. *Theoretically*, these statements are heavily biased by a Durkheimian or Parsonian sociology and its four central, hidden dogmas. First, the conceptualization of societies overestimates the minimally required *degree of societal integration*. Modern, functionally differentiated societies, whether ethnically plural or not, do not resemble well-integrated wholes but can more adequately be seen as loosely co-ordinated patchworks (Unger 1996). The traditional metaphor of the 'cement' of society can better be replaced by the polemical one of a 'heap of sand'. Second, Durkheimian and Parsonian sociology is focused on *normative integration* (action co-ordination through shared principles, norms, and values) and strongly underestimates the other important mechanism of action co-ordination, particularly common interests (Bader 1989: 325 ff.). Most liberal political philosophers share a similar professional deviation: they further restrict normative integration to articulated normative principles and neglect cultures, virtues, and traditions of good practice.[2] Third, integration, cohesion, and social order are thought to require *harmony*, a conception which neglects the huge amount of routine conflicts without 'disintegrative'

---

[1] One of the most remarkable aspects of Nussbaum (1996) is, in my view, that all critical responses to Nussbaum share both basic assumptions: too much unity and integration and too much 'patriotic' allegiance, loyalty, solidarity, and identity (see particularly the responses by Barber, Glazer, Taylor, Walzer) and nobody (including Martha Nussbaum herself) takes a critical stance (Bader 1999a). Kymlicka criticizes both liberal and communitarian views of 'social unity' (1996: 128) but fails to distinguish clearly between 'political unity' and 'social unity' and still asks for too much extra-constitutional social coherence and cultural unity even in his thin concept of cultural membership. Consociational arrangements can do with less.

[2] Even if they explicitly address the levels of culture, virtues, and practices, like Galston, they still hold that 'a modern and multicultural society requires a common set of moral expectations and moral language if it is to remain a society and not a haphazard association or even assemblage of groups and persons ready to do cultural and economic battle with one another at the least inducement' (1995: 111). Not only can 'modern' society absolutely not be characterized as 'Gemeinschaft', there is commonly also too much community talk when it comes to polities or 'political communities'. Modern societies can better be captured by metaphors as 'patchwork' or 'bazar' (Sanchez 1996: ch. 5). And political communities which should clearly be distinguished from the state (Bader 1995a) should also take much more critical distance from this 'truth to which communitarianism as I understand it is principally devoted' (Galston 1995). Galston's conservative 'new progressive stance' is clearly opposed to the more 'conflict-prone' critical notion of community in Unger (1987: ii. 560 ff.). See also Bader (1991: ch. 4) and Galston's conservative criticism of Unger (1991).

effects and, particularly, the binding effects of conflicts.[3] Fourth, integration-talk puts a premium on *stability* as such, underestimating or neglecting (institutional as well as cultural) change. *Empirically*, it is astonishing that the story of a 'loss' or 'decline' of morals, which is told at all times and comes and goes in waves, is so poorly researched, and that the transatlantic export of this talk, which may be partly true for (parts of) the USA (Selznick 1995; Barber 1984) comes so easily to Western Europe (Favell 1996; Joas 1993; Bovens and Hemerijk 1996). Sober sociological reflections about the 'nature of society' should help criticize the hidden or explicit conservative bias of much sociological theory and can de-emphasize alarmist fears. The challenging normative option of a very loosely integrated society allowing for high degrees of institutional separation and ethno-cultural differences[4] is certainly not ruled out by some mysterious general nature of society. Empires have historically been completely detached from ethnos and the question whether a democratic demos can be cannot be answered by sociological theory selling conservative 'truths'. Liberal nationalists and rooted cosmopolitans beware of sociologists bearing gifts. It remains a truism that 'at least some internal coherence' (Parekh 1995: 28) is required for liberal-democratic polities and, particularly, for socialist policies of rough, complex equality. But we can do with much less than most liberal nationalists and all communitarians think and we are unable to give precise, let alone quantifiable, general answers of how much minimal coherence is required or what this minimal integration exactly means.

Does not the 'nature of man', the deep-rooted 'instinct for solidarity' (Nagel 1991) rule out disentanglement of demos from ethnos? Does not social psy-

---

[3] Following Max Weber, Simmel, Coser, and others, Dubiel (1990, 1994) and Hirschman (1994) have rightly criticized communitarian answers to the question 'Wieviel Gemeinsinn braucht die liberale Gesellschaft' (How much civic virtue does a liberal society need?), pointing out that conflicts, conflict-routines, and, particularly, the institutionalization of conflict, make for traditions, allegiances, and even 'communities' (Bader 1991: ch. 10, §§ 4 and 5). Needless to say, this critique should be complemented by a critique of the fashionable takeover of sociology by neo-classical economy as the other extreme.

[4] See Bader (1998) for more options than the 'mosaic' with its presumed centrifugal tendencies and the republican melting pot (even in its 'post-ethnic' or 'trans-racial', 'transnational' forms) with its presumed centripetal tendencies. No general laws hold here (it depends) and the tricky normative and political question is to find context-specific balances of (the centripetal forms of) institutional separation and (the centripetal forms of) cultural differences. Michael Lind, for example, asks for too much extra-political social unity, cohesion, integration as a precondition for political unity and stability and, consequently, can only think of multi-nation states as undemocratic, totalitarian empires or strange anomalies (like Switzerland or Canada). Democratic consociationalism, for him, is simply a non-option or a nightmare. See, in a similar vein, J. S. Mill: 'Free institutions are next to impossible in a country made up of different nationalities. Among a people without fellow-feeling, especially if they read and speak different languages, the united public opinion, necessary to the working of representative government, cannot exist. It is in general a necessary condition of free institutions that the boundaries of governments should coincide in the main with those of nationalities' (Mill 1977: 547–8). See for a critical discussion Dyke (1995: 35) and Tamir (1993: 163–4). The manifestos of Lind (1995) and Hollinger (1995) for a 'post-ethnic' or a 'national democratic America' do not really present new institutional and cultural options and are, as a consequence, somewhat out of phase.

chology tell us that conceptions of liberal nationalists, rooted cosmopolitans, or democratic universalists are impossible, mere utopian illusions, given the 'need feeling of identity'. To be short, it does not. Critical, cognitive social-psychology (Turner and Hogg 1987) has shown that general cognitive, perceptive, and social mechanisms of self-and-other categorization can only explain why the different self-categorizations are—inevitably—positively evaluated. Anthony Smith has coined this, in the case of ethnic groups, 'ethnicism'. However, it does not demand 'ethnocentrism' and cannot explain, and is not intended to explain, when and why which groups and social categorizations emerge, become salient, etc.[5] In particular, they cannot explain which social and *collective identities* become paramount and achieve strong motivational force. Nowadays, it is a fashionable truism that 'we' who live in complex, modern societies, have 'multiple identities'. The salience of 'national identity', common not only to 'nasty' nationalists and most communitarians but also to liberal nationalists, can be criticized from two different perspectives corresponding to the two analytically distinct dimensions of collective identities: societal and political identities. The first criticism questions the assumed salience of political identities in general compared to the many, overlapping social identities developing in old and new international social movements and SMOs in a trans-domestic civil society cutting across national boundaries (Falk 1995; Held 1995). The second criticism questions the focus of political identity on the level of the (nation-)state and stresses local and regional as well as transnational political identities in an era of simultaneous devolution and reconstruction of state sovereignty. Both lines of critique can be fused in order to open broader perspectives on problems of motivation/compliance and to allow for a broader set of remedial options for (assumed) crises of motivation and legitimacy of liberal, democratic welfare states.

The *motives* to comply with, in general, are manifold and mixed: traditional, affective, purely instrumental, and moral (Bader 1989: 325 ff.), and so are the bases of commitment or loyalty to the (nation-)state:[6]

(i)   Long-standing institutions induce *traditions* of compliance (focus of conservative theories of loyalty);

(ii) affective identification stabilizes solidarity, and *pre-political ethnic* or *national* identities are melted with civic or political identities (focus of nationalist theories);

(iii) *local and regional* commitments feed the more abstract national and state-centred imagined communities (focus of communalist theories);

(iv) commitment based on the working of economic, social, cultural institutions (economic or social democracy or civil society) spills over into

---

[5] See for a short discussion Bader (1995*b*: 16–22).
[6] Here I apply my earlier analysis of collective identities (Bader 1991: ch. 4) and national identities (Bader 1995*b*: 105 ff.).

loyalty to state institutions (focus of social-democratic, socialist, and associational theories: *non-ethnic pre-political bases* of political loyalty;

(v) just institutions of the liberal, democratic welfare state and democratic political procedures create and reinforce the corresponding civic, democratic, and social cultures, habits, virtues, and practices of commitment (Bader 1997*e*) and these practices, in turn, will strengthen just institutions and democratic procedures.

The hope that such a virtuous 'dialectics' of institutions and motives really exists is most explicit in republican theories but is also shared by liberal-democratic theories. Both stress the *political bases of political loyalty*.

If one accepts, for the moment, the common presumption of all different versions of theories of citizenship that we are confronted with a crisis of the legitimacy of state institutions and an erosion of the different bases of compliance, my framework enables me to chart the different *remedial options*. Each of the rivalling political traditions tries to strengthen or rebuild its respective favourite base. The conservatives try to conserve traditional institutions and shield them against all (or all rapid) changes; ethnocentrist nationalists try to purify the ethnic or 'racial' bases of the nation and to keep all 'aliens' out; liberal nationalists try to strengthen and develop specific civil and political national cultures; communalists (and most liberal-democratic communitarians) criticize state centralism, ask for more local and regional autonomy, try to rebuild and strengthen local and regional commitments, and ask for more influence on supra-state levels, contributing to the development of multilayered political units, sovereignties, and loyalties. However, their critique of the state stresses parochial political bases of loyalty instead of trans-domestic ones. Associationalists or advocates of civil society try to strengthen the civil pre-political bases of political loyalty and underscore the increasingly trans-domestic (i.e. trans-, supra-, and international) character of new loyalties (Bauböck 1994; Bader 1997*b*).[7] Radical democrats try to strengthen political

---

[7] For Cohen and Rogers (1995) the arenas and identities or solidarities of associative democracy differ from: (i) 'workplace democracy' and traditional European social democracy with its 'organic', 'natural', 'particularist', 'densely culturally textured', 'common pre-political identities', 'rooted in common culture and life circumstance' (pp. 238, 251 ff.); (ii) the 'political' identities and 'solidarities of citizenship' (p. 256) corresponding to the 'formal political arena' which, on the one hand, are also 'fabricated', 'deliberate', 'intentional', rooted in 'common concern, purposes, discussions' and 'less particularistic'. On the other hand, they are still too particularistic and not cosmopolitan enough. Their hope is that new democratic associations and social movements in international civil society will foster 'more cosmopolitan but thinner solidarities': 'An ample supply of this new kind of solidarity . . . at least hints at a way through the present morass of social democratic distemper and increasingly barren exchanges between radical, participatory democrats and statist egalitarians' (p. 252). 'It is true that we are promoting what once marched under the banner of "citizenship". But the fact that it no longer marches indicates the utility of the project . . . Practices within civil society come to look more like the state, even as they are given more autonomy from the state and are assigned a proportionately greater role in governance. Radical democracy and egalitarianism are joined through a state that stakes deeper social roots in a more cosmopolitan civil society' (p. 263). See also Hirst (1994).

bases by designs of micro- and macro-institutions which intend to remove barriers of participation and heighten the quality and deliberative character of democratic institutions and processes (Barber 1984; Offe and Preuss 1991: 165–71).[8] Rooted cosmopolitans systematically try to strengthen trans-domestic institutions and loyalties. Even a broad coalition of communalists, associationalists, liberal nationalists, and radical, rooted cosmopolitans may be possible. If so, it should aim at institutional reforms rather than at moral appeals and moral pedagogy for three reasons: the structurating impact of institutions on habits, attitudes, and motives is, empirically, much higher than vice versa; institutional experimentalism, in a normative perspective, seems to be much more in line with crucial individual freedoms than pedagogic experimentalism; and practical reform, in a short-term or mid-term perspective, is only able to change institutional settings and may hope that new cultures and motives will develop.[9]

Even if the causes of the recent crisis of institutions of liberal-democratic (welfare) states are to be seen in radical changes of the economic and social structure of globalizing capitalism and grave failures of both neo-liberal and social-democratic institutional settings (Hirst 1994; Streeck 1998; Scharpf 1999; Favell 1996), and not in the much deplored 'decline of public spirit', let alone in the increasing ethnic diversity or the often blamed policies of multiculturalism, there is still reason to worry. Some of the most urgent global problems, mentioned above, ask for stronger forms of democracy and require more political commitment than the minimalist commitment arising from conflicts and conflict-regulation. Effective international policies capable of overcoming difficult *paradoxes of collective action* require trust, and common 'ethnic' and 'political' cultures, as well as networks and identities, facilitate their resolution.[10] The crucial questions, then, arise. Which culture? Which identities? Most traditional answers in political theory stress the ethnic/national ones.[11] Within (nation-)states, ethnic and political cultures

---

[8] 'Involvement of a maximum number of citizens in activities and movements where they can practice their 'duties of civility' and learn the 'public use of reason' . . . call for an institutional reform of democracy that encourages such participation by increasing the opportunities of active citizens to make an impact on political decisions. In this way a rights-based approach which focuses on institutional obligations could also pay attention to the motivational conditions necessary for sustaining institutional guarantees of rights' (Bauböck 1994: 311). Quite often the latter two traditions are explicitly combined (Cohen and Rogers 1995).

[9] See, for a similar relationship between institutional and motivational change in recent sociology of work, Sitter (1995) and Christis (1997).

[10] Common political and/or ethnic *customs* and common *history* of a polity are important sources of mutual trust (knowledge of long chains of previous actions and reactions). Political and/or ethnic *solidarity*, a deep-rooted feeling of togetherness, is a second important source of mutual trust absent in the Hobbesian world of rational choice. Common political and/or ethnic *morals* (really shared principles, values, ethos, virtues, and the recognition of mutual obligations) is a third, important source of trust to overcome collective action paradoxes which the strategic gamblers (those lonely monads without history, common allegiances, and morals) are confronted with even if they happen to detect some common interest (Bader 1997*d*).

[11] See quotations of Mill and Mading Deng in n. 5.

may sometimes happily support each other.[12] But when it comes to global problems and dilemmas of global collective action, one is sharply reminded of the inherent tension. Consequently, all morally permissible options on the scale (from liberal nationalism to universalist cosmopolitanism: Bader 1997*e*: fig. 1) are pressurized. Abstract cosmopolitanism faces a serious lack of motivation, does not 'work', and should not be mistaken for the only morally legitimate option. State-centred identities and loyalties of liberal nationalism, on the other hand, are rather counter-productive when the problem is to strengthen compliance with imperfectly allocated global duties (O'Neill 1991; Bauböck 1994; Bader 1997*b*). The reference to national commitment in order to generate enough motivational force commonly serves as a device for getting rid of global obligations or keeping them at a harmless distance. Attempts to appeal to the 'moral usefulness of the (nation-)state' as a source of loyalty and commitment remain ambivalent even if they 'aim at the progressive expansion, but not the abolition, of existing solidarities' (Walzer 1995*a*: 249).[13] They may only help to alleviate the problem if they de-emphasize the ethnic pre-political base by opting for some version of a 'post-ethnic', national, political culture, if they try to strengthen the trans-domestic, civil, pre-political base (for example, international old and new social movements, NGOs), and at the same time try to develop and implement stronger global institutions.[14] Only in such a model of multilayered political units, sovereignties, and political as well as 'reflexive' social loyalties, may transformed loyalties to (nation-)states

---

[12] Systems of 'national' welfare states, institutions, and practices of social security and services are currently under heavy neo-liberal attack. Many social-democratic parties and theorists, in their attempt to defend at least the bare minimum of welfare arrangements, increasingly appeal to ethnic-national sentiments, playing the ethnic-national card (Offe 1998; Streeck 1998). It is highly doubtful whether this can work in the short run, but I think it is evident that, apart from moral conundrums (Bader 1997*b*), it does not solve the problems on the level of interstate distribution and co-ordination, it may be highly counter-productive for their medium and long-term solutions, and it clearly does not contribute to a supportive climate for multi-ethnic politics inside states.

[13] See my reply (Bader 1995*c*: 251). A similar strategy is in principle followed by Tamir (1993: 158–67) and, much more elaborate, Bauböck (1994). See my discussion in Bader (1997*b*). 'Transnational' (from Bourne to Bauböck) rather than 'post-national' is the better term to indicate this progressive expansion of solidarities and obligations. For this reason, I changed the original title of this contribution.

[14] See Hirst (1994: 72*e*3) for limits of associationalism, even taking into account all international associations (p. 71) and 'a relatively strong international civil society' which have drawn attention to and tried to address problems that national governments have preferred to ignore' (p. 72). 'Why does a given political entity have the membership that it does?' Associationalism has no specific answer to this' and 'cannot be peddled as another kind of hope for the World's poor. That would be an obscenity', and a rather defensive one: 'flaw in our morality and in our world. The absence of an easy solution is no excuse to ignore the problem. It would be foolish to abandon advocacy of reform and renewal in Western societies, as if the World's poor would gain by our maintaining the imperfections of our current institutions' (p. 73). This is needlessly defensive, in my view, because associative democracy should be complemented with a design of international organizations beyond 'major charities, sporting bodies, business organizations and political agencies like Amnesty, Pen, International Federation of Jurists, Oxfam, etc.' Hirst and Thompson (1996) are more offensive in this regard. See again Held (1995) and Falk (1995).

be helpful. Yet, realistically, the prospects for such a decisive shift towards trans-domestic loyalties and identities are bleak. Global institutions are weak or absent and supra-national institutions like the EU perform very badly under criteria of efficiency, democracy, and, particularly in our regard, the creation of new political cultures, the 'invention of traditions' and the generation of supra-national loyalties. The development of trans-domestic identities and loyalties, too, depends on appropriate institutions as a social precondition in order to make the positive 'dialectics' work, to enable civil and political participation, and to create new, broader, less parochial, and more cosmopolitan identities.[15]

Democratic Institutions in an Age of Transnationalism

Crouch and Eder have pointed out that one of the most urgent problems of 'new politics of inclusion' is to 'rethink the design of democratic institutions for including citizens on a local, regional, national and European basis' (1996: 14). To facilitate participation, a whole set of participatory social and political institutions is needed. In this section, I want to explore, in a very rough and sketchy way, whether the institutional design of 'associative democracy' in a rooted cosmopolitan perspective is able to start up such a positive dialectic of 'institutions and motives'.

Dominant normative theories of democracy have suffered from a terrible lack of institutional concreteness and only recently have more intensive efforts been made to fill this gap (Cohen and Rogers 1995; Hirst 1994; Unger 1987, 1996; Barber 1984; Streeck 1996). Two characteristics in particular make this developing strand very attractive: (i) the critique of old versions of an inevitable trade-off between democracy and efficiency;[16] (ii) the combination of institutions for 'social democracy' (for example industrial democracy, democratic education, social security, and services) on sectoral, local, regional, and national levels with stronger participatory forms of political democracy, particularly at local and regional levels. However, only very recently more attention has been paid to two important problems: the design of institutions on transnational (supra- and international) levels, and the relationship of

---

[15] See Bader (1997*e*) with reference to Macedo, Barber, and Dewey. 'Civic participation transcends the particularities of history, language, kinship, locality, and occupation. It creates new identities and new solidarities. It does not follow, however, that political democracy is the sole creator of community, or that it can be effective without a non-political infrastructure of association, interdependence, and moral education. A democracy is weak and volatile if citizens are badly divided, or if many are incapable of participating, or are shut out from participating' (Selznick 1995: 132).

[16] See Streeck (1996), Unger (1987), and de Sitter (1995). Crouch, Eder, and Tambini, in their introductory remarks to this volume, seem to stick to the old version of this trade-off.

institutions of associative democracy to problems of ethnic and national diversity within states.

The design of more adequate institutions on transnational levels has to be based on two crucial assumptions. The first is a critique of the traditional treatment of state *sovereignty* and its replacement by an analysis of the differentiated, delegated, and limited 'powers' on communal, provincial, state, or federal levels and on the level of supra- and international organizations (Bader 1995*a*: 211 ff., 1997*c*; Pogge 1992; Ruggie 1993; Held 1995; Falk 1995). In terms of institutional design this allows one to get rid of the old and thoroughly misleading alternatives: a (liberal, democratic, or socialist) 'world state' or the existing state-system or a 'world without states', 'global libertarianism'. The second assumption is a critique of the traditional treatment of *citizenship*, lumping together state membership, citizenship, and ethnicity/nationality, and its replacement by an analysis of social and political conceptions of democratic citizenship which leaves the adequate 'units' open, an analysis of the moral and legal conditions of 'denizenship' (for legalized residents), state membership, and (dual) citizenship which is much better suited for a 'world of global migration'.[17]

The institutional design of 'associative democracy' within states may provide more flexible and context-sensitive solutions of long-standing issues of ethnic and national minorities, if it is combined with institutional designs of *federalism* and of 'consociational' or 'power-sharing' systems. These systems allow for much higher degrees of societal and cultural sovereignty and also for considerable legal, political, fiscal powers.[18] Of course there are 'limits to the *autonomy*' of self-determined ethnic units, national provinces, or states on the one hand. On the other hand, all models of local or sectoral autonomy run up against three well-known problems. First, if societal problems are more and more 'global' and interconnected, small units cannot solve the related coordination problems. This, however, does not exclude 'subsidiarity' and *souvereiniteit in eigen kring* (sovereignty in one's own sphere). Second, federalism and decentralization have been, most of the time, enemies of politics of rough, complex equality. To correct severe economic and social inequalities among cities, regions, or—for example, within the EU—among states, considerable power of the 'centres' is required. Third, old Christian versions of *souvereiniteit in eigen kring* and fashionable neo-liberal versions of privatization and deregulation have never been guarantees of autonomy and democracy, quite to the contrary,[19] nor did they really lead to 'deregulation'. To tackle the entrenched

---

[17] See Hammar (1990), Çinar (1994), Bauböck (1998), and Bader (1995*a*, 1997*c*, 1999*b*).

[18] See Lijphart (1995), Dyke (1995), Hannum (1990), Kymlicka (1997), and Carens (1995, 1996) for the difference between institutionalizing pluralism versus pluralizing institutions. A more detailed treatment is found in Bader (1997*f*, 1998).

[19] e.g. the Dutch version of consociationalism has been highly élitist (Stuurman 1983; Lijphart 1995; Seidman 1995).

power positions of dominant classes and élites in the different societal fields and in local institutions, again much democratic power from the 'centres' is needed.[20] To find a legitimate and feasible balance between central powers and powers of sectoral or territorial units requires, obviously, intimate knowledge of the specific problems and context. No general, ready-made solutions are available and the well-known rules of thumb—as much autonomy as possible, as much centralism as necessary—are really not impressive.

The specific institutions to complement or replace the institutions of 'thin', 'liberal', representative party democracy differ widely if one compares the design of 'strong' democracy (Barber 1984) with 'empowered' democracy (Unger 1987), 'associative democracy' (Cohen and Rogers 1995; Hirst 1994). I cannot discuss these important differences here. They all are, however, varieties of more 'participatory democracy' and share one central hope: that institutions which enable more people to participate more often in more matters crucial for their daily lifes will actually foster more social and political participation and this will, in turn, create deeper and more stable commitments and loyalties. Participation is the central, creative mechanism mediating between institutions and motives (Pateman 1970; Cunningham 1987).[21] Participatory democracy has not only to tackle three structural problems of all forms of democratic control: democratic decisions and control require information, skills, and time. Compared with 'thinner', more centralized varieties of representative party democracy, they have to confront two additional problems. First, they must and do allow for strong *participation* on many levels and in many fields. The well-known bottleneck is whether people are willing and able to effectively participate in this way. The main trouble, it seems to me, is not to counter conservative 'philosophical anthropology' or thin liberal élitism on the one hand, republican fires and overstressed participatory duties on the other. The main problem lies in informed, effective, timely, and coordinated participation 'higher up' and 'far away'. Participatory movements and institutions face many more collective actors in these arenas and have to solve more severe collective action dilemmas. International social movements and NGOs have shown that it is possible to overcome these hindrances.[22] But they still lack much organizational power and strength, compared with multinational corporations, and this situation is worsened by the neo-liberal destruction of institutions and mechanisms of global political governance.

---

[20] The main reason why classical communism and social democracy, which originally shared anti-statist principles with liberalism and anarchism, ended up in 'conquering' and defending strong central states has been, in my view, that they had to compensate for lacking societal power positions by concentrated political and state power.

[21] Here I disagree with Papadopoulos (ch. 8 above).

[22] Actually, taking their 'ethnic, cultural, national, religious' diversity into account, their common cause, networks, and trust have been able to overcome collective action paradoxes much better than the miserable record of performance of state governments in the inter-state arena. Recognizing this should not seduce us into the uncritical optimism characterizing the treatment of international civil society by Held (1995) or Falk (1995).

Social movements and NGOs depend on these institutions and cannot supplant them or act 'leaving them aside'. Second, most models of participatory democracy in political and industrial democracy have had not only a strong local, but also a strongly *parochial* bias at odds with 'transnational citizenship'.[23]

Conclusion

Concluding this discussion, 'we' radical democrats have to face four hard and serious paradoxes:[24]

1. The culture, habits, virtues, and practices of *participatory democracy*, particularly the republican forms, have been historically very thickly embedded in ethnic/national cultures. At times, they have been very strong indeed, but also *highly exclusive*. Morally defensible political cultures in our age of migration have to be much thinner without losing motivational force. We cannot know in advance whether increasing participation in transnational social relations (and hopefully developing international solidarity of 'class', professions, of culture) and in transnational ('old and new') political movements (international SMOs and NGOs) and in developing transnational political institutions like the EU, the UN (and hopefully developing transnational political solidarities) actually will create strong enough social and political commitments and moral obligations to live up to our minimal moral obligations. We can only hope and try.

2. It is possible to criticize misleading dichotomies of *either nationalism or cosmopolitanism* and to imagine morally defensible and empirically stronger versions of liberal nationalism or rooted cosmopolitanism. Politically, however, these 'third ways' are still utopias. Playing the 'ethnic', 'nationalist' cards still seems to be predominant. Finding reasonable and at the same time attractive and stimulating balances between universalism and particularlism is an extremely demanding practical task.

3. In 'normal times', traditional, emotional, and instrumental motives are

---

[23] Barber, for instance, has difficulties in connecting local to state arenas in the USA (and almost completely neglects the problem of citizenship as exclusion and international solidarity). Paul Hirst is much more sensitive in this regard (Hirst 1994: 51 ff.).

[24] Contrary to Crouch and Eder, 'citizenship as a status' and 'as a practice' are not contradictory: the 'status' of civic, political, and social citizenship is not 'conferred', 'given by', or 'granted' by the state. Historically and in actual practice, it is always fought for and it is only as strong as democratic practices are, on the one hand (Somers 1993: 606). And *erkämpfte* and legally guaranteed civil, political, and social 'rights' or 'statuses', on the other hand, are important resources in these actual struggles. I do not see a 'dilemma' here and no need for a trade-off: depending on what 'optimize' means, it is certainly possible to optimize the 'passive' status and the active 'deliberative dimension'. It is a strategic dilemma of all 'institutionalization' (Bader 1991: 242), not a specific dilemma of participatory democracy.

sufficient to explain compliance of citizens and normative consent certainly does not play a prominent role. Customs, solidarities, and interests are the predominant mechanisms of action co-ordination explaining 'social stability' without much reference to normative coherence or legitimacy. In 'exceptional times', crises of 'legitimacy' come to the fore and 'values, norms, or principles' begin to play the role normative sociology and most political philosophy assigned to them. Polities, then, have to show higher degrees of political 'community'. The same holds for politics of democratic experimentalism and more radical institutional transformation. Communitarians of all sorts overestimate the normally required degree of political 'community', but some liberal communitarians have a point in arguing that such a transformational perspective 'commits us to a strong sense of social responsibility. It suggests that the thin theory of community espoused by many liberals is not enough, that we need a stronger idea of community, one that will justify the commitments and sacrifices we ask of ourselves, and of one another, in the name of a common good' (Selznick 1995: 128). However, they make no clear distinction between 'social' and 'political' community and do not restrict the higher degrees of political community and commitment to such transformational strategies.

4. The virtuous *dialectics of institutions and motives* has to *start* somehow. Very often this is presented as a chicken–egg problem: you need motivated people to be able to imagine, design, and implement new institutions and you need new, more participatory institutions to motivate people. Happily, in reality things are more a matter of degree and the supposed vicious circle may turn out to be a more spiral-like figure: some people are motivated to change and we actually live in institutions allowing at least for some participation. Projects of democratic transformation can start at both ends at the same time (Unger 1996; Sabel 1995). However, even if such a virtuous dialectics takes off, the burning question is whether it will be in time. Urgent global problems have to be addressed, the starving and uprooted 'out there' cannot wait, and the institutional misfit prevents timely, co-ordinated, effective action. The development of new institutions takes much time and so does the development of trans-domestic and global moral obligations. Urgent domestic problems of democratic, multicultural incorporation have to be addressed and the development of morally defensible and feasible institutions and policies takes much time and so does the development of tolerant civic, social, and political cultures, habits and practices.

REFERENCES

BADER, V. M. (1989). 'Max Webers Begriff der Legitimität', in J. Weiß (ed.), *Max Weber heute* (Frankfurt: Suhrkamp), 296–334.

BADER, V. M. (1991). *Kollektives Handeln: Prototheorie sozialer Ungleichheit und kollektiven Handelns II* (Opladen: Leske & Budrich).

—— (1995*a*). 'Citizenship and Exclusion', *Political Theory*, 23/2: 211–46.

—— (1995*b*). *Rassismus, Ethnizität, Bürgerschaft* (Münster: Westfälisches Dampfboot).

—— (1995*c*). 'Reply to Michael Walzer', *Political Theory*, 23: 250–2.

—— (1996). 'Incorporation and Egalitarian Multiculturalism', unpublished paper for the 'Blurred Boundaries' conference, Melbourne.

—— (ed.) (1997*a*). *Citizenship and Exclusion* (London: Macmillan).

—— (1997*b*). 'Fairly Open Borders', in V. M. Bader (ed.), *Citizenship and Exclusion* (London: Macmillan), 28–60.

—— (1997*c*). 'Conclusion', in V. M. Bader (ed.), *Citizenship and Exclusion* (London: Macmillan), 175–89.

—— (1997*d*). 'Ethnicity and Class: A Proto-Theoretical Mapping-Exercise', in W. W. Isajiw (ed.), *Comparative Perspectives on Interethnic Relations and Social Incorporation* (Toronto: Canadian Scholars' Press), 103–28.

—— (1997*e*). 'The Cultural Conditions of Trans-National Citizenship', *Political Theory*, 25/6: 771–813.

—— (1997*f*). *Incorporation of Ethnic or National Minorities: Concepts, Dimensions, Fields and Types* (mimeo).

—— (1998). 'Egalitarian Multiculturalism: Institutional Separation and Cultural Pluralism', in R. Bauböck and J. Rundell (eds.), *Blurred Boundaries: Migration, Ethnicity, Citizenship* (Aldershot: Ashgate), 185–222.

—— (1999*a*). 'For Love of Country', *Political Theory*, 27/3: 379–97.

—— (1999*b*). 'Citizenship of the European Union: Human Rights, Rights of Citizens of the Union and of Member State', *Ratio Juris*, 12/2: 153–81.

BARBER, B. (1984). *Strong Democracy* (Berkeley, Calif.: University of California Press).

BAUBÖCK, R. (1994). *Transnational Citizenship: Membership and Rights in International Migration* (Cheltenham: Edward Elgar).

—— (1998). 'The Crossing and Blurring of Boundaries in International Migration', in R. Bauböck and J. Rundell (eds.), *Blurred Boundaries* (Ashgate: Aldershot), 17–52.

BOVENS, M., and HEMERIJCK, A. (1996). *Het verhaal van der moral* (Amsterdam: Boom).

CARENS, J. H. (1995). 'Liberalism, Justice and Political Community: Theoretical Perspectives on Quebec's Liberal Nationalism', in J. H. Carens (ed.), *Is Quebec Nationalism Just? Perspectives from Anglophone Canada* (Montreal: McGill-Queen's University Press), 3–19.

—— (1996). 'Immigrants, Cultural Diversity and Liberal Democracy', paper presented at the European Forum, 'Multiculturalism, Minorities and Citizenship', Florence, 18–23 April.

CHRISTIS, J. (1997). 'Arbeid, Organisatie, Stress', Ph.D., Faculty of Political and Socio-Cultural Sciences, Amsterdam.

ÇINAR, D. (1994). 'From Aliens to Citizens', in R. Bauböck (ed.), *From Aliens to Citizens: Redefining the Legal Status of Immigrants* (Aldershot: Avebury), 49–72.

COHEN, J., and ROGERS, J. (eds.) (1995). *Associations and Democracy* (London: Verso).

CROUCH, C., and EDER, K. (1996). 'Introduction to European Forum Seminar: Social and Political Citizenship in a World of Migration', European Forum Seminar; 22–4 Feb.

CUNNINGHAM, F. (1987). *Democratic Theory and Socialism* (Cambridge: Cambridge University Press).

DUBIEL, H. (1990). 'Zivilreligion in der Massendemokratie? Kritik einer klassischen Theorie posttraditionaler Legitimation', *Soziale Welt*, 41: 125–43.

——(1994). *Ungewißheit und Politik* (Frankfurt: Suhrkamp).

DYKE, V. (1995). 'The Individual, the State, and Ethnic Communities in Political Theory', in W. Kymlicka (ed.), *The Rights of Minority Cultures* (Oxford: Oxford University Press), 31–56.

FALK, R. (1995). *On Human Governance* (Cambridge: Polity Press).

FAVELL, A. (1996). The Return of Civil Political Culture', paper presented at the EUI Conference 'Multiculturalism, Minorities and Citizenship', 18–23 April, Florence.

GALSTON, W. (1991). *Liberal Purposes: Goods, Virtues, and Diversity in the Liberal State* (Cambridge: Cambridge University Press).

——(1995). 'Progressive Politics and Communitarian Culture', in M. Walzer (ed.), *Toward a Global Civil Society* (Providence, RI: Berghahn Books), 107–12.

HAMMAR, T. (1990). *Democracy and the Nation State: Aliens, Denizens and Citizens in a World of International Migration* (Aldershot: Edward Elgar).

HANNUM, H. (1990). *Autonomy, Sovereignity, Self-Determination: The Accomodation of Conflicting Rights* (Philadelphia: University of Pennsylvania Press).

HELD, D. (1995). *Democracy and the Global Order* (Cambridge: Polity Press).

HIRSCHMAN, A. O. (1994). 'Social Conflicts as Pillars of Democratic Market Society', *Political Theory*, 22: 203–18.

HIRST, P. (1994). *Associative Democracy: New Forms of Economic and Social Governance* (Amherst, Mass.: Massachusetts University Press).

——and Thompson, G. (1996). *Globalization in Question: The International Economy and the Possibilities of Governance* (Cambridge: Polity Press).

HOLLINGER, D. A. (1995). *Post-Ethnic America: Beyond Multiculturalism* (New York: Basic Books).

JOAS, H. (1993). 'Gemeinschaft und Demokratie in den USA', in M. Brumlik and H. Brunkhorst (eds.), *Gemeinschaft und Gerechtigkeit* (Frankfurt: Suhrkamp), 49–62.

KYMLICKA, W. (1996). 'Social Unity in a Liberal State', *Social Philosophy and Policy Formation*, 13: 105–36.

——(1997). *States, Nations and Cultures* (Assen: van Gorcum).

——and NORMAN, W. (1994). 'Return of the Citizen', *Ethics*, 104: 352–81.

LIJPHART, A. (1995). 'Selfdetermination versus Pre-determination of Ethnic Minorities in Power-Sharing Systems', in W. Kymlicka (ed.), *The Rights of Minority Cultures* (Oxford: Oxford University Press), 275–87.

LIND, M. (1995). *The Next American Nation: The New Nationalism and the Fourth American Revolution* (New York: The Free Press).

MILL, J. S. (1977). 'Considerations on Representative Government', in J. M. Robson (ed.), *CollectedWorks*, xix (Buffalo, NY, and Toronto: University of Toronto Press and Routledge & Kegan Paul).

NAGEL, T. (1991). *Equality and Partiality* (New York: Oxford University Press).

Nussbaum, M. C. (1996). *For Love of Country: Debating the Limits of Patriotism* (Boston, Mass: Beacon Press).

Offe, C. (1998). 'Demokratie und Wohlfahrtsstaat: Eine europäische Regimeform unter dem Streß der europäischen Integration', in W. Streeck (ed.), *Internationale Wirtschaft, nationale Demokratie* (Frankfurt and New York: Campus), 99–136.

——and Preuss, U. K. (1991). 'Democratic Institutions and Moral Resources', in D. Held (ed.), *Political Theory Today* (Oxford: Polity Press), 143–71.

O'Neill, O. (1991). 'Transnational Justice', in D. Held (ed.), *Political Theory Today* (Cambridge: Polity Press), 276–304.

Parekh, B. (1995). 'Minority Cultures and the Limits of Equality', paper presented at the conference Berg en Dal.

Pateman, C. (1970). *Participation and Democratic Theory* (Cambridge: Cambridge University Press).

Pogge, T. W. (1992). 'Cosmopolitanism and Sovereignity', *Ethics*, 103: 48–75.

Ruggie, J. G. (1993). 'Territoriality and Beyond', *International Organization*, 47: 139–74.

Sabel, C. (1995). 'Bootstrapping Reforms: Rebuilding Firms, Welfare State, and Unions', *Politics and Society*, 23/1: 5–48.

Sanchez, P. Z. (1996). 'Postfoundationalism, Human Rights, and Political Cultures', Ph.D., University of Toronto.

Scharpf, F. (1999). *Governing in Europe: Effective and Democratic?* (Oxford: Oxford University Press).

Schmitter, P. C. (1996). *Is it Really Possible to Democratize the Euro-Polity? And if so, What Role Euro-Citizens Play in it?* (Florence: European University Institute).

Seidman, S. (1995). 'Verschil en democratie in het Westen: Conceptuele en vergelijkende observaties', *Krisis*, 60: 60–74.

Selznick, P. (1995). 'From Socialism to Communitarianism', in M. Walzer (ed.), *Toward a Global Civil Society* (Providence, RI: Berghahn Books), 127–32.

Sitter, U. de (1995). *Synergetisch produceren* (Assen: van Gorcum).

Somers, M. R. (1993). 'Citizenship and the Place of the Public Sphere: Law, Community, and Political Culture in the Transition to Democracy', *American Sociological Review*, 58: 587–620.

Streeck, W. (1996). *The Efficiency of Democracy* (mimeo).

——(1998). 'Einleitung: Internationale Wirtschaft, Nationale Demokratie', in W. Streeck (ed.), *Internationale Wirtschaft, nationale Demokratie* (Frankfurt and New York: Campus), 11–58.

Stuurman, S. (1983). *Verzuiling, Kapitalisme en Patriatchaat* (Nijmegen: SUN).

Tamir, Y. (1993). *Liberal Nationalism* (Princeton: Princeton University Press).

Turner, J. C., and ½ogg, M. A. (1987). *Rediscovering the Social Group: Self-Categorization Theory* (Oxford: Blackwell).

Unger, R. M. (1987). *Politics: A Work in Constructive Social Theory* (Cambridge: Cambridge University Press).

——(1996). *What Should Legal Analysis Become?* (London and New York: Verso).

Walzer, M. (1995a). 'Response to Veit Bader', *Political Theory*, 23/2: 247–9.

——(ed.) (1995b). *Toward a Global Civil Society* (Providence, RI: Berghahn Books).

10

Social Movement Organizations and the Democratic Order: Reorganizing the Social Basis of Political Citizenship in Complex Societies

Klaus Eder

What Does Citizenship Have to Do With Democracy?

Democracy is a cultural project which calls for a form of co-operation among human beings that excludes the use of force and that bases co-operation on collective consent. It was not the Greek city-states which invented democracy. Co-operation based on collective consent has been characteristic for many societies. They simply did not use the word democracy to define what they were doing. But they lived something that we would describe as democracy. The Greek case is particular in one respect. The Greek city-states were the first societies to use the idea of democracy to justify and legitimate a given political order. It was with the Greeks that democracy became an ideology justifying a political order. And applying the so-called Thomas theorem, which is that defining a situation as real has real consequences, I claim that defining a political order as democratic has real consequences. But the consequences—concerning the Greek city-states—were for the time being limited.

The modern form of democracy, emerging from the eighteenth century onward in Europe (and its North American colonies), is again a special case. It is characterized by the fact that European societies from the eighteenth century developed a highly specific institutional order, the nation-state, and used the idea of democracy as its legitimating ideology. This particular combination of the nation-state and the idea of democracy has provoked a series of events, from the French Revolution to Enlightened Absolutism and to the modern nationalist waves ending in fascism, which all belong to the same category of events: attempts use democratic principles for the legitimation of the modern nation-state.

I would like to distinguish two principles that are central to the idea of democracy: first, the principle of enabling the equal participation of people and, second, the principle of collective will formation through rational discussion. The first principle underlies the rule of *universal election*; elections are seen as the mechanism through which people participate in politics, thus self-determining their form of co-operation and of living together. The second principle underlies the rule of *public discussion*; public discussion is seen as a mechanism that ensures that any political action has to pass the test of public consent: political action has to be justified before the public.

These rules which are central for a democratic order have given rise to the two central institutions of a modern democratic order: the first institution is 'citizenship' which includes a series of active political rights of participation; the second institution is the 'public space' which provides an arena for discussing public matters. Both the notion of (political) citizenship and the notion of public space belong to the most widely discussed ideas in modern political theory and modern political discourse. An example of this is the resonance to Habermas's idea of the public space as the forum of free exchange of ideas; another is the resonance that the idea of citizenship has in today's political discourse.

Thus we have identified the two principles that are used to justify and legitimate a modern political order as a democratic one. I emphasize the aspect of legitimation: that is to say that democracy is an idea and an ideal used as a critical standard for evaluating a given political order. Giving up such ideals is the worst that could happen to modern political orders: fascism is one of the frightening examples of the consequences that occur when the reference to democratic principles has been given up. Ideals, however, are not unproblematic either. They do not guarantee a rational political order built on the premises of these ideals.

Problems arise, for example, when people start to *realize* ideals. Historical attempts to realize ideals have produced self-destructive effects, ranging from Jacobinism to Stalinism. It has led to ideological politics, which has been counter-productive for creating and reproducing a democratic order. Avoiding counter-productive effects while realizing principles leads to an alternative way of relating democratic principles to reality: namely *applying* principles to reality while considering the context. *Realizing* principles often leads to totalitarian action; *applying* principles adequately in a given historical and social context means developing procedures which help to prevent principles from producing effects that are contrary to democratic principles. This contextualism can also be called a reflexive use of principles in the construction of a modern political order. The *problem of democracy* is thus not inherent in the principles; the argument that the cruelties occurring in the course of modern history have challenged the pertinence of these principles is stating a false problem. The problem of democracy is a different one: it is one of the adequate application of democratic principles to social reality. The real problem is democracy in context.

This argument has a further implication: it depends on the people who put into practice the principles of the democratic organization of society. It is here that the problem of citizenship comes in. Democracy depends on the people inhabiting democratically organized spaces. As long as we reduce the problem of democracy to creating it (even by making it a long-term project which permanently has to be built, thus never leaving the state of its creation), we do not have the problem of citizenship. We have a problem of the avant-garde creating its conditions and educating the people inhabiting future spaces. When turning democracy into an endless project we avoid the real world of imperfect democratic institutions and imperfect people. And this is what should interest social scientists at least. The institutional forms of reproducing and stabilizing should become the focus and as soon as this happens the imperfection of the people becomes a problem. This is the core of the citizenship debate: how to create democratically organized societies with imperfect people. This problem was removed from the agenda in the new social movements debate. It is not by chance that the discourse on citizenship follows the discourse of social movements that has dominated the intellectual-political debate since the 1960s.

The Problem of Democracy

Situating the Problem of Democracy

The problem of democracy lies in the way in which these principles are applied to context by social actors (citizens). This argument concerns the viability of democratic principles; it is based on doubts as to whether modern political institutions can still embody democratic principles. The two main empirical points are the following. First, elections, the institutional form of participation, have become a ritual; people vote not because they believe in their democratic character, but because they have some diffuse feeling of obligation to do so. Second, the public space as an arena of public debate has become an arena of spectacles staged by the mass media.

The first point can be linked to the phenomenon of the declining importance of elections; electoral participation is declining in the USA and it is expected to decline even further.[1] This decline can be counteracted if élites

---

[1] This was the expectation of Ginsberg and Shefter (1989) in the late 1980s. Since then this trend seems to have remained stable on a low level (with cyclical variations).

succeed in transforming elections into a big public spectacle that nobody wants to miss (good examples are the 1996 presidential elections in the USA or the recent Italian local elections). The collective will of the people then turns out to result from an organized ritual that integrates people into a collective process of ritual dramatization. The second point can be linked to the discussion of the mass media as arenas that do anything but support discursive processes. What the public arena provides are mechanisms that (*a*) distort reality, (*b*) use media communication for instrumental purposes (this is the theory of instrumental actualization), and (*c*) communicate only news that people like to hear. The media do not contribute to rational argumentation, but to symbolic dramatizations of pieces of reality.

Both phenomena are said to block the realization of democratic principles. They violate the legitimating principles of equal political participation and public discussion. The phenomena I have named are part of a widespread critique of existing democracy: Thus the media are condemned to fail their role in modern public debate; thus the people are criticized because they do not fulfil their obligation as citizens to vote. I would like to argue that these critiques are misled and based on an inadequate understanding of the way democratic principles are *applied* to reality. Therefore I will take a more distanced position which leads to the following questions. Are ritualization and dramatization a necessary condition of applying democratic principles to social reality? Does democracy need ritualization and dramatization to gain a stable social basis? Is not what has been criticized as a problem of democracy a constitutive part of the social anchoring of democratic principles?

My answer will not be a simple one. It will be based upon a theoretical perspective that has gained ground in sociology under the label of 'new institutionalism'.[2] The basic idea is that institutions are in fact basically rituals and ceremonies. This also holds for political institutions. Political institutions are fundamentally organizations that organize rituals and ceremonies. These rituals and ceremonies, however, need an idealization that makes these rituals and ceremonies acceptable to people. And here the idea of democracy comes in: democracy is a specifically modern way of rationalizing the rituals of voting and of public debate. This distinguishes modern societies from non-modern societies; the latter rationalize their institutional forms by different ideas (for example, ones that have been prescribed by God and serve only his will); the former rationalize such rituals by reference to universal principles of equal participation and public debate. These rationalizations are more than mere ideological superstructures; they are a social reality themselves and have social effects. One fundamental effect is that they stabilize political institutions. Such beliefs shatter when the link to reality becomes too loose (what-

---

[2] The theoretical ideas I draw upon go beyond new institutionalism (Powell and DiMaggio 1991). The historical institutionalism of Somers (1993, 1995) as well as the historical constructivism of Giesen (1991, 1998) are parallel attempts from which I have drawn heavily.

ever 'too loose' might mean more exactly—but this is a methodological question).

Seen from this perspective, the critique of democratic institutions would be justified on the ground that the existing democratic institutions no longer succeed in staging the rituals of political participation and public debate. Thus central problems of modern societies would be left to the private sphere, to the market, and to economic forces that do not need a democratic legitimation. This disenchantment with political institutions would even destroy the very basis of these institutions: the staging of a collective action of the people. The critique would not be justified on the grounds that these institutions have become mere rituals, 'irrational' ceremonies. What I therefore want to defend is that democratic institutions are—as any other social institution is—ritually organized ceremonies that bind people together in a collective action. They are—and this is the small but decisive difference—democratically legitimated rituals and as such different from non-democratically legitimated institutions. This has some consequences for the empirical critique of public life to which I will turn later.

Reconsidering Democratization

This theoretical perspective allows me to take a fresh look at some of the proposals for a more democratic political order in modern societies to overcome the limits of existing democratic regimes. The main hope that has dominated the discourse on realizing more democracy in modern societies has been put in phenomena which bring back people and discussion to political life: *social movements, collective mobilizations, and new forms of public deliberation*. These phenomena are said to revive democracy, to introduce more elements of grass-roots democracy to modern societies, to induce what has been called 'populist reforms' (Shrader-Frechette 1991).

I agree that these phenomena are central to the transformation of modern democratic institutions. But I disagree with the explanation of why they are important for the development of democratic institutions. The usual explanation is that the social movements that have emerged in advanced modern societies are (or could be) a better and more complete realization of the principles that make up a democratic society. From the theoretical perspective I proposed above these new forms of participation and deliberation are not a new step toward the realization of more democracy, but simply ways of applying democratic principles to modern societies. As such, these new forms are as ritually organized as any existing democratic institution; they are as much part of ceremonial practices as any other existing form of public participation and debate. Social movements and new forms of public deliberation have nothing more inherently democratic than the so-called old forms of parliamentary debate or electoral mobilization. These new forms offer additional social references that can be rationalized in democratic terms.

To mobilize some evidence for this theory I will turn to the phenomenon that has become, in the last two decades, the embodiment of a coming new democratic way of organizing modern society: the new social movements. These movements have been seen as new opportunities for citizens to participate in political life. I would like, first, to show that these new movements do not 'realize' more democracy. Their importance is linked to the following: first, they offer new rituals of participation and debate and, second, these rituals are good for rationalization in terms of democratic principles.

I will turn first to the phenomenon of the new social movements, then describe their institutional potential in providing new ritual forms of collective action, and finally discuss their function in providing democratically organized public spaces. This will be done through reference to the case of modern environmentalism.

Movements as an Element of an Emerging Institutional Order

The Emergence of New Social Movements

The new social movements have often been described as single-issue movements. This is only partially true and misses the distinctive aspect of these movements. The proposition that they are forms of collective mobilization through which citizens succeed in organizing themselves collectively with the aim of influencing and changing the course of the development of modern societies—as Alain Touraine, the most important theorist of social movements, has argued—comes close to the self-understanding of these movements but not necessarily to their real function.

What can be pointed out as their most important characteristics are mobilizations for two types of concerns in contemporary society. The first has to do with the increasing public sensitivity to issues that are common goods (or public goods) problems. Among these common goods one issue has become central and dominant: the environment. It has even become the most disputed example of a common good. Common goods, however, encourage free-riding (Olson 1965). To counteract such tendencies toward free-riding, normative prescriptions that bind individual interests to a common cause and make collective action possible are necessary. Social movements are such a mechanism. The concern for common goods (as manifest for example in environmentalist and ecological movements) can be defined as a normative obligation insti-tutionalized in a social movement.[3]

The second concern has to do with the problem of recognition, which is a double-edged problem. It refers to defensive reactions against the other as well as to mobilizing claims for recognition of minorities or migrants. Collective mobilizations for recognition generate what has been called identity politics. Since identity markers need public mobilization to be recognizable, social movements play an important role in identity politics.[4]

Social movements are in this sense creating an institutional context which is first of all an alternative to the market. The market model of co-ordinating individual interests does not work on its own: it needs stronger normative obligations. In order to commit individuals to contributing to the mainte-nance and enhancement of public (or common) goods or to recognizing the particularity of the other, constraints have to be imposed upon private actors. The traditional solution has been for the state to regulate (and sanction) indi-vidual and collective behaviour. But this solution has led to a paradox: the more the state has to take over such functions, the more it intrudes into the lifeworld, thus creating the paradoxical effect of destroying the normative obligations it wants to establish. Social movements have reacted to this attack on the lifeworld and rejected the state as a solution to the collective action problem. But what is there beyond the market and the state as a solution to creating collective action in matters that are concerned with collective goods?

The third solution is neither the market nor the state, but association.[5] Actors bind each other through associational ties. Both types of new social movements fit this associational model. The first type, the common good ori-ented type such as environmentalism, creates collective action through the identification with a collective concern such as the environment. Such move-ments create collective action by defining a common good problem as their common issue. Thus free-riding is overcome by creating an object for identi-fication. The issue of environmental protection has served this purpose. The same holds for the second type of new social movements, identity-oriented movements that push the gender issue or issues of collective identity in national, regional, or religious movements. The issue of collective identity creates the basis for a collective mobilization beyond interests.

---

[3] This is not to say that there has not been such a concern for common goods in old modern society. Concerns for national identity are certainly of this kind, but obviously have not been solved in a modern way. Therefore we see environmentalism as a key to how these other common good issues might be institutionally regulated.

[4] The movements that can be subsumed under this heading are the feminist movement, nationalist movements, queer movement, ethnic and religious movements. This plurality of concerns contains a common denominator: the quest for a collective identity to be recognized as different by the others.

[5] Knoke (1986) has proposed an analytical model for dealing with this third type of social organi-zation. It has so far, to my knowledge, not triggered further research.

The common good orientation makes the environment a good case for studying the effect of politicizing concerns for common goods. The rise of regulatory agencies within the state reacts to the rise of such concerns; regulatory agencies can no longer claim to represent the common interest against the particularistic interests of civil society; rather, they have to compete with other actors and their concerns for common goods, such as environmental movements and groups. The classic state agencies have to adapt to this situation, and the phenomenon of systems of negotiation outside the traditional institutional framework of politics is a key to the institutional transformation that accompanies the rise of common good issues.[6] The identity concerns produce another and different politicizing effect: the rise of counter-movements to social movements that push identity issues.[7] No longer are social movements the privileged instance to give voice to concerns; counter-movements do so too. And between the two competition for public attention is growing.

These developments point to a shift in how modern societies regulate themselves through politics. Politics is shifting towards a different field: it is no longer tied to the state and the field of action defined by state institutions. Social movements are thus not the result of pressure for more democracy but an element in the development of the new institutional forms of politics in modern societies. They are not only challenging but extending the boundaries of institutional politics, to use Offe's formula (1985). They are also good arguments for democracy. Finally, they even foster the symbolic aspect of politics by extending the public arena and intensifying public communication (ecological communication is one important part of it). So we arrive at the paradox that the increase in ritual politics and symbolic politics fostered by social movements leads to more democracy. This paradox cannot be resolved by a theory of the inherent democratic potential of social movements. It can only be resolved by a theory that explains the institutionalization of organized social movement actors in terms of a neo-institutionalist theory of a democratic political order.

This theory emphasizes two aspects: (1) the increasing participation of consequential organized collective actors[8] in diverse issue fields or policy domains and (2) the intensification of public communication over these issues. Both phenomena will be looked at in the following section in order to prepare the

---

[6] The argument that the state increases its regulatory activities in non-welfare issues has been advanced by Majone. It simply says that, after the interventionist state aiming at issues of social justice, the emergence of environmental policy issues which imply a series of concerned actors has led to a new regulatory style and even an increase in state activities to guarantee the co-ordination of all the groups and actors concerned (Majone 1993). Thus the old argument by Habermas concerning the clash between system and lifeworld gains a completely new and paradoxical meaning.

[7] A good example is the abortion issue which is targeted by pro-choice movements and pro-life movements.

[8] The term 'consequential actors' is taken from Laumann and Knoke (1987).

ground for more questions. Do these phenomena contribute to more democracy? What role do citizens play in such a world?

The Emerging Institutional Context of Movement Organizations

The institutionalization of social movements has been analysed so far mainly regarding the effect upon the internal organization of social movements, that is, the emergence of particular organizational forms of social movements.[9] Another effect (less well analysed) is the effect of the rise of organized social movements upon the external relations of movement organizations, that is, upon the rules governing the interorganizational field of which social movement organizations are a part. This emerging interorganizational field develops some peculiarities which transform the modes of political institutionalization that have developed in modern political cultures. A new type of interconnection emerges between the society as represented by social movement organizations, the economy as represented by industrial organizations (including trade unions), and the government as represented by the administrative organizations of the modern state.

The rise of social movement organizations dealing with public goods creates a strain on the monopoly of the state to provide common goods. The provision of public goods becomes a contested issue in policy-making. Thus movement actors bring the state back in, but not as the key and powerful actor, but as a co-operator or adversary in a controversial policy domain. Market-based organizations, the economic corporations, are defined as those which destroy common goods and are at the same time necessary to provide these common goods (for example, by developing an industry for recycling waste and developing green technologies), which makes these organizations a consequential actor in a policy field. Thus an institutional system emerges in which new rules emerge (most of them beyond the law[10]) which co-ordinate actors through rules that are an effect of movement organizations entering this field.

The emergence of social movement organizations is therefore more than just an addition to an existing political space. It rather entails two specific structural changes. The first is the separation of active movement organizations from their constituencies. Civil society is not the association writ large, but the representation of associations by specialized corporate actors, that is, social movement organizations. This naming is, however, increasingly misleading. Social movements organizations are no longer movements in the

[9] This is the discussed under the label 'social movement organizations' which has been triggered by the work of Zald and McCarthy (1987a, b).

[10] Here the discussion on delegalization and new forms of law has a central place. See for a first cycle of this discussion Abel (1980) and Galanter (1980). A new cycle could be expected after a longer period of theoretical focus on the rule of law and of practical focus on European law.

strict sense of the term. They have become something different for which I would like to propose the term 'public interest group'. The second change is the shift of the institutional locus of control away from state–economy relationships toward a new triangular situation: a state–economy-society relationship.

This emerging constellation is different from the idea of society taking over the state or the economy or both. The dichotomic world-view characterizing social theorizing since the nineteenth century is no longer adequate. The opposition of state and market, of state and society, of system and lifeworld, have given place to a triangular situation of co-ordination of functionally differentiated spheres of modern life. This shifts the locus of control away from spaces specific to either the state or the economy, or some shared (corporatist) space between both, toward some new type of space. The emerging type of society is no longer defined by state intervention into the economy and the resulting welfare state with its specific corporatist arrangements. The state is now intervening in civil society, creating institutional arrangements which can be called 'postcorporatist' (Eder 1996). The space which is shared by these actors is the public space (Habermas 1989 [1962]), a space extending beyond the boundaries of institutional politics.

Table 10.1 gives an overview of the triangular structure of the institutional context emerging in the course of the institutionalization of collective actors representing civil society (social movements). It distinguishes the primary institutional location of collective actors which defines the specific environment for each of the other two actors, and lists some elements constituting the action space of these collective actors. Thus an inventory of the specific environments that organized collective actors provide for each other can be given. This model presents three basic elements of the space constituted by consequential collective actors. It defines the action space of highly complex societies in which old metaphors of people versus the state, of capitalists versus plebeians, of managers versus clients, no longer grasp the institutional reality. Since there is no longer a zero-sum game between two opposing forces, taking the side of one of the collective actors is excluded. There is no option between rationality, justice, and discursivity, between state, market, and civil society. There is only some overlapping space (depending on issue-specific and time-dependent conjunctures) which is the *public space.*

The triangulation of these actors shapes the institutional context of democracy in present-day polities, that is, in polities of the 'post new social movements age'. The state is no longer the exclusive reference for democratic politics (this also holds for the countermodel of economic democracy). The public space emerging in this triangulation requires actors capable and competent to people it. Such people are called citizens. However, the context for such citizenship has become more complicated. Hence the question: what kind of political citizens are needed to serve as a public for triangulated

TABLE 10.1. *A model of organizational democracy*

Specific environments	Institutional location		
	Market	State	Associations (civil society)
Issues	Non-interference into the private sector	Providing public goods and services	Moralizing and politicizing issues
Carriers (collective actors)	Economic corporations, firms	Political parties, policy-makers	NGOs, movement organizations
Social units	Classes	Status groups	Moral communities
Messages	Consumer preferences	Voting behaviour	Protest mobilizations
Media of communication	Money	Votes	Moral frames
Type of public constituency	Consumers	Voters	Opinion-holders (the 'public')
Institutional myth	Formal rationality	Justice	Discourse

political arrangements? What kind of people are necessary to fill public spaces for triangulated institutional systems?

Democracy and the New Institutional Complexity

Shifting Boundaries of the Political

The *interorganizational field* emerging from the co-ordination of pluralized collective actors shifts the boundaries of the political towards the public space. This is the central claim. Its indicators are forms of collective bargaining and procedures of conflict settling and dispute resolution which emerged first in policy areas which are rather new or recent and therefore more open to adaptive changes (such as environmental issues). The normative rules of the game co-ordinate the conflicting actors in a way that is far beyond the old models of settling class conflicts.[11] This process is still less developed when looking at

[11] To situate this type of triangulated order in the evolution of interorganizational forms I have proposed the notion of a 'postcorporatist order' (Eder 1996).

claims for recognition, in spite of attempts to institutionalize multicultural agencies or migrant forums that provide spaces for debating identities. Regarding the latter, the classic public space, the street and ordinary man, indicates a revival of public space that is peopled by a mobilized counter-public.

The changes in the institutional order due to the integration of social movement organizations into institutional politics go even further. The new institutional politics is accompanied by a rise in moral self-presentation by collective actors. A good indicator of this is the rise of the discourse of 'public responsibility' of movement actors and economic actors. Money is still a necessary, but not a sufficient means of regulating the issues that have set into motion all these changes. Markets are no longer simply organized around economic processes of money-based exchange, but are embedded in a context in which symbols of trust and reliability and images of oneself and of others shape market processes. *Identity markets* make symbolic goods the medium of market relations. The logic of such identity markets is moving away from money values and their price towards symbolic values and their resonance. Identity markets even make state intervention and the political regulation of markets subsidiary. Policy-makers themselves have to enter the game of the identity market. Thus the symbolic dimension in the self-regulation of the emerging interorganizational field becomes more and more central.

These developments point to important changes in the way in which different collective actors, including movement organizations, are embedded in or even create a new institutional framework which is characterized by the following elements:

• a new symbolic order expressing concern for collective goods or collective recognition;
• an institutional form beyond the state, market, and civil society, that is, a self-organizing arrangement of actors dealing with common good issues or issues of recognition;
• an interorganizational field in which issues and identities are constantly presented and communicated.

The emerging institutional order is not a civil society—a term that describes an ideal world—and it even poses the question whether this description still serves the function it once had: to produce a self-correcting idea of modernity, that is, reflexive modernity. The civil society concept misses the point that characterizes even in ideal terms what has happened to the public space through the new social movements: a new logic of institutional action which fosters forms of self-organization beyond the state and which thus contributes to a rearrangement of institutions that have served so far as the carriers of modern rationality.[12]

The mechanism reproducing the emerging public space is public communication. It is my empirical claim that social movements have contributed to increasing public communication (Luhmann has called this 'increasing public noise') and thus to an expanding public space of modern societies. By focusing on the public space, its agenda-setting function, and the way in which it co-ordinates the strategies of movement actors with the one of the competing collective actors in policy domains, we will be able to assess the particular role of public debate in the emerging institutional order of modern societies. The theoretical claim is that the expansion of public communication provides a public ritual of debate in which more actors than ever before take part. This has specific consequences for the public space in which these actors communicate their issue definitions and thus monitor each other. I would like to develop this point using the cases of ecological communication and of identity communication.

Extending the Boundaries of the Political:
The Environmental Movement

During the 1980s, the environmental movement in Western societies put the environment on the public agenda. Since then its opponents have appropriated this issue as well. In fact, the environmental movement no longer has to struggle for this discourse to be noticed: it has actually become topical. There are now so many voices that, ironically, it is difficult to be heard. Does this noise change the political culture and the political institutions of modern societies? Does it lead to more democracy? Or does it lead to its decline, due to a post-modern fragmentation of meaning which makes meaningful communication impossible?

To answer such questions we have to understand better the dynamics of public agenda-setting which shapes the public discourse on the environment. Twenty years ago environmental movements put this issue on the public agenda. Once the public agenda has been set, these movements must defend their agenda-setting image. They no longer have the monopoly of representing environmental concerns; competitors emerge in the market of producing and communicating 'green' images. Keeping a public image is bound to a discourse where interactive strategic moves of competing actors begin to define the discursive field. This is changing the environmental movement's image

---

[12] The work of Shrader-Frechette (1991) is pertinent here because she shows that risks, seen as a mode of framing reality by the ecological movement, lead to changes in methodological and procedural forms of dealing with the problems that these risks denote.

and forcing it to stabilize its social position *within* the discourse on the environment. Public discourse is therefore a key to the understanding and analysis of the rise and fall of environmental issues, taking into account the special role protest actors play in it.

The increasing attention to environmental issues has finally caught the environmental movement in a paradox: the movement that created the green public agenda can no longer be sure of being present also on the media agenda. It is bound to this public agenda, which in turn is bound to the symbols of environmental dangers that once resonated deeply and created the culture of environmentalism. On the other hand, the media agenda that increasingly influences the policy agenda has developed its own dynamic, with the tendency to exclude environmental movements from the agenda-setting process.[13] This has contributed to the transformation of environmental movements into cultural pressure groups. In order to survive, they must invest in public discourse (Hansen 1993a; Rossmann 1993), which means engage in public relations activities. The question of whether environmental movements will survive in the market-place of public discourse can already be answered. Environmental movements will certainly not survive as movements of mass mobilization. The action repertoire will change fundamentally, and with it the relationship between movements and their constituencies. They will survive as a collective actor, taking care of needs and risks which are not covered by the traditional public interest groups (such as trade unions). Their survival depends on their capacity to keep control of their stakes in the public discourse. Survival in this market is contingent upon the successful communication of symbolic packages that resonate with the respective constituency.

The example of the environmental movement gives an idea of the effects that new social movements have had on the construction of a public space in modern societies. The effect is a twofold one. The first is the enlargement of the public space by making any issue a contested policy domain. The public space expands by creating issue-specific public spaces in which different coalitions of collective actors emerge. Thus the idea of a big and uniform public space where all people meet is inadequate. We have rather to do with a network of issue-specific public spaces and with issue-specific discourses. At the same time, these public spaces are developing their own modes of functioning: the discourses are the result of communications strategies and even communication campaigns of collective actors that have a stake in an issue. Public

---

[13] The classic statement on the constitutive role of the media for protest activities is Gitlin (1980). In the mean time, however, this role has undergone significant changes. See, concerning environmental protest, the contributions in Hansen (1993b), especially Cracknell (1993), Hansen (1993a), Burgess and Harrison (1993). Another tradition is the one initiated by Gamson (1992). See as an overview Gamson *et al.* (1992). The insertion of movements into an issue agenda thus becomes the focus of interest.

relations and the most modern technologies of communication are used to constitute this network of public spaces. Movement actors engage in symbolic action to attract public attention, business corporations engage in PR activities in policy domains. And policy actors join this ritual of image communication.

The second effect has to do with the extension of the boundaries of the political through such a multiplication of public spaces. The cases I have in mind are cases of horizontal systems of negotiation that have emerged in recent years not only on the national level (especially in Germany), but also on the European level.[14] In Germany *Politikdialoge* (political dialogues) comprise cases such as advisory commissions, energy consensus talks, environmental forums. Somewhat distanced from this institutional level, interorganizational dialogues (between citizen initiatives and enterprises) increasingly play a role. Mediation procedures can be added to both levels of dialogue, bringing a more binding function, with different degrees to which non-adherence to such mediated results can be sanctioned legally. In any case, public attention to such dialogues and eventual mediation procedures provide strong pressures on the participants to behave according to general rules.[15]

These cases can be seen as new institutional forms of political solutions to collective action problems. They do no longer simply challenge the institutional boundaries of the political (Offe 1985), but they extend these boundaries. This extension is linked to the inclusion of a new and particular type of issue. Ecological conflicts are particular because they combine and even fuse distributive questions with value commitments and identity questions. In ecological conflicts it is not just the distribution of risks that is at stake but also the values and identities which should underlie the human relationship with nature. Identities are at stake because the issues are about the extent to which ideas of a good and decent life are recognized as legitimate political claims. At the same time, any decision on collective goods is linked to diffuse pressures regarding the protection of a common or general interest which creates particular legitimation problems.

Environmental problems thus need a public space and involve actors as a public and as bearers of interests and ideas and identities. The result is the paradox I mentioned at the beginning: the more actors participate in the institutional game, the more they have to communicate their views; the more they communicate their views, the more they engage in ritualistic forms of

---

[14] On the European level environmental dialogues and social dialogues have been staged to coordinate citizenship interests in these matters. For an analysis of the ambivalences of such discursive politics in the environmental sphere see Eder (1999).

[15] 'Citizens' juries' in Britain represent the same phenomenon. The different wording has to do with a different national tradition of conceptualizing political forms in which social actors participate. In the German context the word *Staatsbürger* would distort the meaning of those forms that are called there 'discursive institutions'. Habermas's theories have had an imprint on the wording in present-day Germany.

argumentation in dramatizations that solicit the attention of the public, above all of the media. The media turn out to be the public space co-ordinating the networks of issue-specific public spaces. Media communication, however, does not follow the model of rational argumentation, but the model of selective representation of reality. Media are constructing a reality, and the more they do so, the more communication increases. Does this mean more democracy or less?

Extending the Boundaries of the Political: Mobilizing Ethnic Identities

The mobilization of ethnic differences and identities along ethnic lines provides the second case for shifting boundaries of political citizenship. The boundaries are themselves the medium of mobilization. They can emphasize old national boundaries or transgress them. They can turn local and compete with national ones. Cross-cutting cleavages make the political a space in which actors are 'overdetermined' by their memberships in different political fields. A central place in this multiplication of identitarian politics is the rise of ethnic politics.[16]

Ethnic conflicts are not conflicts over interests that are couched in particular language games (such as the environment, which means different things in different cultures—for some cultures nature is bad, for others good). They are conflicts over culture as such. They confront symbolic boundary markers with other symbolic boundary markers, leaving the option of mutual recognition or splendid isolation. The choice is between exclusion of the other or multicultural pluralism. Such options imply a different logic of mobilization and protest.

The first difference has to do with the totalizing character of identity claims. When one group claims recognition the group addressed must answer in the same terms, pointing out its identity claims. Thus mobilization becomes a double process: mobilizing the identity of one group provokes the mobilization of the group addressed. Movements and counter-movements are emerging simultaneously. There is nothing comparable in the workers' movement or the new social movements: for them the 'other' has been institutions, capitalism, or/and the state. Identity mobilization leads to a movementization of society as whole.

This particularity of identity mobilization, the co-occurrence of movements and counter-movements, was already visible in older forms of identity mobilization, such as the romantic movement or the fascist movement. The dialectics of co-occurrence was, however, thwarted in the first case by stabi-

---

[16] Identity politics is discussed in Calhoun (1994, 1995). See also the discussion of the ambivalences of identity politics in Eder (2000).

lizing romantic identity claims as minority positions of a marginalized literary intelligentsia. In the case of fascism, the identity claims became majoritarian (a process supported and fostered by a specific mode of party politics), thus supplanting the competing identity claims by an encompassing one: the elect nation.

Thus we can already see that identity mobilization requires a particular mode of analytical treatment. Its emergence divides the world into separate collective identities. When its dialectics is stopped, identity mobilization runs amok. When its dialectics is marginalized it ends up in the intellectual negation of the world, in cultural pessimism, and intellectual psychosis.

The normal case in the past was marginalization. Fascism was the exception, occurring at a time when a basic institutional condition for identity mobilization was emerging: namely society-wide communication of voices and images, via radio and film. This points to a second specificity of identity mobilization: its dependence on public communication. Identities have to be staged publicly, they have to be enacted in publicly visible rituals in order to be consequential. The contemporary situation makes this communicative presence of the other an everyday possibility. The resurrection of public space and public discourse in the course of the communicative revolution (to which the environmental movement itself has contributed) has provided the necessary institutional means for the evolution of modern society towards identity mobilization.

A third difference is an implication of this logic of identity mobilization. The resolution of identity conflicts is dependent on dealing with conflicting boundary markers. Apart from pure force (genocide), communication is the only means of dealing with identitarian differences. Thus the mode of communication becomes the central field of collective action over 'culture'. The repercussions of this changing field of social conflict in the course of the ethnicization of conflicts can be observed in the present-day philosopher's discourse which offers us the option of particularistic communities (the communitarianists) or of multiculturalism (the new universalists). Culture—to make the point clear—has become the field of collective mobilization and social conflict.

In the analysis of ethnicized conflict, of identitarian movements, a particular form of political citizenship comes to the fore. Political citizenship is based on another element: the struggle over the cultural symbols, frames as the concern of collective mobilization. It is no longer over interests at stake in such issues that collective mobilization takes place. It is rather to self-understanding, to marking boundaries to the others, that collective mobilization refers. The political citizen becomes a citizen who is forced to choose the identity in the name of which he or she will become active. The reflexive citizen chooses the boundaries of the public space by choosing where he or she belongs. He or she can choose which role to play on the public stage, when to watch, and when to act.

Citizenship and Democracy

The Theory of the Public Space Revisited

Does ethnic self-presentation in public contribute to more democracy? The answer to this question is, in both the environmental and the ethnic case, an unconditional yes. To understand and justify this affirmative answer, the underlying theory has to be made explicit. To describe again the phenomenon in theoretical terms: we have to do with an extension of public rituals of movement–state–negotiations and of movement–business–interactions; we have to do with the dramatization of public debates where public resonance decides. This has created public arenas in which public debates go on in form of advertisements, symbolic actions, media dramatizations. All these phenomena, I claim, provide a new social reality for mobilizing democratic claims. The reality of ritual participation and communication is—to go even further—a necessary condition for democratic principles to survive the ambivalent modernization of modern societies.

The first theoretical reason for such a claim is an anthropological one: human beings are narrative animals. They live of and through stories about realities; arguments are always embedded in stories that give meaning to them. These stories are histories, collective memories, individual memories. The second theoretical reason is a sociological one. Social interaction is symbolically mediated and therefore dependent upon symbolic forms which allow ongoing communication to be decoded. Research in symbolic interactionism has shown that arguments, the constitutive element of communication, are always embedded in a meaning-giving frame which has to be invoked and stabilized in each communication. There is no argument outside a story. This is not to deny that social actors are capable of being rational. On the contrary, it is to claim that the reference to a shared knowledge of the world is the condition for rational arguments to enter discourse. But this does not transform discourse into a collective process of argumentation. Ideally, discourse is a collective argumentation. In social reality, however, collective argumentation is culturally bound. It belongs to the historical experience of modern societies that democracy has always been connected to shared cultural beliefs. Democracy was coupled with beliefs and knowledge that could provide for collective identity, for a sense of belonging together, for a sense of trust, for an implicit meaning that everybody can rely upon.

The new issue politics, fostered by issue-specific policy-making, has brought onto the public stage the question of collective concern and of belonging. It contributes even more to the transformation of the public space into a theatre. This metaphor of the theatre is helpful in giving a place to the discourse on collective concern (*Betroffenheit*). In a theatre the actors perform a script, but they know that it is a script. They tell stories. Thus they are reflexive actors. There is no theatre without a public: the actors act in front of a public which evaluates and criticizes what they are doing. This is a metaphorical way of saying that we have to deal with the return of the citizen to the public space.

What Role do Citizens Play in this Theatre?

Citizens are the andience of the performance given in this theatre. They participate as a public to which critical intellectuals (*Kritiker*) give a voice. The critical public judges the performance of scripts played by actors on the scene. These actors on the scene again perform according to a prescribed script. The actors only add the performance of the script. A paradoxical effect is that the actors who have brought such issues back to the public space disappear to the extent that they have been successful. The return of the citizen marks the end of social movements. The citizen returns and takes the place of social movements. But what kind of citizen?

It is not the *Staatsbürger*, the citizen as the subject of the state. Nor is it the *Wirtschaftsbürger*, the marketized citizen. It is the citizen beyond the state and beyond the market. This citizen has been called the political citizen or social citizen. As a political citizen he performs. As a social citizen he is supported in going into the theatre. It is not to be suspected that every spectator will become a performing actor (the stage would be immediately overcrowded). There is some movement (as in modern plays) from the stage to the public and back, but this is the exception. Normally those performing are paid and the others pay (eventually subsidized). Who plays and watches depends on the piece performed. There are pieces which attract a lot of people and need many actors. The environment would be such a piece.

This metaphor avoids the euphemization and delusions of the active citizen (Gilliatt 1995). The active and the passive citizen are the two sides of the same coin: they are the two elements necessary for performing public events. We need performers and spectators, some who talk and some who listen. But this is citizenship in the state of nature. Institutions are necessary to guarantee that performers and actors will meet. We need timetables, spaces, and scripts. Thus to act as a citizen is a complex phenomenon. Citizenship is based on the configuration of these three elements. To mark the difference from *Staatsbürger* and *Wirtschaftsbürger*, this kind of citizen is called the *Bürger*. This is the citizen of civil society, claiming social or political rights according to the role which s/he takes in a specific issue area.

Consequences for a Theory of Citizenship

The institutionalization of an order that integrates social movement organizations, and leads to a more complicated configuration of state intervention, economy, and society, is the structural reason for the shift in contemporary discourses on democracy which turn from social movements to citizens, from collective mobilization to citizenship. Citizens no longer besiege the institutions but are part of them. This opens the discourse to new ideological cleavages. The revival of old ideological battles has begun by giving them new modernist clothes. This applies above all to the contemporary debate on conceptions of citizenship, such as the controversy between the liberal-individualist and the civic-republican conception of citizenship. Neither the idea of a social citizenship protected by the state and enabled by the use of citizenship rights nor the idea of the permanently active and self-disciplined citizen acting on behalf of his community out of a learned duty will be sufficient basis for a theory of citizenship which takes account of the structural and institutional changes reported above.

A new theory of citizenship is needed to make sense of these changes. It is a theory that takes account of the fact that citizens are no longer at the centre of democratic society but only an element in it. That participation is contingent on attention cycles, symbolic staging, and state reaction and economic performance of society. What we need is a *realist theory of citizenship*. Such a realist theory first takes into account the unintended and often perverse effects of the ideas underlying citizenship in the nation-state, the first type of institutionalization of citizenship as a modern institution. This refers to the effects of equalizing citizens, of drawing boundaries between communities of citizens, and of empowering citizens to act on their preferences in a moral way. The perverse effects dominate today's discourse on citizenship: the privatizing effects of social citizenship, the exclusionary effects of building communities of citizens, and the free-riding of citizens in modern citizenship regimes. The solutions proposed have, however, been nostalgic: back to the old virtues of equality of citizens, to willed communities (a euphemism for national communities), to reinstalling (through education?) the moral sense of obligation to a collectivity. The alternative to nostalgia is to redefine the basis of citizenship in late modern times.

Such a realist theory of citizenship can be grounded on three analytical aspects: the constituency of citizenship, the agency of citizenship, and the space of citizenship. The analysis of the constituency of citizenship starts with assumptions about what people are doing when participating in public life.

They follow a daily timetable: the newspaper every morning, the news every evening. They occupy a space which is the private room with television (eventually Internet) through which they are linked to the public world. This constituency is quite different from those publics described in nineteenth-century accounts of the public: the coffeehouse public, the newspaper-reading public, the high culture of politically interested people. To name such people citizens implies a soft notion of citizenship. A citizen is anyone who listens under conditions which set no restrictions on exit. Such people have some basic rights (human rights), some protection against repressive action from authorities, some social rights which guarantee a minimum standard of living.

A stronger version of citizenship takes into account the scripts which actors on the stage perform for the people. Such scripts contain the metaphors which link people to issues and solutions and which allow them to play the game of politics. These are the active citizens, those who organize the support of the many in order to prove their legitimate claims about issues. Such a stronger notion of citizenship introduces a hierarchy into the notion of citizenship: the more citizens are political agents, the more we have a distinction between the ordinary citizen and the political citizen (those who want to be political citizens are only a part of the people).

An even stronger version of citizenship takes into account the real spaces where communication takes place. These are spaces where active political citizens define who is included and who is excluded from the game. Procedures of collective decision-making imply necessarily strict rules on who can participate in such processes. The real political citizen has to pass the entrance requirement of institutional procedures defining the realm of the political. Given the shifting boundaries of the political and the pluralization of spaces where consequential collective actors meet, we will have shifting boundaries of inclusion and exclusion. Inclusion or exclusion from citizenship has become a volatile phenomenon, depending on the constituency which is referred to, on the collective actors speaking in their name, and on the issue-specific power constellation.

The realist content of such a theory of political citizenship in complex societies leads to the simple formula which says that the more democratic decision-making is organized the more exclusive it will be. Political citizenship in complex societies is no longer an institutionally fixed and stable phenomenon. The preconditions for that, an integrated state–economy–society institutional framework such as the modern national welfare state, are no longer to be taken for granted. The structural configurations of citizenship are becoming volatile, they include and exclude in a contingent way.

How can a sense of citizenship be created under such conditions? This question can only be answered by giving up the assumption of unitary and closed collective identities. Political citizenship is national when the configuration of collective actors is tied to national politics. It is local when local community matters bring collective actors together. And it is issue-specific (for example, 'ecologist identities') when issues provide non-national and non-local constellations of collective actors in the virtual realm of a shared problem definition (such as global warming).

This allows political citizenship to be decoupled from a rigid notion of collective identity. There is no single community base to political citizenship, but many shifting ones. Shifting loyalties are characteristic of political citizenship in complex societies.[17] There is, however, a high cost to such shifting loyalties which should be taken seriously. Such a notion of citizenship undermines the normative ground on which citizenship was built, which is its formal legal foundation, the grounding of citizenship on the rule of law. This might be the price to be paid for political citizenship in complex societies. The price would be high if modern society fell back to the natural state of feuding lords characteristic of the age of religious wars. The price to be paid would be payable if a new normative regime were emerging capable of binding any kind of legal rule in each context (including the nation-state) to the test of universalizability. Such a normative order is certainly not a kind of world state formed according to the model of the nation-state but some kind of anarchic normative space in which the force of public self-presentation works as a binding moral force on collective actors. A global public space based on a specific institutional myth would be a solution. Whether such a myth is a global human rights discourse or a discourse of mutual recognition of difference is an empirical question. This is part of the competition of discourses which is the constitutive element of the formation of a global public space.[18]

Conclusion

Democratic discourse needs social embedding. The theory proposed is that public communication is embedded and institutionally regulated through rituals and ceremonies. This means that democracy is impossible without rituals and ceremonies. They provide the social world within which to communicate. The public space is a theatre, and democratic principles allow everybody to act and stage himself in this space, to talk, even to talk nonsense. The new institutional system created by social movements in advanced modern societies has fostered the creation of such public spaces: the media tell stories, good and bad ones, social actors enter the media public, a space which ranges

---

[17] Whether we call this post-national citizenship (Soysal 1994) is secondary. This term simply indicates simply that citizenship is becoming more dependent (or contingent) on context.

[18] The role of the human rights discourse has been emphasized by Soysal (1994) within the debate on post-national citizenship. This is to be seen as an option of institutionalizing democratic forms of social organization in a world of migration.

from advertisements through talk shows to public ceremonies. Thus everybody can observe everyone else.

Such a theoretical notion of communication allows me to give democratic principles a sociologically enlightened social role: democratic principles are used to rationalize these public spaces. And there is a final effect to be mentioned: the ideals of universal participation and of public debate become themselves stories that are invoked in everyday communication by diverse social actors. It is the democratic story that is told to gain legitimacy in the emerging institutional field. The legitimacy of the new emerging institutional system is tied to the story of public debate and equal participation of everybody. Thus democracy itself increasingly becomes a myth. As a modern myth democracy would no longer be something like God, outside the real world and invoked in order to legitimate institutions of collective action. It would become part of the normal, taken-for-granted everyday culture of modern political institutions.

This, however, means to give up the idea of democracy as a set of objective principles. The solution that we need and have to keep consists of institutions which make participation and communication an ordinary phenomenon. This means to ritualize participation and communication in thousands of forums and arenas of (often boring, sometimes insulting, sometimes factually wrong) public discourse and in everyday media dramatizations of persons and issues, whether through talk shows, through news reports, or through caricatures. We have to think democracy socially, as a set of ritual forms and ceremonial events that organize everyday public life. The opposite of democracy is authoritarianism and totalitarianism. Both fear nothing more than to be exposed to rituals of everyday public life. For example, no authoritarian ruler, even less a totalitarian ruler, can live with the mass media rituals of looking for bad news. As the spectators of the theatre we know that we live in a world of dramatization and ritual staging. And empirical research shows, that people make sense of the public theatre.

Democracy is—to conclude—the staging of a public theatre, with hopefully a critical mass of spectators possessing common sense. A realist theory of citizenship is needed to avoid the pitfalls of expecting too much or too little from political citizenship in modern complex societies.

REFERENCES

ABEL, R. L. (1980). 'Delegalization: A Critical Review of its Ideology, Manifestations, and its Consequences', in E. Blankenburg, E. Klausa, and H. Rottleuthner (eds.), *Alternative Rechtsformen und Alternativen zum Recht: Jahrbuch für Rechtssoziologie und Rechtstheorie* (Opladen: Westdeutscher Verlag), 27–46.

BURGESS, J., and HARRISON, C. M. (1993). 'The Circulation of Claims in the Cultural Politics of Environmental Change', in A. Hansen (ed.), *The Mass Media and Environmental Issues* (Leicester: Leicester University Press) 198–221.

CALHOUN, C. J. (ed.) (1994). *Social Theory and the Politics of Identity* (Oxford: Blackwell).

—— (1995). *Critical Social Theory* (Oxford and Cambridge: Blackwell).

CRACKNELL, J. (1993). 'Issue Arenas, Pressure Groups and Environmental Agendas', in A. Hansen (ed.), *The Mass Media and Environmental Issues* (Leicester: Leicester University Press), 3–21.

EDER, K. (1993). *The New Politics of Class: Social Movements and Cultural Dynamics in Advanced Societies* (London: Sage).

—— (1996). 'The Institutionalization of Environmentalism: Ecological Discourse and the Second Transformation of the Public Sphere', in S. Lash, B. Szerszinski, and B. Wynne (eds.), *Risk, Modernity and the Environment: Towards a New Ecology* (London: Sage), 203–23.

—— (1999). 'Taming Risks through Dialogues: The Rationality and Functionality of Discursive Institutions in Risk Society', in M. J. Cohen (ed.), *Risk in the Modern Age: Science and the Environment* (Oxford: Macmillan and St Martin's), 225–48.

—— (2000). *Kulturelle Identitäten zwischen Utopie und Tradition: Soziale Bewegungen als Ort gesellschaftlicher Lernprozesse* (Frankfurt: Campus).

GALANTER, M. (1980). 'Legality and its Discontents: A Preliminary Assessment of Current Theories of Legalization and Delegalization', in E. Blankenburg, E. Klaus, and H. Rottleuthner (eds.), *Alternative Rechtsformen und Alternativen zum Recht: Jahrbuch für Rechtssoziologie und Rechtstheorie* (Opladen: Westdeutscher Verlag), 11–26.

GAMSON, W. A. (1992). *Talking Politics* (Cambridge: Cambridge University Press).

—— CROTEAU, D., HOYNES, W., and SASSON, T. (1992). 'Media Images and the Social Construction of Reality', *Annual Review of Sociology*, 18: 373–93.

GIESEN, B. (1991). 'Code, Process and Situation in Cultural Selection', *Cultural Dynamics*, 4: 172–85.

—— (1998). *Intellectuals and the Nation: Collective Identity in German Axial Age* (Cambridge: Cambridge University Press).

GILLIATT, S. E. (1995). 'Disliking Politics: Philosophical Foundations for a Sociology of the Apolitical', *International Sociology*, 10: 283–98.

GINSBERG, B., and SHEFTER, M. (1989). *Politics by Other Means: The Declining Importance of Elections in America* (New York: Basic Books).

GITLIN, T. (1980). *The Whole World is Watching: Mass Media in the Making and Unmaking of the New Left* (Berkeley, Calif: University of California Press).

HABERMAS, J. (1989 [1962]). *The Structural Transformation of the Public Sphere* (Cambridge, Mass.: MIT Press).

HANSEN, A. (1993a). 'Greenpeace and Press Coverage of Environmental Issues', in A. Hansen (ed.), *The Mass Media and Environmental Issues* (Leicester: Leicester University Press), 150–78.

—— (ed.) (1993b). *The Mass Media and Environmental Issues* (Leicester: Leicester University Press).

KNOKE, D. (1986). *Associations* (Greenwich, Conn.: JAI Press).

LAUMANN, E. O., and KNOKE, D. (1987). *The Organizational State: Social Choice in National Policy Domains* (Madison: University of Wisconsin Press).

MAJONE, G. (1993). *When does Policy Deliberation Matter?* (Florence: European University Institute; mimeo).

OFFE, C. (1985). 'New Social Movements: Challenging the Boundaries of Institutional Politics', *Social Research*, 52: 817–68.

OLSON, M. (1965). *The Logic of Collective Action: Public Goods and the Theory of Groups* (Cambridge, Mass.: Harvard University Press).

POWELL, W. W., and DiMAGGIO, P. J. (eds.) (1991). *The New Institutionalism in Organizational Analysis* (Chicago: University of Chicago Press).

ROSSMANN, T. (1993). 'Öffentlichkeitsarbeit und ihr Einfluß auf die Medien: Das Beispiel Greenpeace', *Media Perspektiven*, 2: 85–94.

SHRADER-FRECHETTE, K. S. (1991). *Risk and Rationality: Philosophical Foundations for Populist Reforms* (Berkeley, Calif.: University of California Press).

SOMERS, M. R. (1993). 'Citizenship and the Place of the Public Sphere: Law, Community, and Political Culture in the Transition to Democracy', *American Sociological Review*, 58: 587–620.

——(1995). 'What's Political or Cultural about Political Culture and the Public Sphere? Toward an Historical Sociology of Concept Formation', *Sociological Theory*, 13: 113–44.

SOYSAL, Y. N. (1994). *Limits of Citizenship: Migrants and Postnational Membership in Europe* (Chicago: University of Chicago Press).

ZALD, M. N., and McCARTHY, J. D. (1987a). 'Organizational Intellectuals and the Criticism of Society', in M. N. Zald and J. D. McCarthy (eds.), *Social Movements in an Organizational Society* (New Brunswick NJ, and Oxford: Transaction Books), 97–120.

——and——(eds.) (1987b). *Social Movements in an Organizational Society* (New Brunswick, NJ, and Oxford: Transaction Books).

11

The Civic Networking Movement: The Internet as a New Democratic Public Space?

Damian Tambini

Introduction

For many, the commercial media are to blame for the current crisis of active citizenship. There is a convergence of opinion that newspapers, radio, and especially television, distort and trivialize deliberation and representation in the public space (Habermas 1989 [1962]; Fishkin 1991, 1995; Garnham 1986; Barber 1984). Others have made the small step from this prognosis to the assertion that new media of communication—the Internet, multimedia, and computer mediated communication (CMC)—can be used to encourage active political citizenship. The heralding of the Internet as a potential 'third sphere' of free public deliberation, untainted by state or commerce, has been accompanied by a boom in experiments using CMC to encourage democratic participation. These projects have attempted to use such 'new media' to offer new channels of access to the main transactions of democracy: information provision, preference measurement (voting), deliberation, and will formation/group organization. Many information-based services are also being delivered via new media. Initiatives range from city web pages, as more efficient means to make political information available to those who use the Internet, to experiments in electronic voting, to encouraging all citizens to use interactive media to organize interest groups and neighbourhood alliances. Although there have been national experiments (for example the White House, which offers direct email to the US President's office and extensive information on the government programme), it is the local experiments—the so called 'civic networks'—that are most advanced, and offer the clearest insights into emerging patterns of political communication.

In this chapter I do not aim to evaluate civic networking in general. The phenomenon is too new for that. Rather, drawing on a longer piece of research in which six city networking experiments were compared (Tsagarousianou *et al.* 1997), I examine civic networks as experiments in the use of CMC to encourage democratic citizenship. I argue that a very broad notion of democracy and participation is necessary in coming to terms with the implications of new media for democracy: CMC has implications not only for information provision, voting and polling, but for the very formation and organization of political identities, especially given that CMC is being made available to a mass public at a particular historical moment when existing media institutions and the very idea of a national public are being redefined. In this context, the new civic networks indeed demonstrate how CMC can be used in a practical way to provide new forms of political participation. They also show that the extent to which they prove able to do so will depend on how media are organized and regulated, and how the public interest is defined in the contemporary context. As I show below, this is by no means clear yet.

The Civic Networking Movement

By 1996, more than 200 towns in the USA and cities had pages on the World Wide Web (Dutton 1996). Although some of these are simply advertisements for regional tourism or business, more than fifty have some kind of civic networking project under way.[1] These projects range enormously in their origins and in their basic architecture and aims, but share the civic republican premise that rewiring the machinery of democracy can reactivate political citizenship. In Santa Monica, a plan to allow town officials to work from home via modems was extended to give all citizens the right to access debate and information about city politics via their home PCs, and then further extended into PEN, the Public Electronic Network, one of the first civic networks of online discussion groups in 1990 (Dutton 1996). In Philadelphia, Neighborhoods Online was set up by community activists with the aim of 'making it easy for groups and concerned citizens to access information about issues relevant to neighbourhood empowerment'; to 'help civic organizations access the internet' and 'create networks of neighbourhood activists' (Schwarz 1997). The Seattle Community Network, in collaboration with local libraries, used CMC to provide the local community with access to information, forums for discussion, and email (Schuler 1996: 333–44, 480–1). Although they were

---

[1] For listings of civic networking projects see the documents of the Center for Civic Networking (http://www.civic.net:2401/ccm.html); the listings of Community Computer Networks and Free-Net Web Sites (http://www.freenet.victoria.bc.ca.freenets.html).

influenced by previous forms of electronic democracy and calls for public
information utilities and rights to information (Etzioni 1972; Arterton 1987;
Sackman and Nie 1970), the projects owe their salience to new technological
and socio-economic conditions. Dozens of think-tanks and institutes have
emerged to 'network the networks' (Schuler 1996), reflecting the consolidation of this new civic networking movement.

Throughout Europe, within varied regulatory and cultural contexts, civic
networking became a key trend of the 1990s. In some cases town governments
made central investments in state-led networks, and in others networks have
been set up by non-government organizations. In the Netherlands alone, over
sixty towns have web pages. Amsterdam's Digital City, with its anarchic, unregulated 'Underworld' of discussion groups, is the biggest civic network in
Europe, and was organized by veteran civic education enthusiasts within the
city government, together with groups of tame hackers (Brants *et al.* 1996).
By 1997, over 45,000 Amsterdammers had registered, visiting the 'virtual city'
on average once a week (Francissen and Brants 1997). The organizers of
Athens's Network Pericles saw civic networks based on home PC access as
élitist and agoraphobic, and therefore introduced a network of information
and voting terminals in public places (Tsagarousianou 1997). The reluctance
of Berlin's city government to sponsor civic networking left a vacuum, which
was, however, filled by students and other enthusiasts who set up their own
grass-roots discussion groups on city issues (Schmidtke 1997). Around the
same time, intellectuals and city officials in Bologna, Italy, offered all citizens
free access to IperBolE: a network of information pages, email links, and
discussion groups designed and operated by the local authority; and in
Manchester, England, a project to improve computer literacy spawned an
Electronic Village Hall as a side product (Tambini 1997; Bryan 1996). These
were by no means isolated cases. Local authorities open new information
systems and civic networks every week.

Civic networking has emerged at the policy level not only because the technology has become more widely available, but because of various policy games
(Dutton and Guthrie 1991): expansionist plans of government information
departments; pressure from new communitarian or civil society think-tanks;
lobbying by telecommunications providers; EU initiatives, promoted because
of subsidiarity problems;[2] and the aims of accountability, transparency, and
efficiency associated with 'new public management' in local government.

Civic networks have been subject to criticism from both left and right. Why
should government, local or otherwise, be involved in a leisure/entertainment
activity already provided for by private enterprise? Can this form of tinkering
affect the real problems for political citizenship such as globalization and

---

[2] There is a growing interest in teledemocracy in the European movement. Bologna's civic network
is half funded by the EU under the Esprit programme with the remit to experiment in new forms of
electronic democracy.

social exclusion? Surely the only beneficiaries of these new forms of electronic democracy are the media and computer firms who seek to create new dependencies on their products, and who will simply monopolize control of new media as they did the old? Previous experiments in 'electronic democracy' in fact have generally flopped due to lack of interest from citizens (Brants *et al.* 1996; Arterton 1987), so why should the current fad differ? Why should democratic communication be carried out in a privileged medium used by a tiny, unrepresentative part of the populace?

The Context: Media and Public

The new civic networking trend, unlike previous experiments in democratic communication, occurs at a moment of particular historical opportunity for reform of communications institutions in the industrialized democracies. Many established media institutions are being redesigned or replaced. In particular, it has been claimed that there is an opportunity here to move away from the previous structuring of political communication around a broadcast model of communication within national public spheres. Current transformations in the communications infrastructure have a political element, in the privatization and deregulation of broadcasting and telecommunications, and a technological/economic aspect which consists in the end of bandwidth scarcity, convergence between telecommunications and broadcasting, and growing access to computers. This dual transformation occurs at a time when many of the institutions of democratic communication, such as a clear sense of national interest and homogeneous culture, are being put into question because of migration and multiculturalism, and civic republican and communitarian ideals—both critical of the 'old media'—become the new normative anchors in the policy debate.

Although CMC is not itself new, mass access and user friendliness are, and mark a turning-point in media development. Not just HTML communications protocols, which render our email and Internet facilities possible; but browsers, message routing, and intelligent agents make information provision much more flexible and interactive than were previous broadcasting and print-based media. Although mass access is not yet a reality, Internet cafés and the connection of public libraries, schools, and hospitals help ensure that those who do not own hardware can, in principle at least, have access to online communication and information facilities. Moreover, as information industries become more central to economies in advanced countries, more have access to CMC in the workplace, which further spurs education and leisure use. Even where CMC and the Internet are not making inroads, video on demand and browser viewing guides are closing the gap between the

structure of broadcast and print communication (one to many) and that of
the net (many to many). Clearly, current trends are not to be dismissed as fads
like 'citizens band' and community radio. The massive investment in information infrastructure has simply gone too far and the numbers of citizens
who use online communications continues to grow. Icon-based and menu-
driven interfaces render literacy a lower hurdle: CMC no longer demands
knowledge of specialist programming languages. Infrastructurally, new alternatives to old-fashioned twisted pair telephone wires: satellite and fibre-optic
technology are in the process of ending bandwidth scarcity and cheapening
communication and information provision. Even where the wires are not
being changed, digital compression is finding ways of sending much larger
amounts of information down them faster (Negroponte 1996). Two key ideas
are questioned: that communication should be organized as far as possible in
the service of democratic citizenship and that democratic citizenship is practised in a national public sphere.

The interaction between questions of (de)regulation and this rapidly
changing mediascape throw many post-war certainties into question. Suddenly the fact that our democratic institutions (not only the 'free press' but
also government information provision, voting, propaganda, and political
organization) are built around a carefully regulated communications infrastructure becomes visible: Blumler, Garnham, and others have read these
current media changes in Europe in terms of a concern with the decline of
public broadcasting, which they see as an imperfect twentieth-century equivalent of Habermas's public sphere (Garnham 1990: 16, 111–14).[3] The regulatory ideals of freedom of speech, impartiality, public service, and universality
of access, they argue, are not safe, especially given the current crisis of public-
service media caused by fiscal, legitimation, and technological squeezes
(Keane 1991: 7) and a corresponding expansion of commercial media in most
European countries.

The problem of regulating media in the public interest, however, does not
stop there. The previous regulatory framework emerged in the context of
industrializing, democratizing, nation-building states, and a broadcast (one-
to-many) model dictated by communications technologies then available.
This led to the institutionalization of ideals such as public service, impartiality, universal access, and national interest/national security for broadcasting
and telecommunications. Whereas in the past the idea of a national 'public',
reflected in the print and broadcast mediascape, was the focus both of demo-

---

[3] 'I want to argue that . . . changes in media structure and media policy, whether these stem from
economic developments or from public intervention, are properly political questions of as much
importance as the question of whether or not to introduce proportional representation, of relations
between local and national government, . . . that the policy of western European governments towards
cable TV and satellite broadcasting is as important as their attitude towards the development of a
United Europe; . . . that political scientists and citizens concerned with the health and future of democracy neglect these issues at their peril' (Garnham 1990: 104).

cratic deliberation and of communications regulation, this conception is ever more deeply questioned and new solutions are sought. Transnational communication and loyalties are increasing (Morley and Robbins 1995; Soysal 1994) and the firm grasp which national public broadcasters once had on their publics has already been loosened by satellite, video, and deregulation (Blumler 1992; Morley and Robbins 1995). Multiculturalism and globalization have been further problems for public and universal ideals in broadcasting. Such processes have been both cause and consequence of the delegitimation of the old élitist idea of the public based on a cultural canon which could be broadcast to other class, ethnic, gender, and regional groupings. The response to this, and to the funding and technological changes all over Europe and beyond, has been marketization of media. An ever greater proportion of information for citizenship is carried by for-profit broadcasters, which only compounds the critique of society and politics as a sport or a spectacle for sale: what Garnham (1986: 48) calls the 'politics of consumerism'[4] and others have called the society of the spectacle, or soundbite politics. With the rise of new, interactive, and high-capacity media these problems are being reassessed, and the relationship between public, nation, and state (local and national) is being renegotiated.

Just how new media can be used and regulated in the service of democratic citizenship, then, remains to be seen. Whereas broadcasting and print media (and also book publishing, telephones, and libraries) were institutionalized around the idea of the national public, or active citizenry, the particular democratic role of new media is only now being explored in practice.

Computer Mediated Communication and Democracy

Are email, interactive CMC, and the Internet qualitatively different from television and the traditional media? What do the new media offer that old media cannot provide? What difference does it make if I talk about politics in a computer discussion group instead of the local coffeeshop? A great deal, if you believe the new gurus of electronic democracy. In 1972 Amitai Etzioni was already calling for 'electronic town halls' to provide forums for deliberation on local policy issues (Etzioni 1972). Ben Barber identified electronic democracy as one way to achieve 'Strong Democracy' in 1984. Stefano Bonaga, university professor and local government officer in Bologna was even more expansive: 'All over the world a new dimension is evolving with unbridled

---

[4] 'Politicians relate to potential voters not as rational beings concerned for the public good, but in the mode of advertising, as creatures of passing and largely irrational appetite, to whose self-interest they must appeal . . . the citizen is appealed to as a private individual rather than as a member of a public' (Garnham 1990: 16).

momentum and making a major impact on democracy and development, stretching the horizons of citizenship: this is the world of new communication and information technologies, destined to revolutionize democracy and the economy' (Bonaga 1994).

The claims for new media and political citizenship centre on the efficiency of new media, their capacity, their interactivity, and on their freedom from time–space constraints. As new media are interactive, they institutionalize citizens' right to reply, to select information, and to communicate directly with one another or their representatives without the gatekeeping influence of editors. Further, rather than receiving a diet of what journalists and editors deem to be important political information, citizens can seek the information that interests them and serves their interests. They are more efficient because by exploiting the growing availability of bandwidth they can offer faster access to more information. The fact that the new media free communication from time–space constraints improves efficiency and permits new forms of direct democracy and deliberation.

In the next section I investigate the various ways in which civic networks seek to use CMC to rejuvenate active citizenship. Since very different visions of democratic participation lie behind each of the civic networking projects, I will use a simple theoretical framework, which distinguishes four key transactions of democracy, and for each ask how new media are being used to reform them.

Information Provision/Access to Information

Citizens need information in order to participate in decision-making, organize interest groups, and make propaganda. New media, according to civic networkers, not only make it cheaper to access and provide more information, but reduce the problems of selectivity and bias, since they overcome problems of space scarcity that are endemic to print and broadcast media. Technologies also permit new ways of sorting and searching the increasing volume of information which is received, and more potential for self-editing of media diet. Indeed, as societies become more complex, and individuals' definitions of their own interests more fragmented and various, existing information infrastructures encounter increasing problems of complexity and overload, which some argue is the key problem of contemporary democracies (Zolo 1992). Whereas conventional media have always involved a process of selection of the information that gatekeepers deemed interesting or important for citizenship, new media, as they offer direct access to the information being used by decision-makers themselves and means to quickly search through it, can potentially ease such problems. They may do so through introducing more immediate and efficient forms of consultation and many-to-many communication, and preventing a situation arising in which local governments are remote, unaware of the needs and wants of their citizens. Such problems of complexity are clearly linked to the current renegotiation of public services mentioned above. The 'public' was defined in terms of universal, homogeneous preferences, which were in turn defined in terms of an authority which could decide questions of taste and representation on behalf of the audience. That uniformity is challenged in multicultural, affluent consumer societies which threaten any 'public' cultural policy. An interactive rather than broadcast media system offers some hope of bypassing these problems, avoiding ever thornier questions of deciding what information citizens need, and letting them decide themselves.

Bologna's civic network, like most, is geared above all to information access and deliberation. Deliberation will be dealt with below. Information is provided on the organization and work of local government on World Wide Web pages, with several layers of links and also email links to the relevant city officials. Citizens can access the city statutes, planning documents, information on the workings of local government, including lists of departmental competencies and some meeting agendas. The organizers of the network also prepare and update a list of some 200 voluntary organizations and pressure groups operating in Bologna. There are some direct email links from the information pages to responsible officers. Costs are reduced, and the volume and quantity of information is greatly increased in comparison with printed material. Hypertext, high-quality graphics, virtual reality maps of the city, and other interactive presentation methods certainly facilitate information provision as a form of civic education.

This has, however, raised questions of bias. That there is no politically neutral information is obvious, and therefore that a degree of power is concentrated in the hands of those that select it (for example, web-page designers) is also clear, but given the nature of the medium (here I refer to Internet-based networks) powers of selection are diminished in comparison to conventional media. In Bologna, the long-term goal was to open as much as possible of Bologna's intranet of local government databases directly to the Internet. These plans have met with technical and legal problems and the information that is available is all selected by the system administrators.

This has led to an argument in favour of grass-roots, voluntarily organized networks, like that in Berlin. The obvious problem with grass-roots initiatives in comparison with state-led initiatives like Bologna, however, is the status and reliability of online information. Information on grass-roots networks does not have the signature of city authorities; as with so much information on the Internet, its providers are less accountable for content and there is a resultant cheapening of information as well as potential for citizen overload. Further, when a clearly state-led civic network is lacking, there is nothing to stop several competing networks being set up alongside one another. The online citizen is then confronted with a confusing array of discussion groups, information, and lists.

Preference Measurement:[5] Referenda, Polls, and Representation

Civic networkers not only argue that new media make voting, opinion polling, and referenda easier for the citizen and cheaper to administer; they further posit that the real-time interactive communication and measurement made possible by CMC can transform a procedure in which a citizen's response is moulded by a preset framework into a process through which citizens design the very categories in which their choices are measured. Some seek therefore to incorporate elements of direct democracy into civic networks, in the process transforming conventional forms such as referenda into new 'interactive' measurements of opinion. One problem with paper-based referenda, they argue, is that those who set the question hold too much power. The wording of the question and preselection of a limited range of responses have, through suggestion, such an influence on respondents that referenda can amount to the 'capture' of citizens rather than consultation. Such instruments of direct democracy often serve merely to legitimize decisions already taken. One response to this problem is to give citizens the right to set up referenda themselves. Citizens in Italy and California, for instance, have the right to demand referenda if they can collect large numbers of signatures. Such referenda petitions, to be successful, need armies of volunteers with clipboards to bother shoppers for signatures. The staging of a referendum often therefore depends more on mobilization resources than on preferences in the population, hence the existence all-purpose referendum parties (for example, the Referendum Party in Italy). These organizations concentrate resources in order to use popular referenda to set the political agenda. In the case of the Italian Referendum Party there is evidence that the overuse of referenda has resulted in their decline. Through online listing of questions, and more widespread access to communications resources, a more genuinely popular, interactive referendum system could be achieved. Thus civic networkers are experimenting with interactive referenda and polls.

Just as the process of setting questions could be democratized by new interactive media, so could answering them, argue civic networkers. Interactivity, particularly coupled with message routing and language recognition, could enable the measurement of natural language responses, and more complex question structures. In Amsterdam the City Consultations project

---

[5] David Miller (1993: 75) saw preference measurement as the key to liberal ideals of democracy, to be contrasted with deliberative views. In this view 'preferences are sacrosanct because they reflect the individuality of each member of the political community'.

experimented with interactive, computer-assisted polling, using 'choice trees' which led telephone voters through a series of choices permitting responses in matters of degree and qualified (if . . . then) answers (Brants *et al.* 1996: 240).

Networkers also hope to transform elections. Citizens are more likely to stay at home when there is bad weather on polling day. The housebound, such as single parents and the elderly, tend to vote less than other groups. Attendance at elections and referenda tends to decline with increased frequency of polls. These facts suggest that participation could be improved by making voting easier, and ideally by making it possible to vote from the home. Voting from home, it is argued, is likely to offset the 'citizen fatigue' and disinterest said to result from frequent polling. The claim that new media can end apathy by making voting easier has been made not only for computer mediated communication, but also in relation to other media such as interactive television and even telephones (Arterton 1987; Becker 1981).

But there is a prior assumption that needs to be addressed. Are citizens politically apathetic because of barriers to participation in civil society? Many civic networking projects seek to remove the costs of participation, assuming that when citizens participate they do so in order to serve their own interests and in pursuit of their own visions of the future, calculated against the costs of participation, such as walking to a polling booth or writing a letter. The 'active participation' so dear to civil society theorists, however, may have more complex, multiple motivations. People use civic networks, for example, for entertainment and education, and few of them are directly concerned with the 'political ends' which network enthusiasts claim motivate citizens.

The funding of Bologna's civic network, provided by a project of the European Commission, was given on the condition that the city would develop and experiment with software for electronic polling and referenda. Although a Bologna software company is working on the software, the IperBolE management does not intend to use any form of polling on their network. They will only do so when interactivity is a reality and conditional responses can be measured; when natural language responses and matters of degree can be measured; when citizens have the right to petition to annul a referendum if they feel unrepresented; and when universal access to the technology is a reality. Computer mediated preference measurement faces even larger obstacles in voluntary, unofficial networks than in state-led initiatives. Grassroots civic networks would not be used for polling and preference measurement because their *ad hoc* organization and non-universality prevents universal access, or even representativity of sampling. In fact, at the time of writing, no civic network has held even an experimental vote on a local issue, and binding referenda or elections seem far off, for reasons of user identity and security.

Deliberation

Eschewing the idea of democracy as measurement of preferences public space theorists suggest that we focus on opinion/will formation, and deliberation as problem solving, thus revealing the links between democratic communication and social learning. As citizens' political preferences do not precede political competition but to a certain extent result from the debates and compromises which occur when citizens and policy-makers puzzle their way through problems, we should focus analysis on these processes of deliberation if we wish to achieve ideals of active political citizenship (Calhoun 1992; Cohen 1989; Habermas 1989 [1962]; Fishkin 1991; Miller 1993). Clearly, within such a view, CMC holds much promise for opening new arenas of debate and discussion.

Discussion groups, familiar to any user of the Internet, offer a new arena of deliberation, which is freer from constraints of time and space and very efficient. A citizen worried about plans for a new car park would not have to sit through discussions of planned tree pruning and school closures while waiting to make her point. She could merely follow some menus through lists of discussion subjects until she finds her debate on car parking and types in her contribution, which can be considered at leisure by the other interested parties. It is this kind of scenario, and the fact that the technology is already cheap and well-known, that has driven many civic networkers to base their city networks around a series of discussion groups.

The Bologna project used standard email, bulletin boards, and list servers to provide a system of discussion groups and email links. Individuals and local organizations can contribute to discussions on local issues such as education, planning, roads, and so forth. The Bologna project illustrates some of the problems of centrally planned networks, such as problems of control and agenda-setting. In IperBolE, an unelected official has the right to censor the discussion groups, the great majority of which she herself decided the themes of. The 'editors' exclude party-political propaganda, material considered obscene, and advertising. This situation, however, should be viewed as a possible but not necessary problem with state-led initiatives. Since PEN project city officials in contrast were reluctant to curtail freedom of expression in any way, the Santa Monica project, which had always been more concerned with discussion than with information provision, ran into deep trouble. A minority that used the PEN network for 'flaming' (online attacks and insults) caused many committed users to cease using the network (Dutton 1996; Docter and Dutton 1997).

Philadelphia's Neighborhoods Online does receive some funding from local government, but it is designed and implemented mainly by one of many American organizations dedicated to civil society, the Institute for the Study of Civic Values (Schwarz 1996, 1997). It is dedicated above all to networking between voluntary organizations rather than individuals. In Berlin, after discussions revealed the reluctance of the local authority to actively support a centrally organized civic network, city-oriented discussion groups made their way onto bulletin boards organized by grass-roots computer enthusiasts. A set of discussion groups with subject headings quite similar to those in Bologna was set up by a group of students in the university. Here the stress was on providing a forum for debate and organization: there are no official connections with local government, and the debate is often much more critical than that on the 'tame' civic network of Bologna (Schmidtke 1997). Discussions were just as radical on PEN, however, where anti-authority statements were common (Varney 1991), and the degree to which discussions criticize positions of authority are more likely to be due to political-cultural factors than to network management.

Although the editors use their considerable agenda-setting powers to encourage debate of local politics, surveys of the content of discussion groups reveal that most users are more interested in using the network to organize leisure and social and only secondarily political activity (Tambini 1997). Pornography had to be banned in the Digital City of Amsterdam, not because the authorities disapproved, but because they generated so much interest that 'traffic jams' disabled parts of the system (Francissen and Brants 1997).

Direct email links between citizens and local government officers in the various departments are another innovation in deliberation. Networks in Bologna, Berlin, and Amsterdam all offer this service, though rates of response by local government officers are low, and the legal and political status of this form of communication is unclear. One advantage of using email rather than letters is that citizens need less knowledge of the internal workings of city hall. With automatic message routing, all messages can be sent to a central postbox, and then distributed on the basis of keyword recognition to the appropriate departments. (This, argue the organizers, allows citizens who understand very little about local government to be heard, since they need not know who to address messages to.) In trials in Bologna a message routing system achieved over 90 per cent success in placing messages (Tambini 1997).

Whereas in Bologna the organizers of the civic network constantly pressurize officials to follow the discussion groups relevant to their department, and the civic network provides direct email links to officers, 'unofficial' networks can make no such claims. Their status, it could be argued is no more significant than a passing comment in a café. No one is obliged to read discussion groups and, although they are encouraged to do so, local government officers are—paradoxically—generally slower to respond to emails in comparison to letters. Again, the problem may be a misunderstanding of citizens' motivation in taking part in discussions.

Will Formation/Organization

A shared interest does not automatically spawn a political organization to represent it. This applies both to institutions, such as parties, movements, and interest groups, and to the states and political systems that form their context. National interest, like any form of political partisanship, is the result of a complex process: in order to translate an identified interest into collective political action, individuals with similar interests must somehow find one another and discover that they share that common interest. They must further form or reform some kind of common will, organizational structure, and identity (Eder 1985; Pizzorno 1987; Melucci 1982; Touraine 1977). For political parties and movements, propaganda has been a key to these organizational requirements: newspapers are set up and distributed, speeches are made in public places, and political groups seek to exploit the mass media by staging demonstrations and lobbying journalists. Communication resources become the key to mobilizing groups in this way, and meeting such 'publishing costs', broadly conceived, is a key to success in forming and mobilizing political identities.

The impact of CMC on mobilization concerns three areas: (i) cost of mobilization (for example, of propaganda); (ii) network logistics (that is, finding those who share your interests); and (iii) stigma or illegality (the need to mobilize secretively). Many have argued that interactive list servers and bulletin board discussion groups can dramatically reduce publishing costs (Myers 1994; Schmidtke 1997). If access to CMC increases, this could greatly democratize access to public attention, as 'desktop publishing' becomes a reality. Using interactive and non-edited media, and the powerful search engines of the Internet, individuals with the most obscure common interests can find one another and communicate. In fact these media are most useful to the most obscure and isolated interest groups. This has been most commented upon with reference to the ease with which the organizational problems of covert groups, such as Neo Nazis and paedophiles have been overcome using interactive media, but the claim that new media ease the process of finding others with similar common interests, and contacting and mobilizing them, appears to be applicable also to more conventional interest groups in civil society. That these media are less effective in constructing and maintaining the larger scale, aggregate collective identities, such as 'nations', is clear. They may in fact contribute to the fragmentation of such national publics.

In Bologna, voluntary and civil society organizations were invited to provide pages for the network, and provided with free email with other citizens and one another in order to 'weave a new fabric of civil society'. A total of over 300 associations, parties, pressure groups, and unions have subscribed. In addition to cheap email, they receive assistance in providing web pages and sharing resources with one another. A similar network was set up in Philadelphia. It is too early to comment on whether presence on such networks has altered patterns of co-operation between organizations, or attracted new support, but this is likely, given the rates of use.

Centrally organized networks may have a tendency to inhibit the emergence of centres of power outside government control or at least to ensure that the network reinforces the position of the local government apparatus as the key provider of information and arena of discussion and decision-making. Independent resource centres such as that of Neighborhoods Online and LibertyNet in Philadephia show how a network which takes the opposite approach can assist voluntary organizations. Provision of easy assess to political information (even such simple things as detailed census breakdowns) can be crucial to the organizations of civil society, as can the cheap and simple provision of access to and lists of other organizations which may face similar problems or work on similar issues. The Philadelphia projects offer subscriptions not to individual users (as did Santa Monica and Bologna) but to voluntary groups. According to Ed Schwarz, activist and civic network organizer:

With Congress and federal departments and even state and local governments starting to go online, the Internet could give us quick access to information about programs and legislation that we could use ourselves and share with one another. Most important, the Internet offered grassroots groups a new way of conveying our own views—first to our fellow citizens, and then to the politicians. In short, using the Internet, we could overcome the sense of isolation, ignorance, and impotence that was holding us back. Its major tools—email and the World Wide Web—were tailor made to deal with these problems. (Schwarz 1997)

Issues in Network Design: Bias, Regulation, and Access

Clearly the most naïve claims of civic networkers—for instance that the new media will erode existing political hierarchies and replace them with a new fabric of civil society—are misleading. The degree to which new forms of democratic participation can be developed using the new media will depend upon how new media are regulated and who has access, and also on the design choices made. Before discussing regulation I will focus on issues of design, and particularly whether networks are centrally designed and administered, or grass-roots-based.

Most of the networks I have mentioned are in fact a combination of local government design and grass-roots initiative. Networks in Bologna, Santa Monica, and Athens have been marked by a particularly strong local government role, whilst Philadelphia and Amsterdam, for instance, combine limited state involvement with initiatives from the public and voluntary sector.

Central control of networks offers some practical advantages. Local government sanctioned, centrally designed civic networks generally offer more accountable, reliable sources of local information and more direct links between online deliberation and government action. Further, if the network is operated by local government it is more likely to have the resources to be proactive in developing universal access, which enables a broader range of democratic transactions to be legitimately provided for. Such top–down networks, however, are open to many of the criticisms previously levelled at public broadcasters. They can be accused of asserting a hegemony through control of information and agenda-setting, of monoculturalism, or of protecting the interests of the bureaucrats.

State control, however, has implications when issues of bias, netiquette, and content regulation arise. The damaging obscenity and flaming that occur in the unregulated discussion groups in the PEN system, for example, indicate that some regulation can be necessary for networks to survive. The tight control and (sometimes automatic) censorship exercised by unelected officers over debate and information provision online in some networks may, however, warrant criticism since some—such as IperBolE—have almost a local monopoly in Internet provision. Whether local providers do need to be regulated in terms of balance and bias will depend not only on the future importance of the medium, but on future developments in bias and agenda-setting in interactive media, phenomena that require further study. Administrators of discussion groups have agenda-setting power as they choose titles of discussion groups and prepare lists of FAQs (frequently asked questions), censor and edit messages (if that is allowed), and so forth. Even where, as in Bologna, the aim is for officers eventually to have no control over content (user-designed discussion groups will replace those selected by the managers), the original designers do have a key role in the development of the culture of the network, and the original design of discussion groups. If we assume that participants are heavily dependent on the information selected for the city's web pages, debate seems likely to be further restricted.

As networks grow, however, the sheer volume of information and communication carried by these media may rule out administrator influence of discussion groups. In 1996 a judge in the Netherlands ruled that the Digital City as Internet provider could not be expected to know what was posted in all its newsgroups and therefore was not responsible for regulation of content (Francissen and Brants 1997). At the same time in Italy, however, administrators were puzzling over whether the new 'Par Condicio' laws regulating political use of media (designed to counter Berlusconi) would be applied to Bologna's civic network. They decided to delete what they called 'ideologico' (party-political) contributions to discussion groups. The very notion of what constitutes balance, agenda-setting, or impartiality in these media remains to be defined.

Attention in this respect must be paid to the software. There appears to be a trade-off here between access and agenda-setting. The more user-friendly a program is, the more agenda-setting power it has. Menu-driven touch-screen interfaces for information provision, deliberation, or preference measurement, such as those on trial in Athens, clearly have a much stronger agenda-setting potential than do, for example, natural language software. Menu interfaces, however, especially the touch-screen variety, require less literacy and therefore exclude fewer from the network. Interfaces are further divided into those that favour a 'virtual city' approach (graphically representing buildings with various functions as in Amsterdam), and those that prefer text. Virtual cities are arguably more user-friendly, but have the disadvantage of structuring interaction into non-existent streets and buildings when there may be no need to do so, undermining the organizational advantages of non-graphical subject listings for civil society and will formation such as that in use in Neighborhoods Online in Philadelphia.

Clearly access is a key, both for the civic networks which have to justify their budgets, and for the inhabitants of the so-called emergent Information Society more generally. If nothing is done to guarantee access, and if the new media do become more important arenas for democratic communication, society will face a new polarization between citizens versed in information technology and able to access politically decisive information and expressive channels, and an uninformed underclass whose opinions and preferences are manipulated by decisions of advertising and PR companies (Murdock and Golding 1989).

For many of the founders of civic networks, especially in Bologna, Manchester, Athens, and Amsterdam, civic networks were seen as a means to open access, through public terminals, to the new means of communication to all citizens. From another point of view, however, these networks could be seen to compound the problem: by offering yet another privileged medium of expression and information to those who can access it, and thereby contributing to impoverishment of other media. One network in particular that has responded to this problem is Bologna's, which from its beginnings has referred to universal access to the network as a right (Tambini 1997).

A key aspect of the IperBolE project was that local government granted a right of access to the Internet (via the civic network) to all citizens of Bologna. Since then the city has been attempting to make that right a reality, promoting access and offering computer literacy education. After three years, over 5,500 private individuals had accounts to use the network, as did over 200 organizations. Since many of these accounts have multiple users, many more log on, although still only a fraction of Bologna's 390,000 population uses the network. PEN, in Santa Monica, was founded in 1990. Since then, the number of registered users (who use the network mainly via modem from home) has risen to over 7,000 (in a population of around 86,000), while the number who use the network at least once a week fluctuates around the 400 mark. Amsterdam's network, which is available not as a right, but for a price, has the highest rates of registration and use, with 45,000 (almost 8 per cent of the adult population) registered to use the system. The slightly anarchic infotainment mix of the Amsterdam network may help account for its popularity, as do the particularly high rates of computer/modem market penetration in Amsterdam (Francissen and Brants 1997).

Public terminals have been provided by some networks to ensure greater access for those without PCs and modems. Budgetary restrictions have limited services, however. The three terminals in Bologna's IperBolE offices often have a queue of users waiting to log on, and the dozen or so terminals situated elsewhere in the city have limited hours, since an assistant is required to help novices. In Amsterdam, the Digital City's initial 'fleet' of twenty-four terminals was later cut to ten, because there was too small a budget for assistance. In Athens, where all access to the network is to be via public terminals, it was estimated that there should be one terminal for every 14,000 citizens (Tsagarousianou 1997), obviously not an optimum for universal access.

Not only do registration patterns of civic networks reveal that access is not universal, but they support the claim that it is unrepresentative: participants in civic networks are overwhelmingly male, young, educated, and professional. Bologna's registration figures for 1996 were similar to the other networks: 19 per cent students, 41 per cent white collar, 18 per cent professionals; 72 per cent were between 20 and 40 years of age and 86 per cent were male.

Discussion

I will draw three conclusions about civic networking. First, I approach the phenomenon in its own terms, as an attempt to encourage democratic participation at the local level. Here I stress that little can be achieved unless access and media literacy are improved. Second, I will note that civic networks have simplistic assumptions about motivations of political participation that should be reviewed. Third, I will stress that, even if access can be generalized, and barriers to participation removed, civic networks' notion of local communities as the principle spheres of political participation needs to be reviewed.

Universal access to civic networks and rights of access are still a long way off. But much of the experimentation in civic networking being currently carried out concerns democratic transactions which require universal access (or at least that users better represent the wider population) if they are to legitimately have any teeth. Online voting and referenda, for example, to be legitimate, must assume that all citizens have suffrage. If information-based services are to be provided via such networks, then surely the infra-structure has to be provided to ensure equal access to them. Similarly, if dis-cussion groups are to have any binding role—equivalent to that of citizens' juries or deliberative opinion polls now being trialed (Fishkin 1991)—then they should be open to all. Where access to CMC is restricted to an unrepre-sentative minority, there is a very strong argument for keeping the key trans-actions of democracy offline. Civic networking under these conditions could be regarded as a further advantage to the information class, and is unlikely to be justified for the use of binding referenda, voting, or opinion polling. Delib-erations that occur in online media under these conditions should be ignored, rather than directed to the attention of local representatives. Only where uni-versal access can be guaranteed is civic networking likely to move beyond its current status, which generally combines innovative information provision with inconsequential, chatline-type discussion groups.

Genuine universal access probably requires state intervention. Just as libraries and schools in the past were deemed necessary for the exercise of political citizenship, there is a growing lobby for similar intervention in new media in the 'information age'. The danger of state-led initiatives, however (apart from bias), is that they invest in infrastructure for local civic partici-pation which no citizen is interested in using, because they misinterpret the motivations of political participation, assuming that participation occurs when it is in individuals' rationally defined interests to participate. A growing body of research argues that it does not, and that contextual factors, access to resources, and mobilization explain participation (Verba *et al.* 1993; Knoke 1990; Whitely 1995; Leighley 1995). Although it is too soon to say whether Athens's Network Pericles has to face the embarrassing prospect of low take-up, the PEN project in Santa Monica saw a decline in usage between 1993 and 1996. In particular, whereas in the early years city officials and opinion leaders were keen to contribute to discussion groups, most had ceased to do so by the time the project reached its sixth year (Docter and Dutton 1997). Low take-up was the fate of civic initiatives using interactive television.[6] Networkers thus tend to share a rather naïve notion of the nature and rationality of political participation. The free-rider conundrum has made us more aware of par-ticipation benefits (benefits from taking part in civic action rather than its policy outcome). It is likely that those who participate in civic networks do so not because they seek to invest in an individual or collective good, but simply for amusement or to learn how to use the new medium, thus these forms of political participation are likely to be unstable in the long-term (Whitely 1995). The erratic individual patterns of PEN participation described by Dutton (1996), for example (obsessive use followed by boredom and neglect), suggest that individuals do not simply use civic networks to further their

[6] For Amsterdam, see Brants *et al.* 1996; for the Quebec project see Fishkin 1991: 21–3.

political interests. As many previous projects in electronic democracy have shown, citizens may simply not be interested in taking part, particularly once the initial novelty of the 'virtual world' has faded. Thus, the argument that making voting easier will make people more inclined to do it, and more likely to participate in frequent polls, is likely to be mistaken. Electoral studies show that very few vote on the basis of gains–losses calculations.

What is community participation in contemporary cities? In order to make sense of these patterns of use, and also of the fact that by far the most popular aspects of civic networks relate to leisure interests rather than local politics, one must place the civic networking movement in its historical context. Not only do civic networkers often have an ill-conceived notion of the motivations of political participation, but many of the hopes held for the local, urban networks I have discussed here tend to reflect anachronistic, even nostalgic, notions of local communities. Civic networks tend to overestimate the degree to which local communities are homogeneous and share common interests. Some networks, the Neighborhoods Online network in Philadelphia for example, have the explicit aim of serving existing communities rather than 'virtual communities' (Thompson 1990). This is indeed one of the often stated aims of the civic networking movement (Schuler 1996), which is strongly influenced by mainstream communitarianism (Etzioni 1995). But clearly there is a problem here. In their nostalgia for the community of the past, and their frequent reference to the New England Town Hall meetings, they neglect the fact that past sense of community responsibility was based on a material interdependence, kin, homogeneity of preferences, and economic ties that simply no longer exist (Friedland 1996). The civic networking movement takes place in the context of a complex renegotiation of political interests and identities due to globalization and multiculturalism. The irony of local community use of these technologies is precisely that their potential—the freeing of communication from spatial constraints—remains unexploited. They are used in towns and neighbourhoods, units in which face-to-face communication is possible. Workers working for the same company in different countries—but getting paid drastically different wages for the same work—in contrast, lack the resources to travel or communicate with one another. Access to cheap and efficient communications of this type could have a much greater material value for them.

The key problem may thus not be distortion of communication, or ease of access to information and voting, but regards actor formation in globalizing society. Whereas the territoriality of modern states and citizenship was reinforced by the broadcast model of media, and national public spheres were relatively stable arenas for representation and deliberation, the new, potentially aspatial media are being introduced in a contemporary context where interdependencies are more difficult to define in territorial terms. Civic networks response has generally been to act local, but not, in general, to think global.

The history of nation-building shows that print media, and in particular the novel and the newspaper, were necessary conditions in the emergence of the nation-state as the principle modern unit of collective action (Anderson 1983). The structure of broadcasting and its coupling with the modern state and vernacular language continued that general process of nationalization of culture (Gellner 1964, 1983). The movement away from broadcasting, and towards many-to-many, increasingly inter- and transnational communication, if it is permitted to continue, arguably goes against that trend since the mediascape no longer reifies geographical or political centres. Whether new media networks can actually be constitutive of interest and identity groups, however, is an open question. Community networkers face a choice: attempt to shore up local communities whose members are no longer economically interdependent, but merely share consumption spaces and the worst effects of social problems, or use the new media to seek to forge new forms of interdependence and will formation that fit contemporary economic realities.

Clearly, the nature of political citizenship in the information age will become a more pressing question, and civic networks may be important in experimenting with forms and technologies of participation. It is perhaps less likely that they themselves will achieve the goal of rejuvenating civil society that they hope for. If current debate is any guide, however, questions of competition and competitiveness of media and communications industries are deemed more important than political citizenship issues. The civic networking movement is in direct conflict with the process of the marketization of public broadcasting and telecommunications services, and it seems more likely that the giant conglomerates such as Microsoft and America Online, rather than any notion of the public interest, will control the future of civic networking.

REFERENCES

ANDERSON, B. (1983). *Imagined Communities: Reflections on the Origins and Spread of Nationalism* (London: Verso).

ARTERTON, F. C. (1987). *Teledemocracy: Can Technology Protect Democracy?* (London and New York: Sage).

BARBER, B. R. (1984). *Strong Democracy: Participatory Politics for a New Age* (Berkeley, Calif.: University of California Press).

BECKER, T. (1981). 'Teledemocracy: Bringing Power Back to the People', *Futurist* (Dec.): 6–9.

BLUMLER, J. G. (1992). *Television and the Public Interest: Vulnerable Values in the West European Broadcasting* (London: Sage).

BONAGA, S. (1994). 'Dalle mura al mondo: Reti telematiche per parlarsi', unpublished Bologna City Hall Document.

BRANTS, K., HUIZENGA, M., and MERTEN, R. (1996). 'The New Canals of Amsterdam: An Exercise in Local Electronic Democracy', *Media, Culture and Society*, 18/2: 233–48.

BRYAN, L. (1996). *Market Unbound: Unleashing Global Capitalism* (New York: Wiley & Sons).

CALHOUN, C. (ed.) (1992). *Habermas and the Public Sphere* (Cambridge, Mass.: MIT Press).

COHEN, J. (1989). 'Deliberation and Democratic Legitimacy', in A. Hamlin and B. Pettit (eds.), *The Good Polity* (Oxford: Oxford University Press), 17–34.

COMUNE DI BOLOGNA (1994). 'Internet per Bologna e l'Emilia-Romagna: Ampliamenti del Progetto Esprit citycard. La society civile in rete a Bologna (local authority PR document).

DOCTER, S., and DUTTON, W. H. (1997). 'The First Amendment Online: Santa Monica's Public Electronic Network', in R. Tsagarousianou, D. Tambini, and C. Bryan (eds.), *Cyberdemocracy: Technology, Cities and Civic Networks* (London: Routledge), 60–83.

DUTTON, W. H. (1996). 'Network Rules of Order: Regulating Speech in Public Electronic Fora', *Media, Culture and Society*, 18: 269–90.

——and GUTHRIE, K. K. (1991). 'An Ecology of Games: The Political Construction of Santa Monica's Public Electronic Network', *Informatisation and the Public Sector*, 1: 279–301.

EDER, K. (1985). 'The "New Social Movements": Moral Crusades, Political Pressure Groups, or Social Movements?', *Social Research*, 52: 869–90.

ETZIONI, A. (1972). 'Minerva: An Electronic Town Hall', *Policy Sciences*, 3: 457–74.

——(1995). *The Spirit of Community* (London: Fontana).

FISHKIN, J. S. (1991). *Democracy and Deliberation: New Directions for Democratic Reform* (New Haven, Conn.: Yale University Press).

——(1995). *The Voice of the People: Public Opinion and Democracy* (New Haven, Conn.: Yale University Press).

FRANCISSEN, L., and BRANTS, K. (1997). 'The New Canals of Amsterdam', in R. Tsagarousianou, D. Tambini, and C. Bryan (eds.), *Cyberdemocracy: Technology, Cities and Civic Networks* (London: Routledge), 18–40.

FRIEDLAND, L. (1996). 'Electronic Democracy and the New Citizenship', *Media, Culture and Society*, 18/2: 185–213.

GARNHAM, N. (1986). 'The Media and the Public Sphere', in P. Golding, G. Murdock, and P. Schlesirger (ed.), *Communicating Politics: Mass Communication and the Political Process* (New York: Holmes & Meier), 37–53.

——(1990). *Capitalism and Communication: Global Culture and the Economics of Information* (London: Sage).

GELLNER, E. (1964). *Thought and Change* (London: Weidenfeld & Nicolson).

——(1983). *Nations and Nationalism* (Oxford: Basil Blackwell).

HABERMAS, J. (1989 [1962]). *The Structural Transformation of the Public Sphere* (Cambridge, Mass.: MIT Press).

HELD, D. (ed.) (1993). *Prospects for Democracy: North, South, East, West* (Cambridge: Polity Press).

KEANE, J. (1991). *The Media and Democracy* (Oxford: Basil Blackwell).

KNOKE, D. (1990). *Political Networks: The Structural Perspective* (Cambridge: Cambridge University Press).

LEIGHLEY, J. (1995). 'Attitudes, Opportunities and Incentives: A Field Essay on Participation', *Political Research Quarterly*, 48/1: 181–211.

MELUCCI, A. (1982). *L'invenzione del presente* (Bologna: Il Mulino).

MILLER, D. (1993). 'Deliberative Democracy and Social Choice', in D. Held (ed.), *Prospects for Democracy* (Cambridge: Polity Press), 75–92.

MORLEY, D., and ROBBINS, K. (1995). *Spaces of Identity: Global Media, Electronic Landscapes and Cultural Boundaries* (London: Routledge).

MURDOCK, G., and GOLDING, P. (1989). 'Information Poverty and Political Inequality: Citizenship in the Age of Privatised Communications', *Journal of Communication*, 39/3: 180–95.

MYERS, D. J. (1994). 'Communications Technology and Social Movements: Contributions of Computer Networks to Activism', *Social Science Computer Review*, 12: 250–60.

NEGROPONTE, N. (1996). *Being Digital* (London: Coronet Paperback).

PIZZORNO, A. (1987). 'Politics Unbound', in C. S. Maier (ed.), *Changing Boundaries of the Political: Essays on the Evolving Balance between the State and Society, Public and Private in Europe* (Cambridge: Cambridge University Press), 27–62.

SACKMAN, H., and NIE, N. (eds.) (1970). *Information Utility and Social Choice* (Montvale, NJ: AFIPS Press).

SCHMIDTKE, O. (1997). 'Berlin in the Net: Prospects of Cyberdemocracy from Above and Below', in R. Tsagarousianou, D. Tambini, and C. Bryan (eds.), *Cyberdemocracy: Technology, Cities and Civic Networks* (London: Routledge), 60–83.

SCHULER, D. (1996). *New Community Networks: Wired for Change* (Reading, Mass.: Addison Wesley).

SCHWARZ, E. (1996). 'An Internet Resource for Neighborhoods', in R. Tsagarousianou, D. Tambini, and C. Bryan (eds.), *Cyberdemocracy: Technology, Cities and Civic Networks* (London: Routledge), 84–9.

——(1997). 'An Internet Resource for Neighbourhoods', in R. Tsagarousianou, D. Tambini, and C. Bryan (eds.), *Cyberdemocracy: Technology, Cities and Civic Networks* (London: Routledge), 110–24.

SOYSAL, Y. N. (1994). *Limits of Citizenship: Migrants and Postnational Membership in Europe* (Chicago: University of Chicago Press).

TAMBINI, D. (1997). 'Universal Cybercitizenship', in R. Tsagarousianou, D. Tambini, and C. Bryan (eds.), *Cyberdemocracy: Technology, Cities and Civic Networks* (London: Routledge), 84–109.

THOMPSON, J. B. (1990). *Ideology and Modern Culture: Critical Social Theory in the Era of Mass Communication* (Cambridge: Polity Press).

TOURAINE, A. (1977). *La Voix et le regard* (Paris: Éditions du Minuit).

TSAGAROUSIANOU, R. (1997). 'Back to the Future of Democracy? New Technologies, Civic Networks and Direct Democracy in Greece', in R. Tsagarousianou, D. Tambini, and C. Bryan (eds.), *Cyberdemocracy: Technology, Cities and Civic Networks* (London: Routledge), 41–59.

——TAMBINI, D., and BRYAN, C. (eds.) (1997). *Cyberdemocracy: Technology, Cities and Civic Networks* (London: Routledge).

VARNEY, P. (1991). 'What's Really Happening in Santa Monica', *Technology Review* (Nov./Dec.): 43–51.

VERBA, S., SCHLOZMAN, K. L., BRADY, H., and NIE, N. H. (1993). 'Who Participates? What do they Say?', *American Political Science Review*, 87: 303–18.

WHITELY, P. F. (1995). 'Rational Choice and Political Participation: Evaluating the Debate', *Political Research Quarterly*, 48/1: 211–35.

ZOLO, D. (1992). *Democracy and Complexity: A Realist Approach* (Cambridge: Polity Press).

12

Conclusions: The Future of Citizenship

Colin Crouch, Klaus Eder, and Damian Tambini

Citizenship develops through the tension between the ideals of citizenship—symbolized in the granting of rights—and the ability and will of institutions to deliver on those ideals. Nation-state membership has consisted, as T. H. Marshall pointed out, in the centrality of the state as guarantor not only of civil rights but of political and social rights (Marshall 1963; Marshall and Bottomore 1992). In the 1980s, historical circumstances once again focused public debate on the degree to which social-democratic welfare states could deliver citizenship in terms both of participation and of equality of status. This opened the way for a series of policy innovations which claimed to rescue the citizenship ideal whilst rejecting the welfare model of state-sponsored citizenship. In this book we have reviewed the two main solutions: those that relocate participation in the market, and those that attempt to encourage participation in representative and deliberative institutions. The current questioning of the nation-state can be understood through these experiments: each of which proposes different institutions as guarantors of different combinations of civil, social, and political rights. No longer 'woven into a single (national) thread' (Marshall), the various institutions and practices of citizenship are once again contested and undermined.

It is clear from the contributions to this volume that these considerations apply across many late capitalist countries. Although these countries followed very different routes to the modern institution of welfare-supported citizenship (Mann 1987), similar structural conditions and ideological movements led to the dismantling of those institutions. The new focus on citizenship was clearly related to a crisis of nation-state institutions. The Marshallian model, according to which the institutionalization of social rights is necessary for the realization of the ideals of political and civil rights, was attacked on a number of fronts. Not only the contradictions of the welfare state, but dissatisfaction with the workings of the institutions of political citizenship (particularly mass democratic institutions in relation to state-run or profit-based communications media) led to a consensus around a critique of existing citizenship institutions, and a will to experiment with new solutions. As these experiments develop, it appears that national citizenship regimes are confronted with a choice between forum, market, and state institutions.

The Ideal of Citizenship

The radical reforms of the 1980s and 1990s, while they attacked existing institutions of social and political citizenship (such as welfare rights), attempted none the less to appropriate the ideal of citizenship. Whereas Marshallian welfare states once took responsibility for making citizens, the state now shifts an increasing proportion of decision-making and distribution tasks to the market. Some attempts are made at the same time to rejuvenate a non-state, non-market notion of civil society. However, as Peggy Somers noted, this was frustrated not only by the dynamic nature of market-seeking capitalism, but by the pervasive binary opposition between state and market in political theory, such that path dependencies constantly work to prevent this 'third sphere' of civil society becoming the site of citizenship participation.

Clearly there is no singular, uniform ideal of citizenship, but a cluster of varied ideals around the central ideas of participation and equality of status. These ideals are differentially served by market and forum solutions under contemporary conditions. In this section we will review the effects of market and deliberative experiments on the ideal and institution of citizenship.

Civic republican, communitarian, and liberal conceptions share a definition of citizenship as involving participation and encouraging equality. Hence the citizenship experiments of the 1990s—carried out in the structural context of declining economic capacities of the state—were couched in terms of 'empowerment', 'freedom of choice', and 'equality of opportunity'. The rising concern for issues of recognition and respect in political philosophy seized on the egalitarian element of citizenship, which had been already evident in Marshall's concern with citizenship as a tool of 'civilization' (Fraser and Gordon 1994). Deliberative and direct democracy were explicitly described in terms of encouraging citizenship (Barber 1984), and where marketization has been the main trend, the reforms were couched in terms of furthering citizenship (for example, in the case of the UK *Citizen's Charter*) through consumer rights. In this way, the welfare state model of citizenship, in which the state shouldered the responsibility for cultivating citizens, was transformed. The policy arenas in which this new consensus on citizenship was formed varied from neo-liberal economics to the citizens forums of the post-communist arenas, but they were united in their attempt to relieve states of the responsibility for citizenship.

Whereas Marshall proposed that the unwinding of the three threads of civil, political, and social rights in the feudal order was followed by their modern national rebraiding, it may be that in the post-Marshallian world the 'threads' of citizenship once again part company. It is not clear that the national state is the guarantor of basic human rights, since transnational organizations and principles take that role, and states appear less inclined or able to take responsibility for making citizens. Neo-liberal privatization policies, which are not being reversed by the so-called 'third way' (Blairism and Shroederism), shift the emphasis to the market, whilst the emerging civic republican and communitarian solutions seek to embed participation and redistribution in the non-state, non-market realm. In sum, the ideal of citizenship may have grown out of a concern with the social and political necessities for realizing ideals of civil rights, but as globalization, complexity, and liberalization allow the threads of citizenship to unwind, there ensues competition over how to reorganize the various elements.

Market, Forum, State, and the Ideal of Citizenship

State solutions were problematized by globalization: not only because the globalization of the production process undermines the capacities of the state, but because migration and cultural globalization undermine the (usually national) identities around which citizenship regimes have been based. The egalitarian aspect of citizenship—citizenship as a univeral status— is redefined in diverse ways by the various solutions. Market solutions are more concerned with efficiency of choice making, neglecting social inequality (whereas state solutions tried to determine the conditions for social participation), and forum solutions assume that deliberation (a focus on the institutions of political citizenship) is able to bring about sufficient equality.

That citizens should have the right and duty to participate actively in the decisions that have an impact on them is a central value invoked in defence of all three solutions for citizenship (states, markets, and forums) and is an aspect of most dominant approaches to the problem. But there is an important distinction here between conservative views, for which participation is necessary because it provides for legitimacy of state institutions, a republican view for which participation is a value in itself, a democratic view for which broad participation is a mechanism for fair representation, and a functional view for which maximizing participation renders rational decision-making more likely.

On all these accounts, marketization has met with problems. Unlike universal citizenship, markets have no implicit mechanism against social exclusion, as Hemerijck discusses in Chapter 7. The underclass tends to grow with the erosion of social rights, and those unlucky enough to find themselves in that class are disenfranchised from market-articulated choice and likely to challenge the legitimacy of states. Further, although markets are subtle and efficient mechanisms of decision-making in comparison with state institutions, this applies only to the collective decisions that can be reduced to a sum of individual decisions. Education is not an issue of such a type as it provides both a social good and an individual one, as Crouch discusses in Chapter 6. As the contributions in Part II make clear, many policy fields can be seen in this light, and the cost of marketization needs to be counted in terms of this balance. Further, many forms of market choice are indirect: the fact that, as Freedland points out, marketization places the citizen in a conflictual, individualistic relationship with the public-service provider, particularly in so far as governments act as purchasers on behalf of citizens, ultimately downgrades the citizen's voice in government.

In the context of privatization and deregulation of public communication and television, for example, mass media solutions appear ever less equipped to provide public spaces for rational decision-making, and new media are likely to exacerbate problems of exclusion as they continue to be the toys of élites. The attempt to reduce the democratic deficit by radically reforming deliberative mechanisms, however, also runs into problems: referenda and deliberative institutions may improve on mass democracy in terms of providing legitimacy, but do less well in terms of co-ordination of decision-making in ever more complex social realities. Electronic democracy might help resolve problems of complexity in democratic communication, but remains illegitimate and unrepresentative if instruments of interactive communication do not become universally accessible, and control of content rests in the hands of the huge communications providers.

Just as welfare tended to undermine individual capacities for control over resources, marketization and individualization of welfare have the converse problem of denying that there is any social or structural origin for problems of poverty, treating them as each individual's own problems. This was demonstrated here in Procacci's analysis (Chapter 3). Equality as a value in itself is not central to every version of the ideal of citizenship, but is referred to in some form by both marketization and forum responses. Both markets and forums, however, have notable disadvantages in relation to social rights in terms of their capacities to foster equality of status. Markets in public services (for example, education) tend to become mechanisms for reproducing inequality and current experimental deliberative mechanisms (since referenda campaigns and Internet access cost money) tend also to be inegalitarian in comparison to a welfare and education backed notion of universal citizenship.

Mechanisms and Interactive Effects

The tripartite distinction that has governed the structure of this book has, of course been unrealistic. Welfare, market, and forum exist alongside one another. Some of our most important findings concern the relationship between them. While theorists since Marshall have been well aware that capitalist markets are dependent on the existence of effective citizenship rights and institutions, markets are now posited as alternatives to citizenship rights. Thus where the developments Marshall described had an implicit leaning towards 'class abatement', such mechanisms are becoming less important. In a context where markets are rarely confined to individual states, and their social preconditions are rooted partly in transnational rights regimes, the institutions linking markets and political membership seek a new equilibrium.

Can markets exist without civil society and the state? Clearly the answer is no, and thus it is increasingly asked what exactly is the new relationship between the three institutional settings of citizenship we have identified. Marketization reforms examined in Part I tend to reduce deliberation by economizing the relationship between citizen/consumer, provider, and state. Hence in marketized service provision deliberation takes place regarding not ends, but means, since the discussion of economized services tends to concern efficiency and value for money rather than the nature of social goods. This tends also to neutralize the social contexts and conflicts that surround social policies, which do not 'count' in discussions of value for money, as Freedland discussed. Clearly, as Crouch argued, given also the well-established perverse inefficiency effects that marketization of public services produces at the level of the system, markets are not enough. Without some form of regulation, and regulation that does more than regulate for more perfect competition, such markets, whilst undeniably forming a stopgap and delivering some efficiency benefits, generate more problems of conflicts of interest, for example between hospitals or schools that now compete for funds, and dump costly 'customers'.

Marketization reforms undermine the status equality through which citizenship had abated the polarization effects of capitalism. 'Consumer' as an alternative status, even when this appears with the proviso of rights or charters, has no such equalizing tendency: it actually serves to reproduce inequality as consumer power differs hugely across socio-economic categories. A defender of current reforms may argue that markets are sufficient in the making of political citizens in today's late capitalist, post-scarcity societies. This argument would propose that marketized societies do make good citizens, since they are more competitive and efficient, regardless of the rise in absolute inequality that they entail. Such a view reflects naïve assumptions regarding political citizenship, however. Equal participants in contemporary society are not to be defined in terms of absolute calculations of the minimum requirements of literacy, shelter, and nutrition, but in terms of relative measures: in particular, those that ensure that no interest group (for example, an underclass) is consigned to a trap of second-class citizenship, reproduced by poor education and other services. That political citizenship in a polity is a matter of degree (and in terms of opposing class interests often a zero-sum game), rather than an absolute threshold to be reached, is a key to evaluating current reforms in terms of citizenship.

There is also the separate question of the concept of the public, the collective, the shared, in contemporary society. The prevailing political temper is clearly to solve the various problems of collective action and public space by reducing the realm of publicness to a minimum. Here neo-liberal politics, neo-classical economics, general disgust with political failure and corruption, a prevailing culture of individualism, and a paradoxical legacy of 1960s anarchism came together. However, not only is it impossible to privatize everything, but the quality of goods and services is sometimes damaged when they are privatized. Certainly for some, as problems of inequality of access again become acute.

Very few political forces see their interests as served by a radical destruction of all senses of the collective. We noted in the Introduction how the neo-liberal British government in the 1980s adopted explicit policies for citizenship after it became concerned that a declining sense of collective responsibility was undermining social order. Military interests also have cause for concern if a thoroughgoing individualization and privatization leads to an unwillingness to serve in defence forces. We do not know how far a society can go in privatization before it becomes incapable of any collective purpose, but it is likely that political forces right across the spectrum would show signs of considerable alarm as that point was reached. Until now, conservatism and neo-liberalism have retained their coalition in nearly all countries, but there would come a point where the former would part company with the continued anti-collectivist drive of the latter. Before that point is reached the feasibility of reconstructing the concern for the public arena (which is the essence of active citizenship) will become a more pressing question. Mid-nineteenth-century England is often looked back to as the true heyday of unfettered market forces, but in fact this was a society deeply bound in tradition, with an intense sense of the importance of public affairs at all levels, from the local town to that of the British Empire. It is certainly no guide to what a contemporary nation-state emptied of the modern state and its welfare policies would look like.

Citizenship Now

The 1980s debate on citizenship was fertile: it spawned not only a new theoretical engagement with citizenship, but also endorsed a series of policies designed to find new ways of redesigning the institutions which constitute citizenship. In terms of the ideals of citizenship, however, there are, as we have seen, many drawbacks with both market and forum solutions. It does not, however, seem that a return to national welfare states is an option, given the structural conditions outlined in the Introduction.

In addition to the experiments investigated here, the 1980s citizenship debate led to a series of innovations such as citizens' juries and deliberative mediation organizations' (Fishkin 1996; Barber 1984). These remained small-scale experiments for the most part, however. Forum solutions had problems with getting beyond apathy (they generally overestimate the desire of individuals to participate) and legitimacy. They also, despite the aspatial potential of new communications technologies, tended to be local in nature, rather than directly engaging with the implications of the globalization of production and markets. It was the marketization reforms that were most widely experimented with. The obvious question, therefore, is whether it would be possible to find a compromise position, incorporating elements of the dialogistic solution into markets. How can consumer rights be institutionalized to prevent the problems of indirectness of market decision-making that Freedland outlined, and also generate a marketized means appropriate to decisions regarding collective goods? And how, as Jenson and Phillips argued in Chapter 4, can the related tendency to individualize relations to the state be reconciled with collective organization in civil society?

What other integrating mechanisms could be conceived, which could be reconciled with the tendencies to globalization, liberalization, and complexity which have haunted the citizenship project in recent years. One way of instituting such reforms would be a bill of rights for the marketized citizen. This would have to differ from the current *Citizen's Charter* model, which cannot cope with social goods, and reduces deliberation to efficiency comparison. In principle there is nothing to stop this from happening. The charter approach could be used to lay down standards for political questions of the quality and level of services, and not just to appraise the performance of lower level staffs. And the establishment of rights in the terms of charters can take a deliberative form, with widespread opportunities for participation and dialogue. At present these experiments are all cast in a managerial form: top management wants to know what customers think about products and services, and they also want to monitor the performance of lower level staff. That is not the only way, nor indeed the most obvious way, in which citizens (a larger notion than 'customers') may wish to express their views about the services of the modern state.

It is notable that much of the public debate over welfare reform has been concerned with the benefit entitlements of social casualties, especially the unemployed. But, at least within Europe, the concept also extends to services which are more universally used and where there are strong incentives for people to care about being involved in discussions of service quality in ways that treat them as citizens: health policy, education, urban transport, and traffic conditions are the most obvious. These remain core areas for staking out the shared business of a community.

The relevant size of such communities varies enormously. Many issues are still intensely local; for others nation-states retain considerable autonomy. In no way does the globalization of the economy suddenly transform all concerns into ones which can only be treated at some remote transnational level, even if some elements of many issues have implications at such a level. Not only are some important local and national matters of no relevance to the global, but there are also the important senses in which the globalization of the economy reinforces the importance of the local. As economic geographers have been pointing out in recent years, globalizing tendencies create powerful incentives for relevant political and economic interests in individual towns and regions to work at strengthening the capacity of their locality to participate in the global competition. Groups come together to discover and assert potential and actual strengths of their areas which give them advantages of niche locations and protect them from generalized, uncontrollable cross-national competition. In so doing they use their local collective recourses and try to develop new ones. They therefore reinvent levels of citizenship. For some of these purposes the relevant 'locality' is in fact the existing nation-state and its set of public institutions.

Of course, localities vary widely in their capacity to engage in this process. While élites in some cities can work to produce desirable high-skilled production locations, others seem able to take on no collective task beyond trying to make local labour as cheap and obedient as possible. Also, the citizen participation that is offered by such developments is usually less than universal; it mainly concerns local élite groups, possibly including labour élites. It is very unlikely to incorporate those already marginalized and defined as 'excluded' or as 'underclass'. Nevertheless, these moves do demonstrate the abiding relevance of a capacity for collective action, for extensive participation in that, and therefore for some forms of citizenship.

While one can see several useful ways in which citizenship may develop in the coming years, it is unlikely that any of these will result in any one Big Idea to rival universal suffrage, or the welfare state. One reason for this is that, if any political vision occupies a hegemonic position today, it is the neo-liberal one, accompanied by the closely related idea that the firm provides the single best organizational form for tackling most tasks. While neo-liberalism is fully consistent with many elements of citizenship, it has great difficulty accepting any extensions of that idea that involve either the state or discursive forums intervening in any way with the free operation of markets. This reduces a possible citizenship agenda to improved information rights, community action against criminality, and probably also recognition of immigrants' rights. Once one reaches subjects that are of particular concern to many of those complaining of defects of citizenship—for example, reforming rather than reducing the welfare state, challenging growing social inequalities, finding collective solutions to environmental damage—neo-liberalism warns against any institutions that might interfere with the market.

The model of the private capitalist enterprise is also very limited in its citizenship potential, though governments are increasingly turning to it as a form of organization as they lose confidence in their own public structures; many previously public functions are being privatized to firms, or government departments and agencies are being required to act as though they were firms. Enterprises can better provide information, choice, and probably a more customer-oriented form of client service than many public bureaucracies, and these are gains for citizenship. There are, however, strong limitations. First, the whole point of capitalist enterprise is to carry out those tasks and serve those populations which bring profit; relatively unprofitable tasks and populations are left undone and unserved. That is why private firms are often more efficient than public agencies, but it is also why they fall short of the criteria of citizenship. Also, in their internal structure they embody the principle of managerial as opposed to democratic control. More constitutional forms of company structure, such as German *Mitbestimmung*, have remained minority experiments.

The Japanese concept of the firm as an alternative community and possibly an alternative form of citizenship to the polity began to attract widespread attention in the early 1990s, as a kind of compromise between democratic citizenship and managerial power. This created some uneasiness among western observers, who saw this as a very deficient form of democracy. However, even this model has been in some decline, at least among former admirers in western business communities. The currently dominant concept of the enterprise stresses flexibility, a minimum of obligations to employees, and ideally no employees at all, just individual self-employed subcontractors who are responsible for their own pensions, sickness care, and even vocational training.

With no currently available alternative social models with the political and economic power to rival markets and enterprises, citizenship experiments will continue to move along the margins of political initiative, either finding ways of becoming incorporated within the terms of markets and enterprises, or establishing small counters to them.

REFERENCES

BARBER, B. R. (1984). *Strong Democracy: Participatory Politics for a New Age* (Berkeley, Calif.: University of California Press).

FISHKIN, J. S. (1996). *The Voice of the People* (New Haven, Conn.: Yale University Press).

FRASER, N., and GORDON, L. (1994). 'Civil Citizenship against Social Citizenship?', in B. Steenbergen (ed.), *The Condition of Citizenship* (London: Sage), 90–107.

MANN, M. (1987). 'Ruling Class Strategies and Citizenship', *Sociology*, 21: 339–54.

MARSHALL, T. H. (1963). *Class, Citizenship, and Social Development* (New York: Anchor).

——and BOTTOMORE, T. (1992). *Citizenship and Social Class* (London: Pluto).

INDEX

Tables are indicated by page numbers in **bold**, and figures by page numbers in *italics*.